## CREATED IN THE IMAGE OF
# GOD

MISSIONARY TO THE CHÁCOBO OF BOLIVIA IGNITES A
REVOLUTION WITHOUT GUNS

# GILBERT R. PROST
COMPLETED AND EDITED BY LORILYN ROBERTS

*Created in the Image of God: Missionary to the Chácobo of Bolivia Ignites A Revolution Without Guns*

Copyright © 2024 Laurel Prost Graf and Gary Graf

Published by Rear Guard Publishing, Inc.

Gainesville, FL

Completed and edited by Lorilyn Roberts

Enhanced cover design by Lisa Vento

Standard licensing agreement

Ver 1.4

NKJV Scripture taken from the New King James Version®. Copyright © 1982 by Thomas Nelson. Used by permission. All rights reserved.

REVISED STANDARD VERSION OF THE BIBLE, copyright © 1946, 1952, and 1971 the Division of Christian Education of the National Council of the Churches of Christ in the United States of America. Used by permission. All rights reserved. License Agreement for Bible Texts - New American Standard

NEW AMERICAN STANDARD BIBLE 1995 (NASB 1995)

NEW AMERICAN STANDARD BIBLE Copyright (C) 1960, 1962, 1963, 1968, 1971, 1972, 1973, 1975, 1977,1995 by THE LOCKMAN FOUNDATION A Corporation Not for Profit LA HABRA, CA All Rights Reserved http://www.lockman.org

THE HOLY BIBLE, NEW INTERNATIONAL VERSION®, NIV® Copyright © 1973, 1978, 1984, 2011 by Biblica, Inc.™ Used by permission. All rights reserved worldwide.All rights reserved.

All Scripture marked with the designation "GW" is taken from *GOD'S WORD*® .© 1995, 2003, 2013, 2014, 2019, 2020 by God's Word to the Nations Mission Society. Used by permission.

Scriptures marked HCSB are taken from the HOLMAN CHRISTIAN STANDARD BIBLE (HCSB): Scripture taken from the HOLMAN CHRISTIAN STANDARD BIBLE, copyright© 1999, 2000, 2002, 2003 by Holman Bible Publishers, Nashville Tennessee. All rights reserved.

Scripture quotations marked CSB have been taken from the Christian Standard Bible®, Copyright © 2017 by Holman Bible Publishers. Used by permission. Christian Standard Bible® and CSB® are federally registered trademarks of Holman Bible Publishers.

Scriptures marked MON are taken from the MODERN ENGLISH VERSION (MON): Centenary Translation: THE NEW TESTAMENT IN MODERN ENGLISH by Helen Barrett Montgomery, 1924.

Scriptures marked ESV are taken from THE HOLY BIBLE, ENGLISH STANDARD VERSION (ESV): Scriptures taken from THE HOLY BIBLE, ENGLISH STANDARD VERSION ® Copyright© 2001 by Crossway, a publishing ministry of Good News Publishers. Used by permission.

Scriptures marked ISV are taken from the INTERNATIONAL STANDARD VERSION (ISV): Scripture taken from INTERNATIONAL STANDARD VERSION, copyright© 1996-2008 by the ISV Foundation. All rights reserved internationally.

Scripture quotations marked MSG are taken from *The Message*, copyright © 1993, 2002, 2018 by Eugene H. Peterson. Used by permission of NavPress. All rights reserved. Represented by Tyndale House Publishers.

*Scripture quotations marked (GNT) are from the Good News Translation in Today's English Version- Second Edition Copyright © 1992 by American Bible Society. Used by Permission.*

Scriptures marked NLT are taken from the HOLY BIBLE, NEW LIVING TRANSLATION (NLT): Scriptures taken from the HOLY BIBLE, NEW LIVING TRANSLATION, Copyright© 1996, 2004, 2007 by Tyndale House Foundation. Used by permission of Tyndale House Publishers, Inc., Carol Stream, Illinois 60188. All rights reserved. Used by permission. Scripture is taken from GOD'S WORD®, © 1995 God's Word to the Nations. Used by permission of Baker Publishing Group.

Easy-To-Read Version (ERV). Copyright © 2001 by World Bible Translation Center All rights reserved.

Taken from the Complete Jewish Bible by David H. Stern. Copyright © 1998. All rights reserved. Used by permission of Messianic Jewish Publishers, 6120 Day Long Lane, Clarksville, MD 21029. www.messianicjewish.net.

The Names of God Bible (without notes) © 2011 by Baker Publishing Group. All rights reserved. No part of this publication may be reproduced, stored in a retrieval system, or transmitted in any form or by any means—for example, electronic, photocopy, recording—without prior written permission of the publisher.

Scripture quotations from the COMMON ENGLISH BIBLE. © Copyright 2011. COMMON ENGLISH BIBLE. All rights reserved. Used by permission. (www.CommonEnglishBible.com).

All rights reserved. No part of this book may be reproduced in any form or by any electronic or mechanical means, including information storage and retrieval systems, without written permission from the author, except for the use of brief quotations in a book review.

Library of Congress Number 2024909816

Printed in the United States of America

ISBN 979-8-9873394-6-6 (ebook)

ISBN 979-8-9873394-7-3 (softcover)

ISBN 979-8-9873394-8-0 (hardcover)

*For Marian, the Love of My Life*

# CONTENTS

Acknowledgments — xiii
The Chácobo Indian Tribe in Bolivia — xv
Gil Prost's Note to Readers — xvii
Introduction — xxix

1. Confronting a Missiological Problem — 1
   *1955*

2. Discovering an Innate Moral Imperative — 10
   *Chácobo Myth - Nahuapaxahua*

3. Does the Game of Life Have An Umpire — 21
   *Chácobo of the Amazonian Rainforest*

4. Chácobo Satire — 24
   *The Story of Pai as a Raisi and Escaping Mother-in-Law Control*

5. A Mind Structured With A Priori Knowledge — 32
   *Innate Meanings Belong to God*

6. The Great Discovery: Chácobo Satire — 38
   *Pëta Rejects the Role of Raisi*

7. The Marriage Trap: Becoming a Raisi — 45
   *Former Raisi Called It a Prison*

8. The Dying Raisi — 54
   *Chácobo Satire*

9. A Cultural Law-Way Sneaked Into History and Has No Place in the Divine Plan — 61
   *"The Law" (Abstract) or "The Law" (Mosaic)*

10. The Concept of Culture — 67
    *Defining an Abstract Noun*

11. The Shaping of Culture — 72
    *Is the "Word of God" a Record of "God-breathed" Words with "Fixed" Inherent Meanings?*

12. Does Culture Determine What One Thinks — 83
    *Social Existence and Elemental Forces of the World*

13. Where Are The Positive Universals — 91
    *A Universal Interpretative System that Echoes God's Right and Wrong*

14. The Long Night — 97
*Chácobo Fable - When the Sun Failed to Come Up*

15. Introducing the Seven-Day Week — 105
*A New Way to Track Time*

16. The Chácobo — 114
*A Maimed Society*

17. Epignosis versus Gnosis — 126
*Unchanging vs General Knowledge*

18. The Need for Etic Analysis — 132
*Chácobo Law-Way*

19. When Did Society Go Its Own Way — 138
*The Husband-Wife Dyad Represents the Universal Covenantal Relationship*

20. There is a Way That Seems Right to a Man — 142
*But Its End is the Way of Death (Proverbs 14:12)*

21. Which Comes First — 151
*Social Existence vs Essence*

22. The Great Awakening — 156
*Inherent or Divine meanings Have Been Replaced With Meanings That "Belong to the People"*

23. Healthy Words — 165
*II Timothy 1:13: "Hold fast the pattern of sound words which you have heard from me, in faith and love which are in Christ Jesus."*

24. The Nuclear Family — 171
*God's Natural Family vs Humankind's Artificial Family*

25. Centripetal Societies — 178
*Natural Roles are Replaced with Ascribed Duties and Obligations*

26. The Rule of Exogamy - Part I — 183
*Exogamy and the First Sin*

27. The Meaning of Gift — 192
*A Universal "Free" Concept vs a Context-Derived Meaning Requiring Reciprocity*

28. The Biblical Understanding of Gift — 203
*Sharing the Gospel in a Different Culture*

29. The Law of Contradiction and the Law of Identity — 211
*The Taxonomist*

30. Culture and Neurosis — 217
*God is the Author of Meanings*

31. Creating a Defensive System Against Anxiety — 221
*The Covenantal Husband-Wife Dyad vs a Biological Dyad*

32. Learning Requires A Priori Equipment Etic Data — 229
*Classificatory Tool Kit*

| | | |
|---|---|---|
| 33. | **A Bible Translator's Dilemma**<br>*Culture is a Kind of Law* | 235 |
| 34. | **The Mandate of Heaven**<br>*China* | 243 |
| 35. | **From Babel to the Amazon**<br>*Confusion of Languages Began by Scrambling Word Orders* | 248 |
| 36. | **Commodity, Money and Freedom**<br>*Chácobo of Bolivia* | 254 |
| 37. | **The Pacahuara**<br>*Bolivia* | 261 |
| 38. | **War Against Positive Universals**<br>*"Acquired" vs "Learned"* | 266 |
| 39. | **Etic Divergence**<br>*Rejecting the Divine Plan* | 271 |
| 40. | **The Right Time**<br>*The Chácobo of Bolivia, the Iñupiat Eskimos of Alaska, and the Sharanahua of Peru* | 277 |
| 41. | **Iñupiat Eskimos**<br>*Alaska and Arctic Slope* | 291 |
| 42. | **The Life Needs New Forms**<br>*Old Wine Skins vs New Ones* | 301 |
| 43. | **The Rule of Exogamy - Part II**<br>*The Concept of Family Around the World* | 311 |
| 44. | **Forms Having No Place In the Divine Plan**<br>*Exogamy in Northern India* | 327 |
| 45. | **The Jívaro People**<br>*Equador and Peru* | 331 |
| 46. | **Sharanahua**<br>*Peru* | 340 |
| 47. | **Miccosukee (Mikasuki)**<br>*Florida, North America* | 347 |
| 48. | **The Trobriand Islanders**<br>*Papua, New Guinea* | 353 |
| 49. | **Kiowa - Apache**<br>*The Great Plains, North America* | 372 |
| 50. | **Do Sound Words Exist**<br>*Taking the Gospel to the World Needs Sound Words* | 379 |
| 51. | **Naturalizing Singing and Dancing**<br>*Aguaruna and Jívaro of Peru* | 385 |
| 52. | **War Against the Law of the Mind**<br>*Winnebago Satire - The War Between the Right and Left Arms* | 390 |

53. Eat Me, and You Will Defecate　　　　　　　　　398
    *Winnebago Satire*

54. "Help! I Need to be Cleansed!" An Analysis of a
    Winnebago Story　　　　　　　　　　　　　　　404
    *Personal Testimony of a Winnebago*

55. The Contextual Shaping of Meaning　　　　　　407
    *Beware Lest Anyone Cheat You Through Philosophy and Empty
    Deceit, According to the Tradition of Men*

56. The Mystery of the One-Flesh Principle　　　　412
    *Japanese Family*

57. Cultural Diversity　　　　　　　　　　　　　　422
    *The Two Become One Flesh*

58. Demolition of Divine Meanings in Progress　　 428
    *Universal vs Relative in Anthropology*

59. The Pirahã of Brazil　　　　　　　　　　　　　433
    *Trickster Story - Don't Trust Your Perceptions*

60. The Nature of Etic Divergence　　　　　　　　 439
    *What it Means to be Created in the Image of God*

61. The Gleaning of Meanings　　　　　　　　　　 445
    *Perceptions, Concepts, Categories, and Language*

62. Innate Universals from the Field of Particulars　　455
    *Constituents of Knowledge—Form and Meaning*

63. Species Versus Kinds　　　　　　　　　　　　　462
    *Chácabo and Chinese Lad*

64. Does a Divine Plan for Living Exist　　　　　　466
    *A Transformation*

65. Chácobo Learn How to Participate in Bolivian Society　474
    *The Beginning of the Revolution Without Guns*

66. The Missiological Crossroad　　　　　　　　　　484
    *"New Wine" of Christianity Demanded "New Skins"*

67. Requires New Forms　　　　　　　　　　　　　493
    *The Chácobo Meaning Attached to the Concept of Marriage Had "No
    Place in the Divine Plan"*

68. Cultural Relativist versus Concept-Innatist　　　499
    *SIL Missed the Mark*

69. The "Yoke of Slavery" Longs to be Broken　　　505
    *Returning the Husband-Wife Bond to Its Rightful Place in God's
    Family*

70. Breaking the Yoke of Slavery　　　　　　　　　509
    *Tearing Down Strongholds*

71. The Battle Lines Are Drawn　　　　　　　　　　518
    *Where Do the Rules of Behavior Come From*

72. Year 1998 in Gainesville, Florida     526
*Return to Bolivia After an Eighteen-Year Hiatus*

73. Discovering "Gold" Among the Particulars     539
*The Miccosukee Translation Project*

74. Allegory of the Cave     548
*From Plato's Republic*

75. A Revolution Without Guns     559
*Making Disciples of Jesus Christ Among All Nations*

Appendix - Email from Gil Prost to Roy [Garren]     571
Afterword by Lorilyn Roberts     575
About the Author Gilbert R. Prost     577
Notes     581

# ACKNOWLEDGMENTS

A special thank you to the following people who made publication of this book possible:

Laurel Prost Graf, Jim Prost, Gary Graf, Bob and Barb Edewaard, Jed and Marian Keesling, Jeffrey and Diane Michel, Tom and Kay Orth, Robert and Lois Wilkinson, and Andy Schreffler

# THE CHÁCOBO INDIAN TRIBE IN BOLIVIA
## PREFACE

In *Created in the Image of God*, a missionary to the Chácobo brings the Gospel to a dying tribe in Bolivia, South America. In the process, he restores God's transcendence rooted in the *husband-wife* covenantal relationship.

Can this miraculous transformation among God's imagers[1] be spread to the ends of the earth in A Revolution Without Guns before Jesus' imminent return?

Part memoir and part academic, *Created in the Image of God* deals with anthropologic/linguistic issues related to Bible translation in endemic Bible-less cultures still needing to hear the Gospel.

# THE CHÁCOBO INDIAN TRIBE IN BOLIVIA

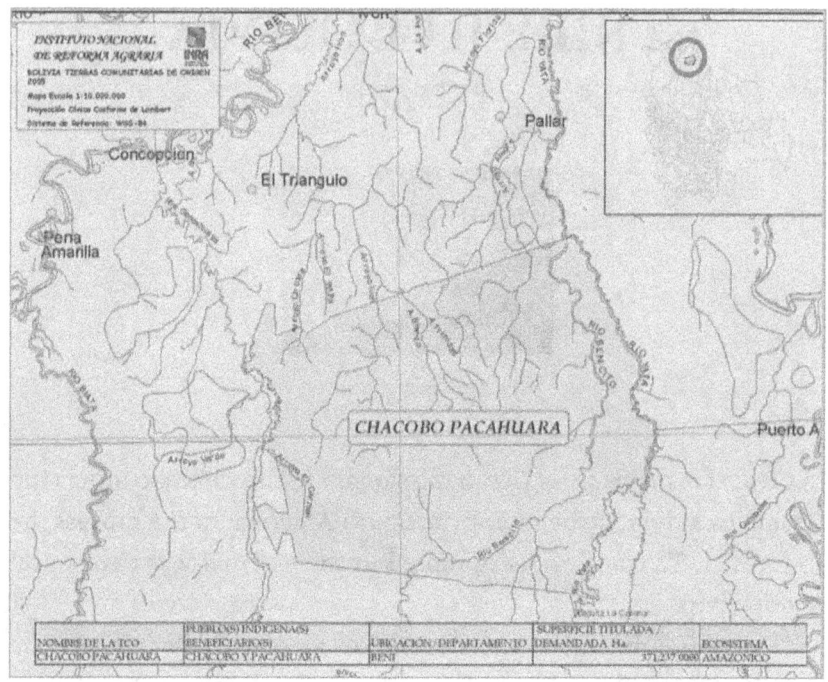

Map of Chácobo Land Title

# GIL PROST'S NOTE TO READERS

BIBLE TRANSLATOR AND ANTHROPOLOGIST

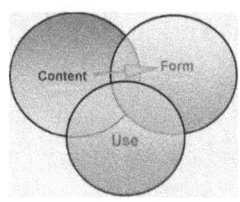

As a Bible translator, my task is to ensure the meaning-content attached to forms (marriage, family, and gift, etc.) "do not belong to the people" but to God.

In the words of linguist Kenneth Pike, every translator's task is to "package them right."[1]

If this is not done, the results will be man's words rather than God's. Packaging form with meaning-content is no laughing matter.

The crucial question that one must ask is: Do concepts held in common by all people have Divine meanings attached to them?

When we examine the claims of the New Testament writers, one thing is clear: They saw themselves as communicators of the true Word of God, not as men delivering "an accurate record of spirit-guided perceptions."[2]

> *For this reason we also thank God without ceasing because when you received the word of God which you heard from us, you welcomed it not as the word of men, but as it is in truth, the word of God, which also effectively*

*works in you who believe. (I Thessalonians 2:13, NKJV)*³

~

## PERCEPTIONS

It must be noted that before a society can talk about "perceptions," they must first be classified using concepts whose meanings "do not belong to the people."

The classification of sense perceptions presupposes a set of innate (inborn), unlearned classificatory concepts, i.e., part of, kind of, same-different, good-bad, male-female, before-after, someone-something, and people-animal.

In the words of cognitive scientist Steven Pinker:

> People in all cultures carry out long chains of reasoning built from links [kind of, part of, same-different, and good-bad] whose truth they could not have observed directly.⁴

For Pinker, these epistemological "tools" are innate. They "do not belong to the people."

In this regard, the Apostle Paul wrote Timothy declaring:

> *All Scripture is given by inspiration of God, and is profitable for doctrine, for reproof, for correction, for instruction in righteousness,*
> *that the man of God may be complete, thoroughly equipped for every good work. (II Timothy 3:16-17)*

He didn't view the Scriptures as being a "record of spirit-guided perceptions."⁵ But he did believe that perceptions could easily be shaped by social influences.

Jesus admonished His disciples before returning to the Father:

> *"However, when He, the Spirit of truth, has come, He will guide you into all truth; for He will not speak on His own authority, but whatever He hears He will speak; and He will tell you things to come"* (John 16:13).

The position taken here is that the Greek word *theopneustos* means not a product of human origin breathed into by God, but a Divine product breathed out by God.[6]

Jesus did not tell them, "The Spirit will guide your perceptions." Isaiah 55:11 (Amplified Bible) states:

> *So shall My word be that goes out of My mouth; it shall not return to Me void (without producing any effect, useless), but it shall accomplish that which I please and purpose, and it shall prosper in the thing for which I sent it.*

One "product" that is "God-breathed" is the Gospel. So convinced that the Gospel was a product of Divine origin, in Galatians 1:9, Paul wrote:

> *As we have said before, so now I say again, if anyone preaches any other gospel to you than what you have received, let him be accursed.*

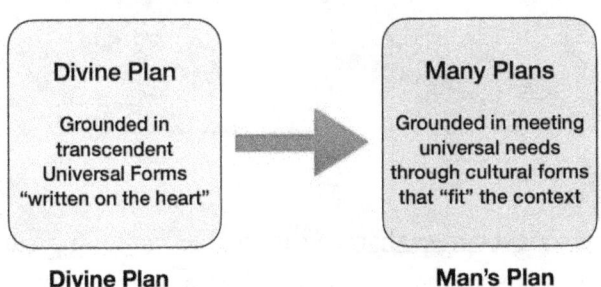

# GLOSSARY OF TERMS USED THROUGHOUT THIS BOOK

- <u>Acquired</u>: Innate (inborn).
- <u>Concept</u>: An abstract idea to which a meaning is attached. If the meaning is inherent, then it represents a Positive Universal.
- <u>Concept-Innatist</u>: Believes there exists within the subconscious of every human being a set of Universal concepts, principles, and categories for living whose meanings are "fixed" and culture-free. Inborn, already-formed ideas.
- <u>Contextualization</u>: The act or process of putting information into context.

Contextualization

- <u>Dialectical materialism</u>: A theory that maintains the Universals for living are derived from material existence;

that is, from biology, one's sense perceptions, and the environment.
- <u>Dualism</u>: The view that the mind and the body (or brain) are two distinct spheres of activity that nevertheless interact. For the theist, the spirit/mind and body are linked together as an inseparable one. For the non-theist spirit/mind and body interact but are not linked. The monist rejects the mind-body dualism and reduces the mind to the brain.
- <u>Dyad</u>: Two individuals, such as husband and wife.
- <u>Emic</u>: Native's point of view of the cultural system under investigation. Represents the values, "rules of behavior," and the ideals of the individual society being analyzed.

## Perspectives

**Emic perspective**

How members of a society perceive and understand their world.

**Etic perspective**

How a Bible translator interprets a group's behavior using etic data of which there are two kinds, mental and material.

- <u>Etic</u>: Relating to or involving analysis of cultural phenomena from the perspective of one who does not participate in the culture being studied. Free from human interpretation.

- *Etic* divergence: Occurs when the Divine meaning attached to a form familiar to all is rejected and replaced with a meaning "that belongs to the people."

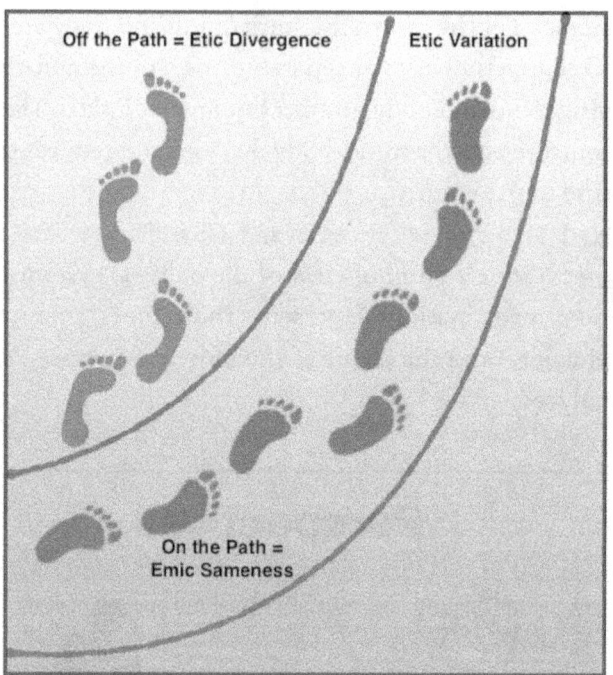

- Empiricist: Believes meaning is derived from context and meanings are variable.
- Empiricism: A theory that all knowledge is derived from sense experience and that the mind is a *tabula rasa* upon which the rules of behavior are written.
- Epistemology: Branch of philosophy concerned with knowledge.
- Essence: The sum total of those attributes that cannot be removed from a being without destroying the being itself.
- Exogamy: The custom of marrying outside the family, clan, lineage, village, or tribe. Otherwise, it would be considered an incestuous relationship.

- <u>Fixed meanings</u>: Meanings that are constant and "belong to God."
- <u>Infrastructure</u>: "The elementary forces of the world," as referred to in Colossians 2:8. "Beware lest anyone captivate you through philosophy and vain deceit, in the tradition of men and the elementary principles of the world, and not after Christ" (Colossians 2:8, MON, Modern English Version).
- <u>Innate (Inborn) Positive Universal</u>: Mysteriously structured in the mind and that Paul describes figuratively as "written on the heart."
- <u>JAARS</u>: Jungle Air and Radio Service.
- <u>Learned</u>: Meanings that are subject to change and "belong to the people."
- <u>Lausanne Movement</u>: A global network of Christians established in 1974.
- <u>Paleologic thought</u>: Faulty thinking.
- <u>Patrilocal</u>: Social system where married couples live in the household of the husband's parents or somewhere closeby.
- <u>*Raisi*</u>: A son-in-law who has promised his Chácobo in-laws he will provide them a daily supply of fish and wildlife in exchange for conjugal rights to their daughter. The position enslaves the son-in-law and hinders his ability to be the head of his wife, as Christ is head of the church.

Raisi

- <u>Sound Words</u>: The Apostle Paul uses this phraseology to describe words that reflect God's authorship of proper communication in culture. *"Hold fast the pattern of sound words which you have heard from me, in faith and love which are in Christ Jesus" (II Timothy 1:13).*

# Do Strong Words Exist?

"Don't listen to him... He believes sound words exist."

"Sound" words

- <u>Status:</u> A collection of rights and duties.
- <u>*Tabula Rasa*</u>: The theory that the mind, before receiving impressions, is a blank tablet completely devoid of innate ideas.
- <u>Taxonomy</u>: A branch of science that uses mental function concepts like same and different, animate and inanimate, part of any kind, and person and thing to group and organize objects having the same qualities under the same genus.
- <u>Transmute</u>: To change in form, nature, or substance.
- <u>Universal-Lexicon</u>: Structured in the unconscious mind and contains Universal forms attached to inherent (God-given, unchanging) meanings.

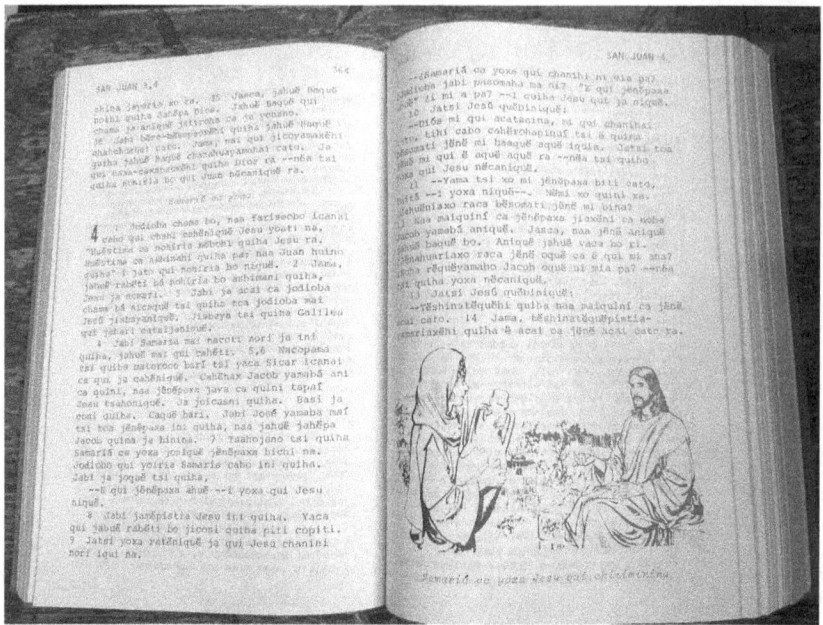

Chácobo Bible

## CONVICTIONS

- The task of every Bible translator is to communicate meaning. Authors John Callow and John Beekman state in *Translating the Word of God*, "All translators are agreed that their task is to communicate the meaning of the original, the texts of the Scripture in the original languages of Hebrew and Greek. There is no discussion on this point."[7]
- If all meanings are derived from perceptions and "belong to the people" and not to God, then there can be no Universal meanings since the perceptions of each person will differ from those of his fellow man. Meanings acceptable in one society will be regarded as totally wrong in another.

- According to Anna Wierzbicka, "Meaning has to do with constants [from God] and not with the variables."[8]

# INTRODUCTION

Bolivian map

# INTRODUCTION

## THE POTENTIAL SON-IN-LAW TEST

Amazonian tribes have an unusual rule. They require daughters to remain home after marriage. Stories abound of jaguars disguised as human beings interested in marrying the daughters of such households. The function of this myth is to counteract Genesis 2:23-24:

> *"This is now bone of my bones*
> *And flesh of my flesh;*
> *She shall be called Woman,*
> *Because she was taken out of Man"*
>
> *Therefore a man shall leave his father and mother and be*
> *joined to his wife, and they shall become one flesh.*

Knowing their daughters are the means to obtain a fish and wildlife provider, the question in the minds of parents who use daughters as "bait" is this:

Is the person who desires to marry our daughter a human being? Or is he a jaguar disguised as a human being who will ultimately take our daughter and set up an independent household, leaving us without a fish and wildlife provider?

In Chácobo culture, anyone who marries a daughter and then removes the daughter from her parent's control must be a jaguar.

To prevent the destruction of a family type explicitly designed to provide a household-of-five with a daily supply of protein, a psychological-biological test was devised to help husband and wife detect if the young man seeking to marry their daughter was a human or a jaguar.

If a human, the prospective son-in-law would abide by the rules and become their fish and wildlife provider; if a jaguar, he would remove the daughter and set up an independent household.

The discovery procedure is simple. It begins with the knowledge

## INTRODUCTION

that behavioral differences exist between humankind and animals. Man can suppress a stimulus and not react if he sets his mind to it; animals can't.

If a native gives you the roasted eyeball of a tapir to eat, you can suppress your shock and disgust, take the gift, eat it, and say, while smiling, "Thank you."

When offered raw cat meat, a jaguar cannot suppress its revulsion. It will not eat its own species.

The test is simple for an Amazonian tribe member who believes that *A* can also be *B*, and wonders if the person who wishes to marry his daughter is a jaguar in human flesh. Invite the potential son-in-law to dinner and feed him a dish of hot spicy food, hot enough to make him react to it.

If he is a human in love with his daughter, he will suppress his desire to drink water to relieve his discomfort while complimenting the mother on how tasty the meal is. If he does this, he will make a good son-in-law whose ascribed function will be to provide fish and wildlife to his soon-to-be wife's family.

However, if the person is a jaguar, it will relieve its discomfort by requesting water. If a couple allows him to marry their daughter, he will take the daughter, set up an independent household, and leave the family without a wildlife provider.

# INTRODUCTION

Bolivia Team, Gil Prost (tall man with glasses) in the back, and Marian is in front of Gil

## CONVICTIONS

- The story provides evidence regarding anxieties within such societies.
- As represented by the jaguar, the ideal must be depicted as dangerous.

# CHAPTER 1
# CONFRONTING A MISSIOLOGICAL PROBLEM
## 1955

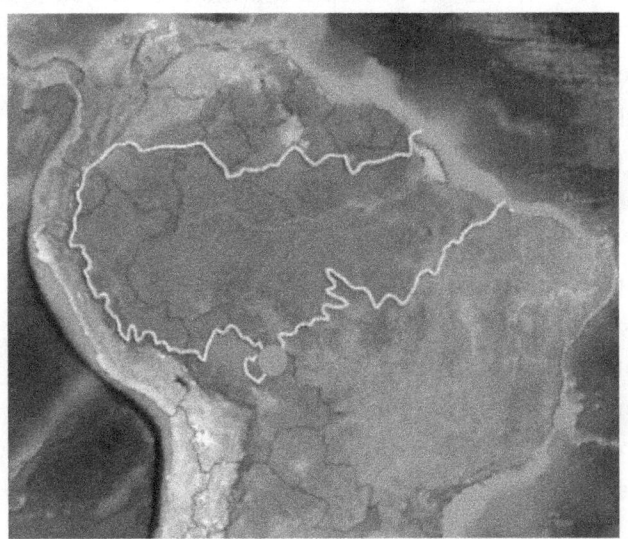

Amazonian Rainforest

My story begins in 1955 in the Bolivian Amazonian Rainforest. Here I am, 65 years later in 2020, writing a book in my 90s to address a missiological problem so controversial that the director of the Summer Institute of Linguistics said: "I do not believe there is a viable role for you in the Branch because of your philosophical position."[1]

The SIL Branch in Bolivia had found academic support from a prominent evangelical missiologist-anthropologist, Charles H. Kraft (1932-), who wrote: "... there is no such thing as an absolute set of cultural forms. The idea must be abandoned."[2]

I had joined the Summer Institute of Linguistics before 1955 in anticipation of serving as an international missionary with Wycliffe. Upon assignment to the Chácobo, my wife, Marian, and I joined the Bolivian SIL Branch. After being a member for almost 20 years, I was asked to be the Associate Director of Field Operations (ADFO) of the Bolivian Branch.

Kraft was right. I didn't "fit" for an important reason: I wasn't a cultural relativist.

I believed "forms" or concepts common to all had inherent or Divine meanings. Society had the freedom to reject and replace those Divine meanings with meanings "that belonged to the people."

As the Associate Director of Field Operations of the Bolivian Branch, I wrote Bolivia's "Scheme for Completing the Task" in 1984. However, to the surprise of SIL and WBT (Wycliffe Bible Translators) corporate leaders, we finished the job three years earlier.

We were the first SIL/WBT Branch to complete the corporate goal, known as the Task; the first to redeploy its members around the world; and the first to turn over its base of operations, *Tumi Chucua*, to the Bolivian government in 1981.

Without many miracles, the story I share here would not have been possible.

## THE FAMILY UNIT

The family structure consists of eight parts or dyads: Hu-Wi (*husband-wife*), Fa-So (father-son), Fa-Da (father-daughter), Mo-So (mother-son), Mo-Da (mother-daughter), Br-Si (brother-sister), Br-Br (brother-brother), and Si-Si (sister-sister).

The *husband-wife* dyad represents a covenantal relationship, and the seven other dyads represent biological relationships.

As I discovered, the Chácobo had replaced the covenantal *husband-wife* dyad with a different kind of dyad that produced a leaderless society. Nothing prepared me for this revelation.

As I learned more about their leaderless culture, I observed no one issued a command that another person would carry out. Husbands were prohibited from living in the same space as their wives; and, most importantly, no husband was head of his wife or his children.

What kind of society had we come to share the Gospel with, and how could we do the job God called us to do when the forms that made Chácobo society operate were foreign to us and the God who created us?

It took many years to grasp how much this impacted the Chácobo Indian tribe. We later discovered that these unbiblical forms were found not only among the Chácobo Indians but among dozens, if not hundreds, of societal groups around the world.

After learning the Chácobo had rejected the biblical nuclear family structure, I became what is called a concept-innatist. I believed in 1955 and still believe that humans are born with already-formed ideas, knowledge, or beliefs.

That discovery compelled me to attempt an experiment: To restore God's Universal to its rightful cultural position. Many years later, I would find out if my experiment succeeded.

THE MOST IMPORTANT thing for the reader to know is that, as a Bible translator and anthropologist, I embrace a biblical worldview. From my perspective, the nuclear family is the basic unit of society. As the Apostle Paul stated in Ephesians 5:23, "For the husband is head of the wife, as also Christ is head of the church; and He is the Savior of the body."

And Adam states in Genesis 2:23:

> "*This* is *now bone of my bones*
> *And flesh of my flesh;*
> *She shall be called Woman,*
> *Because she was taken out of Man.*"

Upon discovering there were Chácobo sages who rejected how their ancestors had structured the nuclear family—making the mother-daughter dyad the dominant dyad—my investigative spirit kicked in. How did the Chácobo sages—critical of the mother-daughter dyad—know the *husband-wife* dyad was God's standard for the nuclear family?

I concluded the only way they could have known that the one-flesh principle of *husband-wife* represented the Universal was because the principle had been "written on their hearts," just as Chinese sages knew that "knowledge of the good" was written on their hearts.

Did not the Word of God declare that the one-flesh principle, as stated in Genesis 2:23-24, is covenantal? In the meantime, I concluded that the unconscious mind in all humans has innate forms with attached Divine or inherent meanings.

God gave humans free will. Men and women have the freedom to reject and replace those inborn meanings with meanings derived from what Karl Marx (1818 - 1883) called social existence, Mao Zedong (1893 - 1976) called social practice, and Charles H. Kraft called cultural context.

The Chácobo had replaced what linguist Kenneth Lee Pike (1912 -

2000) called an "Innate Positive Universal" with a "negative particular action."[3]

I discovered I was in an epistemological battle regarding these forms or customs that I believed had attached to them Divine meanings.

Other anthropologists believed these forms could be replaced with newer forms "that belonged to the people."[4] In other words, they accepted the meanings that society gave to those forms while disregarding the meanings given to them in the Bible.

For example, one might ask: Is there an absolute internal structure to the nuclear family? Or is the nuclear family even structured?

In this regard, Christian philosopher and lawyer, Herman Dooyeweerd (1894 - 1997), wrote: "Membership is absolutely restricted to the parents and their offspring in the first degree."[5]

However, membership in the Chácobo family included parallel cousins classified as brothers and sisters. Their concept of family did not accord with Scripture.

What surprised me was no evangelical anthropologist, to my knowledge, and according to American theologian Cornelius Plantinga, Jr., had declared that such structures were unnatural, "metaphysically untethered to any transcendent purpose."[6]

The Apostle Paul, to my amazement, understood the process. He believed such forms had "crept into" history and had "no place in the Divine Plan."

> *Beware lest anyone cheat you through philosophy and empty deceit, according to the tradition of men, according to the basic principles of the world, and not according to Christ. (Colossians 2:8)*

What had crept in was a new way of thinking that rejected the Rules of Logic. If the social structure, where parallel cousins are viewed as brothers and sisters, is valid, then family membership isn't limited to parents and offspring in the first degree.

Instead, membership is solely determined by social existence, social practice, or cultural context. In the name of science, logical thinking was jettisoned and replaced with environmental determinism.

When I expressed my conviction to anthropologist Kenneth Lee Pike in 1978, his reply was, "Gil, that's the most interesting thing I've heard in twenty years. Now you need to study anthropology to write it up for the academic community."

That is what I set out to do. I believed the nuclear family, as the basic unit of society, had been replaced among the tribes we were working with by other family structures.

In the words of Pike, "A Positive Universal can be replaced with a negative cultural particular."[7]

Each family type shown in the chart at the end of this chapter represents a shift away from logical thinking and declares that, under certain conditions, *A* can be *B*. A cousin can be classified as a sibling, an uncle as a father, and an aunt as a mother.

The North American Branch administrators and SIL anthropologists found my position untenable, ill-founded, and unscientific. The idea that the unconscious mind was actually structured with such knowledge was totally unacceptable to the administrators of the SIL Branch of which I was now a member.

My position was based on Scripture. I believed a law existed that was "written on the heart" (Romans 2:14-15, New International Version):

> *(Indeed, when Gentiles, who do not have the law, do by nature things required by the law, they are a law for themselves, even though they do not have the law.*
> *They show that the requirements of the law are written on their hearts, their consciences also bearing witness, and their thoughts sometimes accusing them and at other times even defending them.)*

This "law written on the heart" compelled Chácobo sages of the past to want to set up independent households free from mother-in-law control, a principle made explicit in the Word of God (Genesis 2:24).

Professor Charles Kraft failed to recognize the existence of a spiritual phenomenon called *etic* divergence. *Etic* divergence occurs when the Divine meaning attached to a form familiar to all is rejected and replaced with a meaning "that belongs to the people."

The concept-innatist believes a set of Universal forms exists with "fixed" and absolute meanings.

An *etic* perspective (psychologist R. H. Wozniak) says, "Phenomenon is the outward expression of essence, the form in which it is manifested."[8]

When it ceases to be an expression of essence, what is being expressed are the ideas, values, and rules for living derived from social existence that "belong to the people" rather than God.

We were working amongst a people group who had given new meanings to words like family, husband, wife, father, mother, daughter, son, father-in-law, mother-in-law, son-in-law, and daughter-in-law, creating cultural forms that prevented husbands and wives from becoming "one flesh."

Unknown to me, I had stepped on a semantic-theological landmine.

Did there exist forms common to all with Divine or inherent meanings attached, or were the meanings attached to words common to all derived solely from social existence?

Except for the late linguist Kenneth Lee Pike, president of the Summer Institute of Linguistics (SIL), most evangelical anthropologists or linguists have rejected the idea that forms common to all have attached inherent or Divine meanings, the most prominent being the late Dr. Eugene Nida (1914 - 2011) of the American Bible Society.

Rejecting the idea of a Universal-Lexicon hardwired into an unconscious mind, Nida wrote:

There is a tendency to regard the "true meaning" of a word as somehow related to some central core which is said to exist (in some Universal-Lexicon), either implicitly or explicitly, in each of the different meanings of a word or a linguistic unit. All the different meanings are supposed to be derivable from this central core of meaning.[9]

Dr. Charles Kraft agreed with him: "Though the forms are parts of culture, the meanings 'belong to the people.' They are not inherent in the forms themselves. They are attached to the forms based on group agreements."[10]

When the Lord breathed into man, man's form became a living, cultural, biological being endowed with language and innate knowledge. Kraft believed "form and meanings always come together in real life."[11]

> *And the LORD God formed man of the dust of the ground,*
> *and breathed into his nostrils the breath of life; and*
> *man became a living being. (Genesis 2:7)*

My discovery of Chácobo satire, critical of their ancestors for restructuring the nuclear family and making the mother-daughter dyad the dominant one, put me in the middle of an anthropological debate. Do concepts common to all have inherent meanings that are "fixed" and belong to God, or are all meanings derived from what Kraft calls "real life" and Marx called "social existence"?

Should I be a cultural relativist, as advocated by evangelical anthropologists, or a concept-innatist?

# CREATED IN THE IMAGE OF GOD

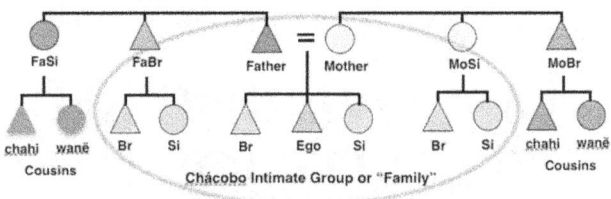

Chácobo family tree

## CONVICTIONS

- The unconscious mind is structured with innate (inborn) forms common to all. There are inherent or Divine meanings that humans can reject and replace with meanings that Karl Marx called social existence, Mao Zedong called social practice, and Charles Kraft called cultural existence.
- Within every culture exists cultural and linguistic forms that have "no place in the Divine Plan." The task of the missionary is to discover what those forms are.

# CHAPTER 2
# DISCOVERING AN INNATE MORAL IMPERATIVE
## CHÁCOBO MYTH - NAHUAPAXAHUA

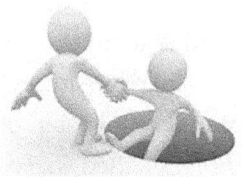

As members of a dual organization, the Summer Institute of Linguistics and the Wycliffe Bible Translators, Marian, my wife, and I left the Windy City of Chicago in 1955 to go to Bolivia, S.A. Our ultimate goal was to translate the New Testament into a non-existent written language in one of its Bible-less tribes. We were assigned to the monolingual Chácobo Indians who lived in Northern Bolivia.

In the vastness of the Amazonian Rainforest, the Bolivian government had informed us the Chácobo lived on the Benicito River in Northern Bolivia. Our plan to contact the Chácobo was simple. Fly over the area each evening before dusk to look for smoke from their cooking fires. They had to cook or roast their food if they were to eat.

Once we discovered the smoke, we made plans to enter the forest at the closest point on the river, which we found, to our dismay, was a marsh separating the river from the land. To get to land, we had to wade through two to three feet of water for about a mile.

When we emerged at the other end, a trail before us led to a village. Thirty minutes later, we entered the small community of *Biiyá* (It-Has-Mosquitos). Our contact was friendly.

However, since the elder Chácobo, to whom everyone went to for advice, didn't live there, they took us farther into the interior. After another long hike down a narrow trail, we arrived at a slight clearing as the sun was setting. In the opening was a single thatched longhouse where Taita Rabi, his daughter, and two other families lived.

Co-worker Perry Priest and I spent the evening attempting to converse in Spanish with a few families whose Spanish vocabulary was distressingly limited. They could be classified as being monolingual. We finally convinced them the reason for our visit was my desire to return with my wife Marian and live with them.

Spending the night sleeping on palm leaves, we tried to keep warm by slowly burning logs nearby, waiting for dawn to come. At around four in the morning, Taita Rabi exited his hammock, lit a torch, and headed off to the village of *Biiyá*.

Early in the morning, Perry and I hiked back to *Biiyá*. Again, I made known my desire to come and live among them and learn their language. Of course, they didn't understand. Assuming I desired to put them to work gathering natural rubber, one elder asked if I was a *pícaro* who mistreated his workers. When I said I wasn't a "patron," they extended an invitation.

The idea that there were individuals who were non-Bolivians, a young couple from another land, who desired to live among them and learn their language, didn't compute. It took a couple of years to explain why Marian and I desired to live with them. We needed to learn to speak their language first.

In the meantime, they would have to wait. Nevertheless, they gave us an invitation, and a week later, Marian and I became members of the village of *Biiyá*.

Our first night in the village was eventful. We listened to a hungry jaguar growl as it circled close by. In the morning, the Chácobo broke into two teams to see if they could find the beast that had kept us awake all night. Since we had guns, Perry joined one team and I the other. It was the team Perry joined that found the jaguar. They encouraged him to shoot the beast with his .22, but he refused.

When I asked where our house should be built, the Chácobo insisted it be next to what I later discovered was the men's clubhouse. While we spent the first month building a home, the men shared their living quarters with us.

The materials used came from the jungle except for the doors, nails, and screening. Instead of shingles, we used palm leaves, and instead of walls and floors made of wooden planks, they were made of split palm. Such planking produced the world's most enormous mosquito trap, our home.

Accompanying the arrival of the rainy season came the mosquitos, and with the mosquitos came a change in living patterns. Late in the afternoon, as the sun set, the Chácobo would pack up their belongings, leave *Biiyá*, and move closer to the water, camping there until morning. The rainy season turned the marshland into a lake.

They said a species of mosquitos lived at the water's edge in the trees rather than near the ground. To escape the mosquitos of *Biiyá*, they spent the night in the treetops, where the species lived. In the morning, they would return. They never complained.

With the increase in mosquitos, we dared not light our kerosene lamps and invite them to come in and taste new blood. So we crawled under our mosquito net and waited for morning and the Chácobo to return.

We soon discovered the idea of privacy did not exist. During the day, we had a continual stream of Chácobo who wanted to know the ways of this "couple" who had dropped in from the sky to live among them. With their faces pressed against the screen, we continually heard the phrase *"Jahuë ni toa."*

It didn't take a scientist to figure out what they meant by *Jahuë ni toa* as they pointed to various objects with their lower lips. They were asking, "What is that? What is that?"

What was interesting about the phrase was the replacement of intonation with the particle *ni* used to mark a question to the words, *Jahuë ni toa* (what-?-that). We then discovered we could end the sentence with other particles like *sa*, which expressed wonderment; *rë*, which expressed sadness; *pë*, which expressed disgust; and *pa*, which expressed surprise. For example, *Jahuë ni toa sá* = What in the world is that?

EVENTUALLY, we ran out of supplies and kerosene for our stove. Restocking meant an hour's trip to the river during the dry season and another hour back. To bring all our supplies back to the village, I asked the men for help, telling them they would be well-paid for their efforts. They all agreed.

However, as we left for the river, a couple of Chácobo men, fully adorned with feathers, walked into the village. They had come from another village, Lemón, to invite the men of *Biiyá* to a beer-fest. Walking there meant at least a four-hour walk.

I quickly learned drinking beer together was a vital feature of their law-way. As we all left, the men told their wives they would return later in the evening.

As we were walking to the river, we could hear the JAARS (Jungle Air and Radio Service)[1] seaplane landing. The men from Lemón immediately took off running. They had never seen a plane before. When I arrived, all our supplies were stacked together on the riverbank, along with enough kerosene to last a month. The men marveled that such a machine could fly.

Then the "owner" of the beer-fest shouted, "*Kanoma ni*" (Let's get going). As they disappeared into the jungle, I wondered how long it would take me to bring all the supplies back to the village. I picked up a couple of five-gallon tins of kerosene and started walking.

As I headed back, however, I heard someone behind me. Maro was carrying a kerosene tin in each hand. He had left his buddies to help a naive kid from Chicago in his time of need. When we arrived in the village, he rounded up the women and asked them to help return the supplies. Then he left.

Why did only Maro leave his drinking buddies to help me? Later, I discovered that long before we became members of *Biiyá*, the Chácobo, to my amazement, were fully aware of the biblical principle, do to others as you would want them to do for you. How was that possible? I discovered the principle when collecting stories, histories, and legends in hopes of gaining a better understanding of the Chácobo law-way.

> *Jesus said, "Therefore, whatever you want men to do to you, do also for them, for this is the Law and the Prophets" (Matthew 7:12).*

## THREE YEARS LATER

On a beautiful day in July 1962, our small SIL Aeronca seaplane was on its way to *Biiyá*. We were low on supplies, and it was time to restock. A trip to the river to pick up the supplies and bring them back to the village would probably take two and a half hours. Of course, I would need help from the men to get the supplies back.

During the height of the dry season, returning our supplies would take five times longer than during the rainy season when the water would reach high up into the treetops, flooding the jungles to the village.

In the rainy season, I would paddle my canoe to the seaplane, which would be waiting on a flooded grassland. Then, we would fill the canoe with supplies, and I would paddle back.

But now the river was at its lowest, only a couple of feet deep in some places. Instead of being three to four miles in width, forming a vast lake, it was now only thirty feet wide.

However, just as five Chácobo men of the village and I were ready to leave on a long trek to the river to meet the seaplane, Huara, from *Nucleo* village, approximately four hours away, arrived with his buddies. As the "owner" of the beer fest, he and his companions had come to invite the men of *Biiyá* to a day of drinking *jënë*, known as manioc beer.

Since the entire Chácobo way of life revolved around the manufacturing and drinking of *jënë*, no Chácobo man in his right mind would turn down such an invitation, even though it meant walking four hours to the other village and then four hours back. They told their wives they would return late in the evening.

We took off toward the river. They were going to a beer-fest, and I would pick up my cargo and bring it back to the village. As we walked, I suspected I was in trouble. If they went to a beer-drinking party, who would help me carry the cargo back? Would the invitation to a beer-drinking party overrule their previous commitment to help me return our supplies to *Biiyá*? I would soon find out.

Since none of the men from *Nucleo* had yet to see the little yellow seaplane that could land on water, when hearing it in the distance, they immediately began running like a bunch of excited kids to see who could get to the river first.

Upon arriving, I discovered that someone had neatly stacked our supplies for the next six to eight weeks on the riverbank. Along with our long-awaited mail and copies of *Time* magazine, there were supplies packed in gunny sacks, boxes, and many five-gallon kerosene tins that we needed to fuel our kerosene refrigerator, stove, and lamp.

When the partygoers had completed their plane inspection, someone shouted, *"Kanoma ni"* (Shouldn't we be going?)[2] They immediately left, disappearing single file into the jungle.

As I watched the partygoers disappear and the Aeronca seaplane take off, banking around the river's bend and flying out of sight, I stared at the stack of supplies. How many trips would it take to return to the village with everything? I picked up two five-gallon kerosene tins and took off. This was going to be a very long day.

Ten minutes down the trail back to the village, I heard the footsteps of someone coming up behind me. It was my neighbor, Maro, again. He caught up to me, carrying a kerosene tin in each hand. Amazingly, this compassionate and caring Chácobo had chosen to leave his drinking comrades to help a young, naive tenderfoot from Chicago in his time of need.

At that time, little did I know about the importance of *jënë* in the life of every Chácobo. Nevertheless, I did wonder what had motivated Maro to leave his drinking buddies to return and help me, primarily since he had never heard the words of Jesus, "And just as you want men to do to you, you also do to them likewise" (Luke 6:31). That question lay dormant in the recesses of my mind for many years. Ten years later, the answer came.

I found it in an unexpected place—some Chácobo mythology. I had been collecting stories and discovered the story of a mythical Chácobo warrior, Nahuapaxahua, fleeing for his life after a skirmish with another tribe. The essence of the story goes like this.

## MYTH OF NAHUAPAXAHUA

When fleeing for his life after a battle with the enemy, Nahuapaxahua arrives at the riverbank, needing help to get across. Seeing the alligator lying by the river, he shouts, "Grandfather Alligator, I need help. You would take me across the river if you were a human."

Hearing his plea for help, the alligator responds, "I am human! Let me take you across."

Knowing full well that all alligators by nature instinctively act like alligators and not humans, Nahuapaxahua is cautious. He places a pole vertically into the back of the alligator's head and then leaps to the top.

As they cross the river, Nahuapaxahua suspects the alligator wants to eat him. As they pass under a tree limb on the river's opposite bank, the alligator snatches at Nahuapaxahua, who leaps from the pole to the tree, escaping in time with his life.

The alligator gets angry, snaps his teeth, and roars, "Without my help, you couldn't have gotten across!"

Next, Nahuapaxahua meets a tapir. He addresses the tapir in the same way. "Grandfather Tapir, if you were a human being, you would take me home to my mother."

To this, the tapir replies, "You are mistaken. I am not a tapir. I am a human being. Your mother lives close by, and I will take you there."

But the tapir, whose natural behavior is to sleep during the day and walk around at night, is in no hurry. He first needs to sleep.

Nahuapaxahua finally gives up on the tapir and continues. Next, he meets an *agouti*, a rodent the size of a rabbit but with short ears and clawed feet. The Chácobo claim the *agouti* stole their manioc to make *jënë* (beer) for themselves.

By now, Nahuapaxahua is very weak and thin and covered with sores and insect bites. Giving him a drink of her *jënë*, Mrs. Agouti asks, "How are you, my Grandson?"

"Fine, Grandmother," he replies. "I am looking for my mother. If you were a human being, you would take me to her."

The next day, Mrs. Agouti, known as the Trickster, takes him a short distance and leaves him stranded in a forest that immediately becomes impenetrable through her magic.

Just then, when he is lost and without hope, he encounters the woodpecker, to whom he says, "Grandfather, if you were a human being, you would take me to my mother."

The woodpecker who lives above the ground replies like the other creatures, "I am not a woodpecker; I am a human being, and I will take you home."

By flying from one dead tree to another, tapping each tree along the way for Nahuapaxahua to hear and follow, Nahupaxahua is guided home by the woodpecker who decides to help him.

I ASKED, "Where did the knowledge of this moral imperative come from? How was it possible for this isolated, "primitive" tribe of the Amazonian Rainforest, a tribe that couldn't count to two, had no concept of a seven-day week, could neither read nor write, nevertheless, know the biblical principle, "Do for others what you want them to do for you" (Matthew 7:12a, Living Bible)? What was the source of this moral imperative to help someone in need?

Knowledge of the principle certainly didn't come from the Jesuits who entered the lowlands of Bolivia in the sixteenth century to "save the souls of the indigenous peoples."[3] Before the Jesuits were able to contact the tribes of Northern Bolivia, they were all expelled from South America in 1773 for political reasons.

On several occasions, the monolingual Chácobo had encountered American Maryknoll priests from the town of *Riberalta* traveling up the Benicito River in large motorboats during high water. They avoided these priests, they told us, believing the creatures wearing these white flowing robes couldn't possibly be *nohiria* (people). Since they were not sure who these creatures in white flowing robes were, they said they avoided them to be on the safe side.

In the early '50s, Tom Moreno of New Tribes Mission and his wife Wanda traveled up the Benicito River and contacted the tribe. Since the Chácobo were monolingual and couldn't be evangelized through Spanish, the Morenos eventually left and settled in the jungle village of *Guayara* Marin where they had a successful ministry.

The point is this: No historical evidence exists that some outsider learned their language and then taught them the moral principle of helping others in need as embedded in the *Myth of Nahuapaxahua*.

Having had zero exposure to the Bible, the law of Moses, and the teachings of Christianity, they nevertheless knew that to be human meant "doing for others as you would want them to do for you."

One thing is clear. They possessed knowledge of this Universal Principle long before any Christians arrived in the Americas. Their knowledge of this Universality, expressed in the *Myth of Nahuapax-*

*ahua*, revealed the existence of an innate Meta-Script "woven into the very fabric of their existence," a script that informed them what it meant to be human.

> *For when Gentiles, who do not have the law, by nature do*
> *the things in the law, these, although not having the*
> *law, are a law to themselves,*
> *who show the work of the law written in their hearts, their*
> *conscience also bearing witness, and between them-*
> *selves* their *thoughts accusing or else excusing* them).
> *(Romans 2:14-15)*

I finally concluded that a Universal Moral Principle "woven into the fabric of their existence" had been "triggered" and brought to consciousness when Maro considered my plight. He decided to leave his buddies and return to help me. I never forgot his kindness.

Replenishing of supplies - Aeronca seaplane

## CONVICTIONS

- Long before we arrived on the scene in 1955, the Chácobo were fully aware of the biblical principle, "Therefore, whatever you want men to do to you, do also to them, for this is the Law and the Prophets" (Matthew 7:12).
- When Maro turned around and left his drinking companions to help carry our supplies back to the village,

he did so, in my opinion, because a Universal Moral Imperative "written on his heart" had been "triggered" and brought to consciousness.

- If true, it meant Maro chose to obey what his conscience informed him to do, while the other men decided not to follow the voice of conscience.
- When I shared the myth and what I believed to be the source of this moral imperative with Kenneth Pike in 1978, he replied, "Gil, that's the most significant thing I've heard in the past twenty years."
- Since they all knew the principle, that if you are a human being, you must help others in need, their consciences would accuse them of that specific transgression in the day when "God will judge the secrets of men by Jesus Christ" (Romans 2:16), even though they had never heard the Universal Principle explained to them by an outsider.
- Every empiricist must explain, how did this Universal Culture-Free Moral Imperative "written on the tablets of their hearts," a Moral Imperative which they as people had the capacity to reject, come to exist in their subconscious where it could be "triggered" and brought to consciousness?
- Psychoanalyst Géza Róheim (1891 - 1953) correctly wrote, "Myth is a reliable indicator of the unconscious."[4]

# CHAPTER 3
# DOES THE GAME OF LIFE HAVE AN UMPIRE
## CHÁCOBO OF THE AMAZONIAN RAINFOREST

When living among the Chácobo of the Amazonian Rainforest, we asked many questions. Was there something deep within them that echoed a yes-no, right-wrong, or good-bad concerning choices?

Where did the binary concepts of yes-no, right-wrong, and good-bad come from? Were they invented? Or were they "triggered"?

The purpose of these Universal binary and dual categories that exist in the mind is to impose order and coherence on society. The forms and categories that shape how the game of life is played are not derived from social existence; instead, they transcend existence. So, how can humans understand how the game of life is played apart from knowing the Umpire's mind?

The question the cultural analyst must answer is: Does there exist *a priori* innate information (*etic* data) metaphorically described by the Apostle Paul as a "law written on the heart" that man and society can reject, modify, distort, and replace with meanings of their own which they then "bequest" to their children?

Romans 2:15 states: "... who show the work of the law written in their hearts, their conscience also bearing witness, and between themselves *their* thoughts accusing or else excusing *them*) ..."

If there is to be a Science of Culture, a Science of Translation, or a Science of Missiology, the analysts must have a set of constants like linguists. In this case, just as it's more proper to say the musical scale was discovered, not invented, the Universal constants could theoretically make up a conceptual framework that the analyst could use to determine what remains to be discovered.

Anthropologist Ward Goodenough hoped such a "fixed-unit," a conceptual framework, would be constructed. He believed: "The *etics* of socially meaningful behavior of all kinds [would] eventually be developed, and the study of other aspects of culture [would] achieve the rigor that we now associate with the study of language."[1]

After 38 years, the dream is dead. It is dead because secular academia continues to reject the fact that Universal forms have attached to them inherent or Divine meanings that sinful humans, to some degree, have rejected and replaced with meanings derived from social existence.

"Sound" words

# CREATED IN THE IMAGE OF GOD

## CONVICTIONS

- Just as the concepts of baseball—pitcher, batter, umpire, shortstop, and outfielder—were meaningless until someone invented the status positions and the rules of the game, the concepts and categories of family, marriage, gift, and status positions of husband, wife, son, daughter, brother, sister, and cousins were meaningless until someone structured the meanings in the subconscious.
- The meanings attached to these cultural concepts must be inherent in the mind rather than in matter and social existence.

# CHAPTER 4
# CHÁCOBO SATIRE
## THE STORY OF PAI AS A RAISI AND ESCAPING MOTHER-IN-LAW CONTROL

When a Chácobo male married, according to their game plan, it was assumed he would become the primary food supplier for his in-laws in exchange for conjugal rights to the mother-in-law's daughter.

A CHÁCOBO MYTH - THE STORY OF PAI AS A RAISI AND ESCAPING MOTHER-IN-LAW CONTROL

On a hunting trip, the village men encountered a herd of pigs running through the jungle. They immediately shouted, "*Yahua, yahua!*" (Let's go.)

So, the men chased the wild pigs, hoping to kill some. After shooting a few, they stopped the chase.

Pai, however, kept on running. He was thinking about his mother-in-law. No matter what he did, she was never satisfied.

After Pai chased the wild pigs for half a day and never shot any of them, a male *yahua* finally stopped running and asked him, "Why do you keep chasing us if you are not going to shoot us? What is your problem? And what do you want?"

"I am Pai," he replied.

And (seeing he had an unhappy marriage) the *yahua* said to Pai, "Take this female to be your wife and join us, and get down on your hands and knees."

So Pai got down on his hands and knees. Before doing this, however, he first placed his bow and arrows against a tree.

The *yahua* took Pai into another forest. As Pai ran, he grew pig's feet, hair, teeth, body, and face. Despite the transformation, he was still able to speak Chácobo.

When it became dark and he failed to return home, his wife began to cry. "A jaguar must have killed my husband," she lamented.

In the morning, Pai's wife and children searched for him. Failing to find him, they returned home weeping.

Eventually, his wife remarried. Sometime later, the Chácobo man who married Pai's widowed wife went hunting. One day, when his mother-in-law (also known as *raisi*) saw him return home without any game, she placed a rubber slab in the tortilla she was preparing. As he entered the house, his mother-in-law asked, "How did it go?"

"Terrible. I didn't see a thing."

His mother-in-law said, "Here is some meat for you to eat. Enjoy it."

He bit into the meat and failed to chew off a piece. He pulled harder. As he pulled, it snapped out and smacked him in the eye.

"Good grief!" He exclaimed to his wife. "A piece of rubber hit me in the eye. Doesn't your mother know what she's doing?"

His wife began to cry.

He told his mother-in-law the following day, "I am hunting for wild pigs. Perhaps the same thing that happened to your former son-in-law will happen to me."

Grabbing some manioc flour [to eat along the way], he left. By noon, he had arrived at a large creek.

A salt slick [that animals visited] happened to be there. His former buddy Pai was also there, but he was unaware of it. As he was making camp, he thought he might be able to shoot a few wild pigs and satisfy his mother-in-law.

Just then, Pai came up behind him and greeted him. "Is that you, Buddy?"

"Yes, it's me."

"This is where you are living?" the new son-in-law asked.

"Yes. This is where I now live," Pai replied.

"While you've lived here in the forest, your former wife and children have wondered about you. They miss you," the new son-in-law said.

"Is that so?" Pai said. "There is no way I am going to return. Besides, I have now sired another family, and returning would be impossible. But what about you? What are you doing here, Buddy?"

"I just needed to get away. My mother-in-law fed me a slab of rubber. When I pulled on it, it snapped back and hit me in the eye. So, I left. I told her that I was going hunting."

The former son-in-law, now Pig Pai, suggested to his friend that he shoot one of the old, large sows and one of her piglets.

"I want you to roast that old sow for our mother-in-law and the piglet for your wife. However, when you bring them home, I don't want you to carry them up to the house.

"Leave the sow on this side of the creek for our mother-in-law to get. But this tender piglet you give to your wife. Bring the piglet up to the house," Pig Pai told him.

So, the young man shot the old sow and piglet to roast. As he was butchering them, a vulture landed in the trees.

"Kill that vulture for me too, Buddy," Pig Pai said.

The young man shot the vulture. He gave the vulture to Pig Pai, who then magically transformed the form [not the content] of the vulture into a partridge [to get even with his ex-mother-in-law, who tried to trick him.] He then placed the partridge [vulture] on the fire-table to roast, saying, "This too is for our mother-in-law."

The young man decided it was time for him to return home. After saying goodbye to Pig Pai, he traveled all day and arrived home the next morning.

When he came to the creek, he set down the heavy package of meat for his mother-in-law before crossing to the other side. His wife's package he brought across the creek, leaving it near the house.

"He's back," they shouted. "Did you shoot any wild pigs?"

Declaring he had shot a few, Buddy told his wife that her package was near the house on "this" side of the creek. He then told his mother-in-law that the larger package was on the other side of the creek. It was too heavy to carry across.

Mother and daughter excitedly left together to get the meat. When his mother-in-law saw the size of her bundle, she called to her daughter, "Come and help me lift the basket so I can carry it back across the creek."

The daughter helped her mother.

"Now, you cross the creek first, and I will follow," the mother told her daughter.

But as the mother crossed the log, it began to break when she reached the middle. The weight of the mother-in-law and the heavy load she was carrying split the log in two.

While holding on to the bundle of roasted meat, she screamed and fell into the creek. As she hit the water, the tooth of the pig cut her on the head with a profusion of blood. So much bleeding spilled that it turned the creek into a large lake.

After hearing the log break, the daughter ran to the water's edge and exclaimed, "Mother has disappeared into the water. She has turned into a porpoise!"

The mother-in-law, now a porpoise and bleeding from the head, swam away.

∼

As shown in the above satire, the Chácobo of another age were critical of their food practice.

Niebuhr wrote:

> Man seeks to protect himself against nature's contingencies; but cannot do so without transgressing the limits set for his life. Therefore, all human life [all cultures] is involved in seeking security at the expense of other life. The perils of nature are thereby transmuted into more grievous forms of human history.[1]

The new form the Chácobo created necessitated restructuring the nuclear family and replacing the *husband-wife* dyad with a mother-daughter one.

Because the Divine meanings attached to the forms of family, marriage, husband and wife had been "triggered" and brought to consciousness, these satirists of another age innately knew that Chácobo newlyweds should be allowed to become "one flesh." They should be free to set up independent households.

The satirist is informing his audience that a mother's rights to her daughter as a "helpmate" are transferred to her husband. The mother-daughter bond must be broken as well as the contractual meaning of the term *raisi* and the institution of the household-of-five.

Sadly, from one generation to the next, the satire fell on deaf ears. A daily supply of beer, the "staff-of-life," transcended the needs of the spirit.

By submitting to the material forces of the Amazonian Rainforest, the Divine Meta-Script "written on their hearts" that informed the Chácobo how to live had been corrupted and was leading them down a path to cultural extinction.

The good news is that, as an outsider, I was able to counsel young Chácobo men that the advice given by their own sages needed to be taken seriously. If it was not heeded, they would find themselves living under the mother-in-law control.

IN THE BEGINNING, I was unaware of how their "social game" was played. My goal was to place a Chácobo bilingual schoolteacher in each village, completely unaware that at the moment these teachers married, we would be confronted with a cultural form that had "no place in the Divine Plan."

Thanks to anthropology professor Francis L. K. Hsu (1909 - 1999), it became clear that the Chácobo had restructured the nuclear family. Besides replacing the covenantal dyad of *husband-wife* with that of mother-daughter, they also created a negative form called *raisi*.

When a Chácobo bachelor married, he didn't become a son-in-law; he became a *raisi*. His duty in life was to supply food for his wife's parents whom he addressed as *raisi*.

His *raisi* in turn promised him conjugal rights to the in-law's daughter and all the beer he could drink. The beer was made by his *raisi* (mother-in-law) and his wife.

Once we figured out how their social security system worked, we realized we had a problem. Our long-range plans were blocked and hindered by Chácobo mothers-in-law who refused to let their married daughters leave home and become "one flesh" with their husbands.

To our dismay, we discovered that when a Chácobo school teacher became a *raisi,* it meant he had to submit to the desires of his *raisi* (mother-in-law). He was expected to live in the village and household where it was his duty to be the main food supplier in exchange for conjugal rights to the mother-in-law's daughter.

This tension between which dyad should be dominant in society, mother-daughter or *husband-wife,* is revealed in the above satire, *The Story of Pai as a Raisi and Escaping Mother-in-Law Control*, created by a *raisi* (son-in-law) who clearly understood that their Chácobo ancestors had replaced Divine meanings with new meanings shaped by social existence in the Amazonian Rainforest.

Sad *raisi* who can't please his mother-in-law

## CONVICTIONS

- At some point in their history, the Chácobo restructured the nuclear family, replacing the covenantal dyad of *husband-wife* with that of mother-daughter. In doing so, they put mothers-in-law in control of all family decisions.
- From an *etic* perspective, the restructuring of the nuclear family and putting mothers-in-law in control had "no place in the Divine Plan."
- Chácobo sages of another era created satire warning their fellow tribesmen not to be tricked. Their ancestors had created a new form called *raisi*, a form which had "no place in the Divine Plan."

## CREATED IN THE IMAGE OF GOD

> *Moreover the law entered that the offense might abound. But where sin abounded, grace abounded much more ... (Romans 5:20)*

- The form reduced sons-in-law to functional cogs weighed down with the duty of being food suppliers for their wives' families.

# CHAPTER 5
# A MIND STRUCTURED WITH A PRIORI KNOWLEDGE
## INNATE MEANINGS BELONG TO GOD

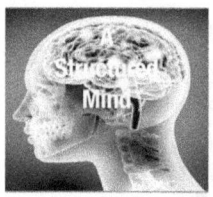

*So God created man in His own image; in the image of God He created him; male and female He created them. (Genesis 1:27)*

Marian and I were assigned to a dying tribe of 133 people that lived in four villages in a remote area of Bolivia. We had come to proclaim a message of hope and deliverance from sin.

While their worldview acknowledged sin, which they called *jocha*, they had no idea of its origin or penalty. We had to fill in the blanks. In time, we discovered we were dealing with "forms common to all."

One such form was that of the family. According to theologian Cornelis Van Til, "The family is the simplest and smallest unit of society and the real foundation of culture."[1]

The fundamental foundation of culture consists of four status positions: father, mother, and their sons and daughters.

In contrast, the Chácobo concept of the family consisted of a father, mother, sons, daughters, and parallel cousins whom they had classified as brothers and sisters. By merging mutually exclusive status positions, that of children of father and mother and children of uncles and aunts, they created a new form of family that "fit" the Amazonian Rainforest.

But why had they classified parallel cousins as brothers and sisters? There had to be a reason. By doing so, they violated the Rules of Logic: $A \neq B$; a sibling cannot be a cousin because their parents are different.

Laws of Logic are important because they are the rules of correct reasoning. "They reflect how God thinks and how we must think if we are to think correctly. Laws of Logic are also called "rules of inference." Correct reasoning can never violate a logic rule."[2]

To my dismay, I discovered that missionary anthropologists had set aside the Laws of Logic, forfeiting their ability to interpret sociological data from a Divine perspective—in other words, "the way God thinks."

Because I refused to accept the missiological dogma "that all meanings belong to the people," I found myself operating outside the bounds set forth by SIL's anthropology department and on the side of those who believed logic was important.

When linguist Kenneth Pike, president of SIL, wrote: "A person may distort Innate Positive Universals into negative particular actions,"[3] in effect, he was saying the God who created man "in His image" has given man the freedom to replace Divine meanings with meanings "that belong to the people."

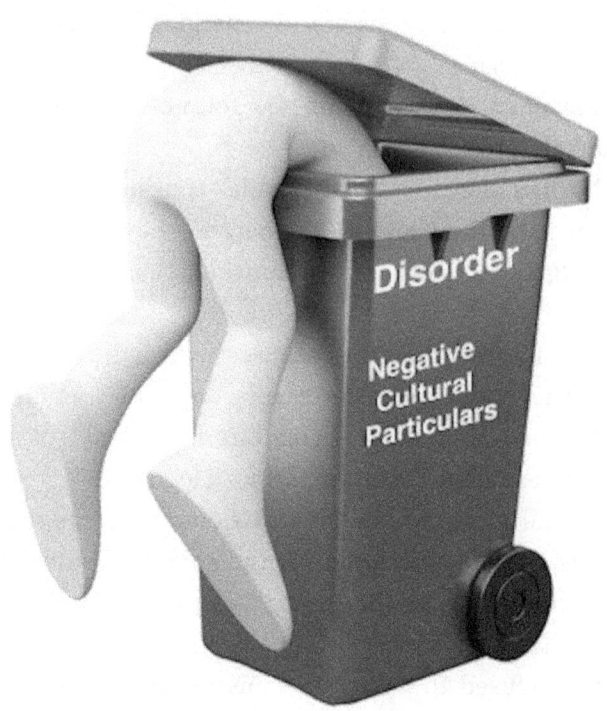

Negative cultural particulars

In other words, humans are free to reject and replace "fixed" and absolute meanings that belong to God with relative meanings that belong to humans. As the Apostle Paul points out, man can reject the Universal Rules of the spiritual game known as culture and "go his own way."

> "... who in bygone generations allowed all nations to walk in their own ways.
> "Nevertheless He did not leave Himself without witness, in that He did good, gave us rain from heaven and fruitful seasons, filling our hearts with food and gladness" (Acts 14:16-17).

For example, Chácobo sages of another age innately knew their fellow tribespeople had restructured the nuclear family, giving it a form that "fit" the environment of the Amazonian Rainforest. They innately knew the Universal, the covenantal dyad of *husband-wife*, had been replaced with a cultural particular. For the Chácobo, the cultural particular was the mother-daughter dyad. It was selected because it "fit" the environment.

The replacement of the Universal, the *husband-wife* dyad, with a cultural particular, that of mother-daughter, meant that when a couple married, every husband/son-in-law became what the Chácobo called a *raisi*; that is, one who promised his in-laws he would provide them with a daily supply of fish and wildlife in exchange for conjugal rights to their daughter.

It was a unique security system designed to reduce a family's anxiety over existence. It was a form that rejected God as Provider.

The discovery of Chácobo satire validated my quizzical hunch. Most of the stories centered around the dominant, controlling mother-in-law. Then, the mother-in-law, a representative of the particular, eventually dies, and couples are free to become "one flesh" and set up independent households.

The existence of such stories compelled me to become an innatist, one who believes the unconscious mind contains knowledge from birth that informs humans how to live.

Upon discovering Chácobo satire, I made it my mission to inform unmarried Chácobo males about the dangers of becoming a *raisi*. Becoming a *raisi* meant the loss of freedom. God was no longer his Provider.

My informant, Rabi, described the form of marriage the Chácobo practiced as a prison. In exchange for a daughter, his mother-in-law would ensure her son-in-law kept his part of the bargain. His duty was to maintain the fire-table filled with fish and wildlife.

When Rabi began serving the entire tribe, his mother-in-law lost control over his life. After a couple of years, his wife and children were taken away. Because he failed to fulfill his duty as a *raisi*, his mother-in-law took her daughter and grandchildren back.

Eventually, Rabi remarried. This time, he married a non-Chácobo (Bolivian) daughter whose parents had become members of the *Alto Ivon* Chácobo village. On my visit to the Chácobo in 1998, Rabi informed me the traditional duty of a son-in-law, to supply his in-laws with a daily supply of fish and wildlife, was to end after one year. Then, couples were free to become "one flesh" and assume new status positions. But in reality, that didn't happen.

> *For the husband is head of the wife, as also Christ is head of the church; and He is the Savior of the body. (Ephesians 5:23)*

Hebrew language

## CONVICTIONS

- Whenever a form familiar to all has a meaning derived from social existence in a particular environment, we not only have a meaning "that belongs to the people," it is a meaning that has replaced a meaning that is "fixed," constant, and absolute. Such a linguistic phenomenon Pike labeled *etic* divergence.

- Every person's mind contains forms common to all. They have attached inherent meanings that belong to God rather than man.
- A Universal-Lexicon structured in the unconscious mind contains Universal forms to which are attached inherent meanings. If such a lexicon didn't exist, no "sound words" such as those described by the Apostle Paul would exist that make positive communication possible.

*Hold fast the pattern of sound words which you have heard from me, in faith and love which are in Christ Jesus. (II Timothy 1:13)*

- Replacing inherent meanings with meanings that "belong to the people" misrepresents the Universal, and therefore, sins against God, the Creator of meaning.

## CHAPTER 6
# THE GREAT DISCOVERY: CHÁCOBO SATIRE
### PËTA REJECTS THE ROLE OF RAISI

The Chácobo family exhibited all the qualities of a mechanistic society with ascribed functions for each member designed to relieve particular existential anxieties. Each member of the system knew what their ascribed function was. Commands were never given. Instead, there were complaints and suggestions like, "Too bad the beer is running out," or "There is no meat on the fire-table."

As a cultural outsider observing the mysteries of Chácobo behavioral patterns for a few years, I concluded the Chácobo socio-economic operating system was maiming them. They were a leaderless, goalless, and dying culture. The question was why?

Providentially, anthropologist Francis L. K. Hsu in his article "Kinship and Ways of Life" provided the answer:

> The total effect of the dominance of the attributes of one structural dyad [within the nuclear family] leads to a particular kind of kinship content, which in turn strongly conditions the pattern of thought and behavior of the individuals reared in the kinship system in society at large.[1]

At some point in their history, the Chácobo had replaced the covenantal-based dyad of *husband and wife* which promoted freedom and self-actualization[2] with the biological dyad of mother and daughter. Their function was to provide beer for the household-of-five and all the men residing in the men's communal house.

However, if the Chácobo were to survive in the modern economy that pressed in around them, they needed a new socio-cultural operating system—one that would free them from the status position of person-things;[3] i.e., cogs assigned specific functions to keep the beer flowing.

The assigned duties masquerading as functions were maiming them. Instead of carrying out ascribed functions, they needed to return to natural roles which would give them the freedom to self-actualize.

After discovering the Chácobo innately knew the primary quality of being human was to love one's neighbor and help him in his time of need, it was apparent it was a moral principle they could not have learned from any outside source.

As I was collecting Chácobo legends from my neighbor, Maro, the stories exposed the maiming effect of the mother-daughter biological dyad as the dominant dyad in their society.

Sometime in the remote past, Chácobo sages, as critical observers of what it meant to be a *raisi* (son-in-law), fully understood that the status position was maiming them. As moral beings, they camouflaged their opposition to the meanings their ancestors had attached to the concepts of marriage and family by creating satire.

They believed the dominant biological dyad of the nuclear family, the mother-daughter dyad, which served a specific function, needed to be replaced with the covenantal dyad of *husband-wife*, a dyad that promoted freedom and self-actualization.

Unknown to them, their lifeways and traditions, in the words of the Apostle Paul, had been shaped by the "material elements of their environment," which was the Amazonian Rainforest. It had produced a new status position called *raisi*.

> *Beware lest anyone cheat you through philosophy and empty deceit, according to the tradition of men, according to the basic principles of the world, and not according to Christ. (Colossians 2:8)*

The discovery was a wake-up call that we needed to set the Chácobo free from ascribed functions so they could survive as a viable culture. It meant Marian and I were in a strategic position of moving away from being the guardians of a dying function-based society to being promoters of an operating system grounded in cultural forms common to all people. Attached to those forms were Divine meanings that would promote freedom.

These Chácobo sages intuitively knew there was something unnatural about their cultural operating system. Their design for living had placed structural restraints on their freedom to live meaningful lives as real husbands and real wives.

Because of their ascribed functions, functions passed down from one generation to the next, the present generation was not free to self-actualize and become school teachers, merchants, community leaders, and church elders. They were a leaderless and goalless society.

Fearing to make their convictions known, they dressed up their convictions with satire. As I collected the stories, it was obvious that few Chácobo recognized the myths as satire. To them, they were just legends, not warnings that they should heed.

When I shared the satire with Rabi, who was now a *raisi* and a food supplier for a Chácobo household-of-five (he was the fifth member), he immediately recognized he was trapped. He had no freedom to self-actualize.

It was a great day when I discovered Chácobo "insiders" who knew their cultural forms of family and marriage were maiming them. I am forever thankful for the verbal records passed down from generation to generation. Each account concluded that the Chácobo lifeway was a prison from which Chácobo males needed to be set free.

The following satire reveals the intense feelings of a Chácobo bachelor who wanted no part in becoming a *raisi* to provide food for a Chácobo household-of-five. To do so would reduce him to a "person-thing."

Pëta was unmarried, and so was the young lady of this story.

∽

## PËTA REJECTS THE ROLE OF RAISI

Pëta is a lovely fellow. One day, he meets a young lady in the forest whom he takes home. She becomes his wife. After living together for several months, his wife becomes pregnant, and she gives birth to their first child.

One day, Pëta's wife says, "I want to go home and visit my mother. I'm taking our son with me."

"My wish is that you do not go, but go and see her if you so desire," Pëta replies.

So she takes their son and leaves.

After his wife has been gone for some time, Pëta decides to make his wife return since he doesn't want her to visit his mother-in-law. He is determined that she not visit her mother [because she might be compelled to remain].

So, Pëta transforms himself into a small bird. He flies past his wife and son and lands on the trail ahead. By now, she is halfway there. She never sees Pëta fly by. Pëta sits down on the trail and growls like a jaguar.

"Listen, my son; a jaguar [is ahead of us]," his wife exclaimed. "Let's get back to your father."

So, she runs back as quickly as possible. When she arrives home, she sees Pëta making arrows on his stool. She is disappointed that she couldn't visit her mother.

"How did it go?" Pëta asks. "Did you see your mother?"

"We never arrived," she replies. "There was a dangerous jaguar on the trail."

He answers, "Didn't I warn you the trail is full of jaguars?"

"You were right, and I didn't believe you. It was frightening!"

Some time passes, and Pëta's wife says again, "I want to see my mother."

Pëta tells her to go but refuses to accompany her.

[The informant then adds: Pëta was probably embarrassed to see his in-laws because he had taken their daughter away.]

So the wife goes the second time, and the same thing happens again. This time, Pëta's growl sounds like two tigers. Hearing the growls, she runs back home. When she arrives, she sees Pëta sitting on his stool, working on his arrows.

"What happened?" He asks. "Don't tell me you decided to come back again."

"It is dangerous to travel alone. Too many jaguars. I think you need to take us."

"That would be impossible," he says, and Pëta refuses to go.

Jaguar in the Amazonian Rainforest

## CONVICTIONS

- Psychoanalyst Geza Róheim is correct when he writes: "Myth [especially satire] is a reliable indicator of the unconscious."[4]
- The story of *Pëta* reveals the sentiments of a sage who refused to become a *raisi* because the status position suppressed freedom and self-actualization. The satirist rebelled against being reduced to a functional cog when he married.
- *The Dying Raisi* (chapter 8) and *Pëta Rejects the Role of Raisi* (chapter 6) imply the existence of internal Universal Principles for living that can be "triggered" and brought to consciousness; namely, that the foundational basis of society is the nuclear family and not some other family type.
- There is no more dangerous idea in missiology than the notion that God loves multiculturalism, validated by the existence of hundreds of family types around the world, as long as they functionally meet the needs of society.
- Failure to recognize the "one-flesh" covenantal principle that makes the *husband-wife* dyad the dominant dyad of the nuclear family is a recipe for failure in church planting and community development.
- Unless the function of "mother's helper" ascribed to Chácobo daughters and the function of food supplier for the household-of-five ascribed to sons-in-law was terminated, it meant our efforts to train a core of young people having the skills and know-how to lead the Chácobo people into the 21st century would fail.
- Contrary to what contextualizing missiologists like Charles Kraft proclaim: "There is no such thing as an absolute set of cultural forms ... that would imply the

existence of some sort of absolute cultural structure [i.e., some set of absolute cultural forms] are so misleading that they must be abandoned."[5]

- Every person has a set of absolute cultural forms to which are attached Divine meanings that fallen man can reject and replace with meanings "that belong to the people."
- The story of *Pëta* reveals the sentiments of a married man who refused to become a *raisi* because the status position would suppress his freedom and ability to self-actualize. The creator of the satire rebelled against being reduced to a functional cog in a food supply system that robbed him of his independence when he married.

# CHAPTER 7
# THE MARRIAGE TRAP: BECOMING A RAISI
## FORMER RAISI CALLED IT A PRISON

Socially, politically, and economically, the Chácobo status position within Bolivian society was that of the "tail." Many Bolivians considered them to be savages rather than people. We soon learned they could only count to two and only had four colors: black and white, *shini* (red, orange, yellow), and *niaba* (blue, green, brown).

They had no concept of a seven-day week, were strangers to a market-money economy, and lived inland away from the rivers to avoid contact with the outside world. They numbered 133 members and lived in four villages.

While they filled our minds with existential questions of all kinds, the big unanswered question in their minds was why we had come to live with them. However, we had to learn to speak Chácobo before we could tell them, which took time.

In a few years, they would learn why we had come to live among them and why we wanted to learn their language. In the meantime, they feared what they called the *Carayana*, those who tapped the trees for rubber.

There were times when we returned to the village after being gone for a few months, only to find the small village of *Biiyá* completely empty.

Because the Chácobo feared being captured by some ruthless rubber baron or the Bolivian military, they retreated to the safety of the Amazonian Rainforest, awaiting the day we returned. Unknown to us, we had become their security blanket.

Yet, the linguistic task before us appeared to be doable. First, we had to determine how many phonemes made up their alphabet. Next, we needed to uncover the grammatical forms of their language.

Then, SIL expected us to produce publishable grammar, make primers, write readers, translate the New Testament, lead some to Christ; and, finally, witness the birth of a local church.

After deciding how many phonemes comprised the Chácobo alphabet, we published our first primer, and Marian held our first reading class. It was a class of only four students.

Fourteen years later, two of the students, Rabi and Cana, would be serving their communities as bilingual school teachers approved by the Bolivian government.

Because we both came from a church that gave birth to the AWANA Youth Program, our missiological strategy, unlike that of our colleagues, which began with adults, was to start with kids "because kids matter to God."[1]

As an eight-year-old attending the first AWANA Club in America, they constantly informed me that Approved Workmen Are Not Ashamed. From my perspective, what the Chácobo needed besides the Bible was a core of young people who were not ashamed of their language, their way of life, their attire, or the One who had come to earth to save them from a law-way that led to spiritual and material death. In time, they would become adults with the skills and know-how to help their people transition into a world they did not yet understand.

In 1962-1963, when the Bolivian president came to *Riberalta*, we took our best student, Rabi, along with his father, to meet him. The purpose of the visit was twofold: first, to show President Victor Paz Estenssoro of Bolivia some of the positive fruits of SIL's presence in the country; and second, to introduce the Chácobo to the world beyond the indigenous Indian tribe. After our brief chat with the Bolivian president, I explained to Rabi's father, Caco, the need for a core of bilingual-bicultural Chácobo who could lead their people into the future. I then expressed my desire to send his son to a Christian boarding school near our SIL Center. His father and mother approved. There, he would learn the ways of a culture his parents feared.

In time, young Rabi would become an adult who, like Moses, would lead his people out of a cultural operating system that suppressed the emergence of men who could serve the whole community.

In 1964, we enrolled Rabi in a Norwegian Pentecostal Mission School upriver from our SIL Center. The following year, we enrolled Paë, and the next, Carmelo, followed by others. Because of the skills and know-how they would acquire and the fact they would be bilingual and bicultural, I assumed the community would select them as their leaders.

But unknown to me, there existed in the background a cultural form that would attempt to torpedo our plans to produce a core of Approved Workmen Who Are Not Ashamed of their language and culture, young men with the skills and know-how to lead their people into an economy they didn't comprehend at that time. It was a cultural form that promised them food security in exchange for their freedom.

∼

## ONE-FLESH UNION IS A SPIRITUAL UNION

When the Bible says, "A man leaves his father and mother and is united to his wife, and they become one-flesh" (Genesis 2:24, New International Version), the reference is not only to sexual relations "... but also, and more especially to the spiritual relationship."[2]

This clearly is the interpretation the Apostle Paul gives to this passage in I Corinthians. 6:16:

> *Or do you not know that he who is joined to a harlot is one body* with her? *For* "the two," *He says,* "shall become one flesh."

Like most of humanity, the church at Corinth interpreted the sexual union to be merely a physical act that did not affect a person spiritually.

Clearly, it is God, not man, who determines the structure and meaning of marriage. Ignored by humankind is the fact that marriage takes place under the decree of the Creator, for Jesus said: "Therefore what God has joined together, let not man separate" (Matthew 19:6b).

When the Apostle Paul corrected the Corinthian church regarding their immoral sexual behavior, he defined the one-flesh principle of Genesis 2:24 in terms of a spiritual union, a union even the pagan Corinthians, who did not have the Scriptures, should have known.

The Apostle Paul's statement suggests that sexual intercourse itself should have "triggered" the principle and brought to consciousness its spiritual meaning.

∼

THE MOTHER-DAUGHTER DYAD did not manifest itself as a form until the day "my kids" married. According to the Apostle Paul, the form had "no place in the Divine Plan." In fact, to my amazement, it was a cultural form that Chácobo ancestors had warned their tribe about.

However, aware that they could be expelled from the community, these brave Chácobo sages of ages past used satire to raise a red flag, signaling that replacing the *husband-wife* dyad with that of mother-daughter was a dangerous idea. They ignored the warning.

The cultural form that had "no place in the Divine Plan" had to do with a residence rule. This rule declared that no daughter could leave her father and mother at marriage. She was her mother's helpmate and needed for producing beer, the Chácobo staple of life. It was a form that remained hidden until the day one of "my kids" married.

As an outside observer, I considered it my task to understand the Chácobo law-way. The food-beer delivery system they created enabled members of one village to collectively provide enough food and beer to hold a Five-Day New Moon Fiesta.

When the women harvested the manioc, they would gather not only to harvest the manioc, but to convert part of the manioc into manioc flour and part into manioc beer. After each harvest, the partying began, each village taking turns inviting another village over. After enough manioc beer was made and fish and wildlife roasted, the Chácobo community would invite an adjoining village over to share in the bounty.

Arriving in their bark canoes, the men trekked to the village, followed by the women. The men danced into the village and to the men's communal house while the women followed, carrying all their worldly possessions. The women set up camp outside the men's communal house.

Before the men began to eat, drink, and dance around a large pot of manioc beer in the center of the village, the local shaman offered communion to each man. The elements consisted of a beer sip followed by a meat pinch. It was a closed communion provided for only men.

Eventually, these yearly festive events dedicated to the *Bird Above* ceased to exist. Chácobo Christians recognized these rituals had "no place in the Divine Plan."

## IN NON-LITERATE SOCIETIES NO WRITTEN CONTRACTS EXIST

All contracts are verbal. Before a Chácobo bachelor marries, he must make a contract, not with his potential wife, but with his potential in-laws.

When the verbal agreement is sealed, as previously explained, they call each other *raisi*, meaning one did not become a son-in-law, father-in-law, or mother-in-law at marriage. Instead, one became a *raisi*.

Since Caco Pistia, the first Chácobo believer, married someone whose parents were deceased, he was not obligated to supply his wife's parents with fish, wildlife, food from his garden, and help around the house in exchange for conjugal rights. He was free to serve the Lord. He didn't acquire the role of *raisi*. It also meant his wife was free to be her husband's helpmate.

As I observed the behavior of the Chácobo, it became apparent that Chácobo women ruled. They ruled covertly. They ruled by complaining. "The meat on the fire-table is running low. Go hunting."

As I gained knowledge of the meanings attached to Universal concepts like father, mother, son, daughter, son-in-law, etc., to my surprise, the meanings they attached to these Universal concepts differed from mine. This knowledge dramatically changed how I approached evangelism, church planting, and community development.

This tension between which dyad should be the dominant dyad in the family, mother-daughter or *husband-wife*, is revealed in the satiric piece *The Story of Pai as a Raisi and Escaping Mother-in-*

*Law Control* (chapter 4, "Chácobo Satire"). Pai understood his ancestors had replaced the inherent meanings attached to Universal concepts of husband, wife, family, and marriage with new meanings shaped by social existence in the Amazonian Rainforest.

In the story, the satirist informs his audience the mother should be removed from the jealousy triangle where the son-in-law and mother-in-law compete for the same woman's allegiance.

Such a story couldn't have been conceived unless the one-flesh principle of *husband-wife* had been written in a Universal-Lexicon structured in the unconscious mind.

Because the Divine meanings attached to the concepts of family, marriage, husband, and wife were "recorded" in the unconscious mind and made accessible by being "triggered" and brought to consciousness, the satirist innately knew that newlyweds should be allowed to become "one flesh."

They should be free to set up independent households.

However, in doing so, it would strike a blow to a very creative food delivery system designed to provide older people with a constant supply of fish and wildlife.

In the words of theologian Reinhold Niebuhr (1892 - 1971), Chácobo society was "involved in seeking security at the expense of other life;"[3] namely, the freedom of married sons and daughters.

By imposing such a system, "The perils of nature are thereby transmuted into more grievous forms of human history."[4] One former *raisi* called it a prison, like having the police watch one's every move.

The satirist informs his audience that a mother's rights to her daughter should be terminated when the daughter marries. The mother-daughter bond, the contractual meaning of the term *raisi*, and the institution of the household-of-five (the son-in-law becomes the fifth member), must be broken.

But sadly, from one generation to the next, the satire fell on deaf ears. The need for a daily supply of manioc beer, the Chácobo staff-of-life, along with a daily supply of fish and wildlife, transcended the spirit's needs.

By submitting to the material forces of the Amazonian Rainforest, the Divine Meta-Script "written on the heart" transmuted into a more grievous form of history, leading the Chácobo down a path toward cultural extinction.

The good news is that I, as an "outsider," could counsel young Chácobo men that their sages' advice needed to be taken seriously. More importantly, the perspective on marriage in the Word of God supported the one-flesh principle of *husband-wife* as previously quoted in Genesis 2:24.

Chácobo culture

## CONVICTIONS

- When the Chácobo created the status position of *raisi*, they made a form that not only suppressed husbands and wives from becoming "one flesh," they created a form that had "no place in the Divine Plan."[5]
- The Chácobo replaced God as their Provider with a status position they called *raisi*.

- They used their daughter to gain a fish and wildlife provider. Pity the family that had no daughters.
- Sages of the past would have never created *The Story of Pai as a Raisi and Escaping Mother-in-Law Control* (chapter 4, "Chácobo Satire") if the one-flesh principle of *husband-wife* had not been structured in the unconscious mind where it was "triggered" and brought to consciousness.

# CHAPTER 8
# THE DYING RAISI
## CHÁCOBO SATIRE

Who will provide the food and bear?

## CREATED IN THE IMAGE OF GOD

I was surprised to discover the Chácobo innately knew that they should love their neighbors as they loved themselves.

> *"'You shall not take vengeance, nor bear any grudge against the children of your people, but you shall love your neighbor as yourself; I am the LORD"* (Leviticus 19:18).

For the Chácobo, the primary quality of being human entailed loving one's neighbor and helping them in their time of need. This rule for living was not "learned." It was innate.

As I collected Chácobo myths from my neighbor, Maro, I discovered many humorous stories critical of how they had structured their villages. Some elders used these funny stories to expose the maiming effect of a family type that compelled all the men to live in a men's communal house separated from their wives. By physically separating husbands from their wives, no husband was the head of the family.

What had maimed these Chácobo satirists was the *raisi* form. The moment they made the contract, he and his new wife lost the freedom to self-actualize.

The Chácobo had replaced a Positive Universal with a negative cultural particular. They replaced the *husband-wife* dyad with that of mother-daughter. What the *raisi* would get in return would be a roof over his head, meals supplied by his mother-in-law, and all the manioc beer he could drink.

As I collected the satires they had created, it was obvious that few, if any, Chácobo recognized them to be satires. Instead of recognizing these stories as warnings that they needed to heed, they were just stories.

However, Rabi was surprised when I pointed out that the meanings we attach to the marriage form were not the same as his. I said when he married, he became a *raisi*, someone who had made a contract with his in-laws to be their food supplier in exchange for conjugal rights to their daughter. When I married, I became a son-in-law who married their daughter.

He immediately recognized he had been tricked. He had no freedom and eventually called the cultural form a "prison."

Never did I expect to uncover such satire. I am forever thankful for the verbal records that were passed down from one generation to the next. Each account concluded that the Chácobo lifeway was a prison from which they needed to be set free. They expressed their sentiments in the following story, *The Dying Raisi,* and previously in chapter 6, *Pëta Rejects the Role of Raisi.*

## THE DYING RAISI (SON-IN-LAW)

His troubles began when he married. When he took their daughter as his wife, his in-laws were initially very content. Then, things at home began to change.

He first noticed he was getting thinner and thinner. In dismay, he asked himself, "Why am I becoming so thin?"

He said to his wife: "I am not sick. But for some reason, I am getting weaker and weaker. If this keeps up, I can no longer feed you all."

He began to hear his mother-in-law complain to his wife, "I see your husband is not taking care of you. I wonder what is making him so thin? He has stopped hunting. If he wastes away like this, how in the world will we survive?"

The *raisi* was sad. He could only wonder why he was getting so thin when he wasn't sick. He would talk to his wife about it. She had no idea.

One night, he concluded he was going to die, although he had also concluded there was nothing wrong with him. Yet, he continued to waste away.

"I always need to rest. I cannot get strong again," he told his wife.

Then, one night, when he could not sleep, he noticed his mother-in-law, sleeping next to him, getting out of her hammock. As she rose, she turned her buttocks toward his nose and released potent gas from her anus. It was the strongest, foulest smell he had ever experienced. It frightened him. "Could it be my mother-in-law is trying to gas me to death?"

Three more times that night, she released gas in his direction so he would inhale and swallow it. "I think I am wasting away because of smelling this powerful gas," he concluded.

In the morning, he asked his wife for his bag made of bark where he kept everything he needed to make arrows. "I want my roll of beeswax," he said.

"What do you want this for?" she asked.

"I want to fix my arrows for hunting. I think I am going to get well."

His wife handed him the bag containing his beeswax roll for gluing feathers to the arrow shaft.

When his wife left, he took out the beeswax and softened it.

His wife had gone out with her mother to gather firewood, so she did not see what he was doing. As he pretended to be working his arrows, he thought, "My *raisi* is trying to kill me. I need to stop her."

When his mother-in-law, wife, and everyone else were away, he warmed the beeswax over a fire to make it soft and pliable. He pulled and stretched it, forming a long plug. Then he laid it aside.

When night came, he lay awake. He was going to plug up his mother-in-law.

By midnight, everyone was asleep. Then his mother-in-law farted and released flatus in his direction. It was the same as the others—strong. He inserted a beeswax plug between the hammock strings into her rectum when she was sleeping.

Immediately, the young man's arms became stronger. When his mother-in-law got up again to release gas in his face, it backfired, and his mother-in-law fell dead into her hammock.

When the *raisi* saw what happened, he exclaimed silently, "Oh, good grief! Now, I have killed my mother-in-law. If her children from another *raisi* find out, they will kill me."

When morning came, her sons, daughters, and their spouses got up. They all left her alone, not wanting to wake her. Her daughter (his wife) finally asked, "I wonder why mother is sleeping so long? Kids, go wake her up."

The grandchildren ran to Grandmother and shouted, "It's time to get up, Grandma. The sun is up." They shook her hammock, "Why are you still sleeping?"

She was silent. Her body was stiff and cold.

In the meantime, the son-in-law said to himself, "Good grief! I killed my mother-in-law." The *raisi* felt ashamed.

After they examined the body, they concluded they would never know what killed her. His wife cried for months because she was very loyal to her mother.

After a few months, the *raisi* regained his weight and began supplying wildlife for his wife and children.

∼

## MARO: MY INFORMANT'S PERSPECTIVE

Maro interpreted the satire: "Daughters are very loyal to their mothers. This is customary among the Chácobo."

Maro's closing remarks were revelatory. He was stating a cultural norm. In marriage, no couple becomes "one flesh." Mothers-in-law rule.

How could the satirist who wrote the story, *The Dying Raisi*, know that when their ancestors created the status position of *raisi*, they were "transgressing the limits set for his life?"[1]

By creating the cultural form of *raisi*, the Chácobo had instituted a new lifeway designed to reduce anxiety about how their daily food needs would be met. Perhaps an amazing design, but the Apostle Paul describes it as having "no place in the Divine Plan."

Becoming a *Raisi*

## CONVICTIONS

- The above stories imply the existence of a Universal Rule for living structured in the unconscious mind, a rule brought to consciousness by being "triggered" in a socio-linguistic situation.
- The story of *The Dying Raisi* reveals the sentiments of a *raisi* who realized his mother-in-law was not happy with the amount of food he supplied the household-of-five. If she gassed him to death, her daughter could remarry, and she could gain a "better" food provider.

- Contrary to what contextualizing missiologists like Kraft proclaim,[2] existing in the mind of every person is a set of absolute cultural forms common to all people. Attached to them are Divine meanings that fallen man can reject and replace with meanings "that belong to the people."

# CHAPTER 9
# A CULTURAL LAW-WAY SNEAKED INTO HISTORY AND HAS NO PLACE IN THE DIVINE PLAN

## "THE LAW" (ABSTRACT) OR "THE LAW" (MOSAIC)

Define law

Missionaries today are told that no form has an inherent meaning. Instead, according to anthropologist Charles Kraft, "God seeks to use and cooperate with human beings in the continued use of relative cultural forms to express absolute supra-cultural meaning."[1]

That is a controversial statement. Not only is it contentious, but it is a statement that should be rejected because it is impossible to express what is true by using forms whose meanings are derived from social existence known as culture.

Therefore, every missionary must ask: Is the unconscious mind of every child coming into the world structured with forms or concepts to which there are attached Divine meanings that are "fixed," constant, and absolute? Or, are all meanings derived from social existence as posited by Karl Marx, Mao Zedong, and anthropologists like Charles Kraft?

If the mind of every child that comes into the world is a blank slate with no "fixed" meanings, then meaning is a material phenomenon, and all meanings must be abstracted from experience and the five senses. In other words, no Universal Truth exists.

Applying this to other analogies, a husband can be a female; a fetus can be a glob of meaningless cells; the color of one's skin can be a moral organ. Such meanings clearly "belong to the people."[2]

According to the Apostle Paul, such "law-way sneaked into" history and has "no place in the Divine Plan" (Romans 5:20), translating νόμος (absent the Greek article), as having the quality of abstract law rather than concrete law. I translate Romans 5:20 as:

> *A cultural law-way of living [νόμος absent article],*
>   *which has "no place in the Divine Plan," "sneaked*
>   *into history," bringing about an increase in sin. But as*
>   *sin increased, God's grace increased even more.*

Compare the above translation with the translations at the end of this chapter. When one compares my translation of Romans 5:20, the meanings rendered are vastly different.

Whereas I translate νόμος absent the article as an abstraction, a "law-way of living," every English translator renders νόμος absent the Greek article, as either "the law" or "The Law."

I adhere to a grammatical rule from the *New Testament Greek for Beginners* that states: "Where the Greek article does not appear, the definite article should not be inserted in the English translation."[3] They ignore the rule.

In this regard, Greek scholar James Moulton (1863 - 1917) points out, "For exegesis, there are few of the finer points of Greek which need more constant attention than this omission of the article when the writer would lay stress on the quality or character of the object."[4]

Greek scholars Dana and Mantey agree with Moulton: "When identity is prominent, we find the article; and when the quality of character is stressed, the construction is anarthrous."[5]

The Apostle Paul intentionally absented the Greek article before νόμος (law) because he was dealing with νόμος (law) as an abstract.

Almost 100 years ago, Arthur Slaten wrote:

> Recognition of the qualitative usage of nouns [signaled by the absence of the article] is significant in the translation and interpretation of the New Testament. That the significance of this usage is not generally recognized is apparent not only in many renderings of the Revised Version but even in critical commentaries upon the Greek text and in the standard grammars of the New Testament.[6]

Unfortunately, as Slaten points out, Bible scholars, Bible translators, and theologians, with a few exceptions, have glossed over the fact that the absence of the article before νόμος carries with it semantic content; namely, the intrinsic qualities of law.

For example, every culture reflects rules, values, and customs that portray a particular law-way. The Chácobo called their law-way of living *noba jabi*. The Chácobo were not law-less.

Even though they were not law-less, their particular law-way of living, according to the Apostle Paul, clearly had "no place in the Divine Plan."

Historically, between Adam and Christ, there "sneaked" into history παρεισῆλθεν (diverse cultural law-ways) for doing things, law-ways which not only had "no place in the Divine Plan," but law-ways that increased sinning. The word παρεισῆλθεν translated as "sneaked in," occurs only one other time in Scripture.

It occurs in Galatians 2:4, where the Apostle Paul describes false believers who came in by stealth, infiltrated, "sneaked in," and came in secretly.

> *And this occurred because of false brethren secretly brought in (who came in by stealth to spy out our liberty which we have in Christ Jesus, that they might bring us into bondage)*

Since the word παρεισῆλθεν occurs only twice in the Bible, one would think that translating these two verses into English would not present a problem for the translators. But it does.

Disregarding the rule of Greek grammar that explicitly states: Where the Greek article does not appear, the definite article should not be inserted in the English translation, the vast majority of Bible expositors and translators interpret νόμος absent the article as the Mosaic Law.

They include biblical scholars like Douglas Moo, who says, "The anarthrous νόμος [also known as νόμος absent the article] but clearly the Mosaic Law;"[7] expositor H. Moule asserts that what "came in" was "articulated at Sinai;"[8] expositor John Murray affirms it was "the law, as revealed by Moses;"[9] F. L. Godet, "νόμος (the) law, undoubtedly denotes the Mosaic Law."[10]

In contrast, there is expositor Charles Hodge, who interpreted νόμος absent the article, as "The law stands here for the whole of the Old Testament economy, including the clear revelation of the moral law and all the institutions connected with the former dispensation."[11]

For Hodge, νόμος specifically stands for a Jewish cultural lawway that includes its customs, institutions, values, and principles for living. Instead of all cultures, Hodge gives νόμος a specific identity, Jewish culture.

Greek scholar and expositor R. C. H. Lenski (1864 - 1936) was aware of the problem. He notes that νόμος, as it occurs without the article in Romans 5:20, "should not be conceived as being a mere set of formulated decrees, a code, but as a power that affects something."[12]

He failed to recognize that the power that affects something is the power of cultural forms, such as marriage rules, residence rules, and rules of worship.

Finally, νόμος (a kind of cultural system) with παρεισῆλθον (slipped in with unworthy motives), and which, according to Arndt and Gingrich, was a form "that had no primary place in the Divine Plan."[13]

Whatever kind of law that slipped in between Adam and Christ, it certainly was not the law of Moses. What slipped in were diverse cultural ways of living, that had "no place in the Divine Plan."

| New King James Version | English Standard Version |
|---|---|
| Moreover the law entered that the offense might abound. But where sin abounded, grace abounded much more, | Now the law came in to increase the trespass, but where sin increased, grace abounded all the more, |

Romans 5:20

| New international Version | New American Standard |
|---|---|
| The law was brought in so that the trespass might increase. But where sin increased, grace increased all the more, | The Law came in so that the offense would increase; but where sin increased, grace abounded all the more, |

Romans 5:20

## CONVICTIONS

- As humans filled the earth, and as they entered diverse ecosystems, sin multiplied as the meanings attached to forms common to all were replaced with meanings derived from social existence and which belonged to the people.
- Diverse ecosystems produce diverse cultural law-systems.
- Scholar James H. Moulton: "There are fewer finer points of Greek that need more constant attention than this omission of the article when the writer would lay stress on the quality or character of the object."[14]
- English translators of Romans 5:20 failed to render a correct translation of this vital passage because they failed to adhere to the Greek grammar rules.

# CHAPTER 10
# THE CONCEPT OF CULTURE
## DEFINING AN ABSTRACT NOUN

In the early '50s, anthropologists A. L. Kroeber and Clyde Kluckhohn undertook the formidable task of defining culture. They collected definitions from the leading anthropologists and non-anthropologists of the day.

In 1952, *Culture: A Critical Review of Concepts and Definitions*[1] was published. In this informative book, I discovered 162 definitions of culture.

Despite their efforts, I concluded that no one could provide a convincing, concise definition. Why not? There had to be a reason. What is this phenomenon we call "culture"?

I concluded that the concept of culture is indefinable because it's an abstract noun. The concept of culture is similar to the concept of law, which legal theorist H. L. A. Hart (1907 - 1992) also declared to be indefinable.

Another more recent reference is by Matt Ellis on the Grammarly writing website:

Abstract nouns represent intangible ideas—things you can't perceive with the five main senses. Words like *love, time, beauty,* and *science* are all abstract nouns because you can't touch them or see them.[2]

Both concepts, law and culture, cannot be clearly defined because everyone inherently knows what they mean, just as everyone knows that an elm is a kind of tree and a sparrow is a kind of bird.

This presents a real problem for lexicographers who believe every concept can be defined but end up using circular reasoning. For instance, "need" is defined as to need, "freedom" as liberty, and tree by its numerous species. The concepts of genus or kind are at the heart of the human categorization of the world's species. As abstract nouns, they are indefinable.

~

## THE IMPOSSIBLE TASK OF A LEXICOGRAPHER

Lexicographers, therefore, have the impossible task of defining the indefinable. In this regard, legal philosopher H. L. A. Hart notes: "[Any] definition of law that starts by identifying law as a specie or rule usually advances our understanding of law no further."[3]

The same can be said of culture. Unless concepts like rights, traditions, customs, kinship systems, principles, rules, obligations, and duties can be assigned to some genus that is already understood, understanding what constitutes culture and law is not possible.

For the "primitive" Chácobo, law and culture were described as *jabi* (a way of doing things). What constituted "their way" were traditions, customs, allegiance patterns, obligations, rights, values, rules, prohibitions, and ascribed functions masquerading as duties.

Any anthropologist or missiologist who attempts to define culture in terms of species, i.e., its regulations, duties, obligations, rights, prohibitions, values, traditions, and customs, doesn't advance our understanding of culture.

It would be like defining a tree by pointing to an elm, pine, or palm tree; or defining people by pointing to Christians, Jews, Muslims, Buddhists, Chácobo, Trobriands, Japanese, or Pacahuara. Or defining culture by pointing to an artifact or tradition.

Return to the 162 definitions of culture compiled by Kroeber and Kluckhohn. Every definition of culture, with a couple of exceptions that I will address later, is defined in terms of species, customs, habits, behavioral patterns, institutions, artifacts, rituals, kinship systems, and so forth, all of which are learned. But if every abstract noun is intangible and indefinable, the same holds for the concept we call culture, which is an abstract noun.

## CULTURE AS AN INDEFINABLE ABSTRACTION

I finally realized that culture for the Chácobo was an abstraction. It could not be seen, heard, touched, smelled, or tasted. Their customary way of doing things, i.e., culture, was manifested obliquely in their customs, rituals, values, rules, rights, obligations, artifacts, and institutions.

In addition, their word *jabi* (a way of doing things) was also their word for law. Both exhibited similar qualities. But when a rule, right, or custom is codified, it becomes law, something tangible and concrete rather than abstract. Theologian George Ladd (1911 - 1982) supports this perspective. He said, "Law is fundamentally custom, hardening into what we call law."[4]

While all humans innately recognize what law and culture are, virtually all anthropologists and missiologists seem convinced these two related concepts can be defined in terms of their species. However, because they are abstractions, Professor Hart suggests they can't. I agree.

With the abstract semantic super-category we call Genus, a taxonomic category that exhibits certain qualities of being, it is possible to make sense of the many species in nature. As an abstraction, Genus represents a class of things with common characteristics and can be divided into different kinds.

While a materialist would classify people as a kind of animal, no Chácobo would. For the Chácobo, people cannot be reduced to a type of animal because they exhibit qualities like language, culture, and the ability to categorize things according to their kind. To classify people as a sort of animal would be illogical, absurd, and crazy.

Without abstract super-semantic categories like people, animals, birds, flowers, and trees, which exhibit inherent, known qualities that are not learned, we would not be able to talk about related things.

Aware of this problem, Christian philosopher Gordon Clark (1902 - 1985) wrote:

> Unless we can use concepts and talk about groups of things, philosophy would be impossible. If only individual things existed, and every noun was a proper name, conversation and even thinking itself could not be carried on ... all thought and speech depends on classification, and no epistemology can succeed without something like Platonic ideas.[5]

From left to right, Boca, Maro, Cuya, "Papa" (Gil), Caco, Rabi

## CONVICTIONS

- When God created man and woman, He created taxonomists. He did this by equipping humankind with classificatory binary concepts like male-female, good-bad, someone-something, and part-of-kind-of. All thought and speech depend on classification.

# CHAPTER 11
# THE SHAPING OF CULTURE

IS THE "WORD OF GOD" A RECORD OF "GOD-BREATHED" WORDS WITH "FIXED" INHERENT MEANINGS?

## THE LAW OF IDENTITY

The Law of Identity insists that each thing—animate or inanimate—is composed of its own unique set of characteristics, qualities, or features, which the ancient Greeks called "essence."

People, for example, share the same qualities or essence. Unlike animals, people cook their food, write books, marry, raise families, and communicate in language.

They can communicate with other people groups because their words share the same meanings. If a cultural form had no inherent meaning shared by all humanity, cross-cultural communications and Bible translation would not be possible.

As Christian philosopher Gordon Clark points out, "A given word must not only mean something, but it must also not mean something."[1]

In other words, a queen cannot be a "he," and a someone cannot be a "something."

## CONCEPT-INNATIST

The concept-innatist believes humanity's rejection, distortion, and replacement of Positive Divine meanings with a misrepresentation of those meanings is the cultural stuff of history.

## PARALLEL EPISTEMOLOGICAL (ORIGIN) SYSTEMS

As a result, historically, there are two parallel epistemological (origin) systems: One that declares "essence precedes existence" and one that declares "existence precedes essence."

Postmoderns of every type clearly advocate the latter. A concept-innatist, like myself, believes that "essence precedes existence."

## CULTURE - THE WAY SOCIETY DOES THINGS

According to the concept-innatist, culture is shaped by two forces:

- The law of the mind, which shapes behavior and worldview. "For I delight in the law of God according to the inward man" (Romans 7:22).

- External forces, what anthropologist Marvin Harris (1927 - 2001) called "infrastructure," and what the Apostle Paul referenced as "the material elements of the world."

    *Beware lest anyone cheat you through philosophy and empty deceit, according to the tradition of men,*

> *according to the basic principles of the world, and not according to Christ. (Colossians 2:8)*

The theist believes "essence precedes existence." Essence constitutes the intrinsic qualities that reflect what it means to be created "in the image of God." Without essence, concepts like culture, nature, husband, wife, and science would not exist.

As expressed by British-American cognitive scientist Peter Carruthers, essence implies *a priori* knowledge of categories. This knowledge is "acquired" and brought to consciousness by being contextually "triggered" rather than "learned."[2]

Theologian-concept-innatist R. C. Sproul believes "when experiencing the phenomena of this world, we do it through the lens of our *a priori* categories of thought [i.e., essence]."[3]

> *And the LORD God formed man of the dust of the ground, and breathed into his nostrils the breath of life; and man became a living being. (Genesis 2:7)*

Adam's mind was not a blank slate. Instead, categorizing forms structured his mind. With this *a priori* knowledge, Adam could classify the animals and birds according to their kinds.

The concept-innatist also acknowledges that whenever humans and society diverge from what the Apostle Paul classifies as the "law in the mind," their cultural law will be shaped primarily by social existence in a particular environment. Such a divergence from principles—the law in the mind—will produce social disorder and cultural diversity.

## THE MATERIALIST

The materialist believes infrastructural pressures determine a society's way of doing things.[4] According to existentialist Jean-Paul Sartre (1905 – 1980), "existence precedes and rules essence."

The materialist claims all concepts, categories, values, and social structures are created by existence.

## ACADEMIA'S CONCLUSION: A STANDARD FOR JUDGING CULTURAL FORMS DOES NOT EXIST

Social scientists, anthropologists, and psychologists are all searching for the Holy Grail, an absolute, "fixed" culture-free standard by which to judge the validity of cultural forms[5] to know what ought to be.

Unlike present-day social scientists, the Greeks recognized the existence of such a culture-free Universal standard. They called it *epignosis*.

According to Greek scholars Arndt and Gingrich, *gnosis*, or knowledge with the preposition *epi-* denotes "to know exactly, completely, through and through."[6] The Greeks believed a transcendent standard existed for judging the validity of cultural forms.

Cultural psychologists Norenzayan and Heine point out that culture-free standards "provide the only legitimate criteria by which any particular socio-cultural practice or belief may be judged."[7]

Recognizing the problem, anthropologist Robert Lawless wrote:

> Any comparison of other societies by the standards of one's society, any evaluation of the behavior and beliefs of another society through the perspective of one's folk model, simply labels those other behaviors and beliefs as wrong, crazy, irrational, or stupid.
>
> If we are bound by the perspectives of our particular folk model,

we will learn nothing about why other people behave and think differently from us. Such a sterile viewpoint is called ethnocentrism. Analytic models must have a trans-societal perspective.[8]

Dr. Lawless, my anthropology advisor at the University of Florida, was correct. "Analytic models must have a trans-societal perspective."

Our analytical models should incorporate "fixed" and unchanging, culture-free principles, as advocated by Norenzayan, Heine, Lawless, and others, when evaluating the beliefs, institutions, values, behavior, and social arrangements of others.

Where do missionaries, Bible translators, anthropologists, psychologists, and social scientists go to find this culture-free knowledge? Why does such an analytical research model not exist? While recognizing the problem, none of these observers of human behavior have given us an answer.

There is an answer: Academia has failed to recognize that Divine meaning-content attached to Positive Universals has been replaced with meanings "that belong to the people," thereby relativizing all models.

While Lawless says, "We can never achieve the total outsider's view," which is undoubtedly true, the writer, a concept-innatist, assumes that one can nevertheless approximate a culture-free analysis of cultural forms if one starts with the principle that: "The task of science is to reveal the essence, the internal, deep, and underlying processes behind the multitude of phenomena, outward aspects, and features of reality."[9]

It is a perspective that assumes:

- The cultural analyst confronts a "multitude of phenomena" that contains both representations and misrepresentations of the Universals. In other words, every society can reject, distort, and misrepresent a

Positive Universal whenever it satisfies a perceived social need.
- Despite the mixture of representations and misrepresentations, Universals can be gleaned from carefully examining the particulars.
- For example, investigating Chácobo mythology revealed humanity on display when a person assists one's neighbor in need. The principle didn't need to be "learned." It was "written on the heart."
- A Bible translator discovered the Universal Principle when intrigued with the mysteries of Chácobo law-ways.
- *A priori epignosis* (knowledge in the mind) can be "triggered" and brought to consciousness in a sociolinguistic environment, in which case the Universal meaning attached to the Universal form is "acquired" rather than "learned." This innate knowledge enables every child to look at reality from a Divine perspective.
- Knowledge of what a society thinks ought to be is derived from cultural context. Such knowledge is relative. It is imported into the mind where it seeks to overthrow the Universals or the "law written on the heart."

## A POSTMODERN SHIFT FROM ONE TRUTH TO MANY TRUTHS

Social scientists, including contextualizing missiologists, are fully aware that native beliefs, institutions, values, and practices that one may judge to be morally wrong and invalid may, from the perspective of the native, be perfectly rational, moral, and valid.

Therefore, the dilemma social scientists face, but especially missiologists, is highlighted by this conundrum:

According to Charles H. Kraft, if there is no outside culture-free standard for judging what ought to be, then neither the Ten Commandments nor the Sermon on the Mount can provide us with a "trans-societal perspective" because the meanings of words, i.e., "that belong to the people ... are not inherent in the forms themselves."[10]

For the bottom-up, outside-in structuralist-functionalist, the idea that a concept like marriage has an inherent meaning that can be "triggered" and brought to consciousness is rejected. No "acquired" knowledge exists.

From their viewpoint, all meanings, like the meaning of marriage, are derived from social context, "belong to the people," and therefore, are learned.

For these academicians, no Divine meaning can be revealed in any text.

In contrast, the theist sees what the "finger of God" wrote on tablets of stone on Mount Sinai and the words Jesus expressed on the Mount, which all speak to what ought to be.

Each word and phrase represented Divine meanings free from cultural contamination, but meanings that sinful society had the freedom to reject, distort, and replace with meanings "that belong to the people."

## SOCIAL SCIENTISTS THROW IN THE TOWEL

Because social scientists eventually concluded that the standards they were using to judge the cultural forms of other societies were shaped and contaminated by their own cultures, most gave up their search for a culture-free standard.

In the words of anthropologist Martin Ottenheimer, the cultural analyst must now "benefit from multiple perspectives achieved through the use of multiple frameworks."[11]

However, how can the social scientist "benefit" from a theory that has detached Universal meanings from Universal forms and must now approve of whatever meanings a society attaches to them?

For example, as a Universal form, should singing and dancing be reduced to a function in nature that helps the crops grow, the rain fall, and the animals walk within range of one's arrow?

For the functionalist, the meanings of Universal forms like singing and dancing "belong to the people." Ottenheimer believes they serve perceived needs. The result: "A relativistic approach does not recognize an absolute framework of analysis and does not insist that there is one proper framework for examining cultural data."[12] Kraft, as a functionalist, would agree with that statement.

I, as a concept-innatist, agree with the Greeks and writers of the New Testament, who believed that such a Divine framework does exist.

However, since all meanings are now assumed to be derived from context, all missionaries, especially Bible translators, have a severe problem.

The translator must ask: Is the Word of God "a record of the sense perceptions of spirit-guided men" living in Palestine as advocated by contextualizing missiologist Charles Kraft,[13] or is it a record of "God-breathed" words with "fixed" inherent meanings?

How do I translate...

## CONVICTIONS

- If there exists no "absolute framework" for examining and classifying cultural forms as either health-producing or death-producing, then no missionary, religion, ideology, or ruling class has the authority to condemn cultural forms like adultery, female infanticide, widow burning, slavery, honor killings, rape, incest, jihad, and so on. All is relative.

- The Apostle Paul clearly understood the problem of judging the validity of cultural forms. In his letter to the Philippians, he wrote:

*And this I pray, that your love may abound yet more and more in knowledge [epignosis] and in all judgment; that you may approve things that are excellent; that you may be sincere and without offense till the day of Christ ... (Philippians 1:9-10, King James 2000)*

- Without "more and more knowledge," Paul understood that it would be impossible for the Philippians to discover by testing whether a cultural form was good or bad. There would be no means of knowing what was best or true. Likewise, every missionary depends on *epignosis* (knowledge) to judge the validity of a cultural form.
- The task of the missiologist is to bring to light the Universal framework of culture-free standards that the Greeks and Scripture writers assumed existed.
- A society's culture is about a particular way of living that is at war with the "law in our minds." Immanuel Kant (1724 – 1804) called it *noumenon* (*a priori* knowledge of "fixed" and constant principles). These innate law principles in the mind are brought to consciousness by being "triggered" in a socio-linguistic environment. They are "acquired," not "learned."
- Whenever these "acquired" Divine principles in the mind are rejected, a spiritual phenomenon called *etic* divergence occurs. It manifests itself as a rejection of the "fixed" principles in the mind and the Divine meanings attached to forms common to all people. They are replaced with meanings "that belong to the people."
- Humankind and society, while seeking to relieve their existential anxieties produced by the material forces of a

particular environment, have the freedom to reject what it means to be created in the image of God and diverge from those intrinsic qualities that make up personhood.
- Essence promotes human freedom. Social existence shaped by the forces of the environment reduces people to functional things and increases social disorder.
- A society whose law is shaped by "the material elements of the world" (Colossians 2:8) will be anxious.

## CHAPTER 12
# DOES CULTURE DETERMINE WHAT ONE THINKS

SOCIAL EXISTENCE AND ELEMENTAL FORCES OF THE WORLD

The Chácobo kinsfolk, when I met them for the first time, were among the thousands, perhaps millions, who had rejected the Divine Plan since Adam and Eve. In Acts 14:15-16, the Apostle Paul said:

> *"Men, why are you doing these things? We also are men with the same nature as you, and preach to you that you should turn from these useless things to the living God, who made the heaven, the earth, the sea, and all things that are in them,*
> *"who in bygone generations allowed all nations to walk in their own ways."*

This human inclination manifests itself in many ways, including (a) creating new types of families by restructuring the nuclear family, e.g., replacing the covenantal dyad of *husband-wife* with one of seven biological dyads: (a) Fa-So, Fa-Da, Mo-So, Mo-Da, Br-Br, Si-Si, and Br-Si; (b) the rejection of logic as manifested in the belief that a cousin can be a sibling, an uncle a father, and a nephew a son; (c) the rejection of God as Provider and the need to pray, "Our Father who art in heaven ... give us this day our daily bread;" and (d) the belief that no form held in common by all has inherent meanings that humans may reject and replace with meanings "that belong to the people."

Rejecting the idea that forms have inherent meanings, Mao Zedong wrote: "Where do correct ideas come from? Do they drop from the sky? No. Are they innate in the mind? No. They come from social practice and from it alone."[1]

In 1859, Karl Marx introduced to the academic world a new way of looking at how concepts common to all come into conscious existence. He wrote: "It is not the consciousness of men that determines their existence, but, on the contrary, their social existence determines their consciousness."[2]

Marx believed the mind is structured with rules, values, patterns, and ideas derived solely from social existence rather than from God.

Anticipating the appearance of such thinking, the Apostle Paul wrote:

> *Be careful that no one takes you captive through philosophy and empty deceit based on human tradition, based on the elemental forces of the world, and not based on Christ. (Colossians 2:8, Holman Christian Standard Bible)*

What Marx called social existence, the Apostle Paul described as the "elemental forces of the world," which could shape our thinking and behavior. According to Paul, such environmental forces are natural. Still, a society may attach meanings to these forms that are "not based on Christ," implying society can replace God's design with values "that belong to the people."

Agreeing with Marx was Mao Zedong. Starting with the five senses—seeing, hearing, tasting, smelling, and touching—he said:

> At first, knowledge is perceptual. The leap to conceptual knowledge, i.e., to ideas, occurs when sufficient perceptual knowledge is accumulated. When sufficient perceptual knowledge is accumulated, a miracle occurs. Man and society begin to think logically and rationally.[3]

According to Mao, "All genuine knowledge originates in direct experience."[4] For the theist, all genuine knowledge originates with God.

Rejecting the idea that "all genuine knowledge originates in direct experience" is the late philosopher-theologian Gordon Clark:

> Unless we had concepts or categories of quality [hard and soft], of quantity [one, few, or many], and of relations [front and behind,

past, present, and future), we could not think of botany, baseball, or anything else.[5]

Following in the steps of Marx and Zedong is anthropologist Marvin Harris. He called the "elementary forces of the world" infrastructure (Colossians 2:8).

Harris believed "the elementary forces of the world" consisted of the material constants of one's environment, such as weather patterns, soil fertility, technology, and social media. He believed "infrastructure" determined one's behavior, personality, beliefs, who one marries, and where one lives.

Harris says, "The forces characteristic of the imperial periods in which Jesus and Gautama lived created their personalities."[6] The material forces of our postmodern culture create our personalities.

In contrast, the theist believes the Word of God, fellowship with other Christians, and the leading of the Holy Spirit are all important forces in a believer's life. Such was the perspective of SIL's Chairman of Anthropology.

Following in the footsteps of Marx, Zedong, and Harris emerged a prominent evangelical anthropologist, Marvin K. Mayers (1927 – 2015). He called "the elementary forces of the world" culture. But is culture the only influence that determines how one thinks and behaves? The late Dr. Mayers, who was also a committed cultural relativist, believed it was. He wrote:

> Culture can be defined in hundreds of ways, but the point is that every thought a person thinks, every hope he has, every step he takes, every belief he holds, and every interaction he takes is controlled by his culture. Every move he makes is programmed into him by his culture.[7]

But lest one's every move is programmed by culture, the Apostle Paul wrote:

# CREATED IN THE IMAGE OF GOD

*And do not be conformed to this world, but be transformed by the renewing of your mind, that you may prove what is that good and acceptable and perfect will of God. (Romans 12:2)*

In effect, Dr. Mayers believed "There exists no objective, external standard for right and wrong that is valid for everyone." Instead, contextual social existence, or one's culture, determines our every move.

What the Apostle Paul described as "the elementary forces of the world," anthropologist-missiologist Charles Kraft calls context. Like Mao Zedong, Kraft tackles the problem of meaning by declaring, "A cultural form does not have inherent meaning, only perceived meaning. And this meaning is context-specific."[8]

For Kraft, nothing is more certain in life than one's perceptions. However, theologian-philosopher Gordon H. Clark (1902 – 1985) points out, "If all knowledge is based on experience [perception] alone, then there can be no knowledge of any necessary truth."[9]

Our perceptions must first be sorted into categories using the semantic "tools" that are innate (present at birth) and not learned, *a priori* information that every child coming into the world has.

Consider these words of Clark, "If I do this." These words imply causality, which is a category, an *a priori* concept, a form of knowledge that, instead of being learned from experience, must be known prior to experience so as to make experience possible.[10]

The inexplicable existence of such *a priori* classificatory knowledge structured in the unconscious mind baffles the materialist.

Linguist Kenneth Lee Pike (1912 – 2000) believed, "Our categorization of elements of our universe allows us to have a particular understanding of the universe."[11]

Without this ability to categorize, we would know nothing. The world was designed to be categorized, thus making it a meaningful place for humans to live.

In contrast to the previous five, Pike believed two perspectives of reality exist. He labeled them *emic* and *etic*.

An *emic* perspective represents the values, structures, "rules of behavior," and ideals of the individual or society being analyzed. An *emic* perspective represents the beliefs, customs, structures, and practices specific to a given culture. This perspective differs from every other way of perceiving the world.

The *etic* perspective is free from human interpretation. This culture-free framework of perceiving reality consists of "Innate Positive Universals," according to Pike,[12] mysteriously structured in the mind and that Paul describes figuratively as "written on the heart."

> *(Indeed, when Gentiles, who do not have the law, do by nature things required by the law, they are a law for themselves, even though they do not have the law.*
> *They show that the requirements of the law are written on their hearts, their consciences also bearing witness, and their thoughts sometimes accusing them and at other times even defending them). (Romans 2:14-15, NIV)*

Pike believed two kinds of meanings exist: meanings that are "acquired" and meanings that are "learned." The "acquired" meanings are "fixed" and belong to God. Meanings that are "learned" are subject to change and belong to man.

"Acquired" meanings exist as Innate Positive Universals structured in a Universal-Lexicon. Entries or existing definitions in this Universal-Lexicon can be "triggered," bringing them to consciousness. Man and society have the freedom to replace these Innate Positive Universals with negative particular actions that are learned.

For example, the nuclear family consists of eight dyads: Fa-So, Fa-Da, Mo-So, Mo-Da, Br-Si, Br-Br and Si-Si. In the words of anthropologist Francis L. K. Hsu (1909 - 1999):

When one dyad is elevated over other dyads in a given kinship system, the attributes of the dominant dyad tend to modify, eliminate, or at least reduce the importance of the attributes of other structural dyads.

The hypothesis further states that the total effect of the dominance of the attributes of one structural dyad leads to a particular kind of kinship content, which, in turn strongly conditions the pattern of thought and behavior of the individuals reared in the kinship system [and lifeway] in the society at large.[13]

Cultural diversity, also known as *emic*-ization, began when meanings common to all were replaced with new meanings shaped by the environment. Cultural diversity emerged in earnest when distinct language groups began to fill the earth after the Tower of Babel (Genesis 11).

As people entered different ecological environments, they permitted the elementary forces of each environment to shape their values, ideals, family structures, and allegiance patterns, thereby slowly replacing inherent meanings attached to forms common to all with meanings shaped by context or social existence.

As stated previously, Pike called this replacement of inherent meanings with meanings "that belong to the people" *etic* divergence. Materialists like Marx, Zedong, and Harris, as well as evangelical anthropologists like Mayers, Kraft, and Lingenfelter, rejected the existence of such a spiritual phenomenon.

Chácobo school children

## CONVICTIONS

- The unconscious mind contains cultural and linguistic forms common to all. Attached to them are Divine meanings that humans can reject and replace with meanings derived from culture.
- Pike labeled *etic* divergence as replacing a Divine meaning with a meaning "that belongs to the people."
- God has equipped every person semantically to be a taxonomist.

## CHAPTER 13
# WHERE ARE THE POSITIVE UNIVERSALS
### A UNIVERSAL INTERPRETATIVE SYSTEM THAT ECHOES GOD'S RIGHT AND WRONG

On a university campus, students learn that science is about making decisions based on "fixed" standards, measurements, and constants. But the same cannot be said of the Liberal Arts fields, including anthropology, sociology, religion, history, psychology, economics, political science, semantics, and missiology.

Social scientists, anthropologists, psychologists, and missiologists find this troubling. They see the need for Universals with "fixed" meanings to judge the validity of an action, concept, belief, value, custom, tradition, structure, or rule.

To begin this controversial topic, we must first note that knowledge, in the words of Christian philosopher Gordon Clark, "is always a combination of form and content. We cannot know the form without the content."[1]

For example, when we see a creature with wings, feathers, and a beak, we identify it as a bird.

Likewise, learning to speak Chácobo, a form of communication, meant learning new subject-verb-object patterns, a new phonological system, new ways to ask questions, and new ways to express sadness, surprise, and disappointment. Learning to speak Chácobo meant learning the grammatical features that rendered it different from every other language.

When a meaning is "fixed" and constant—when an attached meaning is inherent and belongs to God—we have a Positive Universal. Many believe such Universal forms exist in a Universal-Lexicon found in the unconscious mind, along with a Universal Grammar.

However, when these positive inherent meanings are rejected and replaced with meanings derived from social existence, society creates a negative particularity. Such meanings have "no place in the Divine Plan."

Kenneth Pike called replacing a "fixed" and constant positive meaning with a meaning "that belongs to the people" *etic* divergence. Such negative actions increase cultural diversity and multiply sinning.

Linguist Kenneth Pike, the coiner of the terms *emic* and *etic*, "was interested in establishing a set of *etic* Universals;"[2] that is, a set of Positive Universals common to all. He wrote, "A person may distort Innate Positive Universals into negative particular actions."[3]

According to philosopher Gordon Clark:

> ... men do not come into the world with blank minds. It [theism] must assert man's endowment with rationality, innate ideas, and *a*

*priori* categories ... his ability to think and speak were given to him by God for the essential purpose of receiving verbal revelation, of approaching God in prayer, and of conversing with other men about spiritual realities.[4]

Pike believed every child is endowed with "fixed" meanings and absolute Universals. The empiricist's task is to prove Pike wrong.

To my surprise, Pike avoided using the word "meaning," replacing it with the word "sense."

For example, instead of word pairs exhibiting contrasting meanings, they "display contrasting senses."[5] He excludes forms like concepts, family, standards, feelings, ideas, thoughts, and principles from his theory of *etic* Universals. I believe he is mistaken, and I am not alone.

Differing with Pike is semanticist Ana Wierzbicka (1938 -) who says the analyst's task is to "reach for the Conceptual Universals."[6] Conceptual Universals are innate (not learned). Cognitive anthropologist Ward Goodenough (1919 - 2013) agreed with Wierzbicka.

No one was more frustrated over the lack of a framework of conceptual Universals than Goodenough, who wrote:

> There are relatively few subject matters for which we have well-developed bodies of *etic* concepts capable of describing the basic *emic* components of the behavioral systems about these subject matters (anthropology, psychology, religion, missiology).
>
> Culture-free *etic* standards provide the [only] frame of reference, the conceptual constants, through which to examine the similarities and differences among different behavioral systems.[7]

I wholeheartedly agree. Such a body of *etic* concepts would provide analysts with a Universal Interpretative System for judging the validity of meaning. But a culture-free Interpretative System does not exist because social scientists, I contend, have been looking in the wrong places. Nevertheless, such false systems continue to be created. For Kraft, "An *etic* perspective is that of an informed outside analyst."[8]

I'm afraid I have to disagree. Such a perspective is derived from the investigator's culture and is not culture-free.

Cultural materialist Marvin Harris believed he found the constants in what the Apostle Paul described as "the elemental forces of the world" (Colossians 2:8).

The Apostle Paul warns us against creating interpretative systems grounded in the elemental forces of the environment, saying such interpretations "do not concur with Christ."

Nevertheless, Harris discovered that "the elementary forces of one's environment" could shape the meanings attached to Universal forms. I have to concede that Harris was right. The elemental forces of the Amazonian Rainforest, its sandy soil, abundance of manioc, and warm climate, shaped how the Chácobo structured the nuclear family and created values different from mine.

One reason the Chácobo didn't release their daughters after marriage was because they needed to help their mothers produce the essential staple of life: manioc beer. If manioc had not been prevalent, there would have been no manioc beer. Chácobo demand for manioc beer compelled them to restructure the nuclear family, making the mother-daughter relationship the dominant dyad. Daughters were not permitted to leave their fathers and mothers at marriage because they needed to remain home to help their mothers make the manioc beer.

Just as "the forces characteristic of the imperial periods in which Jesus and Gautama lived [which] created their personalities,"[9] according to Harris, the elemental forces of the Amazonian Rainforest created the Chácobo's personalities and the way they thought and behaved. It was "the constraints of infrastructure"[10] that determined their lifeways.

Harris believed the analyst's task was to uncover the environmental elements that shaped a society's lifeway. One form that Harris excluded from his constraints of infrastructure was revelation.

Such revelatory knowledge (apart from what we learn in the Bible) is found in the unconscious mind as "innate knowledge." No child enters the world with an unstructured mind devoid of meaningful forms. Something "triggers" the innate knowledge into consciousness.

For example, Chácobo sages of another era created satire critical of how the Chácobo had formed the nuclear family, recommending that the mother-daughter dyad be replaced with the *husband-wife*. Such actions implied the existence of a Universal Interpretative System with conceptual constants, "laws written on the heart," and what Pike called *etic* data. When I explained this phenomenon to Pike, he responded, "Gil, that is the most interesting thing I have heard in twenty years."

My discovery implied the existence of an *etic* Universal interpretative structure in the unconscious mind. To counter assertions that social practice or social existence determines human essence and the meaning of life, we need evangelical linguists, anthropologists, and psychologists committed to "gleaning the Universals from an examination of the particulars,"[11] as quoted by R. C. Sproul. This means that Positive Universals are waiting discovery in every culture.

The first Positive Universal I found was in the *Myth of Nahuapaxahua*. (See chapter 2, "Discovering an Innate Moral Imperative"). What amazed me was the Chácobo knew he expressed his humanity by helping those in need.

The starting point is an unconscious mind structured with a Universal-Lexicon that contains forms to which Divine meanings are attached. This perspective provided me the theoretical basis for creating a plan for restoring the Universals and stopping the Chácobo's slide to cultural extinction.

*Tumi Chucua*, SIL Bolivian base for 27 years

## CONVICTIONS

- "They show [by their actions] that God's law is not something alien, imposed from without, but woven into the very fabric of our creation. There is something deep within them that echoes God's yes and no, right and wrong" (Romans 2:15, The Message).
- What is "woven into the very fabric of our creation" is a Universal Interpretative System containing forms to which "fixed" and constant inherent meanings are attached.
- Cultural materialist Marvin Harris is guilty of "permitting the material things of which the world is created to form its standards" (Meyer 1885).[12]
- Cornelius Van Til: "In the midst of multitudes of perspectives, there must be a criterion by which these opinions can be judged."[13]

# CHAPTER 14
# THE LONG NIGHT
## CHÁCOBO FABLE - WHEN THE SUN FAILED TO COME UP

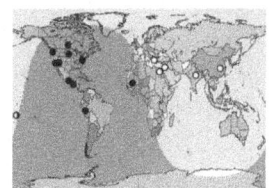

What Marian and I missed during our first two years of living among the Chácobo was a way to preserve food. While the Chácobo had fire-tables for roasting, thereby preserving their meat for a couple of days, we relied on meat provided to us by the Chácobo (that we ate within 24 hours) or meat that arrived in tin cans. The idea that meat could be stored in cans surprised the Chácobo.

The day came when we bought a kerosene-powered refrigerator to preserve our food supply, but there was a problem. When it arrived at *Tumi Chucua*, the SIL Bolivian base, the kerosene fridge would not fit inside the Aeronca seaplane. Transporting it to the Chácobo village via the plane would have taken an hour. Traveling by river in a canoe would take at least a week!

If we were going to have ice cubes for the tribe, it meant finding and buying a wooden canoe wide enough to transport it. I expected to discover such a wide canoe in the jungle town of *Riberalta*.

So, I loaded the refrigerator on an oxcart and transported it from *Tumi Chucua*, our base, to the River Beni. I then loaded it onto a river boat traveling downriver to *Riberalta*. The next day I scoured the tiny city looking for a canoe large enough to carry the fridge.

Disappointed, I found none and asked God why. At *Riberalta*, the Beni River flowed into the *Madre de Dios*. The next day, we traveled downriver to another town, *Portachuleo*.

From there, I disembarked with my refrigerator. Again, I scoured the town, looking for a large canoe to carry it. And again, I found none, and again, I asked God why.

I brought the refrigerator to a Maryknoll Mission Station, where a Maryknoll American priest invited me and my companion, Bill Richmond, to spend the night.

As we were talking, someone informed the priest that a truck was traveling to the Yata River to pull the loading ramp to a higher ground lest it floated away with the rising river. Without the loading ramp, ferrying rubber to Brazil and merchandise back to Bolivia would not be possible.

Not knowing what to do, I loaded the refrigerator on the truck and drove it to the Yata River where I hoped to find someone who would guard it for the night.

Traveling down a crude road, pushing back the encroaching jungle, we finally arrived at the rising Yata. I jumped from the truck bed, expecting to see someone living there. I saw nothing but the jungle. Then I looked across the river. Someone was putting into the Yata River a brand-new canoe large enough to transport my refrigerator to *Biiyá*. How was that possible?

Once it was in the water, the stranger paddled this 3-foot-wide, 15-foot-long canoe to my side of the river. When he arrived, I asked him if he would please sell me his canoe so I could transport my refrigerator upriver to the Chácobo.

He answered, "Yes. Unload the refrigerator. Let's place it in the canoe, and I will take care of it."

After paying for the canoe, we unloaded the refrigerator and placed it in my brand-new canoe.

The next morning, I returned with lumber, a hammer, and a saw.

After building a transom, I attached my 5 hp Mercury outboard motor.

I TRAVELED UPRIVER, thanking God for unexpectedly providing me with a canoe. The timing was incredible. After traveling a couple of hours up the Yata River, we dropped our canoe provider off at his homestead, thanking him for what he had done. Then Bill and I continued traveling upriver for two more days, arriving at the village of *Biiyá* as the sun set.

In 1959, the socio-economic environment around *Biiyá* changed dramatically. The rubber-rich jungle surrounding the village began to attract entrepreneurs who came from the nearest community, five days away on the Brazilian border, to harvest natural rubber.

With the price of natural rubber achieving new highs, an influx of rubber tappers came, each working for a particular "patron" who hired them.

The patron's task was to provide for them. Instead of paying workers with Bolivian currency, the patron paid for food and the necessities of life. Seldom were these *Sinringeriros* or rubber tappers paid in cash.

To avoid higher prices, the *Sinringueiros* turned to their Chácobo neighbors for basic necessities, like manioc, bananas, corn, and roasted manioc flour. Within a few months, the Chácobo discovered their law-way was threatened. There weren't enough bananas, corn, and manioc to trade for soap, salt, and cloth, and have enough to meet their needs.

Besides, unlike the Bolivian nationals, the Chácobo staple of life was manioc beer. Everyone, including children and babies, drank manioc beer, which they called *jënë*. Suddenly and without warning, the Chácobo law-way was threatened. Taking away their *jënë* meant not only the end of their staple of life but also the end of a law-way.

This would terminate a law-way where the village men occasionally gathered for a beer-drinking fest. Each beer-drinking fest had an owner, the provider of the manioc beer.

Whenever a gourd filled with manioc beer was offered to the guest by the owner of the event, the guest never refused it. If the guest had consumed too much beer, he would insert his fingers into his mouth, press down, and regurgitate what he had previously drunk. Then, he would drink what the host offered him.

Only once did I observe a drunk Chácobo which was because he failed to vomit and urinate away enough manioc beer to keep himself sober.

THEN CAME THE GREAT AWAKENING. Unknown to Marian and me, we had become the de facto security blanket for a dying tribe of 140 members who lived in four villages.

Before we finished translating the New Testament into their language, we had to figure out why the Chácobo were a dying tribe that retreated into the forest whenever something threatened them. If we didn't, there would be no readers for the New Testament we hoped to someday publish. Understanding their law-way or what they called *noba jabi* would take time.

As mentioned before, I had begun collecting legends and stories passed down by Chácobo ancestors to better understand their *jabi*. One of the first stories was *The Long Night*, when the sun was delayed coming up, and the animals in the rainforest entered the village.

My informant, Caco Pistia, viewed the event as history handed down for generations. But was he telling me history or a fable? If I were not a Bible translator, I would have chalked it up to a Chácobo story. Most anthropologists would classify it as pure myth.

Who was right? My informant, a young teenager who was learning to read, write, and count; or the educated materialists who claimed there was no God? The event, which I assume to be accurate, places the Chácobo in the Amazonian Rainforest in 1450 BC.

The story that follows is the Chácobo fable of *The Long Night*.

## CHÁCOBO FABLE - WHEN THE SUN FAILED TO COME UP

Caco recounted a time when the sun failed to come up, an event that frightened not only the Chácobo but also all the birds and animals living in the rainforest. As the night grew longer and the sun failed to rise, the villages began to fill up with every kind of animal—primates, wild boars, tapirs, and jaguars.

Even the animals of the rainforest instinctively knew something unusual had happened. Of course, today, all naturalists would consider the idea that such an event occurred in history absurd, contrary to the laws of nature, or a figment of the imagination.

JEWISH SCHOLAR IMMANUEL VELIKOVSKY (1895 - 1979) agreed. In his controversial book, *Worlds in Collision*, of which I own a copy, he wrote: "Because the scientific mind cannot believe that man can make the sun and moon stand still, it also disbelieves the alleged event."[1]

The scientific mind, therefore, must cancel the long-day account recorded in Joshua 10:12-14 as a historical event.

Velikovsky logically declared: "If effect *A*, then effect *B*, 'allowing for the difference in longitude, it must have been early morning or night in the Western Hemisphere.'"

Assuming he would discover long night accounts in the Western Hemisphere, he began examining "the traditions of Central America," assuming this knowledge was "written in the pictographic script by their forefathers."[2]

The Mexican *Annals of Cuauhtitlan*, also known as *Codex Chimalpopoca* for the empire of Culhuacan and Mexico—written in Nahua Indian in the sixteen century—relates a cosmic catastrophe that occurred in the remote past. The night did not end for a long time.

"If effect A, then effect B," I continued to search on the World Wide Web. East of the Chácobo, living in the mountains of Peru, lived the Incas. I discovered they also had a long night story. The story was recorded by Spanish priest-historian Fernando de Montesinos, who resided in Cusco from 1630 to 1641. His goal was to reconstruct the history of the Incas going back to the times of Inca Ruler Pachacuti II (BC 1418 - 1471). According to Montesinos, during the third year of his reign, the sun was hidden for nearly 20 hours.

When examining the myths recorded by anthropologists of tribes living in the same latitude, I discovered other tribes, like the Inca, also had long night stories. They were the K'iché of Guatemala, the Aztec of Mexico, the Omaha of the Great Plains, the Ojibwe living in Wisconsin, Michigan, and Canada; the Wyandot living around Lake Ontario; the Dogrib of the Northwest Territories; the Kwakiutl and Tlingit of Northwest Canada, and the Tsimshian of Alaska.

According to anthropologist Franz Boas (1858 - 1942), these tribes believed "daylight was kept in a box by a chief and liberated by a raven," also known as Trickster.[3]

In this case, the Great Trickster was defending mankind's right to sunlight. Trickster, no doubt, was contending with Yahweh the Chief, saying, "It is unjust for half the world's population to be deprived of sunlight."

The "long day" event that occurred around 1450 BC in the Western Hemisphere, also known as *The Long Night*, clearly placed the Chácobo in the Amazonian Rainforest when it happened. That was approximately 3,500 years ago—amazing!

Transporting refrigerator

## CONVICTIONS

- Long night stories in the Western Hemisphere prove that Joshua's "Long Day" recorded in Joshua 10:12-14 took place. It was not an eclipse, as some claim. It was a supernatural event in history.

  *Then Joshua spoke to the LORD in the*
  *day when the LORD delivered up the Amorites*
  *before the children of Israel,*
  *And he said in the sight of Israel:*

  *"Sun, stand still over Gibeon;*
  *And Moon, in the Valley of Aijalon."*
  *So the sun stood still,*
  *and the moon stopped,*
  *Till the people had revenge*
  *Upon their enemies.*
  *Is this not written in the Book of Jashar? So*

*the sun stood still in the midst of heaven,
and did not hasten to go down for about a
whole day.*

*And there has been no day like that,
before it or after it, that the LORD heeded the
voice of a man; for the LORD fought for Israel.*[4]

- I could tell Caco that the event handed down to him by his ancestors was not a fable.
- Christian philosopher Russell Grigg states: "Those who balk at this account are almost invariably those who have already rejected six-day creation through compromise with evolution's fictitious long ages and have thus rejected the authority of the Bible."[5]

# CHAPTER 15
# INTRODUCING THE SEVEN-DAY WEEK
## A NEW WAY TO TRACK TIME

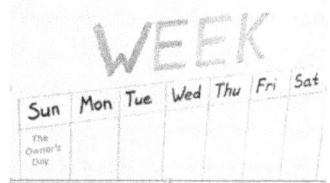

## A SOCIETY WITHOUT DAYS AND WEEKENDS, AND MONTHS WITHOUT NAMES

Most societies structure their social, religious, and economic environments around the seven-day week cycle. While there have been many kinds of weeks in history, including the eight-day Roman week, the twelve-day Chinese week, the thirteen-day Aztec week, the ten-day French Revolutionary week, and the Communist Russian five-day week, the seven-day Judeo-Christian week cycle has become the de facto standard around the world. The secular world has arranged all its social, political, economic, and religious activities around it.

However, the more I thought about the nature of the seven-day week, the more obvious it became that I would be involved in a religious and political act of revolutionary proportions. Helping the Chácobo integrate into the world's tracking of time meant a shift from the rhythms of nature into a Divine Order that transcended nature. If adopted, it would change the rhythm of their lives forever.

Anthropologists warn "outsiders" like ourselves against doing this, claiming it will destabilize the equilibrium established between a societal group and the particular environment in which they live.

On the other hand, if they were to shift away from the rhythms of nature to a Divine Order, they would need to learn to count at least to seven and memorize the names of each day of the seven-day week cycle.

Unknown to most, introducing the Chácobo to the seven-day week calendar was a "religious" act of immense proportions. No longer would they be anxious about having a communion service to the *Bird Above* at the new moon.

As sociologist Eviatar Zerubavel (1948 -) points out, introducing the seven-day cycle is the first step in "increasing the distance between human beings and nature," thereby constraining mankind from "worshipping the heavenly bodies, especially the moon."[1] The Chácobo's communion service to the *Bird Above* always coincided with the new moon's appearance.

But the seven-day solar calendar week does more than increase the distance between human beings and nature. It also positions man above nature as its master. Of course, the naturalists who place man totally in nature can only assume that the seven-day week was a "Jewish invention" that finally gave humans the opportunity to "break away from being prisoners of nature."[2]

All societies would eventually learn that the seven-day week cycle originated with God, not man, as described in the Bible. They would know that it was a personal God who, after creating heaven and earth in six days, "on the seventh day God ended His work which He had done, and He rested on the seventh day from all His work which He had done" (Genesis 2:2).

However, on the "special day" for the Chácobo, God was not absolute and personal but rather impersonal and finite. Unlike us, their worship revolved around the vague, impersonal *Bird Above*, who had a bird's-eye view of what they were doing.

While their reality construct implied the need for a personal transcendent Being positioned above and distinct from nature, their rituals were directed to the impersonal *Bird Above*, which was merely a part of nature.

Unlike most of the world, the Chácobo were unaware that all social, political, economic, and religious activities of the world operated within the framework of the Judeo-Christian seven-day week cycle. For them, there were no weekends to look forward to. There were no birthday parties to get excited about, no Monday "back-to-work" days to dread, no looking forward to Friday pay-days, and no notched wooden posts in their homes to indicate they were keeping track of time. No one ever awoke in the morning, saying, "I wonder what day it is?" There were only days and days without names.

While the Chácobo were anxious about many things in life, being worried about what could happen on a specific day of the week or month was not one of them. There were just days and cycles of the moon, both without names. What regulated their lives was not a 24-hour timepiece with a second hand or the Judeo-Christian calendar and seven-day week cycle, but the position of the sun during the day and the position of the moon at night. For the Chácobo, there were two seasons: the rainy season and the dry season.

∼

## TIME TO ADJUST TO THE PRESENT AGE

It was the start of the dry season, the beginning of May 1959. We had lived with the Chácobo for almost four years and reasoned that if this small tribe, which had grown to about 145 individuals, was to escape self-extinction, it meant some kind of integration with the outside world of which they knew very little.

Common sense dictated they needed to learn to count at least to seven and memorize the seven days of the week to survive in the 21st century. The odds were against them. They were a society of only 145 individuals without leaders in four communities on three rivers.

The more we considered it, however, the more obvious it became that we would be involved in a religious/political act of revolutionary proportions. Helping the Chácobo integrate into the world's system of tracking time and keeping seasons, if adopted, would change the rhythm of their lives forever. As I said, anthropologists warn outsiders like us against doing it.

On the other hand, as it became increasingly obvious, their anxieties over existence had led them to submit to environmental pressures that set limits on their capacity to exist. The new political and economic environment was beginning to engulf them. It was time they learned to count and understand the significance of the seven-day week.

Their "mechanical" ascribed function-based cultural operating system that operated without chiefs and family heads was a hindrance to their future survival. They would need freedom to develop new skills and investment capital for schools and start-up businesses.

I was slowly concluding that their leaderless society would self-destruct unless they had some "bridge leaders" with new skills who could lead them into the future.

Their social-economic-political operating system couldn't possibly handle the stress and pressures of modern society, which was beginning to encroach upon them. In the meantime, it seemed prudent that they at least learn to count to seven and learn the seven days of the week.

Like introducing them to fiat money for trading, matches for starting fires, metal pots for cooking, and outhouses to prevent the spread of germs, we would now introduce them to a Judeo-Christian way of counting time and regulating their lives. This would be a highly religious and political act.

It would inform them when to rest, when to work, and when to worship, implying that all secular and religious activities were to be framed in reference to the last and first day of the seven-day week cycle. In a society accustomed to plenty of rest days, the seven-day week cycle would mean six days of work, not the customary four or five.

∼

## ORIGIN OF THE SEVEN-DAY WEEK

As we began to teach them to count and name the days of the week, they learned that the seven-day week had two special days: *Sabado*, the last day of the week, and *Domingo*, the first day of the week. They would learn after the Creator of the world completed His work, He rested on the seventh day: "Then God blessed the seventh day and made it holy, because on it he rested from all the work of creating that he had done" (Genesis 2:3, NIV).

As the pressures from the modern world crept in, they increasingly looked to us for help to seek relief from these new anxieties. We alone were the ones who understood this external force called civilization. We knew the actual value of the ten-peso Bolivian bill traders were beginning to pawn off on them for a valuable jaguar skin or food. We knew they had "rights" to exist and function as Chácobo in Bolivian society.

They had to learn the concept of "rights." Once they understood how the outside world operated, there would no longer be a need for them to flee on occasion and hide in the jungle—we hoped.

In the years ahead, they would learn that all commercial and social activities in Bolivian society were closed on the first day of the week. But our goal was not only to introduce them to the seven-day cycle by which the entire world now regulated its social, economic, and religious activities; we wanted to teach them a new kind of rest that would set them free from their present anxieties over existence and survival.

The time had also arrived for us to explain why we had come from Chicago to live among them. It certainly was not to help them update their social and economic operating system.

## THE SIGNIFICANCE OF THE CONCEPT OF XËNIPIA - THE CHÁCOBO YEAR

As we approached the beginning of the dry season in 1959 and the water that flooded the lowlands receded, the catfish season arrived. One afternoon, when the fire-tables in the *Biiyá* village were bare, all five men in the village decided it was time to go fishing for catfish. Since catfish search for food at night, this meant the fishing trip was going to be at night.

To me, it sounded like fun. Perhaps I could learn something new. So, I surprised them by saying, "I would like to go along, too."

That memorable night, I certainly did experience something new. I left Marian and my daughter alone in the village.

The first thing this kid from Chicago learned was that their concept of property rights was different from mine. As we approached the river where I had my large dugout canoe tied up, they all started running as fast as they could. "What's the big hurry?" I wondered.

I would soon find out. When I arrived a minute or two later with Rabi, the father of Caco and Boca, I was surprised to see they had commandeered my large 19-foot-long by 3-foot-wide dugout canoe for themselves. Sitting in the bow of my canoe was Caco, my neighbor. Evidently, they hadn't anticipated my coming.

Pointing to what clearly was a one-man bark canoe that looked like it could sink if the occupants made any mistake, Caco proceeded to tell me I could go fishing with his younger brother, Boca.

I realized that for the Chácobo, our Western notion of "private property" was a fluctuating concept with vague semantic boundaries. The semantic boundaries were clear to me. I had purchased that canoe with my money which meant it was under my control. For them, the answer was "Yes, but it also exists for all of us."

So did I or did I not have "rights" over "my canoe" when they commandeered it for their purposes? Apparently not. But what about my shotgun? Did the only shotgun in the village belong to me or the village? If bows, arrows, toucan feathers, and headdresses were classified as "private property," then I reasoned, so was my gun. But what about my boat on the river bank? Did they classify my canoe differently because I tied it up on the river bank and not in my house? How was I going to reply in this situation?

Instead of saying, "Move over, Caco. This is my canoe," which I certainly felt inclined to do, I decided this would not be the wisest thing to say at the moment. I nodded and climbed into Boca's small bark canoe, thinking, "This will be a long and unbearable night." It was.

Before embarking, however, I made sure Boca had packed each end of the canoe a couple of inches above the water line with enough mud to keep the water out. Fortunately, on that memorable night, I caught one eight-pound catfish without sinking the canoe.

## SEEING THE XËNIPA

About an hour before dawn, we all gathered together on the river's west bank to examine what we had caught. They knew it was a good catch, but unlike the disciples, they couldn't count past two, so they had no way of knowing exactly how many catfish they had caught. They immediately began to roast some of the fish because, by now, they were very hungry.

While the fish were roasting, they excitedly looked toward the Eastern sky, causing me to ask: "What are you looking for?" They said they were looking for the *xënipa*. Then one of them shouted, pointing to the horizon, "There it is!"

Appearing in the dawning Eastern sky, I could see three bright stars on a straight 20-degree angle approaching the horizon ahead of the sun. It was the Belt of Orion, known as *Las Tres Marias* in Spanish and *Sirius* by the Egyptians Then they informed me it was time to begin thinking about preparing their *huais* for planting.

For the Egyptians, it signaled the flooding of the Nile. For the Chácobo, the *xënipa* informed them the New Year had arrived, and it was time to think about cutting down a hectare of land. After drying and burning, they would plant their crops.

The time was also approaching when I needed to teach them every *xënipa* was divided into 12 months filled with days that had names.

As our ability to speak Chácobo increased, the time for us to explain why we had come to live among them arrived. It was July 1959. Not only were we going to introduce them to our Lord Jesus, but we were also going to introduce them to the seven-day week, the Lord's Day, and how to count to seven.

Unlike other tribes in Bolivia, the Chácobo could not count past one. They had only one numeral, the number one *huëstita*. Subtract the last syllable and replace it with the syllable *-ma*, and one had *huëstima*, not one but many. Besides *huëstita, huëstima*, there was *rabëta*, a few.

Our initial goal was to teach them that each *xënipa* year had twelve months, each month had four weeks, each week had seven days, each day had 24 hours, and each hour had sixty minutes. Learning to count meant birthdays, holidays, weekends, and months would eventually become important.

They thought my wristwatch informed me where the sun was positioned in the sky. When hunting on a cloudy day, they would ask me where the sun was positioned in the sky, thinking my wristwatch could magically tell me. The sun and the shadow it cast was their timepiece. This meant hunting on a cloudy day could be dangerous.

Because birthdays were important in the new time system, Marian began recording each child's birthday. Thus, we introduced them to a practiced custom, recording the day of one's birth. If they were to integrate into the world's system of tracking, it meant a shift from the rhythms of nature into a Divine Order that transcended nature.

The men's communal house

# CONVICTIONS

- The fact that the seven-day week doesn't "fit" any natural cycle clearly points to God as its Creator. Rejecting God, the Creator of the seven-day week, their ancestors also rejected God's way of reckoning time.

# CHAPTER 16
# THE CHÁCOBO
## A MAIMED SOCIETY

One of the many blunders I made when living among the Chácobo was to assume that each Chácobo village had a chief who could give an order. However, I observed that no adult gave a directive to another with the expectation that somebody would carry it out. There were neither leaders nor followers.

As an outsider, this reminded me of the biblical passage: "In those days, *there was* no king in Israel; everyone did *what was* right in his own eyes" (Judges 21:25).

I eventually discovered that the only superordinate-subordinate (S-s) relationship was parent-child, and I learned that the mother-daughter dyad was the dominant dyad in the nuclear family. Covertly, women ruled their daughters, and through their daughters, their sons-in-law.

No daughter left her father and mother to be joined with her husband at marriage. She remained at home. Her duty was to serve as her mother's helpmate in beer production. She was indispensable.

Years later, it became apparent that the internal structure of the Chácobo nuclear family had been shaped by what Karl Marx called social existence, Mao Zedong called social practice, anthropologist Marvin Harris called infrastructure, SIL anthropologist Marvin Mayers called culture, and missiologist-anthropologist Charles Kraft referred to as contextual interaction.

The Apostle Paul called these forces "the elementary forces of the world" (Colossians 2:8). The types of family structures these elementary forces created had one thing in common: They didn't accord with Christ. They had "no place in the Divine Plan."

For the Chácobo, these background elementary forces consisted of a humid climate and sandy soil, making manioc beer the staple of life for the Chácobo and every tribe living in the Amazon. The Chácobo permitted their need for manioc beer to shape their entire lifestyle, from the production of enormous clay pots needed for brewing beer to the need to keep daughters at home to help in its production.

Years later, after I heard Marvin Harris explain how cultural sameness produced cultural diversity, I concluded that Professor Harris was right. Cultural diversity resulted from "infrastructural" pressures, material pressures that produced "appropriate thoughts."[1]

When the different language groups dispersed after the Tower of Babel, the people entered different ecological niches where the "infrastructural pressures" differed.

After graduating from the University of Florida with my Masters degree in anthropology, I discovered that long before Marvin Harris published his thesis in *Culture Materialism: A Struggle for a Science of Culture* (1980), and before Marian and I arrived in the Amazonian Rainforest (1955), a couple of non-anthropologists, two theologians, F. W. Dillistone and Christopher Dawson, were saying the same thing.

In *Religion and Culture* (1948), Dawson states, "Culture is a way of life adapted to a particular environment."[2] Dillistone wrote in *The Structure of the Divine Society* (1951):

A society gradually takes shape within a particular physical environment. The character of the environment influences its [cultural] forms—whether it is fertile or hard country, whether the climate is equable or extreme, whether the mineral and waterpower is abundant or scanty.

The shape Chácobo society took was to replace the covenantal dyad of *husband-wife* with that of mother-daughter. It was a shift from freedom to being "organized on mechanistic principles ... [in which] every part must be made to function smoothly within the totalitarian whole."[3]

Submitting to these forces produced an ontological shift from freedom to ascribed duties, from natural roles to a tribe organized and based on ascribed functions.

By replacing the covenantal one-flesh principle of *husband-wife* with the biological one-flesh principle of mother-daughter, they, in the words of philosopher Herman Dooyeweerd (1894 - 1977), had "violated the structural law of the family."[4] The Chácobo lifeway had become mechanized, as predicted by Dillistone.

Before our eyes, these kind and generous people lived in bondage shaped by what Paul called "the elementary forces of the world" (Colossians 2:8), and Galatians 4:3: "Even so we, when we were children, were in bondage under the elements of the world." Every part functioned smoothly within a totalitarian whole.

However, before sitting under anthropologist Marvin Harris and reading Dillistone, my understanding of how powerful the environment could be was not part of my missiological research strategy. Sadly, neither is it part of the missiological strategies used by many missiologists.

Unaware of Harris, Dawson, and Dillistone's perspectives, I nevertheless concluded the structure of the nuclear family had been altered. For some unknown reason, the Chácobo had replaced the covenantal *husband-wife* dyad, which maximized human freedom, with the biological dyad of mother-daughter, which suppressed it.

For me, a theist, this internal restructuring of the nuclear family represented a divergence from the Universal stated in Genesis 2:23.

With no anthropological training, my primary focus was to learn to speak the language, reduce it to writing, make primers, hold reading classes, uncover all grammar rules, expand my Chácobo lexicon, and finally, translate the New Testament.

Nevertheless, as an outside observer of their behavior and lifeway, I came to the conviction that a flaw in their social operating system needed to be corrected. There had to be a reason why they were a leaderless, goalless, and dying society. If we didn't help them, who would?

As I attempted to figure out what was maiming them, other missiologists were preaching the doctrine of "sociocultural adequacy,"[5] or cultural forms that "fit" the environment. In the words of Charles Kraft, their message was: One should accept the adequacy and the validity of that culture whether one's own set of values predisposes one to approve of the behavior of that group (or individual).[6]

Cultural relativists recommended we use the very forms that were maiming them!

AS THE YEARS PASSED, evidence mounted that the Chácobo were not only a maimed society, but why were they leaderless? Why were they following the same trajectory of death that other Amazonian tribes had followed?

As I scanned the literature, I discovered that neither Christian nor secular anthropologists provided an answer.

As external pressures threatened not only their food supply but also their lifeway, tethered to the production of *jënë* (beer), the time had come to contact the village of *Nucleo* at the headwaters of the *Arroyo Ivon*.

Ivon River

When we arrived in 1955, the village had just moved inland three days from the Benicito River to preserve their lifeway and avoid conflict with the rubber tappers beginning to occupy their land. I needed to check it out.

The purpose of the trip was four-fold. First, I wanted to see if land was available downstream where the *Biiyá* village could eventually move.

Second, if available, we would apply to the Bolivian Government for the land title. Having title to the land would give the Chácobo some protection from outsiders who would eventually covet their resources, including rubber, Brazil nuts, and cedar. This would require SIL to inform the Bolivian Government why the Chácobo needed a piece of land they could call theirs.

Third, if land was available, the Chácobo could be introduced to the modern cash economy tethered to rubber and Brazil nuts. This would involve teaching them the skill of tapping rubber, arithmetic, money handling, and business with the outside world.

Finally, even though we had cast our lot with the kids of Rabi—Pai and Carmelo, whom we had enrolled in a mission boarding school—we needed to evaluate whether it was worth our time to teach adults to read, count, and handle money. So, I planned a trip to *Nucleo* village.

I could get to *Nucleo* from *Biiyá* either by walking—a four-day trip—or by canoe from *Tumi Chucua*, our SIL Center. It would take the same amount of time. But if I took the canoe route, I could take more stuff, including a stack of primers and a two-way radio. The trip would involve traveling down the Beni River to the *Arroyo Ivon* and then up the *Arroyo Ivon*. JAARS airplane mechanic Elmer Ash and Carmelo's father accompanied me.

ON A MONDAY MORNING in June 1963, when the rivers were high, we set off for *Nucleo* village in my Grumman canoe propelled by my faithful 5 hp Mercury Outboard. The first three nights we spent living under the roofs of Bolivian families who were rubber tappers working independently of the patron system. Until the last day of the trip, the river was debris-free.

At the end of day three, we arrived at *Alto Ivon*, the last Bolivian homestead.

Living at *Alto Ivon*, to my surprise, was a Bolivian Christian family whose livelihood depended on natural rubber and Brazil nuts like other families living on the *arroyo* (river). Upon our arrival, we were thrilled to hear that the Chácobo lived upstream.

It immediately became obvious that *Alto Ivon*, the last Bolivian settlement on the *arroyo*, would be an ideal place for the village of *Biiyá* to move, provided the Christian family was willing to sell their rubber trails. When asked, they informed us they would like to move to *Riberalta* and were happy to know they had a buyer.

The following day, we set out for *Nucleo*, a Chácobo village. Jungle debris, including fallen trees, clogged most of the *arroyo*. We heard children playing as we approached *Nucleo* late in the afternoon. To everyone's surprise, "Papa" had come to visit them. After greeting us, our host Huara immediately provided a place for us to hang our hammocks under his roof.

On our first night and every night after that, our host would awaken his kids at three in the morning and tell them to dip in the creek. I could hear them run to the creek without protesting, jump in, and come shivering back. Amazing kids! When I asked them why they jumped into the creek each night, they answered, "Our parents want us to grow up tall."

We camped there for the next two weeks. Each morning, we held an adult reading class, and in the afternoons, we held classes for the kids. Since the dry season was ending and we had just a couple of weeks to spend with them before the *arroyo* began to dry up, we had to make plans to leave.

After two weeks, I decided the future lay with the kids attending the Norwegian Pentecostal Mission School across the river from *Tumi Chucua*, the SIL Center. Having been sent out from the church in Chicago that gave birth to the Awana Youth Program, my instincts told me to "stick with the kids."

Foreseeing a time when SIL's work in Bolivia would be finished, an important need would exist for indigenous, bilingual, bicultural leadership that had the skills and know-how to help the Chácobo integrate into the Bolivian way of life.

After leaving *Nucleo*, we stopped at *Alto Ivon* and informed Senior Coqui and his wife that we wanted to purchase his rubber trails. Eight weeks later, after selling me his rubber trails and tin cups, I led the village of *Biiyá* to the settlement of *Alto Ivon*.

The line consisted of men carrying their bows and arrows and other household valuables, followed by women loaded down with all their earthly possessions, some carrying nursing babies and children. We stopped and camped for the night when we arrived at a creek. The creeks along the way provided an opportunity to catch minnows and other small fish needed to sustain us. The trip to *Nucleo* took five days.

I, too, was loaded down. In my pack, I carried a two-way radio, a battery pack provided by JAARS, a string hammock that was much lighter than a jungle hammock, a few packages of soup, a bag of manioc flour, and an axe and shovel for making an airstrip. I carried no gun.

My plan was to fly out. But if I were to fly out rather than walk out, my Lord would have to provide a place for me to make a 300-meter airstrip.

Four days later, we arrived at *Nucleo*. While everyone remained in there for a few days, I pressed on to *Alto Ivon* with my two-way radio, an axe, and a shovel, wondering where I could build a 300-meter airstrip to fly out rather than walk. The most obvious place would be where this Christian family had planted their slash-and-burn *chacos*, manioc roots, corn, and bananas the year before.

I was taken across the *arroyo* through a grove of Brazil nut trees and to a large, cut-down area, much of it grown back. It was where they had planted their crops. Since the prevailing winds came from the Northwest, I needed to build the airstrip from the Northwest to the Southeast.

To my amazement, before me were two *chacos* that had been harvested months before. Dead branches and tree stumps covered the two fields with some stumps three, four, or five feet in diameter. Instead of the two *chacos* being laid out North to South, which is what they usually did, someone had laid them out diagonally.

Just as the Lord had provided a brand new canoe large enough to carry a refrigerator, He gave me two burned-out *chacos* in the precise Northwest-to-Southeast direction needed for an airstrip a little longer than a football field.

As I worked on the airstrip, I collected the debris of dead branches, placed them around the stumps, set them on fire, and then waited as they slowly burned down to the roots. What was left were huge holes in the ground that I filled with dirt and tamped down.

As I worked alone on the airstrip, leveling small hills and the ground, the *Biiyá* men made their *chacos* at each end.

The location of their *chacos* served a dual purpose: First, it provided an airstrip, and second, it provided a field to plant their manioc roots, corn, bananas, and rice. As they waited for harvest time, they depended on hunting, fishing, and help from their upstream neighbors. In the meantime, life was difficult. When I finished the airstrip, I radioed JAARS to pick me up.

Except for the approaches, I built an airstrip in the heart of the Amazonian Rainforest in six weeks. The only place in the entire Amazonian Rainforest where one could build a 100-meter airstrip alone in six weeks was at a place where a Bolivian Christian rubber tapper had cut down the virgin jungle and created two *chacos* which he felt compelled to lay out diagonally Northwest to Southeast. Again, my Lord provided.

Before leaving, I had the Chácobo build me a 20-foot by 15-foot temporary shelter where the Prost family could live while I built a mosquito-proof home with an aluminum roof rather than leaf.

Two weeks later, I made my last trip to *Biiyá* to pick up our household effects, including our kerosene stove and refrigerator, kitchen table, mattress, daughter's bed, blankets, pots, pans, silverware, etc. Without the help of JAARS, this move from *Biiyá* (It has Mosquitos) to *Alto Ivon*, a place of few mosquitos, would not have been possible.

Unlike other mission agencies, SIL had an office in the *Ministerio de Asuntos Campesinos* (Ministry of Matters Rural) building in downtown *La Paz*, the Bolivian capital. The Bolivian government and SIL shared linguistic and educational goals. Both believed tribal communities should be integrated into the national economy and lifeway and be able to pursue their social, cultural, political, economic, and spiritual goals without sacrificing their ethnolinguistic identity.

With the move from *Biiyá* to *Alto Ivon* came the problem of meeting the food demands of 35 people. Again, I turned to Dave Farah, SIL's government man in *La Paz*, Bolivia, for help. Harvesting the planted crops would take at least two months.

When I expressed to Dave the temporary food needs of the Chácobo, he immediately took action. Within a week, a shipment of salted halibut, powdered milk, and other staples was coming. The givers? To my surprise, it was the Norwegian government.

However, unknown to SIL and the Bolivian government, the Chácobo were a goalless, dying society. Why were they dying? I had no answer other than my conviction they were a leaderless society which couldn't count to two; and, to my utmost distress, I had become their de facto leader.

By moving to *Alto Ivon*, as their de facto leader, I had assumed the responsibility of introducing the leaderless Chácobo to the national economy. The Bolivian jungle economy, tethered to rubber and Brazil nuts, would provide the means. What I purchased was more than trails of rubber trees; it was also the tin cups attached to the trees waiting to collect the bleeding latex. In the coming months, they would quickly learn how to tap the rubber and create rubber balls ready for sale in *Riberalta*.

The only way for the Chácobo to access the world's goods, like guns, ammunition, pots, pans, cups, knives, machetes, ax heads, salt, and eventually sewing machines, bicycles, radios, and even Bibles, was by earning cash—tapping and collecting the latex, processing it, and selling it to a buyer.

That buyer was "Papa." In their eyes, I had become their "patron."

As their patron, I now needed to supply the Chácobo with tin cups and worldly goods. The Brazilian border was the cheapest place to buy these goods.

On November 22, 1963, as I was busy buying these goods, going from store to store, someone asked me if I was an American. When I told him I was, he replied, "Your president, President Kennedy, has been assassinated." I was shocked.

My role as a rubber buyer and seller of goods was temporary. Besides translating the New Testament, my fundamental task was training a core of bridge leaders to guide their people into the future. It would take time. "My kids" had to grow up. In the meantime, the question of why the Chácobo were a leaderless society that could not count to two remained a puzzle.

Meeting their spiritual needs, however, was more important than meeting their material needs. So, every *Ibobá Bari* (Lord's Day), I would prepare a Bible lesson from one of the four Gospels and present it either in the men's communal house, school house, or visiting space under our bedroom.

More than five years had passed since our first Bible presentation in July 1959, and still, there was no response to the Gospel. After each presentation on Jesus' life, I would encourage them to meet with me afterward when I would explain what it meant to accept Jesus as their Savior and *Ibo* (Lord).

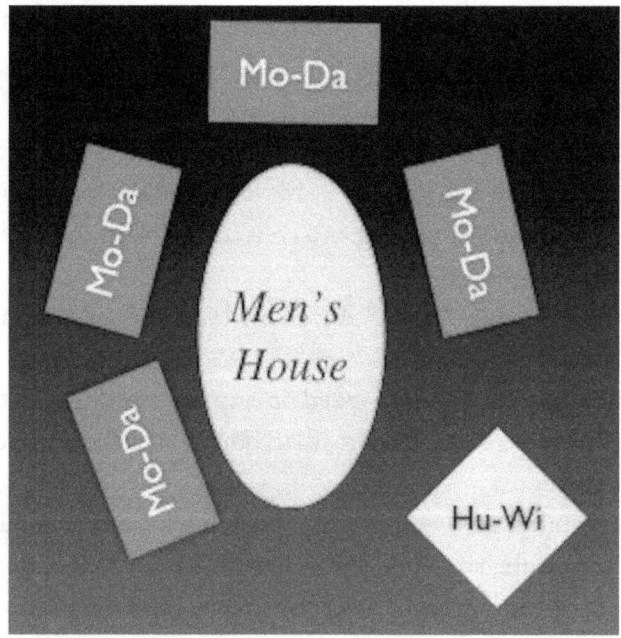

Arrangement of Chácobo village

Caco Pistia, the first Christian

## CONVICTIONS

- Submitting to the elementary forces of the Amazonian Rainforest, the Chácobo restructured the nuclear family and thus created a family type that maimed them.
- By informing the Chácobo that their family type had "no place in the Divine Plan," I also refused to accept the relativist's perspective that cultural forms that satisfied a particular need must be construed as valid.
- The Chácobo nuclear family was "defectively realized because of sin."[7]

# CHAPTER 17
# EPIGNOSIS VERSUS GNOSIS
## UNCHANGING VS GENERAL KNOWLEDGE

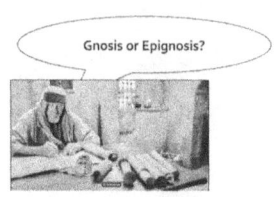

After Alexander the Great's conquests (356 - 323 BC), Koine Greek became the Eastern Mediterranean's lingua franca (commercial language). It was also the mother tongue of most Jews living outside of Judea. Unlike the Jews of Judea, they were now handicapped. They could no longer read the Scriptures in Hebrew.

To make the Scriptures available to these Greek-speaking Jews spread throughout the Roman empire, 70 Hellenistic Jewish scholars gathered in Alexandria, Egypt, to translate the Old Testament into Greek. These scholars carried out the project between the third and first centuries before Christ. Like all translation projects, the Greek-speaking translators faced problems common to all Bible translators.

As Hellenistic Jews, they knew that the Greek language had two primary terms for knowledge: *gnosis* and *epignosis*. Which word would they choose when translating the Hebrew word for "knowledge," which was *daath*? Would they select *gnosis*, which denoted general knowledge, or *epignosis*, which denoted precise, unchanging knowledge?

This problem became especially acute when they came to the phrase, "There was no *daath (*knowledge) of God in the land" (Hosea 4:1b). If these translators rendered *daath* as *gnosis,* it would mean there was no knowledge of God whatsoever in the land, and that was not the case. Israel still possessed a general knowledge about the nature of God.

The problem was that Israel's knowledge of God had become distorted and blurred, and they no longer had a full *epignosis* (knowledge) of God. The LXX translators therefore chose *epignosis* (full and accurate knowledge) rather than *gnosis*. "No longer was *epignosis* (true knowledge) in the land."

A similar translation problem occurs in Hosea 4:6, where the Hebrew word *daath* occurs twice in the same verse, each with a different meaning, which is not reflected in our English translations but in the Septuagint.

> *My people are destroyed for lack of knowledge. Because you have rejected knowledge [*epignosis*], I also will reject you from being priest for Me; Because you have forgotten the law of your God, I will also forget your children.*

When Israel rejected the Scriptures, its lifeway was emptied of God's standards and guidelines for living. Their way of life was no longer shaped by the knowledge that could inform them what ought to be, namely, *epignosis* (knowledge). They no longer had a way of living that relied on *epignosis* (knowledge), which was "fixed" and constant.

In this regard, the Apostle Paul wrote: "I can assure you that they are deeply devoted to God; but their devotion is not based on true knowledge" (Romans 10:2, Good News Translation).

Like present-day America, Israel's "knowledge of the Bible had diminished to the vanishing point."[1] In the process, they lost their *epignosis* (knowledge of God). A lifeway that once manifested a true *epignosis* (knowledge of God) no longer existed.

Fully aware that the true and exact meaning of the Gospel revealed to him could be distorted, Paul declared in Galatians 1:11-12:

> *But I make known to you, brethren, that the gospel which*
> *was preached by me is not according to man.*
> *For I neither received it from man nor was I taught it. But*
> it came *through the revelation of Jesus Christ.*

The Apostle Paul declares that the Gospel he was preaching did not derive its meaning from man, from social practice, or empirically through the five senses; it came through revelation.

Israel, at the time of Paul, no longer had a "fixed" framework of *epignosis* on which to build a positive culture. Instead, they had replaced inherent meanings (meanings that belonged to God), with meanings belonging to man derived from social practice.

Like all societies that reject, blur, and distort the Universals, the consequences for Israel were catastrophic. They were, because of their unbelief, dispersed throughout the world. To my amazement, there was a Jewish family living in *Riberalta*.

## EPIGNOSIS (UNCHANGING) KNOWLEDGE VERSUS GNOSIS (GENERAL) KNOWLEDGE

When Francis L. K. Hsu described the behavioral attributes tethered to four different dyads, that of father-son, mother-son, brother-brother, and *husband-wife,* his hypothesis made great sense.

After reading about the behavioral traits and allegiance patterns manifested by these four dyads, I immediately knew the dominant dyad of the nuclear family for the Chácobo was mother-daughter. I was dealing with a family problem.

From a theistic perspective, it was clear that the Chácobo had restructured the nuclear family sometime in their history, replacing a Positive Universal with a negative particular.

After reading Francis L. K. Hsu's article, "Kinship and Ways of Life,"[2] I knew we could probably finish by 1984. But it would take a revolution. Suddenly, stories like *The Dying Raisi* (chapter 8) and *The Story of Pai as a Raisi and Escaping Mother-in-Law Control* (chapter 4, "Chácobo Satire") made sense. It explained why the first Christian was someone who wasn't a son-in-law.

The messages of these storytellers of the past were clear. Sons-in-law needed to be freed from mothers-in-law control. This would involve returning the *husband-wife* dyad to its rightful place in the nuclear family.

I pulled out a folder and wrote on it the words: "A Revolution without Guns." I would note in it the ideas that I thought would help the Chácobo to restore the Universal.

I later discovered British philosopher Peter Carruthers (1952 -) supported such a strategy. He wrote: "Our Universal concepts can be thought of as prerequisites for successful social life."[3]

Restoring the Universals became the prerequisite for a successful social life, and this was necessary for "A Revolution without Guns" to succeed. This meant creating a framework of concepts to which are attached inherent meanings that are "fixed" and constant. For anthropology to become a science, analytical models must have a Divine perspective.

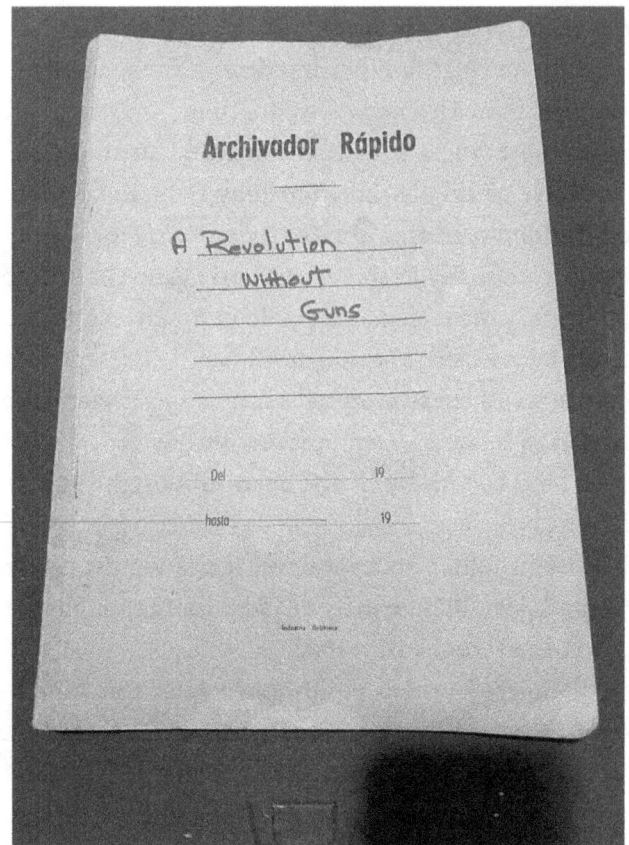

Gil Prost penned these words over 60 years ago, and hence, became the subtitle of the book *Created in the Image of God*

## CONVICTIONS

- Two kinds of knowledge exist: Knowledge in which the meanings of words are "fixed," trustworthy, and constant; and knowledge in which meanings are relative, derived from social practice.
- Hosea was aware of these two kinds of knowledge: Knowledge shaped by the character of one's environment, which was "learned," and knowledge

# CREATED IN THE IMAGE OF GOD

"acquired" and brought to consciousness through a "triggering" process or the reading of the Word of God.

# CHAPTER 18
# THE NEED FOR ETIC ANALYSIS
## CHÁCOBO LAW-WAY

Besides translating the New Testament and producing readers who could read it, we were also tasked with helping the Chácobo return the *husband-wife* dyad to its proper place in the nuclear family. For the cultural relativist, like Kraft, who believes every missionary should accept the "sociocultural adequacy" principle and that "words and all other cultural symbols derive their meanings only from their participation in the cultural context of which they are a part,"[1] such a strategy would be considered ill-conceived.

For the cultural relativist, no Innate Positive Universals exist that a society can reject and replace with negative cultural particulars.

At some point in history, what they called their *jabi* "sneaked into" the Chácobo law-way, and according to the Apostle Paul, these cultural forms had "no place in the Divine Plan."

Thanks to anthropology professor Francis L. K. Hsu, I discovered that mothers-in-law controlled the cultural operating system. I began to understand why men ate together, slept together, and drank manioc beer together in a men's communal house that separated them not only from their wives but also from their mothers-in-law.

Then I discovered sages that warned against such a law-way. However, the Chácobo ignored their warnings.

I began to understand how the mother-daughter dyad's dominance reduced the *husband-wife* dyad's importance. It also explained why mother-daughter houses circled the men's communal house and why they merged the mutually exclusive status positions of siblings and parallel cousins.

However, Hsu failed to point out in his analysis that every one of the eight familial dyads except one was grounded in consanguinity (relationship by blood or a common ancestor). These were father-son, father-daughter, mother-son, mother-daughter, brother-sister, brother-brother, and sister-sister dyads. The exception to the patterns was that of *husband-wife*. It represented a covenantal relationship.

Nevertheless, Hsu's article forever changed how I viewed a society's kinship system and how it structured the nuclear family. The key to understanding a society's law-way and worldview starts with understanding how the nuclear family is internally structured. Hsu explains it this way:

"When one dyad is elevated over other dyads in a given kinship system, the attributes of the dominant dyad tend to modify, eliminate, or at least reduce the importance of the attributes of other structural dyads."[2]

SOCIAL SCIENTISTS, anthropologists, and psychologists are all looking for the Holy Grail, an absolute, "fixed," culture-free standard they can use for judging the validity of cultural forms.[3] Without this, it becomes impossible to know what is right and what is wrong.

Cultural psychologists Ara Norenzayan and Steven J. Heine were aware of the problem. They pointed out that culture-free standards "provide the only legitimate criteria by which any particular sociocultural practice or belief may be judged."[4] I agree.

Recognizing the problem, cultural anthropologist Robert Lawless (1937 - 2012) wrote:

> Any comparison of other societies by the standards of one's own society, any evaluation of the behavior and beliefs of another society through the perspective of one's own folk model, simply labels those other behaviors and beliefs as wrong, crazy, irrational, or stupid.
>
> If we are bound by the perspectives of our own folk model, we will learn nothing about why other people behave and think differently from us. Such a sterile viewpoint is called ethnocentrism. Analytic models must have a trans-societal perspective.[5]

A trans-societal perspective transcends the totality of cultural needs-based perspectives in the world. Such a perspective reflects the ideal, the perfect, the absolute. And there is no way to make sense of life without such a perspective.

However, possessing such a perspective will still fall short of God's perspective, which is perfect. In this regard, linguist Kenneth Pike agrees, stating: "The minute you equate truth with precision, you have gone to *etic* exactness. There is no true statement in any of our experiences because, if we measure it within a millionth of an inch, it would always be different."[6]

While we can never achieve God's perfect perspective regarding linguistic and cultural forms, we can nevertheless approximate a culture-free, outsider's perspective if we start with the principle that meaning precedes existence.

However, if we reverse the process and say existence precedes meaning, all meanings "belong to the people." The result? No Divine perspective exists, the Bible is not the Word of God, and the idea that a cultural analyst could glean Universals from the field of particulars, as suggested by Socrates, must be set aside since no ultimate truth exists.

On the other hand, if meaning precedes existence, it presupposes that life has meaning—namely, purpose and language. "And the LORD God formed man *of* the dirt of the ground, and breathed into his nostrils the breath of life; and man became a living being" (Genesis 2:7).

God used two kinds of substances: the dust of the ground and His Breath. When the two came together, God formed a cultural language-speaking being who could converse with his Maker.

On the other hand, when God created the beasts of the field, He used only one kind of material: the dust of the ground.

When one compares these two similar creation events, he will note that the words for "formed" are not identical. When forming man in Genesis 2:7, the word "formed" contains two Yods (the tenth letter of the Hebrew alphabet), whereas when He created the beasts of the field, the word "formed" has only one Yod (Genesis 2: 19).

The Lord God did not breathe the constituents of language and culture into the life of the beast. The verb "to form" is missing a Yod. Only man lives a meaningful, purposeful existence; a meaning one can express in language.

Meaning comes through forms—a word, a smirk, a smile, a handshake, a gift, or a statement. Forms have either God-breathed meanings or meanings "that belong to the people."

As a Bible translator, I discovered some forms with Divine meanings at some point were replaced with meanings "that belonged to the people." A few examples are:

- Like many societies, the Chácobo classified parallel cousins as siblings. In doing so, they violated the Rules of Logic. Such thinking has "no place in the Divine Plan."
- People living in Northern India applied the Rule of Exogamy to the village. This means one must "marry out"

lest one commit incest. Since Joseph and Mary came from the same town, they would have labeled Jesus a "bastard." Such thinking has "no place in the Divine Plan."
- Tribes living in the Vaupés province of Colombia apply the Rule of Exogamy to each language group. This means one must marry someone who speaks a different language lest one commit incest. But such thinking has "no place in the Divine Plan."
- Children of Trobriand parents are instructed to address the man who takes care of them as the "husband of my mother" lest they "trigger "and bring to consciousness that the man taking care of them is their father. Such thinking has "no place in the Divine Plan." It makes the Bible translator a liar.

> *For God so loved the world that He gave His only begotten Son, that whoever believes in Him should not perish, but have everlasting life. (John 3:16)*

According to the Apostle Paul, humans and society invented the above cultural forms which have "no place in the Divine Plan." They increased sinning.

Romans 5:20 (Prost translation):

> *A law-way which had "no place in the Divine Plan" slipped into history, bringing about an increase in sin. But as sinning increased, God's grace increased even more.*

# CREATED IN THE IMAGE OF GOD

Chácobo learning to read

## CONVICTIONS

- When God breathed into Adam, He breathed into man cultural and linguistic forms with attached Divine meanings.
- The breath of God included the freedom to reject and replace inherent meanings with alien meanings "that belonged to the people."
- Meaning precedes existence.
- If existence precedes meaning, then the two Yods in the Hebrew word "formed" are meaningless, and human existence would be pointless.
- If anthropology is to become a science rather than an art, a framework of *etic* concepts must be developed to know which meanings belong to man and which meanings belong to God.
- According to Robert Lawless, "Analytic models must have a trans-societal perspective."[7]

# CHAPTER 19
# WHEN DID SOCIETY GO ITS OWN WAY

## THE HUSBAND-WIFE DYAD REPRESENTS THE UNIVERSAL COVENANTAL RELATIONSHIP

It will make you wise.

Was there a specific time when the world's nations began "to go their own way," as stated in Acts 14:16, and cultural diversity began? Was there a time when the covenantal one-flesh principle of *husband-wife* was replaced by one of seven biological one-flesh dyads like father-son, mother-son, father-daughter, mother-daughter, etc.? Was there a time when ideas, values, and concepts preceded existence?

For Professor Hsu, the answer would be a resounding "no."

To my knowledge, Francis L. K. Hsu did not attempt to answer the question, "Where do the rules and the behavior come from?[1] Are there ideas, values, and concepts structured in the unconscious mind that can be "triggered" and brought to consciousness?

Having said that, as a cultural anthropologist, Francis L. K. Hsu did acknowledge that the *husband-wife* dyad created an unusual type of people that "have advanced science both qualitative and quantitatively to a height undreamed of by the rest of the world ... and have developed harmony in music systematically and intensively; they have a wider variety of instruments, more precise instruments, and instruments which are capable of covering a wider musical range than any other people ... the tendency of the individual in this type of society is centrifugal. Many of them cannot wait to move out somewhere else or up the social or economic ladder."[2]

For Francis L. K. Hsu, the materialist, there existed no transcendent form nor Divine structure from which a society could diverge. Yet materialist Marvin Harris points out a time when "out of sameness differences emerged."[3]

For the concept-innatist, there was a time when no society merged mutually exclusive status positions like siblings and cousins, fathers and uncles, and mothers and aunts.

As a committed materialist, Hsu also rejected the idea that man lives in two spheres: The sphere of freedom and the sphere of necessity.

While promoting the idea that only one dyad, that of husband and wife, fosters independence and creativity and has "advanced science to a height undreamed of by the rest of the world," he rejected the idea that the nuclear family could be restructured. Nevertheless, his discovery that it could be structured in various ways is significant.

If he had acknowledged that there existed an ideal form of the nuclear family from which a society had the freedom to diverge and "go its own way" (Acts 14:16), his status as professor emeritus would have been questioned. Nevertheless, Pike recognized the phenomenon and called it *etic* divergence.

In addition, Hsu failed to point out in his analysis that every one of the eight familial dyads except one was grounded in consanguinity. These were father-son, father-daughter, mother-son, mother-daughter, brother-sister, brother-brother, and the sister-sister dyads.

The exception to the above patterns was that of *husband-wife*. While seven dyads were grounded in biology, one wasn't.

The *husband-wife* dyad represents the Universal covenantal relationship. According to Derrick S. Bailey, "It is the union of the entire man and the entire woman. In it, they become a new and distinct unity, wholly different from and set over against other relational unities"[4] such as the family-of-five, lineage, band, clan, village, totem, etc.

The distinction between covenantal and biological is essential because it explains why we have cultural diversity.

Such societies create what Francis L. K. Hsu calls "deep-seated centripetal tendencies ... the place of the individual in the 'web of kinship' is inalienable and perpetual."[5]

In such societies, individuals will find it difficult to set up independent households and escape the "web of kinship" ties that suppress their freedom to serve others.

# CREATED IN THE IMAGE OF GOD

Jesus answered, "I am the way and the truth and the llfe" (John 14:6a, NIV).

## CONVICTIONS

- I've discovered that the web of interrelated ascribed functions is a powerful force that constrains human freedom and individuality.

## CHAPTER 20
# THERE IS A WAY THAT SEEMS RIGHT TO A MAN
### BUT ITS END IS THE WAY OF DEATH
### (PROVERBS 14:12)

On a university campus, students learn that science is about making decisions based on "fixed" standards, measurements, and concepts.

For example, each sound listed on a phonetic chart has constant and "fixed" physical properties. These sounds were discovered, not invented. We are dealing with a material phenomenon that occurs in the mouth.

But what about meanings? In this case, are we dealing with a non-material or material phenomenon? Are there meanings attached to words that are innate, "fixed," constant, and that belong to the realm of the spirit? Or do all meanings tethered to the five senses "belong to the people"?

Anthropologist Marvin Harris was convinced that such a standard could be found in the "regularities of nature."[1]

Missiologist Charles Kraft believed he had found the standard in environmental "fitness." He wrote:

The appropriate evaluation criterion would seem to be the concept of "fit" or fulfillment. How well does this cultural form "fit" or "fulfill" such and such a function?[2]

For the theist, relying on the Word of God should be the standard one uses. Should that standard be grounded in nature's regularities, environmental "fitness," social adequacy, or the Bible? Should the missionary become a cultural relativist and accept the postmodern view of multiple perspectives?

Theologian-philosopher Cornelius Van Til says: "No. In the midst of multitudes of perspectives, there must be a criterion by which these opinions can be judged."[3]

I wholeheartedly agree. If one's criterion is grounded in sense perceptions—one's biological needs or contextual environment—then one is left with the norms of one's particular culture for judging the validity of other cultural forms.

In the words of Cornelius Van Til: "Unless as sinners we have an inspired Bible [having words whose meanings are 'fixed' and constant], we have no God interpreting reality for us. There is no true interpretation at all."[4]

## EMPIRICISM OR CONCEPT-INNATISM?

When I discovered that the function of the Chácobo men's communal houses was to separate husbands from their wives, I immediately recognized that this was invalid because it violated the one-flesh principle of husband and wife.

Nevertheless, a contextualizing missiologist has declared the form "adequate" because it satisfies a need, and any attempt on my part to introduce "new wineskins" would upset the equilibrium of the cultural operating system and make acceptance of the Gospel more difficult. So, the standard for evaluating an artistic form is critical. It indeed troubled me.

Wherever one looks, this "fixed" standard is directly linked to what one believes about God, man, nature, and the Bible. If the analyst is convinced that there is no God, that man is a kind of animal, and that the Bible should be treated as a metaphor, he looks for this "fixed" standard in biology and one's environment. It is the standard used by empiricists.[5]

On the other hand, if one sees man as a unique being created in the "image of God," his starting point will not be biology, environmental "fitness," need satisfaction, or one's perceptions, but instead, the Divinely revealed data found in the Scriptures, innate knowledge, which is manifested in human behavior and observable. For the concept-innatist, this is the starting point.

The concept-innatist believes a personal Creator not only "wrote" the rules for living but also endowed man with *a priori* knowledge, without which it would be impossible for man to categorize his sense experience and create knowledge.

Cognitive scientist Steven Pinker (1954 -) recognizes that without innate (inborn) conceptual "tools," which he calls "function concepts," like same and different, someone and something, part of and kind of, there would be no knowledge whatsoever.

According to Pinker, knowledge of these innate "tools" is Universal. They are free from environmental, social, political, and religious control. Without these tools, a missionary can't judge what should be. Pike called such innate information *etic* data.

For those unfamiliar with these academic words, let me briefly examine the features of each standard, the one used by empiricists (data is derived from experience only) and the one used by concept-innatists (inborn knowledge endowed by the Creator).

## THE TERMS EMIC AND ETIC

The terms *emic* and *etic* represent an "inside perspective" and an "outside perspective."

From the cultural analyst's perspective, the insider's perspective represents the worldview of the native whose behavior, traditions, and customs are being analyzed.

In contrast, defining the outsider's perspective is both controversial and problematic. For example, does it mean a) that the analytical concepts used by the investigator are "derived from the culture of the investigator"[6] as proposed by psychologist John W. Berry; or b) that the analytical concepts used by the investigator represent culture-free Universals that have been discovered by observing human behavior?

In this case, an "outside perspective" means innate ideas or forms exist with attached meanings that are not derived from sense experience. If true, it means the *etic* standard for judging the validity of cultural forms is discoverable. Such a standard, if discovered, would make a "culture-free" analysis of culture possible.

However, according to anthropologist Martin Ottenheimer, a "cultural-free analysis is an illusion, and it [must be] recognized. *Etic* concepts are nothing more than the notions from the external analyst's culture. The anthropologist must stop thinking in terms of "one true framework."[7]

For linguist Kenneth Pike, who coined the terms *emic* and *etic*, culture-free analysis is not an "illusion." It is empirically possible. If linguists are able to create a phon-*etic* chart, then the goal of every anthropologist, psychologist, linguist, and sociologist should be to discover the behavioral archetypes structured in the unconscious mind that inform society how to live.

Before Pike coined the terms *emic* and *epic*, psychoanalyst Carl Jung popularized the term "archetype," also known as innate or Universal concepts to which there are attached meanings that are "fixed," absolute, constant, and free from cultural contamination.

"He (Jung) took an *etic* approach to his studies. Jung studied mythology, religion, ancient rituals, and dreams, leading him to believe that archetypes [also known as *etic* data] can be identified and used to categorize people's behaviors.

Archetypes are Universal structures of the collective unconscious that refer to the inherent way people are predisposed to perceive and process information."[8] In this regard, theologian Francis Schaeffer writes:

> If there is no absolute moral standard, then one cannot say in a final sense that anything is right or wrong. By absolute, we mean that which always applies and provides a final or ultimate standard.
>
> There must be an absolute if there are morals, and there must be an absolute if there are real values. If there is no absolute beyond man's ideas, then there is no final appeal to judge between individuals and groups whose moral judgments conflict. We are merely left with conflicting opinions.[9]

Present-day academia has rejected Schaeffer's idea of an "absolute moral standard," with the exception of linguist-anthropologist Kenneth Pike and those interested in uncovering the constituents of this absolute moral standard, which manifests itself phenomenally in human behavior.

Initially, the meaning of the term *etic*, coined by linguist Kenneth Pike, denoted discrete units of sounds that were Universal, "fixed," and constant, and which the linguist could use in creating a "scientific alphabet" for any sound system of language.

The term *etic* was abstracted from the word phon-*etic*, referring to discrete units of sounds that make up the phonetic alphabet. The qualities that made up each of these discrete sounds were discovered. Then, they were charted according to their qualities, as illustrated in the chart.[10]

the international phonetic alphabet (2005)

| consonants (pulmonic) | LABIAL | | CORONAL | | | | | DORSAL | | | | RADICAL | | LARYNGEAL |
|---|---|---|---|---|---|---|---|---|---|---|---|---|---|---|
| | Bilabial | Labio-dental | Dental | Alveolar | Palato-alveolar | Retroflex | Alveolo-palatal | Palatal | Velar | Uvular | | Pharyngeal | Epi-glottal | Glottal |
| Nasal | m | ɱ | | n | | ɳ | | ɲ | ŋ | N | | | | |
| Plosive | p b | | | t d | | ʈ ɖ | | c ɟ | k g | q ɢ | | | ʔ | ʔ |
| Fricative | ɸ β | f v | θ ð | s z | ʃ ʒ | ʂ ʐ | ɕ ʑ | ç ʝ | x ɣ | χ ʁ | | h ʕ | H ʕ | h ɦ |
| Approximant | | ʋ | | ɹ | | ɻ | | j | ɰ | | | | | |
| Tap, flap | | ⱱ | | ɾ | | ɽ | | | | | | | | |
| Trill | B | | | r | | | | | | R | | | | |
| Lateral fricative | | | | ɬ ɮ | | ɭ | | ʎ | | | | | | |
| Lateral approximant | | | | l | | ɭ | | ʎ | L | | | | | |
| Lateral flap | | | | ɺ | | | | | | | | | | |

Where symbols appear in pairs, the one to the right represents a modally voiced consonant, except for murmured ɦ.
Shaded areas denote articulations judged to be impossible.

As a theist, Pike was convinced that the discovery process used in uncovering what constituted the constants in phonology could also be used to find the constants manifested in language and culture. Whether it was sociology, psychology, economics, or anthropology, for Pike, it was Universal constants, also known as *"etic* data [which] provide access to the system—the starting point of analysis."[11]

Pike's "outside perspective" or "absolute moral standard" was tethered to *etic* data, also known as archetypes. The existence of such mental data or archetypes cannot be observed directly but can be logically inferred by looking at religion, satire, myths, dreams, art, and language. This information is not learned; it is discovered.

According to anthropologist Ward Goodenough, once these absolute values, ideal behavioral patterns, and principles are discovered, such *etic* concepts will "provide the frame of reference, the conceptual constants, through which to examine similarities and differences among specific behavioral systems of that type."[12]

Possessing such *a priori* information enables every analyst to uncover when an inherent archetype has been replaced with a standard "that belongs to the people."

In this regard, like Jung, Pike postulated the existence of such Universal ideas, concepts, or forms that are "fixed" and constant and that "do not belong to the people." In the words of linguist Anna

Wierzbika, "We should specify that 'meaning' has to do with the constants, not with the variables."[13]

Both materialists and contextualizers like Kraft strongly disagree, insisting that meanings "belong to the people."[14]

For such, no culture-free world of ideas exists. Instead, truth has been reduced to a social construct. Constants have been replaced with variables. There exists no absolute order of understanding, no Universal-Lexicon, no "sound words" (II Timothy 1:13), and no "law written on the heart" (Romans 2:15).

No Meta-Script exists that manifests itself phenomenally in human behavior. In the social sciences, including missiology, an *etic* perspective has come to mean the perspective of "an informed outside analyst." Presently, this is the prevailing view in academia.

Most, if not all, professors and researchers in the above fields are convinced that the only approach if it is going to be "scientific," must be a bottom-up, outside-in biological-environmental approach. In this case, empiricists would ascribe to the theory that no child is born with mental content or information. The mind is described as being a *tabula rasa* (blank tablet devoid of innate ideas).

The rules for language and culture are written on a blank slate, and they come from the outside via one's sense experiences that are converted into concepts. These rules are then learned by succeeding generations. For Harris and Kraft, all the rules of culture are learned.

Professor Harris believed the starting point is "the regularities of nature." This would include birth rates, pollution, famines, farming, soil fertility, ranching, rainfall, war, technologies, etc.

Unlike thought, such phenomena can be observed, measured, tested, and weighed. These regularities of nature exist outside the mind. They are first perceived through the five senses, then categorized (using function concepts), and classified by the mind. Afterward, they are magically transmuted into rules for living.

However, there are problems with the empiricist's[15] position. First, one needs "function concepts" to create knowledge. An example is how Chácobo children learned to read. If innate function concepts like "kind of and part of" were not in their spiritual DNA, it would have been impossible for these children to learn to read.

Second, the regularities of nature are not "fixed" and constant. They are in continuous flux. If everything one perceives is constantly changing, like the flowing water in the river, then there can be no Universals for living.

Since one's ecological, technological, and economic environment are in constant flux, for the empiricist, so are the ethical rules for living and the meanings they attach to words.

The question about standards and human behavior troubled Harris because he wrote, "The central question is where the rules and the behavior come from.[16] In Harris' *Struggle for a Science of Culture,* the subtitle of his book, *Cultural Materialism,* Harris set out to prove that the rules for living were formed, shaped, and determined by one's environment or what he called "infrastructure." The Rule Maker for Harris was impersonal.

A language problem also exists. Can that which is impersonal be the subject of a personal verb like "write" or "make rules"? If there are Universals for living, then who gives these Universals ultimate meaning? Nature, man, or God?

The empiricist believes meaning is derived from context and meanings are variable. If that is true, then the author is neither man nor nature.

The concept-innatist believes true meanings are inherent in Universal concepts that are "written on the heart." They are "fixed" and constant. The concept-innatist believes "There is a way *that seems* right to a man, But its end *is* the way of death" (Proverbs 14:12).

Marian and I were fully aware that the cultural ways of the Chácobo and the Pacahuara (to whom we were providentially sent) were slowly leading them to cultural and spiritual death. When we contacted the Pacahuara, only ten members were left in the tribe.

Then one died. The Chácobo were down to 133 members when we moved into the village of *Biiyá* to live among them.

CONVICTIONS

- Two kinds of knowledge exist: a) knowledge that is relative because it has been abstracted from sense perceptions, and b) knowledge structured in the unconscious mind that is "fixed," constant, and absolute.
- If there are no concepts common to all that have inherent meanings, then all of life will lack meaning, coherence, and logical consistency.
- There exists an innate moral standard that informs a society how to live.
- "*Etic* [mental] data provides access to the system … the starting point of analysis." ~Kenneth Pike

## CHAPTER 21
# WHICH COMES FIRST
### SOCIAL EXISTENCE VS ESSENCE

Every social scientist must ask two questions: Does social existence precede essence? Or do Universal ideas (essence) precede social existence?

If social existence precedes Universal ideas, then the meanings attached to Universal ideas like family, marriage, husband, wife, father, mother, son, daughter, brother, and sister must be shaped by social existence in a particular material environment. In this case, all meanings would be relative. They "belong to the people."

For example, one society may define the family as one's "linguistic group," another as the "village," and another as one's "clan." To avoid the sin of incest, this means marrying someone who speaks a different language, lives in a different village, or belongs to a different clan.

In this case, social existence in a particular material environment shapes and determines the meaning of family. The starting point cannot be the nuclear family and its internal structure.

If, on the other hand, Universal ideas and their attached meanings precede existence, then every child coming into the world comes equipped with a Universal-Lexicon whose meanings are brought to consciousness when "triggered" in a socio-linguistic situation.

According to Herman Dooyeweerd, in this case, the child innately knows that "membership [in the family] is absolutely restricted to the parents and their offspring in the first degree."[1]

But then, as the child matures, if social existence precedes Universal ideas, the cultural script for living learned from the parents will be in fundamental opposition to the Universal meaning "written on the heart."

In deviant societies that have abandoned the covenantal *husband-wife* relationship as the dominant dyad, children are taught to merge mutually exclusive status positions like father and uncle, mother and aunt, and siblings and cousins. The cultural analyst is tricked into thinking that the starting point can't possibly be the nuclear family.

What the materialist fails to consider is a spiritual phenomenon linguist Kenneth Pike calls *etic* divergence. He says, "A person may distort innate Positive Universals into negative particular actions."[2]

In other words, a society, within limits, may replace a constant with a new meaning "that belongs to the people," making it a relative meaning shaped by environmental pressures.

After finishing our task among the Chácobo in 1980 and, at Pike's request, earning a degree in anthropology at the University of Florida, our next assignment took us to the Miccosukee[3] tribe of South Florida.

This assignment would provide an opportunity to test my assumption that each child coming into the world comes equipped with a cultural-free script.

According to Professor of Law Herman Dooyeweerd, "Membership [in the family] is absolutely restricted to the parents and their offspring in the first degree," but I was also aware that rebellious humans have the freedom to diverge from the script "written on the heart."

After my Chácobo experience, *etic* divergence, replacing a Positive Universal for a negative cultural particular, was a given. How the "divergence" manifested itself phenomenally needed to be uncovered.

Sadly, my approach to uncovering the meanings attached to cultural forms was at variance with SIL's anthropology department.

After discovering that the Chácobo had replaced the one-flesh principle of *husband-wife* with that of mother-daughter, my primary question was: What was the dominant dyad of the Miccosukee nuclear family?

Since the Miccosukee had been classified as a matrilineal society, I hypothesized that the brother-sister dyad had probably replaced the *husband-wife* dyad. My new assignment provided the opportunity to find out. I will share that story a little later in the book.

## THE STARTING POINT

Holding to a top-down, inside-out epistemology meant that I, as a cultural analyst, was dealing with material and spiritual phenomena. It is phenomena that anthropologists and missiologists ignore, believing that "science" is all about a material phenomenon.

Like Pike, who declared, "I reject any analysis that treats all behavior as exclusively physical,"[4] I, too, was marching to a different drumbeat. From a top-down, inside-out perspective, my starting point as a theist was the existence of "laws written on the heart," also known as *etic* data. I also assumed that such data should manifest itself phenomenally in human behavior.

As an anthropologist interested in the social phenomenon of cultural diversity, my starting point was the family unit consisting of a man and his wife and their child or children.

For anthropologist Lévi-Strauss, "There is no more dangerous idea."[5] He could not, in the words of Jewish evolutionary biologist Richard Lewontin (1929 - 2021), "allow a Divine Foot in the door."[6] It implied the existence of *etic* data structured in the subconscious from which society could diverge.

I wasn't surprised to learn that the Miccosukee had merged the status positions of siblings and cross-cousins. However, I was surprised to learn that they had classified the children of the mother's brother as "sons" and "daughters" and the children of the father's sister as "uncle" and "grandmother."

But more surprising was to discover they had no possessive pronouns.

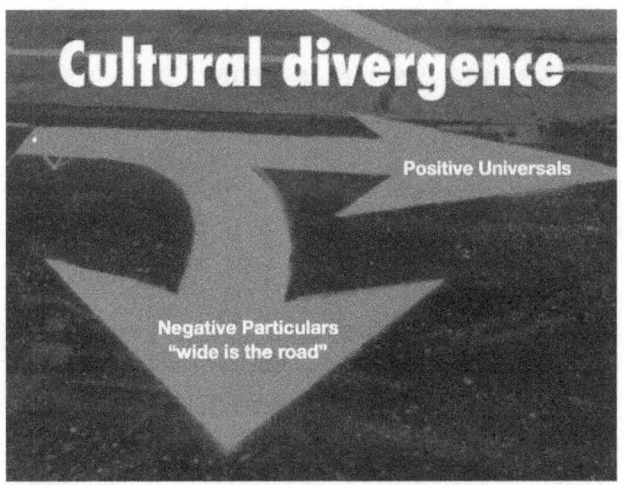

Cultural divergence (sin)

## CONVICTIONS

- Whenever a society chooses to diverge from Universal ideas (essence) "written on the heart," the first effect will be a reconfiguring of the nuclear family, a rejection of the one-flesh principle of *husband-wife*, and replacing it with a biological dyad.
- In the Western world, a paradigm shift has taken place. Instead of Universal ideas (essence) preceding social

existence, in academia, social existence now precedes Universal ideas.
- If "truth" is an effect of social existence as proposed by existentialists, then the Bible ceases to be the Word of God.

# CHAPTER 22
# THE GREAT AWAKENING
## INHERENT OR DIVINE MEANINGS HAVE BEEN REPLACED WITH MEANINGS THAT "BELONG TO THE PEOPLE"

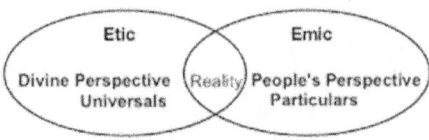

## THE GREAT AWAKENING

After taking a course under Marvin Harris, it became clear that what Harris was teaching was similar to what missiologist Charles H. Kraft taught in his book *Christianity in Culture: A Study in Biblical Theologizing in Cross-Cultural Perspective*.

Both advocated a bottom-up, outside-in materialistic approach to explain how meaningful concepts and rules for living are structured in the mind. What Harris called "appropriate thoughts" were structured in the mind by "infrastructure."

For Kraft, "meaning is [all about] the structuring of information in the minds of persons;"[1] and this information is derived from "context." In both cases, the mind is a *tabula rasa*.

This means if one's starting point is biology, environment, and need satisfaction, then the author of the law "written on the heart" can't be God but the impersonal forces of nature.

There can't be what the Apostle Paul calls "sound words" whose meanings represent an Ideal meaning that is "fixed" and constant.

In Kraft's words, "they [meanings] are not inherent in the forms [words] themselves."[2] Of course, this would mean that God does not speak through words having Divine meanings because "meanings are not inherent in the form [words]."

This interpretation would imply that no word carries a Divine meaning that is "fixed" and constant, which is terrible news for the missionary and every Bible translator who believes in verbal inspiration.

∽

## STANDARD OF SOUND WORDS

When the Apostle Paul wrote to Timothy, he desired that Timothy:

> *Retain the standard of sound words [ὑγιαινόντων λόγων] which you [Timothy] have heard from me, in the faith and love which are in Christ Jesus. (II Timothy 1:13, New American Standard Bible 1995)*

In this passage, Paul encourages Timothy to use "sound words" or "healthy words" in his church-planting ministry. Paul was experiencing the same problem we face in our postmodern culture: Expressing concepts that have been drained of their inherent meanings.

The sickness of our age is this: Inherent or Divine meanings have been replaced with meanings that "belong to the people."

The existence of "sound words" implies the existence of a Universal-Lexicon structured in the unconscious mind in which every entry has a "fixed," constant meaning. In the postmodern age of confusion, "sound words" are under attack. Daughters can marry and acquire "wives." Sons can marry and acquire "husbands." Males who declare they are females can compete in women's sports. In the words of Lenski, "We must [now] substitute categories and patterns of thought which the 'wisdom' of our day produces."[3]

Was it possible for Timothy to use unhealthy words in his church planting ministry? That is, words whose meaning had been distorted, twisted, and replaced with new meanings? Was it possible that what had happened to me personally when I unconsciously spoke of the "gift of God," not knowing that their word for gift carried the Chácobo meaning of reciprocity, was also taking place in Paul's outreach to the Gentiles throughout the Roman empire?

Perhaps the Chácobo carried with them the Asian meaning of gift when they came to the New World across the Bearing Straits. After all, Confucius's advice on religion was: "Respect all gods and spirits, but keep them at a distance," especially if this God wants to give you a gift you can never repay.

If not aware that words' meanings could be distorted, why would Paul encourage Timothy to "retain the standard of using healthy words"? The answer is simple: Using unhealthy words would distort the Gospel.

I believe the Apostle Paul was fully aware that inherent meanings of words could be distorted and replaced with meanings "that belonged to the people." For this reason, the Apostle Paul encourages Timothy to:

> *Hold firmly to the true [meanings of] words that I taught you, as the example for you to follow, and remain in the faith and love that are ours in union with Christ Jesus. (II Timothy 1:13, Good News Translation)*

I can envision Paul specifically instructing Timothy that there existed words where the Divine meanings had been replaced with meanings "that belonged to the people," especially the word "gift." One cannot have "healthy" or "sound" teaching if one uses unhealthy words in which Divine meanings have been replaced with the people's meaning.

The Apostle Paul, an Old Testament scholar, must have known that the true meaning of a word could be corrupted. After all, Moses spoke of those who corrupt the words of the righteous: "And you shall take no bribe, for a bribe blinds the discerning and perverts the words of the righteous" (Exodus. 23:8).

When the true meaning of a word has been twisted, distorted, corrupted, and lost, the Laws of Logic also go with it.

For example, the Law of Non-Contradiction would not exist if innate concepts like same and different did not exist as concepts in one's data bank. Without such data, it would be impossible to distinguish a hand from a foot or the consonant *B* from *P*.

Suppose our minds lack the concepts of someone and something. In that case, we might believe that the young man who desires to marry your daughter might actually be a jaguar, or the village shaman could be a jaguar that could harm you if you deviate from the cultural way of doing things.[4] If these function concepts are innate, so is the Law of Contradiction.

∼

## THE LAW OF CONTRADICTION

The Law of Contradiction annihilates all notions of relativistic thinking.

When Adam and God conversed in the garden, they understood each other because they used words with the same meanings.

> *Out of the ground the LORD God formed every beast of the field and every bird of the air, and brought* them *to Adam to see what he would call them. And whatever Adam called each living creature, that* was *its name. (Genesis 2:19)*

Having a logical discussion with people without agreement on the meanings of words is impossible.

- The Law of Contradiction precludes and rules out a man from declaring himself a woman or a woman declaring herself to be a man.
- The Law of Contradiction rules out the merging of mutually exclusive concepts, including status positions like siblings and cousins, fathers and uncles, mothers and aunts, sons and nephews, and daughters and nieces.
- The Law of Contradiction implies the existence of concepts with inherent meanings that are "fixed" and constant.
- The Law of Contradiction implies the existence of innate knowledge.
- The Law of Contradiction implies that every child comes into the world equipped with a framework of conceptual constants that make thinking logical.

Embracedbytruth.com offers this thought: "By innate knowledge is meant the knowledge, concepts, forms, and Universals that are an essential and intrinsic part of the makeup of the mind, and by which man processes that which he studies and experiences. Without this rational framework, knowledge would be impossible, for data could not be incorporated into the mind nor processed by the mind. Man is born with this framework—part of the *Imago Dei*—hence, the two words "innate knowledge."[5]

According to apologist Edward J. Carnell, the Law of Contradiction must be innate if truth is possible. If we do not have an innate knowledge of rules for right thinking, right thinking cannot start, but right thinking can start. Therefore, the rules are innate.[6]

Without innate concepts like "same and different" and "someone and something," there could be no such law.

However, missiology has other starting points as it is taught today. Because secular universities trained them, missiologists tend to be empiricists who believe the mind is a *tabula rasa* upon which, after sense perceptions have been transmuted into information, this information is then constructed in the mind, which happens to be empty. In the words of Kraft: "By information, we [contextualizers] designate the raw materials from which messages and meanings are constructed."[7]

The problem is that these "raw materials" are derived from sensory data within a particular environment and do not produce "fixed" standards for separating truth from nonsense.

## INNATISM

> Without *a priori* knowledge of the *rationes* ["fixed" standards], sense perceptions cannot report anything meaningful ... with the *rationes* ["fixed" standards], we are able to separate the true from the false, the bad from the good, the ugly from the beautiful (Edward J. Carnell 1952).[8]

I concur with the conclusion of Christian theologian Edward John Carnell (1919 - 1967). If the standard of sound and healthy words that have inherent meaning is lost, so are the Rules of Logic. Psychologically and emotionally, despite the evidence, men are now no different from women, and women are no different from men.

I just learned that the "deposit" I make to my checking account is also an "unsecured loan," which can be taken from me if the bank defaults and the government needs what I thought was "my money."

In our present age, it has become fashionable and scientific to reject the Law of Non-Contradiction and accept the people's meaning of a word, not only in our postmodern culture but also in missiology. In regards to this important passage (II Timothy 1:13), Greek scholar and expositor R. C. H. Lenski wrote:

> Here we have Paul's verdict on modernism [and postmodernism] with its claim that all these words are "outworn categories of thought, old thought patterns" that we have long ago outgrown ... we must [now]substitute categories and patterns of thought that the wisdom of our day produces, that are derived from our science, democracy, sociology, philosophy; although just what these new patterns are to be is as yet in the process of determination.[9]

## THE TRICKSTER'S STRATEGY

The best way to alter a society's way of thinking is to change the meaning of a word and ignore the Law of Non-Contradiction, which says, in its simplest form, *A* cannot be *B*.

When the first Chácobo accepted Christ as Savior and *Owner* (Lord), the shaman whispered in his ear, "If you don't reject Christ as your *Owner*, I will turn into a jaguar and kill you some night."

This new believer was convinced *A* could also be *B*, that the village shaman could be a jaguar in human disguise. However, the threat didn't work. When he expressed his concern to me, I didn't respond by trying to explain the Rule of Non-Contradiction. Instead, I encouraged him by showing him the Scriptures in his language: "The one who is in you is greater than the one who is in the world" (I John 4:4b, NIV).

The words of Scripture encouraged him. Whatever these "new patterns of thought" are, they all have one thing in common: They seek to set man and society free from "fixed" and constant standards for living.

These new patterns are primarily about how man and society

can relate differently to God, family, kin, non-kin, and nature. They involve stripping away the inherent meanings of important relational concepts like husband, wife, father, mother, son, daughter, marriage, family, and gift, and replacing them with meanings derived from sense experiences "that belong to the people."

Any move away from a Positive Universal to a negative particular will always have unintended consequences, the primary one being the creation of what anthropologist Francis L. K. Hsu calls a "centripetal society." Hsu describes such a society as a "web of kinship [in which] the individual has no freedom; he is hedged in on all sides."[10]

> People living in this type of kinship system will be satisfied with the status quo and are conservative. There is no urge within society to fission. On the contrary, there are deep-seated centripetal tendencies.[11]

Like a spider web, it will entangle and trap those who enter it. The trap consists of a set of ascribed functions and duties that one is morally bound to fulfill lest the mechanistic operating system ceases to function. For moral reasons, their allegiance is to the group that provides them with security.

Unlike American society, centripetal societies tend to compel their offspring to remain at home, where they are needed to fulfill the functions ascribed to them. The Chácobo, I discovered, were such a society. When the young couple married, they immediately became trapped in a household-of-five with its reciprocal obligations, rights, and ascribed functions explicitly designed to "fit" the pressures of living in the Amazonian Rainforest.

We will examine this in more detail when we examine chapter 40, "The Right Time," and chapter 64, "Does a Divine Plan for Living Exist?" and how the rules distort the meanings of husband, wife, father, mother, son, daughter, marriage, and family.

# GILBERT R. PROST

Pacahuara Indians

## CONVICTIONS

- Change the environment, and the design of the web must be different.

## CHAPTER 23
# HEALTHY WORDS

II TIMOTHY 1:13: "HOLD FAST THE PATTERN OF SOUND WORDS WHICH YOU HAVE HEARD FROM ME, IN FAITH AND LOVE WHICH ARE IN CHRIST JESUS."

Paradigm shift

The Apostle Paul was aware that he lived in an age when the meanings people attached to words mattered. Based on self-interest, epistemology, and philosophy, people could replace an inherent meaning with a meaning that, according to Karl Marx, was derived from social existence. Such meanings "belonged to the people." Such meanings were selected to satisfy existential needs but, as a result, they multiplied sinning.

There are also meanings that "do not belong to the people." They belong to God. According to Peter Carruthers, figuratively, these meanings are "written" in a Universal-Lexicon structured in the unconscious mind and brought to consciousness by being "triggered" rather than "learned."[1]

They, too, inform one how to live. Such positive lifeways are constructed using what the Apostle Paul called ὑγιαίνουσιν λόγοις (healthy words).

> II Timothy 3:16a (ESV): "All Scripture is breathed out by God..."
> II Timothy 1:13: "Hold fast the pattern of sound words which you have heard from me, in faith and love which are in Christ Jesus."
> I Timothy 6:3-5: "If anyone teaches otherwise and does not consent to wholesome words, even *the words of our Lord Jesus Christ, and to the doctrine which accords with godliness, he is proud, knowing nothing, but is obsessed with disputes and arguments over words, from which come envy, strife, reviling, evil suspicions, useless wranglings of men of corrupt minds and destitute of the truth who suppose that godliness is a means of gain. From such, withdraw yourself.*"

We define a healthy word as having a form common to all to which is attached an inherent or Divine meaning.

An unhealthy word likewise has a form common to all, but its inherent or Divine meaning has been replaced with a meaning derived from social existence.

A list of such Universal forms that have had their inherent meanings replaced with meanings derived from social existence include gift, family, father, mother, brother, sister, husband, wife, singing, and dancing. For example:

- The tribes of the Great Plains dance to make it rain.
- The Jívaro of Peru sing to make the crops grow.

  "I am a woman of Nunguí.
  Therefore, I sing so that the manioc will grow well.
  For when I do not sing there is not much production.
  I am a woman of Nunguí.
  Therefore, I harvest faster than others."[2]

- In the USA, a male can be a wife, and a female can be a husband. "Transportation Secretary Pete Buttigieg announced Saturday that he and his husband, Chasten, have officially become parents of two children."[3]
- Among the Trobiand Islanders, no child has a biological father. Christian missionaries are seen as liars. "They [the missionaries] talk that seminal fluid makes a child. Lie! The spirits indeed bring [children] at night time."[4]
- At an early age, children of a Trobriand household are instructed to address the man living in the household, their biological father, as "husband of my mother."
- People living in the province of Uttar Pradesh, India (see chapter 44), must select a bride or groom living in one of the 400 villages outside of their village. They are compelled to do this because the people of a village consider themselves brothers and sisters. This means

everyone attending one's school is either a brother or sister. It also means one will be put to death by the elders of the village if one marries a classified sister or brother.
- Most people of the world believe a gift must be repaid. In doing so, they cancel out the inherent meaning of the word "gift."

TWENTY-FIVE YEARS HAD PASSED, and the time for our departure had come. We had finished the task and were moving on. As we were packing our stuff, something unusual happened. An elder of the village came over, sat down, and began talking. And, he kept talking.

He recounted when Marian and I arrived. He remembered the day they all came down with the flu, which they called the *nati* (the killer). Two Chácobo died. He recalled the day his wife was sick and recovered because Marian gave her medicine. He shared the day when they were hungry, and we supplied them with food. He said, "You did this for the village, and this for my family, and this for my boys."

I finally noticed that he was using the benefactive "for us," "for my wife," "for the village," and "for …"

A day later, it dawned on me that he had come to say thank you in the only way he knew how. Having no word for thank you, he used the benefactive. What compelled this Chácobo elder to come over and express his gratitude for what we had done for them during our twenty-five years living with them?

His conscience told him to do so. Though they had deleted the concept of thanksgiving from their lexicon, they could not delete the form from a Universal-Lexicon structured in their unconscious minds.

When released, the idea of gratefulness was "triggered" and brought to consciousness that we would no longer be around to help them.

# CREATED IN THE IMAGE OF GOD

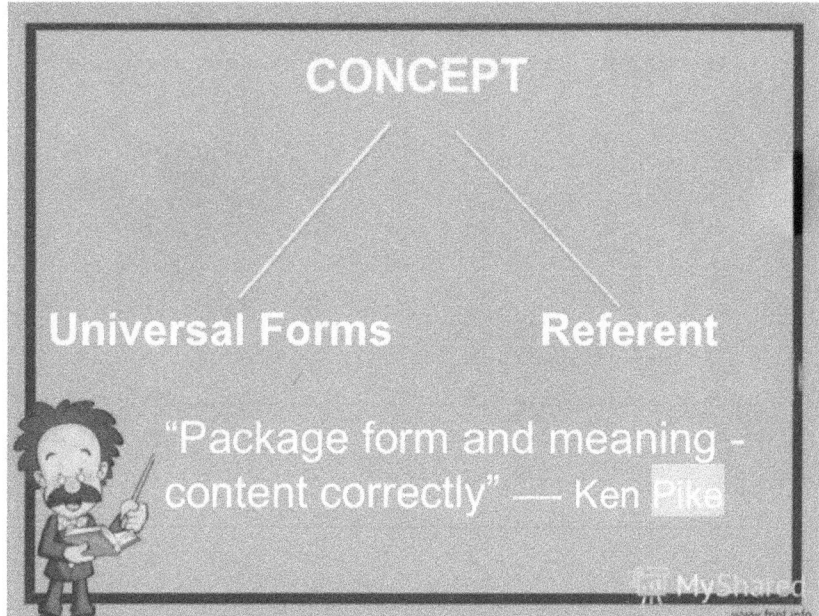

Knowledge = form and content

## CONVICTIONS

- For linguist Kenneth Pike, "form and meaning tied together" reside in the mind as "Positive Universals."[5] Forms common to all have inherent meanings attached to them. When they are replaced with meanings derived from what Karl Marx called social existence, we end up with "negative universals."
- Missiologist-anthropologist Charles Kraft declared: "[All] meanings 'belong to the people.' They are not inherent in the forms."[6] In effect, he was promoting the use of unhealthy words.
- Since Timothy, a disciple, would be confronting a world in which many meanings attached to forms "belonged to the people," the lexicons of the Gentiles would be filled with "unhealthy words," skewing the truth of their

message. Fully aware that such words existed, the Apostle Paul encouraged Timothy to use "healthy words."[7]

# CHAPTER 24
# THE NUCLEAR FAMILY
## GOD'S NATURAL FAMILY VS HUMANKIND'S ARTIFICIAL FAMILY

What Francis L. K. Hsu did, most likely unknown to himself, is reveal how a society estranged from God can restructure the nuclear family by replacing a Positive Universal with a negative cultural particular. A restatement of his hypothesis would say that the attributes of the covenantal dyad of *husband-wife* will lose their importance whenever they are replaced by one of the biological dyads that make up the nuclear family.

Whenever a society rejects and replaces the covenantal *husband-wife* dyad with a biological dyad, it must increase its family size by merging mutually exclusive status positions. The new family type will take God's place as the provider.

The nuclear family concept presents social scientists with a challenging existential question. Does a family form exist that is "fixed," absolute, and that can serve as the foundation upon which to build a creative, positive society regardless of its socioeconomic environment?

Professor of Law Herman Dooyeweerd says yes. He states there exists an "Inner Structural Law of the Family" in which "membership is absolutely restricted to the parents and their offspring in the first degree."[1]

Agreeing with Dooyeweerd is theologian Henry R. Van Til (1906 - 1961). Van Til wrote: "The [nuclear] family is the simplest and smallest unit of society and the real foundation of culture. If this foundation remains pure, man's culture has promise, but if it becomes polluted, all the rest will turn to dust and ashes."[2]

According to French anthropologist Claude Lévi-Strauss (1908 - 2009): "There is no more dangerous idea ... that the biological family constitutes the starting point from which every society elaborates its system of kinship."[3]

Many anthropologists, linguists, and missionaries reject the idea that a "fixed" and absolute family form exists with the *husband-wife* dyad as its dominant dyad. They declare that no form exists with an inherent meaning common to all, that is, a meaning that belongs to God.

While many societies have replaced the *husband-wife* dyad with another dyad, thus creating a new type of family structure, one society has replaced the concept of family with the idea of *Kage* (couple).

In my mind, they have deleted the concept of father and mother and brother and sister from their lexicon. That society is the Pirahã people living in the Amazonian jungles of Brazil.

Anthropologist Marco Antonio Gonçalves and several other anthropologists (see citation) describe the *Kage* in the following terms:

> The couple is the most perceptible unit; using this unit, the fragmentation of social life gains cohesion and a systematic form.
>
> *Kage* is the term used for a relationship between two people of the opposite sex, not necessarily implying sexual relations and/or children.
>
> The couple's autonomy is evident in fishing and gathering expe-

ditions; the couple remains alone for days or weeks, suggesting that this is sufficient to constitute a social life.

On the one hand, the couple produces fragmentation, stimulating an autonomous, non-gregarious lifestyle marked by a provisional mode of living (constant relocation, fragile shelters, and few goods).

On the other hand, the couple appears as a fundamental unit, operating as a regulator of sexual relations, weaving, however tortuously, the social fabric.

Coupling begins when a man and a woman spend an intimate night in the jungle. The choice of staying together or not is then made. This occurs whether the patron is single or not. No relationship is required or necessarily expected to be lifelong. After spending a night with another woman, a taken man either stays with the new woman or the original.

The extent of punishment a wife might give her companion (considering he has returned) is confinement in their hut together, but the issue is otherwise not worried about for long. Grudges aren't common on the matter.[4]

Instead of a community of mothers and fathers, brothers and sisters, and aunts and uncles who take responsibility for the care of their family members, it is the responsibility of the community to take care of its members.

However, some theologians see it differently. No ideal family form exists for cultural relativists like Mayers, Kraft, and Everett. How the family is structured internally is a function of what the Apostle Paul calls the "elementary forces of the world."

However, whatever shape the divergent form of the family takes, the Apostle Paul makes it clear, "It does not accord with Christ" (Colossians 2:8).

As explained earlier, the nuclear family becomes polluted whenever man and society replace the covenantal dyad of *husband-wife* with a biological dyad and then increases the size of the family by merging the status positions of father, mother, son, daughter, brother, and sister with collateral relatives.

Agreeing with Henry R. Van Til is Dooyeweerd, who describes the nuclear family this way:

> The narrowest circle of blood relationship is formed by the ascendants and descendants of the first degree, who were once united in one conjugal family, which was dissolved when the children became of age and left the paternal home.[5]

In time, I discovered that the institution we call the nuclear family was anathema to the Chácobo. They suppressed the natural family lest it destroy their defensive system against anxiety.

Their village design for living manifested their rejection of the natural family. The function of the men's communal house was to separate husbands from their wives and mothers-in-law.

From a functionalist's perspective, i.e., Charles H. Kraft, the family's form should "fit" the environment; in this case, the ecology of the Amazonian Rainforest. For Kraft, the validity of a cultural form is determined by how well it satisfies a need.

Since the Chácobo family concept "fit" the environment and the form adequately met their need for manioc beer, Kraft classified their concept of family as valid regardless of what the Word of God declares.

Evangelical anthropologists Stephen A. Grunion and Marvin K. Mayers point out that it is a "need satisfaction [which] forms the foundation step for interpersonal relationships."[6]

People tend to respond to their needs by creating what psychoanalyst Géza Róheim calls "defensive systems against anxiety." Cultural forms that satisfy needs are "the stuff that culture is made of."[7]

But should such need-based relationships serve as the foundation for a healthy society? Need satisfaction led the Chácobo to create cultural forms and relationships that had "no place in the Divine Plan."

Besides solving the problem of who was going to make the manioc beer, who would provide them with their daily bread, also known as fish and wildlife? At some point in their history, they came up with an awesome, unheard-of idea. They would create a new status position that would replace that of son-in-law and in-law. They called the status position *raisi*.

Instead of using the descriptive phrase *ahuiní bënë* (husband of daughter), they used the term *raisi*. Since they could neither read nor write, the contract was verbal. Not only were sons-in-law called *raisi*, but so were the in-laws.

To gain a daily food supplier, they needed only to persuade a potential son-in-law that he could acquire conjugal rights to one of their daughters if he promised to be their daily meat provider. His only other option was to remain a bachelor or marry a non-Chácobo for whom such marriage rules were non-existent.

The deal also meant he would become the fifth member of their household. While it sounded like a good deal, it was anything but. As theologian Reinhold Niebuhr (1892 - 1971) points out, "Anxiety is the precondition of sin."[8]

This means the Chácobo sinned when they created the status position of *raisi*, made the mother-daughter dyad the dominant dyad of the nuclear family, merged the status positions of cousins and siblings, and separated husbands from their wives by compelling them to live in separate quarters. The more one sins, the less freedom he or she has to serve others.

Unknown to me at the time was the extent to which Chácobo behavior was influenced and shaped by the elementary forces of the Amazonian Rainforest and the cultural form *raisi*. I was unaware, as expressed by F. W. Dillistone:

A society gradually takes shape within a particular physical environment. Its forms are influenced by the character of the environment—whether it is fertile or hard country, whether the climate is equable or extreme, whether the mineral and waterpower is abundant or scanty.[9]

However, as society's design for living takes the shape of its physical environment, the more it sins, the more it loses its freedom. Ontologically, humankind lives in two spheres: the sphere of necessity and the sphere of freedom.

Humans tend to be anxious as transcendent beings juxtaposed between freedom and necessity. "It is the inevitable concomitant of the paradox of freedom and finiteness in which man is involved."[10]

This positioning means only man can contemplate his future existence and sense that his long-term security may be threatened. Only man can sin by stepping outside the boundaries set for his life by creating a defensive system against anxiety.

Chácobo of Bolivia circa 1980s

## CONVICTIONS

- The Divine Plan positioned the *husband-wife* dyad as the dominant dyad of the nuclear family, a plan that Chácobo ancestors rejected.

- When the Chácobo replaced the nuclear family with the family-of-five and the covenantal dyad of *husband-wife* with the mother-daughter dyad, they diverged from the absolute, also known as *etic* data, and increased the amount of chaos and cultural diversity we see in the world.
- Structured in the unconscious mind is a Universal form called marriage. As part of the Divine Plan, it consists of the union of male and female. In the words of Jesus, the Designer of the Plan: "So then, they are no longer two but one flesh. Therefore what God has joined together, let no man separate" (Matthew 19:6).

## CHAPTER 25
# CENTRIPETAL SOCIETIES
### NATURAL ROLES ARE REPLACED WITH ASCRIBED DUTIES AND OBLIGATIONS

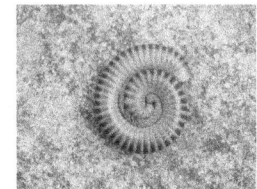

### PUZZLE PIECES

Probably unknown to the missionary evangelist and church planter, centripetal societies will naturally have social rules for living that will constrain evangelism, church planting, and economic development.

In pre-Mao China, according to Francis L. K. Hsu: "The web of relations foredoomed the sustained development of any scientific spirit and inquiry, despite an early history of science and history."[1]

When one goes back to the first Chinese dynasty at the time of Abraham. when the rulers lived under The Mandate of Heaven and Chinese creativity was flourishing, one can't help but wonder if the cultural superstructure at that time was not grounded in the one-flesh principle of husband and wife and the nuclear family. What existed before Mao was a centripetal family grounded in ascribed duties, obligations, and rights, which suppressed individual freedom and the desire to move out and explore the world around them

Whenever personal existence is all about ascribed functions, obligations, duties, and rights within the web of relations, it will be tough for someone to give their primary allegiance to anyone outside the kinship web.

Fortunately, the first Chácobo who became a Christian lived outside the web. The man was an orphan and married another orphan. When he married, he was not obligated to make a contract with his in-laws over conjugal rights to their daughter in exchange for his service as a food provider. He was free to be the head of his family. Neither was his wife under the control of her mother. They were free to become "one flesh."

One way to create a web of relations is for someone in authority to promise family and kin that they would be better off if they redefined what it means to be a "family." Natural roles would be replaced with ascribed functions/duties and obligations.

It was necessary to push the nuclear family into the background and deprive it of its fundamental role in society. The procedure was simple: Begin to distort and corrupt the words of the righteous whose meanings represent a "fixed" Universal idea or meaning.

One would take words like husband, wife, father, mother, son, daughter, brother, and sister and replace their Divine meanings with meanings derived from social context. Instead of rejecting these family concepts, they retained the form and changed their meanings, creating what the Apostle Paul called "unhealthy words."

In doing so, they sanctified what they created as moral and good. Note that the kind of relationship web a society produces is contingent on the kind of economic, ecological, technological, and security pressures it allows to shape the size and function of its security web.

The concept-innatist fully recognizes that one's contextual environment can highly influence how one thinks, especially when one rejects God as their Provider.

There is always a downside whenever a society chooses to go its own way. Every kind of relationship web humans create will suppress individual freedom and creativity. It will put power into the hands of certain members of society and compel individuals to remain in the web, claiming it will provide for everyone's needs.

## PUZZLE SOLVED

Zoologist Desmond Morris was puzzled by why tribal societies like the Chácobo and Pacahuara were centripetal societies instead of centrifugal societies. He wrote: "The simple tribal groups living today are not primitive; they are stultified. Something has happened to hold them back, working against the species' natural tendencies to investigate the world around it."[2]

Another scholar who recognized that something indeed had gone wrong with tribal societies is psychoanalyst Franz Alexander (1891 - 1964). Like Morris, he expressed similar sentiments when he wrote:

> Primitive civilizations are characterized by their static nature and highly rigid organization. They are, in comparison to our (Western) world, well nigh petrified. The static nature of these cultures manifests itself in a stable structure that precisely defines the individual's social place, function, and attitudes with a rigidity unknown in the dynamic societies of the Greek-Roman type or the European and American civilizations.[3]

These, indeed, are interesting observations made by a zoologist and psychoanalyst. In this age of cultural relativity, very few anthropologists, and even missiologists, would dare make statements such as these. Yet, contextualizers (like Kraft) encourage missionaries to "accept the fact that ours is but one of many essentially equal cultures."[4]

Accept this as a fact? If so, here is another point. In centripetal societies, the kinds of social webs they create to relieve their anxieties over existence work against natural tendencies to investigate the world. That internal rigidity will naturally constrain evangelism and church planting.

What went wrong with the Chácobo was their rejection of concepts with "fixed" meanings, which constituted a "fixed" framework for building a positive society. This began when healthy words with inherent meanings were replaced with new meanings "that belonged to the people."

They were a leaderless society. That greatly troubled me. The verdict of some of my colleagues was that both societies would eventually be absorbed into the fabric of the dominant Bolivian culture and cease to exist as a viable society.

Marian and I were more hopeful. We were beginning to plan and implement a strategy to turn things around. For the empiricists who reject concept-innatism, it was a strategy that could only bring, according to Marvin Harris, "disorder arising primarily from the economic processes which allocate labor and material products of labor to individuals and groups."[5] In other words, he believed it would bring chaos and disorder to a well-functioning mechanistic social order.

Marian teaching and strategizing

## CONVICTIONS

- Slowly, these unhealthy words produced a centripetal society that constrained human freedom and deleted all superordinate-subordinate status positions from the Chácobo social operating system.

# CHAPTER 26
# THE RULE OF EXOGAMY - PART 1
## EXOGAMY AND THE FIRST SIN

The following year, everything changed. Providentially, I understood, to some degree, why the Chácobo was a dying, leaderless culture. I studied every theology book available, looking for answers as to why they had no leaders.

In desperation, I went to our small SIL library, where there were a fair number of anthropology books that our first Branch director, Harold Key, in his wisdom, brought with him from Mexico.

Who could provide me with answers to personal questions that screamed for an answer? After browsing through several books on social anthropology, I picked up a reasonably large volume, *Psychological Anthropology,* edited by Francis L. K. Hsu. The title suggested some anthropologists had an idea of how the mind worked. I signed for the book, took it home, and began reading, although my interest in psychology was zero.

Hsu's article, "Kinship and Ways of Life," caught my attention. It was about the source of cultural diversity and a society's particular "lifeway."

In explaining the existence of different "ways of life," Hsu hypothesized that among the eight familial dyads in the nuclear family, *husband-wife*, father-son, father-daughter, mother-son, mother-daughter, brother-sister, brother-brother, and sister-sister, one dyad would be dominant, reducing the importance of every other dyad. He wrote:

> When one dyad is elevated over other dyads in a given kinship system, the attributes of the dominant dyad tend to modify, eliminate, or at least reduce the importance of the attributes of other structural dyads. The hypothesis further states that the total effect of the dominance of the attributes of one structural dyad leads to a particular kind of kinship content, which in turn strongly conditions the pattern of thought and behavior of the individuals reared in the kinship system in the society at large.[1]

Emanating from each dominant dyad was a different cultural operating system, each having a different set of values, allegiance patterns, customs, myths, anxieties, and family structure. He explained why cultural diversity existed in the world. What remains a mystery is the fact that the Rule of Exogamy protects each family type.

Whatever dyad the social group selects to be the dominant dyad of the nuclear family will be protected by the Rule of Exogamy, which some call "the first rule."

Most individuals would be surprised to know that anthropologists have asked: What was "the first rule" and the first sin? According to the materialist, "the first rule" was: One shall not marry a member of one's family; one must "marry out."

The Universal Rule to "marry out" was called the "Rule of Exogamy." For the materialist, the first sin occurred when someone had sexual relations with a sister or brother, mother or father, or son or daughter. Real or classificatory, this rule is not learned; it is innate.

For the non-theist, the first sin did not occur in the Garden of Eden when Adam and Eve ate the forbidden fruit; the first sin occurred when the first human had sexual relations with a member of their family. The sin of incest is so vile that in some societies, the punishment is death.

The Universal Rule of Exogamy is important for the materialist and the theist because the prohibition, in the words of anthropologist Claude Lévi-Strauss, "provides the only means for maintaining the group as a group."[2]

For the theist, only one "group" or family-type exists, and the Rule of Exogamy should protect it; it is called the "nuclear family."

In contrast, the materialist believes whatever "family" social existence produces must be valid because the Rule of Exogamy protects it.

For example, note the family-type of social existence produced on the Great Plains. The Indians call the "band" a family and protect it by the Rule of Exogamy. From a theistic perspective, it also represents a divergence from the Universal.

In addition, whenever the Divine meaning of family is replaced with a meaning produced by social existence "that belongs to the people," it must violate the Rules of Logic.

For tribes living on the Great Plains, a father's brother can be a father, a mother's sister can be a mother, cousins can be brothers and sisters, and nephews and nieces can be sons and daughters.

From a concept-innatist's perspective, the type of family structure illustrated at the end of this chapter that merges the above status positions cannot be valid.

First, it violates the Rules of Logic. Siblings ≠ Cousins; Father's Brother ≠ ego's Father; Mother's Sister ≠ ego's Mother.

Second, the Divine meaning attached to the "family" form has been replaced and shaped by a force labeled "social existence" by Karl Marx.

Agreeing with Marx is evangelical missiologist-anthropologist Charles H. Kraft, who declares that meanings "belong to the people."[3]

The dominant Cheyenne family-type is brother-brother, not *husband-wife*. The result: they replaced a Positive Universal with a negative cultural particular created by social existence on the Great Plains.

For the cultural materialist, the biblical idea that there should be one and only one foundational unit of society, the nuclear family, is perilous. Cultural materialists believe that the type of family a society has must "fit" the environment. In the words of missiologist-anthropologist Charles H. Kraft, "Every missionary should learn to employ more important criteria such as 'fit' and adequacy."[4]

Since the Cheyenne family structure (illustrated at the end of this chapter) was adequate for hunting buffalo, it must be valid according to the cultural materialist. No missionary should declare it invalid because they would be, according to missiologist-anthropologist Sherwood G. Lingenfelter, "distorting the diversity of God's creation ... forcing upon people our standards."[5]

Lingenfelter also agreed with Karl Marx when Marx declared, "It is not the consciousness of men that determines their existence but their social existence that determines their consciousness."[6]

Chácobo men and children

## CONVICTIONS

- Sinful society uses the Rule of Exogamy to protect family types that are in fundamental opposition to the Divine Plan.

~

## DEVIANT FORMS

Whenever a society has a family type that "fits" the environment, it will also have a family type that rejects the Rules of Logic that declares: $A \neq B$. Logic is simply God's means for keeping man from sinning and "going his own way" (Acts 14:16, Prost Paraphrase).

Whenever a society uses its freedom to deviate from the Divine Plan, as stated in Genesis 2:23-24:

> *"This is now bone of my bones*
> *And flesh of my flesh;*
> *She shall be called Woman,*
> *Because she was taken out of Man."*
> *Therefore a man shall leave his father and mother and be*
> *joined to his wife, and they shall become one flesh.*

It creates a new family structure, and using the Rule of Exogamy, protects the deviant form, a misuse of the rule.

Whenever one violates the internal structure of the nuclear family, a shift occurs from order to disorder, and the Marxist belief that social existence rules and precedes essence.

Anthropologist Lévi-Strauss believes the Rule of Exogamy can be compared to a bridge that provides "the fundamental [first] step by which ... the transition from nature to culture is accomplished."[7]

Without the rule, the cultural concept of family could not exist.

When that transition occurred, Lévi-Strauss confesses: "No empirical analysis can determine the point of transition between the natural and cultural facts."[8]

What if, as a Jew, he had not treated the Torah as allegory? He would have realized that such a transition from nature to culture never occurred. Pre-humans did not become humans for whom the first sin was incest.

God created man, Adam, to live above nature as a transcendent cultural being while existing in nature with a body subject to the elements of nature.

Adam, created in the image of God, committed the first transgression when he broke God's Divine Rule: "... but of the tree of the knowledge of good and evil, you shall not eat, for in the day that you eat of it you shall surely die" (Genesis 2:17).

Adam ate, and the Apostle Paul writes in Romans 5:12: "Therefore, just as through one man sin entered the world, and death through sin, thus death spread to all men because all sinned—"

The fundamental shift in social disorder arose with the birth of Seth's son, Enosh, Cain's nephew. With the birth of Enosh, a new era began. Not only was it the "time *men* began to call on the name of the LORD" (Genesis 4:26), but new status positions came into existence, like uncles, aunts, cousins, nephews, and nieces.

With the birth of Enosh, marrying outside the nuclear family became a possibility. The Rule of Exogamy depends on the existence of collateral relatives; that is, someone who is not a father, mother, brother, sister, son, or daughter.

With the birth of Enosh, the Rule of Exogamy came into existence to prevent social chaos. Cultural diversity exists because the rule was used to protect what should not be protected—the merging of mutually exclusive statuses like siblings and cousins, an irrational process needed to create new types of families.

For the materialist, the Rule of Exogamy serves a function; for the theist, it has a purpose. The question that demands an answer is: When did the Rule of Exogamy begin to be applied?

Materialists like Livi-Strauss have no answer; the theist does. It started with the birth of Enosh, the first collateral relative, Enosh being the first nephew and Cain the first uncle.

~

## PROCLAIMING PARADOXES IS A SIN

For the theist, the existential question is: Do family structures exist that should not be protected by the Rule of Exogamy because they merge mutually exclusive status positions like siblings and cousins and thus violate the Rules of Logic?

The Rules of Logic do not matter to the materialist and functionalist; they do to the theist.

For example, although a Kiowa-Apache has only one biological father and mother, he can say, "I respect all my fathers and mothers." Biologically, this sentence is irrational and absurd and violates the Law of Identity, which says *A* (aunts and uncles) cannot be *B* (mothers and fathers).

For the theist, biology matters. For the functionalist, biology does not matter. Therefore, the classification of aunts and uncles as parents is valid if it satisfies a need.

For Christian philosopher Gordon Clark, logic matters: "Using straight-line logic is a virtue; curbing logic and proclaiming paradoxes is a sin."[9]

Classifying cousins as siblings and aunts and uncles as parents not only creates paradoxes, but the process also violates the Rules of Logic. Biologically and linguistically, as Herman Dooyeweerd points out, "Membership [in the family] is absolutely restricted to the parents and their offspring in the first degree."[10]

But for the materialist who rejects logic, whatever family type social existence creates by merging mutually exclusive status positions must be good for society because it satisfies an existential need.

## THE IMPORTANCE OF THE RULE OF EXOGAMY

How important is an unlearned Universal social rule that requires an individual to marry outside his intimate group called family? In the field of missiology, it is crucial. No rule in life better defines who we are as individuals and as a society.

From a top-down, inside-out epistemology, the purpose of this unlearned Universal Rule of Exogamy is to protect the nuclear family and the integrity of its internal structure. However, since man is a transcendent being positioned to exist above nature in freedom, he can misuse his liberty.

He can use his freedom to rearrange the internal structure of the nuclear family and create new types of families by defying the Laws of Logic and merging mutually exclusive statuses. However, for theologian Reinhold Niebuhr: "No philosophy or religion can change the structure of human existence. That structure involves individuality as the only basis of meaning."[11]

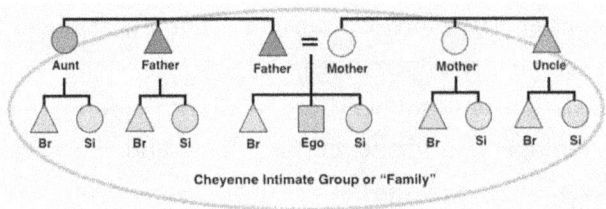
Cheyenne Intimate Group or "Family"

## MORE CONVICTIONS

- The Universal Rule of Exogamy protects the nuclear family and the integrity of its internal structure.
- The Rule of Exogamy was woven into the very fabric of our being when God created Adam in His image. As a

Divine Principle, it is brought to consciousness by being "triggered" in a socio-linguist situation, informing ego to marry outside the family lest one commit incest.
- Whenever a society uses its freedom to deviate from the Divine norm, as stated in Genesis 2:23-24, and creates a new family-type structure, it will use the Rule of Exogamy to protect the deviant form. It represents a demonic misuse of the rule.
- Whenever the structural law of the family is violated, a shift occurs from order to disorder and the functionalist's belief that "existence precedes essence,"[12] as described by Jean-Paul Satre. The rule became innate after it was learned that incest was destructive to society. Its innateness, like language, is a feature of the essence, or what it means to be a human being, living under what Professor of Law Herman Dooyeweerd called the "Inner Structural Law of the Family."

## CHAPTER 27
# THE MEANING OF GIFT
## A UNIVERSAL "FREE" CONCEPT VS A CONTEXT-DERIVED MEANING REQUIRING RECIPROCITY

The meaning of gift

Every society is involved in some form of gift-giving. Why do humans give gifts? Merriam-Webster defines a gift as "something voluntarily transferred by one person to another without compensation."

Is the meaning, cited in Merriam-Webster, "learned" or "acquired"? And why do most people groups reject the meaning of gift?

∼

## THE CHÁCOBO GIFT

The concept of "sound words" to which are attached Divine meanings that are not "learned" but "acquired" by a "triggering process" has been rejected by naturalists. What has replaced "sound words" are "unhealthy words" whose meanings have been shaped by context.

The spiritual war between context-derived meanings—meanings that are relative and that "belong to the people" and meanings that are "fixed," constant, and belong to God—surfaces when we ask, "What is the meaning of gift?"

The meaning the Chácobo attached to the concept of gift was in fundamental opposition to the meaning in my head, which is an item given to someone without the expectation of payment or anything in return. The Chácobo believed every gift needed to be returned. Social meaning shaped its existence.

∼

## GIFT-GIVING AMONG THE JAPANESE

When a missionary in Japan was about to give a gift of money to a needy street person, his wife reminded him that he should not do it.

"How in the world will he ever repay you?" she remonstrated her compassionate husband. She was thinking like a Japanese; he was thinking like an American Christian. The rules of culture prohibited the husband, a messenger of Good News, from being kind. The meaning attached to the form called a gift in Japanese culture demands a return.

No people on earth feel this compulsion to reciprocate more than the Japanese. From childhood, they are taught to believe two things about gift-giving. First, some gifts can never be repaid. This kind of gift they call *gimu*.

Second, there are gifts called *giri*. *Giri* gifts "have to be repaid with mathematical equivalence to the favor received, and there are time limits."[1] It was the tit-for-tat kind of giving the Chácobo women practiced whenever they made manioc flour.

According to anthropologist-author Ruth Benedict (1887 - 1948) three kinds of gift-giving exist in the minds of the Japanese: *gimu*-giving, *giri*-giving, and *on*-giving,[2] leading to some interesting behavioral patterns.

∽

## BANNING OF GIFT-GIVING

According to American historian Gail Lee Bernstein (1939 -), a Japanese hospital in the small town of Bessho banned gift-giving.

> Residents of Bessho had agreed not to give or expect to receive gifts when hospitalized. They had found that hospitalized patients risked relapse if they tried to return all the presents they had received.[3]

Gift-giving was banned because of the adverse psychological and physical effects it had on the patients.

## A RELUCTANCE TO RECEIVE A GIFT

According to jurist Takeyoshi Kahuashima (1909 - 1992), the Japanese concept of a gift is "indebted by a limitless obligation to reciprocate."[4]

∽

## STRANGE WAYS TO EXPRESS THANKSGIVING

The Japanese have a problem with verbally responding to the receipt of a gift. This problem shows up in how they react to having to repay "with mathematical equivalence."

Anthropologist Ruth Benedict noted that the Japanese are extremely wary of getting entangled in *giri* and obligations where gifts must be repaid.

American historian Gail Lee Bernstein says even the offer of a cigarette from a person with whom a man has no previous ties makes him feel uncomfortable, and the polite way for him to express thanks is to say, "*Kino Doku*" (Oh, this poisonous feeling).[5]

Politeness requires an expression of discomfort when receiving a gift, not joy. While the Japanese have several ways of saying "Thank you" in situations where the gift must be repaid, politeness requires one to express his own mental discomfort when receiving the gift. How can the gift ever be repaid if one is a stranger?

*Sumimasen* is probably the most common word used.[6] When used, it expresses frustration, meaning something like, "It doesn't end here, but what can I do about it?"[7]

Haruko, the wife of a farmer living in the village of Biiyá, expressed the same frustration. Since "the receipt of a gift, however small, called for reciprocity, within four months, Haruko had exchanged five such gifts. After the last one, Hauroko became exasperated. 'There is no end to this.'"[8] The gift *(giri)* had become toxic.

According to Kahuashima, the Japanese concept of gift "indebted [one] by a limitless obligation to reciprocate."[9]

What does this have to do with missiology? For the Japanese, it means receiving God's gift to humanity would be equivalent to taking poison. It is the kind of gift that can't be repaid and should, therefore, be avoided at all costs. How could anyone ever repay God?

## GIFT-GIVING AMONG THE ARCTIC CIRCLE ESKIMO

For the Eskimos of the Arctic Circle, any expression of thankfulness for a gift received, like the Japanese, was viewed as slave-making.

On a walrus hunting trip in the barren, treeless Arctic, Norwegian explorer Peter Freuchen had placed before him a pile of meat by the hunter who had thrust his harpoon into the walrus. This final act made him the owner of the walrus. His task now was to cut up and distribute the meat to others in the party.

In the process of thanking the hunter for his gift, Freuchen relates how the village shaman "took it upon himself to put me straight. 'You must not thank for your meat; it is your right to get meat. In this country, no one wishes to be dependent upon others. Therefore, no one gives or gets gifts, and you become dependent on them. With gifts, you make slaves; just as with whips, you make dogs.'"[10]

But these very same Eskimos, who viewed gift-giving as a kind of poison that enslaves every recipient, nevertheless offered "small thank-you presents to Torngarsuk, the Master of the Universe, thanking him for his hospitality."[11]

One thing is clear: The Eskimos attach two meanings to the Universal gift form. One is "slave-making," and the other is "giving without any expectation of reciprocation."

We contend one meaning is "learned," and the other is "acquired," which raises an epistemological question: Does a gift concept exist in a Universal-Lexicon not shaped by social existence? Contextualizers, materialists, functionalists, and existentialists all say no. Whatever its meaning, it is "learned."

Amazingly, while they viewed any expression of thankfulness on earth as death-dealing, these same Arctic Circle Eskimos innately knew it was good to express thanksgiving to the Master of the Universe because it was life-giving. For the life-giving gifts from the Master of the Universe, verbal expressions of thanksgiving were expressed annually. Such gifts could never be repaid.

However, the life-giving meat from a fellow hunter was classified as a human right.

∼

## GIFT-GIVING AMONG THE NATIVES IN PAPUA NEW GUINEA

The tension between the context-derived meaning attached to the concept of a gift existing in the head of natives versus the Merriam-Webster meaning of a gift existing in the head of the missionary is revealed in the unexpected behavior of native leaders in one tribe in Papua New Guinea.

After professing faith, being baptized, attending church, and outwardly behaving like Christians for several years, the natives confronted the missionary, "We ought to have done enough by now to repay Jesus for his death."[12]

They returned to their pagan ways. What went wrong?

Missiologist Wayne Dye provided one answer, concluding that the blame probably lay with the missionary's message. He rhetorically asks:

> Had they (the natives) ever known real conviction of sin and forgiveness? Or had they only heard about the things that would have been sinful to the missionary if he had lived with them?[13]

Dye's statement implies the meaning the natives attached to the word "gift" existing in the natives' heads was the same as that existing in the missionary's head. The very fact that these natives wanted to become Christians and experience forgiveness from sin implies they indeed were convicted, but this forgiveness, they thought, was not free. There was no such thing as a "free" gift.

When we fill in the implied words "for our sins" to their statement so that it reads, "We ought to have done enough by now to repay Jesus for His death for our sins," it is clear they thought God's gift was attainable through going to church, being baptized, and tithing. The meaning they attached to the gift compelled them to believe it had to be repaid.

In contrast, we contend, unknown to the missionaries, the natives had replaced the inherent meaning attached to the Universal form called "gift" with a context-derived meaning of reciprocity. Because social existence shaped and constructed the meaning of the gift, they never understood what the Gospel was all about.

A contextualized theology for the Chácobo would mean the meaning they attached to the concept of "gift" would reduce the Good News to bad news.

Suppose the contextualizer is correct and all meanings come from sense perceptions. In that case, the Word of God is "a record of the sense perceptions of spirit-guided men," and no "sound words" exist, also known as "God-breathed" words with constant, inherent meanings.

∼

## THE FREE GIFT OF SALVATION AMONG THE CHÁCOBO

In our case, we waited ten years before the first Chácobo realized God's gift of salvation was free. Replacing the meaning of "belonging to the people" with its inherent meaning may take time. Only then will they begin to understand grace.

One Sunday in July 1965, almost two years after the assassination of President Kennedy, Caco Pistia, my language informant, stayed behind and expressed his desire to accept Jesus as his Savior and Lord.

Caco was raised as an orphan, and he married an orphan. As I later learned, this meant he had no need to become a *raisi* to obtain a wife. If he were a *raisi*, it meant having a mother-in-law from whom he had to take orders.

Caco was free from what anthropologist Francis L. K. Hsu called a "web of kinship" responsibilities and duties." The Chácobo replaced the nuclear family with a family that classified parallel cousins as brothers and sisters.

The following day, after his confession of faith and as we were waiting for our JAARS pilot to pick us up and bring us to our SIL Center for a break, the *Nucleo* village men danced into the village, fully adorned for the occasion. They had come to invite everyone to a religious feast dedicated to the *Bird Above*. We immediately knew Caco's faith would be tested. Would he or would he not partake in the communion service to the *Bird Above*?

We would have to wait three months before we could hear his story, and what a story it was. Before the dancing and eating began, as was their custom, they held a communion service to the *Bird Above*, the one who sees and knows everything. When the communion elements were presented to Caco, he said, "I can no longer partake in this communion service because I have a new *Ibo* (owner)."

Many in the group wanted to attack and beat him up. How dare he diverge from a practice central to their customs as Chácobo. Then, a few men from *Alto Ivon* stepped forward and defended him, saying, "Leave him alone. We're thinking of making Jesus our *Ibo* also."

Thus, the birth of the Chácobo church. It began with an orphan who had married someone whose parents had died. Marriage to an orphan meant freedom from a mother-in-law's control.

Without me informing him as to what he should do, he innately knew he was a different man. When he refused to partake in the communion service, the shaman, Taita Rabi, leaned over and whispered into his ear, "If you refuse to partake in this service, I will transform myself into a jaguar some night and devour you."

Caco looked into my eyes and asked, "What do you think, Papa?"

The question surprised me. Knowing they all believed that, under certain circumstances, *A* indeed could become *B*, that shamans could become jaguars, I turned to I John 4:4 and read: "You are of God, little children, and have overcome them, because He who is in you is greater than he who is in the world."

After ten years of waiting, God had broken the enemy's hold on the Chácobo.

Learning to read

## CONVICTIONS

- For the Eskimos of the Arctic Circle, there are two kinds of gifts: (a) gifts that "trigger" a response of gratefulness and thanksgiving, and (b) gifts that must be

reciprocated, and no expressions of thanksgiving are expected.
- According to missiologist-anthropologist Kraft, the Japanese are not attracted to Christianity because "they are too proud of their own country."[14] I beg to differ. I propose the Japanese are not attracted to Christianity because when they think of a gift, they think of the kind that demands a "limitless obligation to reciprocate." For the Japanese, the question is: How can one repay God for His gift?
- When the natives of Papua New Guinea returned to their pagan ways, they did so because their concept of gift prevented them from understanding that the "gift of God" could never be repaid. It is free.
- When a society replaces the inherent meaning attached to the form "gift" with its own meaning that "belongs to the people," the contextualization of "gift" distorts the Gospel and there is no Good News.
- Doing positive missiology means considering that the Universal form called gift has two different meanings. One meaning is derived from social existence and "belongs to the people." The other meaning exists in a Universal-Lexicon structured in the unconscious and belongs to God.
- Could it be that the only exchange possible would be that of expressing thanksgiving, implying the existence of another innate rule "written on the heart" that informs the ego that it is good to give thanks to those who have been kind, helpful, and eager to please without any thought of being repaid?
- If, as proposed by missiologist Charles Kraft, "It is people who attach meanings to the forms of culture they use,"[15] why would Merriam-Webster's definition be rejected? Their rejection raises the question: Do definitions exist

that "do not belong to the people," definitions inscribed in a Universal-Lexicon structured in the unconscious mind? Such definitions are brought to consciousness by being "triggered" in a linguistic-social situation and are therefore not learned but "acquired."

- What I find interesting is that most societies in the world reject the above definition of the word "gift." For example, when we gave gifts of food to the needy Chácobo, no one ever thanked us for the gift. In fact, absent from their lexicon is the word "thank."
- Goodenough's vision of an *etic* framework of conceptual constants analogous to a phonetic chart used by linguists will materialize once academia recognizes the dual mind-body nature of human existence.
- The constants needed to transform Bible translation, missiology, and anthropology from an art into a science are found in what Pike calls an *emic-etic* approach to knowledge. In other words, access to *etic* knowledge depends on gleaning the Universals (*etic* data) from semantic and cultural particulars (*emic* data).
- From a top-down, inside-out perspective, a bank of *etic* data exists in the mind that expresses itself phenomenally in words, structures, and cultural forms in daily life.
- Goodenough is correct when he says: "Considerations of meaning are not only irrelevant but, for scientific rigor, taboo."[16] They are "taboo" because meaning is not material data but spiritual and non-material. In the words of Anna Wierzbika, "Meaning has to do with the constants, not with the variables."[17]
- In Robert Lawless's words, "If we are bound by the perspectives of our own folk model [*emic*], we will learn nothing about why other people behave and think differently from us."[18]

# CHAPTER 28
# THE BIBLICAL UNDERSTANDING OF GIFT

## SHARING THE GOSPEL IN A DIFFERENT CULTURE

Unless one is familiar with the New Testament Greek, a distortion of a conceptual constant by the Apostles is likely. I present the following thought-provoking narrative for Bible translators and expatriates desiring to share the Gospel in a different culture.

The Apostle John penned the words:

> 'Come! Let the one who is thirsty come; and let the one who wishes take the free gift of the water of life.' (Revelation 22:17b, NIV)

He had the choice of two related Greek words: *dorea* and *doron*.[1]

John the Apostle chose the word *dorea* rather than *doron* for a specific reason. He wanted to be sure his readers did not read into the concept of "gift" any notion of reciprocity. To avoid this possibility, he chose a word that represented the Universal, not a word that represented the customary habits of the people.

*Dorea* specifically means a "free gift." In contrast, *doron* could mean some reciprocity.

As Revelation 11:10a states, "And those who dwell on the earth will rejoice over them, make merry, and send *doron* (gifts) to one another ..."

So, when Jesus said: "Therefore, if you are offering your *doron* (gift) at the altar [a Jewish custom] ..." (Matthew 5:23a, NIV), He was declaring the act was not to be performance-based because God would not be deceived. It was highly probable that the *doron* (kind of gift-giving) might lie outside the semantic strike zone of what it meant to give a gift.

Again, when Jesus addressed the woman at the well, He chose the word *dorea*, not *doron*. "If you knew the *dorea* (free gift) of God and who it is that asks you for a drink, you would have asked him and he would have given you living water" (John 4:10, NIV).

The Apostle Peter was fully aware of a possible distortion of the concept of gift when he addressed Simon the Sorcerer who thought he could acquire the same healing power as the Apostles. The Apostle Peter said, "May your money perish with you, because you thought you could buy the *dorea* (free gift) of God with money" (Acts 8:20, NIV)!

Like the Apostle Peter, the Apostle Paul was aware of a possible communication problem regarding the concept of gift. Like Peter, he avoided *doron* and chose the Greek word *charisma* or *dorea*, neither of which could imply some kind of reciprocity.

Like many other concepts, *doron* was far easier to distort. If the Apostle Paul had used the word *doron*, there existed a high probability that the readers might have thought they needed to repay God for His wonderful gift of salvation. Instead, He chose *charisma* or *dorea*, as illustrated in the following verses.

> *But the* charisma *(free gift) is not like the trespass. For if many died through one man's trespass, much more have the grace of God and the dorea (free gift) by the grace of that one man Jesus Christ abounded for many.*
>
> *And the* Dorea *(free gift) is not like the result of that one man's sin. For the judgment following one trespass brought condemnation, but the* charisma *(free gift) following many trespasses brought justification.*
>
> *For if, because of one man's trespass, death reigned through that one man, much more will those who receive the abundance of grace and the* dorea *(free gift of righteousness) reign in life through the one man Jesus Christ. (Romans 5:15-17, ESV)*

Here are three more examples:

> *For the wages of sin is death, but the* charisma *(free gift) of God is eternal life in Christ Jesus our Lord. (Romans 6:23, ESV)*
>
> *I thank God for his* Dorea *(gift) that words cannot*

> *describe. (II Corinthians 9:15, GOD'S WORD Translation)*

> *It is impossible for those who have once been enlightened, who have tasted the heavenly gift [implied, which is free,* dorea*], who have shared in the Holy Spirit, who have tasted the goodness of the word of God and the powers of the coming age and who have fallen away, to be brought back to repentance. To their loss they are crucifying the Son of God all over again and subjecting him to public disgrace. (Hebrews 6:4-6, NIV)*

## UNDERSTANDING THE GOSPEL IS DEPENDENT ON "SOUND WORDS"

If the meanings a society gives to words are solely determined by how well the meaning satisfies a basic need, then there can be no innate Universal-Lexicon of conceptual constants having inherent Divine meanings. Only relative culture-specific meanings would exist because no two contexts are the same. If Divine Truth exists, it is unknowable.

If true, then there is no Gospel because the meaning of the gift is determined solely by humankind, whose thoughts and values have been shaped by context, i.e., one's particular environment. No longer does God rule in the affairs of men because they have chosen "to go their own way" (Acts 14:16).

Physical and psychological necessity determine what truly is. But if the meaning of the word "gift" constructed in the hearers' minds signifies the gift must be returned, what kind of Gospel will one preach?

## DISCOVERING A MISREPRESENTATION OF THE CONCEPT OF GIFT

A retired lawyer friend of mine tested Pike's hypothesis that Positive Universals can be distorted into negative particulars with some international students attending the University of Florida.

At a picnic attended by students from all over the world, the majority of whom came from the People's Republic of China, he suggested to a small group of Chinese students that their culture had probably distorted the meaning of the word "gift."

That caught their attention. "How could that be possible?"

He then proceeded to use the following example: He pointed to a student and said, "I know someone stole your camera, and I would like to give you mine. Here, take my camera. It is now your camera. It is a gift from me to you. You need it. I don't. I have another one. Now you can send pictures back to your family in China."

To his amazement, the student replied, "But then I would owe you."

He explained that she owed him nothing. The kind of gift he was talking about was one that did not have to be repaid. That caught their attention.

From there, it was easy to explain that this was the kind of gift God offered them in the form of His Son, who offered up His body to be nailed on the cross for their sins. Whereas a free gift brings joy and gratitude and establishes positive relationships, a reciprocating gift destroys brotherly love and grace while generating anxiety over how the gift is to be replaced.

The meaning these Chinese students had given to the word "gift" produced an unhealthy word in their minds, a misrepresentation of the Universal true meaning. It also produced anxiety over how the gift would be repaid. Unknown to them, the true and exact meaning of the word "gift" had been distorted and replaced with a falsehood, a meaning that implied reciprocity.

~

## THERE ARE NO UNHEALTHY WORDS FOR THE CONTEXTUALIZER

If the word's meaning satisfies a need, it is classified as a "sound word" when, in fact, this shift from its Divine meaning to a meaning "that belongs to the people" is the first stepping stone from truth to falsehood and grounded in empiricism. Linguist Norm Chomsky quoted American philosopher Jonathan Lear:

> Whatever script a society writes, word meanings, sentences, and behaviors "must be based on experience and sensory evidence of all types to which we have over time been exposed ... positing mental objects named by words gets in the way of an explanation."[2]

In contrast, the existence of a culture-free perspective starts with what I call innate principles (unlearned principles that are constant). For the theist, part of the analytical process must include an awareness that sinful man and society have the capacity to create "unsound words" that misrepresent positive internal unlearned principles of the soul.

This occurs when humans and society reject innate laws and Universal concepts "written on the heart" and begin replacing them with rules, principles, and cultural forms that "belong to the people."

It is therefore assumed that when a society chooses "to go its own way," it permits the meanings of words to be shaped by "the tradition of men, according to the basic principles of the world, and not according to Christ" (Colossians 2:8).

The results are cultural law-systems that not only separate man from God but attempt to reduce existential anxiety.

Regarding the Apostle Paul's phrase "written on the heart" in Romans 2:15, Greek New Testament scholar R. C. H. Lenski writes:

> The passive idea in "written" points to God as the writer ... here we have no moral evolution, no herd ethics, no social convention as to what society may decide as right and wrong, what changes as society changes; here we have what is left of the general image of God in the heart of man after the fall ... if no work of the law were written in the hearts of these pagans, no conscience would exist to testify, no moral debating in self-condemnation would be possible.[3]

## MENTALISTS VERSUS NON-MENTALISTS

The label "mentalist" is a dirty word among empiricists, materialists, functionalists, and contextualizers. Both Pike and Lenski were "mentalists" who maintained that innate principles encoded in the subconscious are real and can be rejected, distorted, and replaced with a misrepresentation of what is Universally true.

If, however, no law "written on the heart" exists, there can be no misrepresentation of the law "written on the heart." All meanings and concepts would be derived from context and social existence.

Neither should there exist conflicting thoughts about right or wrong behavior. No Universal rule book would contribute to humans' spiritual psychic unity. All truth would be relative.

Suppose one establishes the difference between a top-down, inside-out mentalist approach to missiology versus a bottom-up, outside-in biological-environmentalist "fitness" approach to missiology, as Kraft, Nida, Mayer, Lingenfelter, and others proposed. In that case, an explanation of the difference between a representation of an innate conceptual constant and a misrepresentation must be given.

For example, if a bribe does not misrepresent the meaning of a gift, since its meaning satisfies a need, our politicians should not be punished when they receive such gifts. What could be wrong with being "... a friend to one who gives gifts" (Proverbs 19:6)?

But more importantly, no Gospel in any society defines a gift with reciprocity.

If the word "gift" does not represent a conceptual constant, it means what Paul called an "unhealthy word." The Apostle Paul admonished Timothy to use "healthy words."

II Timothy 1:13 tells us to: "Hold fast the pattern of sound words which you have heard from me, in faith and love which are in Christ Jesus."

The gift of eternal life through Jesus Christ

## CONVICTIONS

- One must hold fast the pattern of sound words when sharing the Good News with the weary and the downtrodden and not allow unsound words to destroy the message of the Gospel. The Good News depends on "sound words."
- John 3:16: For God so loved the world that He gave His only begotten Son, that whoever believes in Him should not perish but have everlasting life.

# CHAPTER 29
# THE LAW OF CONTRADICTION AND THE LAW OF IDENTITY
## THE TAXONOMIST

Unlike the Rule of Exogamy, the Law of Contradiction necessitates a data bank of *a priori* knowledge hardwired into the unconscious mind for classifying the content of the world's information.

In this regard, the Lord, who created planet earth, informs us in Isaiah 45:18, NIV:

> *For this is what the LORD says—he who created the heavens, he is God; he who fashioned and made the earth, he founded it; he did not create it to be* tohu *(empty), but formed it to be inhabited—he says: "I am the LORD, and there is no other."*

Isaiah affirms that the world was not to remain in a state of *tohu*; that is, a perpetual disorganized chaos. Instead, the Lord intended for the content of planet earth—every animal, bird, plant, vertebrate, and invertebrate creature—to be categorized, named, and "ruled over."

God told Adam and Eve to "fill the earth and subdue it" (Genesis 1:28).

The planet's species were to be classified according to their kind, but without *a priori* knowledge of what constituted "a kind," the earth would have remained in a confused state.

The first man, Adam, had the ontological equipment, the classificatory tools, to understand concepts like "part of," "kind of," "same and different," "husband and wife," "good and bad," "vertebrate and invertebrate."

Without such binary concepts, which the present-day religion of Wokeism is attempting to cancel, it would have been impossible for Adam and his descendants to become taxonomists, classifiers, namers, and rulers.

Adam's ability to categorize and name birds and animals reveals that God equipped humankind not only to live under a Law of Identity that man did not create but also to use features of that Law to make sense of the world.

The Law of Contradiction and the Law of Identity precluded any possibility that Adam would classify a jaguar as a bird; his wife, Eve, as a male; or his sons, Cain and Abel, as primates. It would preclude a man from declaring himself to be a woman or a woman from declaring herself to be a man, as if one's sex is simply a matter of what one desires it to be. It would preclude someone with *XY* chromosomes from being classified as a female with *XX* chromosomes.

Without this innate knowledge of concepts, rules, and values common to everyone that can be "triggered" and brought to consciousness in a socio-linguistic environment, there could exist no world in which every species has most likely been classified by someone.

The Law of Contradiction implies that every child comes into the world ontologically equipped with conceptual constants that make communication and logical thinking possible. The sparrow flying above must be perceived as a kind of bird, not as a kind of animal.

In the words of Larry Arnn, president of Hillsdale College, "The Law of Contradiction is the basis of all reasoning, the means for making sense of the world. It is a law that says *X* and *Y* cannot be true at the same time if they are mutually exclusive."[1]

The Law of Contradiction and the Law of Identity also end all possibilities of relativistic thinking. Yet relativistic thinking rules in academia. It has compelled missiologists like Charles Kraft to declare: "Every missionary should learn to employ more important criteria (such as 'fit' and adequacy)."[2]

According to the contextualizer, a form must be valid if it "fits" the environment.

One of the first steps in introducing cultural diversity into the world, along with chaos, began when humankind classified collateral relatives as brothers and sisters.

The Law of Contradiction says no cousin can be a sibling because their parents are different. Yet, for political and economic reasons, many societies have rejected the Law of Contradiction and merged the mutually exclusive status positions of cousins and siblings.

Not only does the Law of Contradiction inform us how to think logically, Gordon Clark adds:

> The Law of Contradiction claims to be ontological as well as logical. It assumes something about being. [It] requires a knowledge of reality before and independent of the law.[3]

The job of the taxonomist involves gathering, studying, and identifying plant and animal species. It was a task given to the first man, Adam, and God has equipped every individual to be a taxonomist.

God told man:

> *"Have many children so your descendants will live all over the earth and bring it under their control. I am*

> *putting you in charge of the fish, the birds, and all the wild animals"* (Genesis 1:28, Good News Translation).

But without knowledge of what constituted a kind, it would have been impossible to classify the earth's species.

Adam's ability to categorize and name birds and animals reveals that humans were not only to live under a Law of Identity that they did not create but also to use features of that law to make sense of the world in which they lived.

Without this innate knowledge of concepts, rules, and values common to all, which can be "triggered" and brought to consciousness in a socio-linguistic environment, no world in which someone has classified every species could exist.

The Law of Contradiction and the Law of Identity also eliminate all possibilities of relativistic thinking. For example, a duck, even though it flies, shouldn't be classified as a bird because it has web feet, lives on the water, and has a flat, wide beak.

The Law has been "woven into the very fabric of our existence" (Romans 2:15, The Message).

# CREATED IN THE IMAGE OF GOD

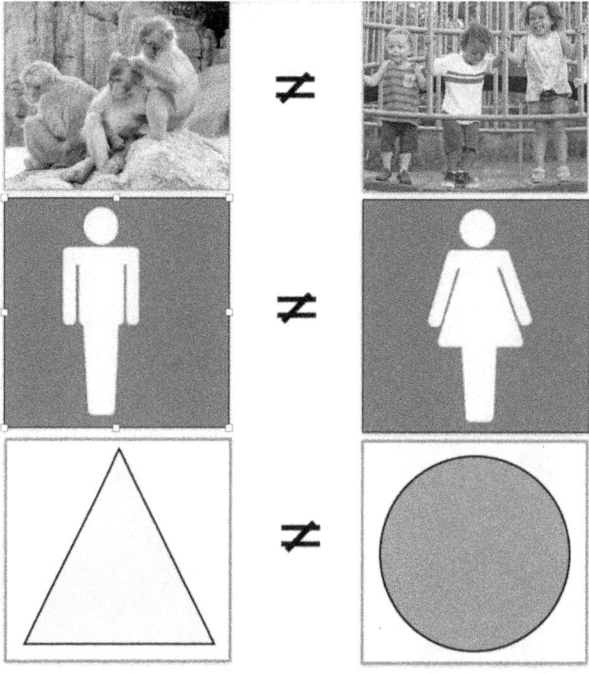

The Law of Contradiction and the Law of Identity

## CONVICTIONS

- One cannot know anything truly if the Law of Contradiction is only a suggestion.
- In the words of Larry Arnn, "The Law of Contradiction is the basis of all reasoning, the means of making sense of the world."
- The Law of Contradiction rules out the merging of mutually exclusive concepts, including status positions like siblings and cousins, fathers and uncles, mothers and aunts, and sons and daughters with nephews and nieces.
- Theologian Reinhold Niebuhr states: "No philosophy or religion can change the structure of human existence.

That structure involves individuality regarding a particular body and the spiritual fact of self-transcendence."[4]

# CHAPTER 30
# CULTURE AND NEUROSIS
## GOD IS THE AUTHOR OF MEANINGS

Among the 162 definitions of culture put forth by Kroeber and Kluckhohn in *Culture: A Critical Review of Concepts and Definitions*,[1] one definition made a great deal of sense. It was that of psychoanalyst Géza Róheim. He proposed: "Every culture, at least every primitive culture, can be reduced to a formula like neurosis ... culture involves neurosis which we try to cure."[2]

His definition of culture made it clear what our "Revolution without Guns" was all about. Along with translating the New Testament and producing readers who could read it, it was about returning Positive Cultural Universals, also known as absolutes, to their primary place in the Divine Plan. At some point in history, these cultural absolutes had been rejected and replaced by negative cultural particulars.

For the empiricist, the idea that Positive Cultural Universals have meanings that belong to God is madness. He believes perceptions precede meaning and determine it. If true, this means every missionary should be a cultural relativist because, in the words of missiologist Charles Kraft, "God seeks to work in terms of cultural forms (which are relative) ... it is for the purpose of leading people into a relationship with Himself."[3] These relative forms have attached meanings "that belong to the people."

In other words, the empiricist believes all knowledge originates in experience and that no form can have an inherent meaning.

Imagine you are an evangelist attempting to lead someone to Christ, and you mention that the parents of Jesus grew up in the same village. Unless the meaning attached to the form called family belongs to God, no Good News exists. For them, Jesus, the Creator of forms and inherent meanings, is an illegitimate being. He should not exist.

For the concept-innatist, like myself, meaning precedes perception. God is the Author of meanings attached to forms common to everyone. The empiricist, however, believes no form can have a Divine meaning. All meanings, according to Kraft, "belong to the people."

The result is cultural relativism. In today's world, people will say, "Your truth, my truth, and their truth."

According to linguist Daniel Everett, in the Pirahã tribe of Brazil, truth excludes history. What is real is what one perceives in the present. Objective truth cannot be known since truth is built on the shifting sands of human perceptions.

The more I observed the behavior of the Chácobo people, the more apparent it became that they had rejected the Rules of Logic. The Chácobo rejection of logical thinking manifested in their merging of two mutually exclusive concepts: siblings and parallel cousins.

Logical thinking implies certainty; for the cultural relativist, nothing is certain. However, the Chácobo invented a new status position called *raisi* to achieve certainty regarding their daily bread. It was a cultural form that suppressed human freedom and creativity and put mothers-in-law in control.

I EVENTUALLY DISCOVERED I was living amongst a people whose cultural operating system was very different from mine. While I ate with my family, no Chácobo husband ate with his family. While I slept with my wife in the same bed in the same room, no Chácobo husband slept in the same room as his wife.

When they asked me if Marian was my cross-cousin, they wondered why when I said she wasn't. Whenever someone showed me kindness, I would say "thank you." Whenever we showed them kindness, there was silence.

To my surprise, they had no word for thank you in their lexicon.

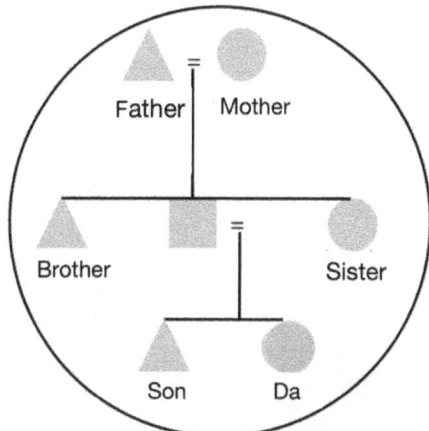

**First Degree Relatives. = Nuclear Family**

Nuclear family - First degree

## CONVICTIONS

- When one thinks logically, one thinks like God, the Author of logic.
- Aspects of Chácobo culture involved "neurosis which needed to be cured."[4]

- When the Chácobo returned the *husband-wife* dyad to its Divine place in the nuclear family, positive things began to happen. It ended their slide into cultural extinction.

## CHAPTER 31
# CREATING A DEFENSIVE SYSTEM AGAINST ANXIETY
### THE COVENANTAL HUSBAND-WIFE DYAD VS A BIOLOGICAL DYAD

It was providential when I was assigned to the Miccosukee language project in South Florida in 1984. Unexpectedly, I discovered that the Miccosukee had a dual set of pronouns.

The discovery provided linguistic evidence that human existence was dual. This dual kind of existence manifested itself in two types of selfhood. The transcendent self is expressed by the pronoun *-ele*, I, and the material self is expressed by the pronoun *cha-*, I.

The *-ele* pronoun positioned the self outside nature in culture and freedom under God. The *cha-* pronoun positioned the self in nature, the sphere of stimulus-response behavior.

Contrary to the materialists, the dual pronoun system declares that man is more than a body and a brain. This natural duality supports what the Word of God declares in Psalm 8: 5-6:

> *For You have made him a little lower than the angels, And You have crowned him with glory and honor.*

*You have made him to have dominion over the works of
Your hands; You have put all things under his feet,*

Human needs must be satisfied in nature if man and society are to survive. This means only man can contemplate his future existence and sense that his long-term security may be threatened. When threatened, humankind and society become anxious.

Because these threats to our existence are real, humans everywhere make decisions regarding economic, political, social, technological, and ecological pressures that affect their well-being.

For example, since people are not animals, from a theistic perspective, they do not instinctively store away their seed/corn to survive the following year. Instead, they arrive at the proper choices by deductive reasoning.

Unlike animals, God created and positioned people under Him to calculate, reason, think logically, and make plans regarding their existence regardless of their environments. When diverse linguistic groups left Babel and began to fill the earth, they entered territories where natural environments were very different.

Some lands were arid, and humans needed to irrigate them to survive. Other lands experienced a great deal of rainfall, and the infertility of the soil compelled communities to pack up and move when the land no longer produced a good crop despite the abundant rainfall.

## ANXIETY - THE FOUNTAINHEAD OF CULTURAL DIVERSITY

It slowly became evident that human anxiety caused by environmental pressures was the Mother of Cultural Diversity. What a particular cultural lifeway is anxious about is also what society is anxious about.

Man, in his struggle to eliminate anxiety from daily life, has consequently busied himself in designing socio-economic, political, and religious systems that will hopefully achieve that goal.

Cultural diversity is nothing more than a manifestation of the various defensive schemes humankind has devised to reduce human anxiety over existence apart from God's decrees and providential care. In the words of psychoanalyst Géza Róheim, "Defensive systems against [existential] anxiety are the stuff that culture is made of."[1]

∼

## ANXIETY REDUCTION MAN'S WAY

Historically, the primary means for reducing a society's existential anxieties has been creating a cultural defensive system based on kinship. In the words of anthropologist Robin Fox (1934 - 2024):

> These defensive systems' stuff were needs-based. They were responses to various recognizable pressures within biological, ecological, and social limitations ... they are there because they meet certain needs.[2]

The first step in creating a defensive system against anxiety is rearranging the internal structure of the nuclear family. This occurs when a society replaces the covenantal dyad of *husband-wife* with a biological dyad. Depending on the need, this is followed by the merging of mutually exclusive status positions and the rejection of the Law of Identity.

Such merging gives birth to what anthropologists call the classificatory kinship system. For example, when Israel entered the Promised Land, Jehovah spoke to Moses, saying in Leviticus 18:3:

> *'According to the doings of the land of Egypt, where you dwelt, you shall not do; and according to the doings of*

*the land of Canaan, where I am bringing you, you shall not do; nor shall you walk in their ordinances.'*

What exactly were these practices? The context gives us the answer. It is all about maintaining the moral integrity of society's basic unit: the nuclear family. If they reject the nuclear family as normative, they are guilty of creating new types of "families."

Israel lived in a social environment in which every nation surrounding them had reconfigured the internal structure of the nuclear family. They did this by merging mutually exclusive status positions, as manifested in the Egyptian family. The Egyptians, at least the ruling class, classified cousins and all uncles and aunts as brothers and sisters.[3]

If Israel had followed the practice of restructuring the nuclear family as was the custom of the surrounding nations, it would have signaled that they no longer believed that Jehovah would "... bless her [Israel] provision; I will satisfy her poor with bread" (Psalm 132:15).

Rejection of the Divine Ideal, where the nuclear family serves as the foundation of society, has consequences. Society's anxiety over existence will compel humans to suppress the Universal and construct a new type of family structured to satisfy specific needs and values.

The number of defensive systems based on the merging of status positions, each designed to relieve some existential anxiety and meet needs, staggers the imagination. The function of each family type in the world is to specifically achieve certain goals and relieve certain anxieties that are shaped by environmental pressures.

The only kinship system not shaped by environmental pressures is the biblical kinship system sketched out in Leviticus 18. It rejects the merging of status positions to relieve existential anxieties.

However, a man estranged from his Creator can use his freedom to violate the Rules of Logic whenever he rejects the Law of Identity and begins to merge mutually exclusive status positions to increase the size of his family.

~

ACCORDING to Francis L. K. Hsu, society's cultural operating system can be traced to how each society has structured the nuclear family. We should congratulate Hsu for his discovery in this regard.

However, Hsu failed to explain the "elementary principles" that compelled the Chinese to make the father-son dyad the dominant dyad or the Hindus to make the mother-son dyad the dominant dyad.

Years later, I asked, what were the elementary forces that compelled the Chácobo to select the mother-daughter dyad, the Miccosukee of South Florida the sister-sister, the Sharanahua of Peru the father-daughter, and the tribes living on the Great Plains the brother-brother? Hsu provided no answers.

Nevertheless, since I knew what biological dyad had replaced the *husband-wife,* I also knew why the Chácobo were a leaderless society heading toward cultural extinction. Instead of being the caretaker of a dying tribe, I became the promoter of social change. And it would start with "my kids," none of whom were married.

As I considered the implications of Acts 14:16-17, NIV:

> *In the past, he [God] let all nations go their own way.*
> *Yet he has not left himself without testimony: He has*
> *shown kindness by giving you rain from heaven and*
> *crops in their seasons; he provides you with plenty of*
> *food and fills your hearts with joy.*

It became evident at some point in history, the Chácobo chose to create a defensive system against anxiety. Their defensive system, I discovered, involved replacing the *husband-wife* dyad with that of the mother-daughter. When I pointed this out to "my kids," along with the opinions of Chácobo sages of the past who agreed with me, they scratched their heads in disbelief.

Although I knew they had restructured the nuclear family, I had yet to figure out what compelled them to make the mother-daughter dyad the dominant dyad rather than some other dyad. I eventually learned:

A society gradually takes shape within a particular physical environment. The character of the environment influences its forms—whether it is fertile or hard country, whether the climate is equable or extreme, whether the mineral and water power is abundant or scanty.[4]

Physical and mental environmental factors were the particular elemental forces that lured the Chácobo to replace the Positive Universal with a cultural negative. The existential questions for the Chácobo were: Who will make the beer? And who is going to provide the fish and wildlife?

# CREATED IN THE IMAGE OF GOD

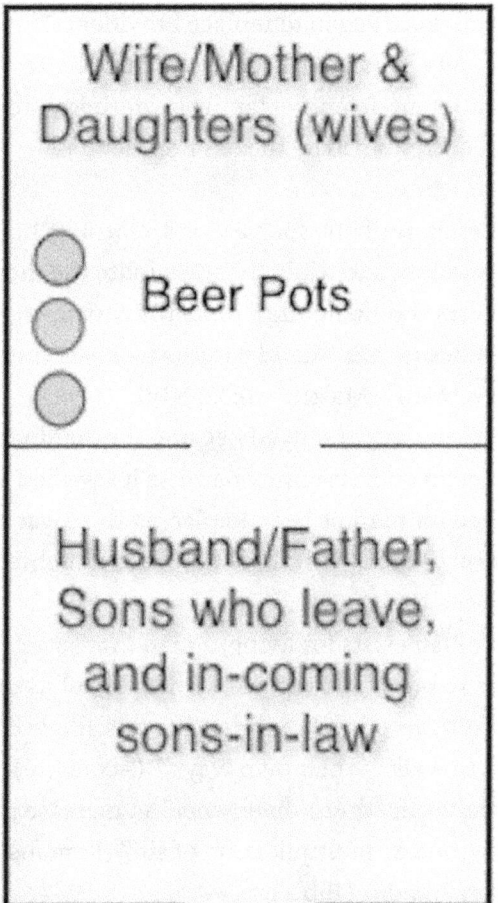

Chácobo family structure

## CONVICTIONS

- The fall gave birth to anxiety. From that day forward, man's needs have been primarily met by "the sweat of the brow," the rejection of the one-flesh principle of

*husband-wife*, and the restructuring of the nuclear family. Social existence began to replace Providence.
- As humanity began to fill the earth after the Tower of Babel, different defensive family forms began to be created, each shaped by the environment's characteristics.
- The necessities of life, such as food, clothing, housing, transportation, and a job, that dominate the thoughts of unbelievers should not dominate the thoughts of God's children. Jesus said, "...and your heavenly Father knows you need them" (Matthew 6:32, NIV).
- The mother-daughter dyad became the dominant dyad of the Chácobo nuclear family because it satisfied a need: their need for manioc beer. Replacing the covenantal *husband-wife* dyad with that of mother-daughter had "no place in the Divine Plan."
- A Divine Plan exists for living, a plan that society has the freedom to reject and replace with a plan of its own making. "'... who in bygone generations allowed all nations to walk in their own ways'" (Acts 14:16).
- What is the effect? *Etic* divergence, an increase in cultural diversity, and a "multiplication of sin" (Romans 5:20, Christian Standard Bible).

## CHAPTER 32
# LEARNING REQUIRES A PRIORI EQUIPMENT ETIC DATA
## CLASSIFICATORY TOOL KIT

Cognitive scientist and naturalist Steven Pinker states:

People in all cultures carry out long chains of reasoning built from links [kind of, cause and effect] whose truth they could not have observed directly. Philosophers have often pointed out that science is made possible by that ability.[1]

When an environment is [becomes] stable, there is a selective pressure for learned abilities to become increasingly innate ... evolution has made computational units of language innate.[2]

For Pinker, these "computational units of language" were not a qualitative feature of being created in "God's image." They were the product of what Karl Marx called "social existence," the pressures of the environment, and natural selection.

In other words, for Pinker, man's capacity to create knowledge by classifying his sense perceptions is a phenomenon brought about by a magical force called Natural Selection.

In contrast, a theistic perspective believes that every child comes into the world equipped with a set of classificatory tools that give each child the capacity to classify sense perceptions and become a creator of knowledge.

Even Pinker acknowledges that knowledge creation depends on possessing these classificatory tools. As Christian philosopher Gordon Clark points out, "learning requires *a priori* equipment."[3]

"Unless we had concepts or categories of quality, quantity, and relations, we could not think of botany, baseball, or anything else."[4]

The set of classificatory tools includes the following concepts: "The Doctrine of the Image of God in man ... is an assertion of innate equipment."[5] Categories reveal the existence of such innate equipment. Even Pinker acknowledges it exists.

Features of the categories include: Meanings are not learned. They are brought to consciousness by a "triggering" process that occurs when a sense experience needs to be categorized.

In addition, English philosopher Peter Carruthers proposed, "Such knowledge will make its appearance at some particular stage in normal cognitive development."[6]

For example, before a child can learn to read and write, the child first needs to acquire knowledge of classificatory concepts like part of, kind of, same and different. Chácobo children learning to read need to understand that a syllable is part of a form called a "word," and the syllables of *ca* and *pa* that are different make up the word *cape*, which means squirrel.

If the concepts "part of" and "same and different" were not part of their "classificatory tool kit," there would have been no readers of the Chácobo New Testament. Features of this classificatory tool kit are:

- All people are equipped with this kit. The God who equipped humans with the necessary classificatory tools to arrange "sense perceptions under concepts" and "concepts under categories" did so so that man could not

- only take dominion over the earth and subdue it but also receive revealed truth.
- These innate concepts are indefinable: All attempts to define a classificatory concept are always circular. For example, part of = piece of; exact = identical; exist = be alive; thing = whatchamacallit; listen = give one's attention to a sound; husband = a married male; and culture = principles for living.
- These innate concepts are irreducible: Regardless of humankind's capacity to detach inherent meaning-content from shared Universal forms and replace them with meanings that "belong to the people," the reality is that a "someone" cannot be reduced to a "something," or a "person" to a "kind of animal," or a "being" to a "non-being."
- Conceptualization: Requires *a priori* equipment.

AWARE that the Chácobo had restructured the nuclear family, I needed to devise a strategy to restore the Universal to its rightful place. Until such a strategy became a reality, Marian and I busied ourselves to help the Chácobo become part of the national economy, which they did not understand.

In this regard, I reluctantly assumed the role of *patrón*, the buyer of Chácobo rubber, Brazil nuts, and supplier of goods. They would roll in large 70-100 kilo rubber balls that I weighed, and instead of paying for them in goods, I paid in cash, known as monopoly money, which they could spend in the small store I built under our bedroom.

In the event that Bolivians defrauded them, we delayed paying them in Bolivian pesos until they learned that the numbers on the bills carried meanings. This was the method we used to teach them how to count, add, and subtract.

Unknown to me then, our venture into the rubber business, as illustrated by wives sitting on rubber balls (see photo at end of chapter), was strengthening the *husband-wife* dyad and weakening the mother-daughter dyad. When sons-in-law sold their rubber, they were paid cash, and instead of turning their money over to their mothers-in-law in exchange for conjugal rights to their daughters, they shared it with their wives.

In the process, they unconsciously strengthened the *husband-wife* relationship and God's design for the family. This began the long process of returning the *husband-wife* dyad to its rightful place within the family. Unknown to me, "A Revolution without Guns" had begun.

It wasn't until they learned that different bills had different values that we introduced Bolivian currency. In the meantime, all transactions were carried out using monopoly money when purchasing needed goods, which included an assortment of necessities such as shotguns, ammunition, radios, pots, pans, machetes, knives, salt, and certain medicines from the small store we set up under our bedroom. After we had built a road connecting the villages of *Alto Ivon*, *Nucleo*, and *California*, they demanded bicycles.

Besides operating the store, Marian kept busy teaching Chácobo children to read and write. As a teacher, she depended on the unconscious minds of the students structured with a set of semantic tools for learning—concepts like "part of the whole." Otherwise, it would be impossible to know, for example, that my fingers are part of my hand or that a wing is part of a bird.

The same holds for a syllable. A syllable is part of a meaningful word. For example, when put together, the two syllables ca + pa create the meaningful word "squirrel." We used the syllable method to teach Chácobo children how to read and write.

Needless to say, without this set of unlearned classificatory tools provided by a caring Creator whose desire for humankind is that they live in a meaningful world, Marian would not have been able to teach Chácobo children how to read and write. There would be no readers of the Chácobo New Testament. The fact is that learning requires *a priori* mental equipment.

Chácabo women and children sitting on rubber balls

Marian teaching reading using *a priori* equipment

## CONVICTIONS

- It would be impossible for man to think and conceptualize without first being equipped by God who wanted to see the earth categorized, "who ... created it not to be chaos, but formed it to be lived in" (Isaiah 45:18, Complete Jewish Bible).
- There would be no readers if Chácobo children had not been mentally equipped with categorizing tools.
- "Learning requires *a priori* equipment"~Gordon Clark.
- The publication *Ethnobotany of the Chácobo Indians* by Brian M. Bloom could never have been written if the Chácobo lacked the mental equipment to categorize all plant life existing in their environment of Northern Bolivia.

CHAPTER 33

# A BIBLE TRANSLATOR'S DILEMMA

## CULTURE IS A KIND OF LAW

By the end of 1970, I had translated two-thirds of the New Testament, but we had practically no readers. When I came to the book of Galatians, to my surprise, a translation problem and a missiological issue of immense proportions confronted me. Who had Christ come to redeem from the rule of law?

The passage in Galatians 4:4-5 (NKJV) is typically rendered as:

> *But when the fullness of the time had come, God sent forth*
> *His Son, born of a woman, born under the law,*
> *to redeem those who were under the law, that we might*
> *receive the adoption as sons.*

When the Apostle Paul carried the Gospel into Galatia, he was confronted for the first time with people who had no written law; yet, like the Chácobo, Yaminahua, Guaraní, and hundreds of other people groups, they were not lawless. How is that possible?

When translating Galatians 4:4-5, I had to answer the question: Whom had Christ come to redeem? Was it just the Jews, which nearly every English translation of Galatians 4:4-5 implies, or all people?

If, for example, the NKJV presents the reader with a faithful rendering of the text, then what message was the Apostle Paul attempting to convey to his non-Jewish readers living in Galatia?

The meaning I glean from reading the New King James Version is this: "Only those who live under the law[1] can be redeemed and become God's children" because, as Greek scholar Merrill Tenney points out, "Only Jews could be said to be under the law; the Gentiles were not."[2]

Was the Apostle Paul really saying, "Unless you Gentiles first become Jews, submit yourselves to the Law of Moses, worship on the Sabbath, and get circumcised, Christ can't redeem you"?

Was the Apostle Paul informing the Galatians that since they were not Jews "living under the law," it was impossible for them to be adopted into the family of God? And as the bearer of "Good News," why would Paul, the Apostle to the Gentiles, devote his life to bringing such news that was bad rather than good?

FOR ME, the above translation implied that I needed to change my missiological approach. It meant bringing the "Good News" to the Chácobo would be complicated, long, and drawn out. It meant that before Christ could "set them free from the law," they first had to become Jews, the very process Paul and the Apostles denounced (Acts 15).

If evangelism meant teaching them "the way of Moses," such a missiological strategy would take a few years.

First, we would have to teach them to count to seven since their counting system had only two words, *wëstita* (one) and *wëstima* (not one).

After teaching them to count to seven using Spanish numerals, we would have to teach them the concept of a seven-day week cycle and that each day of this seven-day cycle had a name. Learning that each day had a name would certainly be a novel idea since they only gave names to people, things, and villages, never to days.

Next, we would need to teach them that the Jewish way of doing things meant they would need to rest on the last day of this series of seven days we call a *Semana*. The name of that day was *Sabado*.

This Jewish way of doing things meant they could only rest one day out of seven rather than two or three days out of seven, as was their custom. Up until now, they never awoke in the morning wondering what they were going to do on the "weekend" like the rest of the world.

Finally, there was the custom of circumcision. The sign of being "under the law" was circumcision. Yet, the Apostle Paul in Galatians 5:2-3 declares:

> *Indeed I, Paul, say to you that if you become circumcised,*
>   *Christ will profit you nothing.*
> *And I testify again to every man who becomes circumcised*
>   *that he is a debtor to keep the whole law.*

After learning how to obey the whole law, they would be prepared to be set free from the law. This meant they would have to stop resting and worshipping on the last day of the week and begin resting and worshipping on the first day of the week, a day we called "Owner's Day."

The Gospel now sounded like bad news instead of Good News. I asked myself, is this the appropriate way to do evangelism among a people moving toward self-extinction? Did Christ only come to redeem those who were living according to "the Way of Moses"?

I concluded the translators had all failed to render the meaning of νόμος (law) absent the Greek article correctly. Since this was a linguistic problem, it meant unraveling the mysteries of the Greek article in the same way we had to uncover the rules of syllable absence in the Chácobo language.

Did the absence of the Greek article, like the syllable absence in the Chácobo language, carry semantic content, a meaning-content that New Testament translators failed to unmask?

While early church scholars, beginning with Origen, felt that the absence of the article before abstract nouns was a clue to its meaning in the Apostle Paul's epistles, today, Greek scholars, Bible translators, and theologians, with a few exceptions, gloss over the fact that absence of the article before νόμος (law) carries with it semantic content; namely, the "intrinsic quality of law-ness."

If forms, e.g., customs, traditions, rules, rights, duties, allegiance patterns, obligations, values, codes, and commandments didn't have the "intrinsic quality of law-ness," like a sparrow having the inherent attributes of bird-ness and a jaguar having the innate qualities of animal-ness, there could be no genera called law, bird, or animal. One would not be able to distinguish between what kinds of behavior were lawless and what kinds were lawful.

As biblical Greek scholars throughout history studied the writings of the Apostles, they noticed that of the 72 times νόμος (law) occurs in the book of Romans, 39 times it occurs without the article, or 55 percent of the time.

In the book of Galatians νόμος (law) occurs 26 times, ten times with the article and 16 times without it. They assumed the absence of the article before νόμος (law) in the writings of a scholar like the Apostle Paul was no accident. It had to be intentional.

It is dangerous for the translator to assume that the noun is sufficiently definite without the article. I contend the article was absent because the Apostle Paul had absented it for a reason. There was no other way to speak of law as a genera.

As a linguist and Bible translator, the question that deserved an answer was: Why did Bible translators ignore this essential grammar rule? It was, I contend, ignored for a reason.

These translators, including biblical scholars, no doubt had trouble believing that the absence of the Greek article could carry meaning, especially when the translator omitted the article before the noun νόμος (law). They failed to recognize that culture is a kind of law.

When New Testament Greek scholars H. E. Dana (1888 - 1945) and J. R. Mantey (1890 - 1981) attempted to analyze the function of the Greek article, they concluded, "We are entering one of the most fascinating fields of linguistic research."[3]

They voiced the sentiments of another Greek scholar, A. T. Robertson (1863 - 1934), who wrote: "The development of the Greek article is one of the most interesting things in human speech."[4]

Having personally wrestled with the function of subtraction of the last syllable of all three syllables within words of a Chácobo sentence and how the absence of a single syllable completely changes the meaning of the sentence, I believe Dana and Mantey are correct in their assessment when they say ignoring the absence of the article would be a "serious blunder."

In their opinion, "Scholars have not accorded it sufficient attention nor sought with proper diligence the real genius underlying its various usages."[5]

We contend the absence of the article in Greek and the absence of a syllable in Chácobo both carry semantic meaning and that meaning needs to be translated into the receptor language.

In this regard, Dana and Mantey point out:

An object of thought (i.e., noun) may be conceived of from two points of view: as to "identity" or "quality."

To convey the first point, the Greek uses the article; for the second, the anarthrous [or absence of the article] construction is used.[6]

Likewise, James Moulton writes, "For exegesis, there are few of the finer points of Greek which need more constant attention than this omission of the article when the writer would lay stress on the quality or character of the object."[7]

Accordingly, if the writer's meaning and intent are to unmask and accurately convey, then translating the semantic content of "absence" becomes obligatory.

Arthur Slaten arrived at the same conclusion over a century ago when he wrote:

> Recognition of the qualitative usage of nouns [signaled by the absence of article] is of extreme importance in the translation and interpretation of the New Testament. That the significance of this usage is not generally recognized is apparent not only in many renderings of the Revised Version but even in critical commentaries upon the Greek text and in the standard grammars of the New Testament.[8]

With a few exceptions, nothing has changed since he wrote those words. Absence of the Greek article before νόμος (law) has, for the most part, been ignored by Bible translators. Nevertheless, I was convinced, not based on some theological perspective, but based on the Greek rules of grammar governing the use or absence of the article, that the true meaning of Galatians 4:4-5 could be unmasked.

Νόμος (law) absent the article, I concluded, could not possibly denote a specific law like the Law of Moses that was written on tablets of stone, but rather an abstraction. As an abstraction, νόμος (law) absent the Greek article, meant a law-way-of-living, a way filled with duties, obligations, customs, and values.

The Chácobo word for this "law-way-of-living" was *jabi*, also known as culture. The Chácobo were not a lawless society. They lived under the rules, customs, and values of Chácobo society. I had no trouble believing that grammatical absence carried meaning since it was manifested in the Chácobo language.

On Dr. Eugene Nida's (American Bible Society) trip to Bolivia, I showed him my data on the absence of a syllable in the Chácobo language. When he saw my information, he considered it to be unusual.

It would have been impossible for us to communicate meaningfully in Chácobo if we did not observe a grammatical rule that stated: Whenever a three-syllable noun like *ínaka* (dog) or *kamano* (jaguar) occurs as the object of a sentence, the last syllable is subtracted. But whenever they are the subjects of a transitive verb, a verb which takes an object, the last syllable of the word is accented.

Inaká kama akë, "dog-jaguar-killed" = the dog killed the jaguar.
Ina kamanó akë, "dog-jaguar-killed" = the jaguar killed the dog.

Aware that absence carried meaning, I didn't go to a commentary looking for an answer to the question, does the absence of the Greek article carry meaning? Instead, I went to *A Manual Grammar of the Greek New Testament* by Dana and Mantey and submit the following translation:

> *But when the right time came, God sent his Son. Being born of a Jewish mother, he was subject to a Jewish law-way (νόμος absent article) so that he might set free both Jews and Gentiles from their man-created law-ways (νόμος absent article). This God did for us to become his children.*

To test how well one could read and see if my translations made sense, I would tape portions of the Word of God I had translated to the store's shutter. I also posted them to "trigger" a desire to read. In the picture, I am testing Cana, one of our first Chácobo school teachers, on how well he could read and understand.

Gil Prost testing translation

## CONVICTIONS

- American clergyman and educator Arthur Slaten summed it up like this: "Recognition of the qualitative usage of nouns [signaled by the absence of article] is essential in translating and interpreting the New Testament. The significance of this usage is not generally recognized. It is apparent not only in many renderings of the Revised Version but even in critical commentaries upon the Greek text and in the standard grammars of the New Testament."[9]

# CHAPTER 34
# THE MANDATE OF HEAVEN
## CHINA

During the period of the Old Testament Patriarchs, long before God's Law was given to Israel at Mt. Sinai, Chinese sages lived who believed that in the unconscious mind of every person was a Meta-Script containing principles that informed man how to live. They called this Meta-Script for living The Mandate of Heaven.[1] Pike called it *etic* data, or inborn information, which provided the starting point for analysis.

The principles contained in this Meta-Script were not learned; they were "triggered" and brought to consciousness in a sociolinguistic situation. According to Wing-Tsit Chan (1901 - 1994), the principles of the Meta-Script are: "... innate ... rooted in the heart of all men, demonstrated by the fact children know how to love their parents, and when men suddenly fall into a well, a sense of mercy and alarm inevitably arouses in their hearts."[2]

The first duty of a new ruler, according to author and jurist, John C. H. Wu, "is to rectify the abuses or perversions of its mandate, and by overthrowing the lawless oppressor, through carefully observing the dictates of natural law, The Mandate of Heaven will be perpetually kept intact."[3]

Since the principles of this moral code are structured in the unconscious mind, they can be obeyed, ignored, rejected, and replaced, but not deleted. As these Universal Principles were lived out, they served as representations of principles that existed in Heaven, in the mind of God. Ignore the principles and suffer the consequences.

When Israel received the Law at Mount Sinai, the Chinese lived under the standards of another law "written on the heart" (Romans 2:15). They called it The Mandate of Heaven.

The Chinese people were fully aware that, as a society, they could diverge from The Mandate of Heaven and that rulers who diverged needed to be overthrown. Linguist Kenneth Pike labeled such a divergence from Divine precepts a spiritual phenomenon called *etic* divergence.

Even though the Chácobo lacked a descriptive term like The Mandate of Heaven which recognized the existence of these precepts "written on the heart," they were nevertheless aware that helping a person in a time of need was one way to demonstrate such a principle.

It was through satire that these Chácobo sages of the past made known that such a Meta-Script structured in the unconscious mind existed. They were, through satire, informing their people they had to restore the Universals from which they had diverged. If not, they would suffer the consequences.

When Marian and I arrived on the scene, the Chácobo tribe had dwindled to 133 members. They were reaping the consequences—a dying culture.

While the Chinese had no written code like the Magna Carta or the Law of Moses, like the Chácobo and thousands of other people groups, they were not a lawless society. They lived under a recognized law. The Chácobo called it *Noba Jabi* (our way of living). The Chinese called it The Mandate of Heaven.

Chinese people knew the only force capable of constraining the accumulation of political power into the hands of the few was The

Mandate of Heaven. As a stratified society, Chinese jurist and author, John C. H. Wu, stated:

> The emperor's powers were severely restricted by immemorial, constitutional customs ... under the old [unwritten system], all persons were equal before the law.[4]

However, this equality before the law disappeared when a ruler put his interests above the people.

For present-day contextualizers, materialists, functionalists, and existentialists, however, the unconscious mind is not structured. Instead, all meanings are derived from social existence or social practice. A contextualizing missiologist-anthropologist insists the idea of a structured mind must be abandoned. For a concept-innatist like myself, I say they are mistaken.

The late Christian philosopher Gordon Clark agreed with the Chinese sages of another age, adding: "Man's mind is not initially blank. It is structured. In fact, an unstructured mind is no mind at all."[5]

For the Chinese, the unconscious mind was structured with a Meta-Script that informed them how to live.

When the Apostle Paul wrote, "Do we then make void the law through faith? Certainly not! On the contrary, we establish the law" (Romans 3:31).

The translator must ask: What kind of law was the Apostle Paul talking about? Note the following answers:

1. The Ten Commandments.
2. The five books of Moses.
3. The Old Testament.
4. The moral law of God.
5. God's will.
6. The whole of the Jewish religion.
7. All cultural law-systems, Jewish and pagan.

8. Uncertain since "Paul uses the word 'law' in so many senses, it is doubtful which one is principally intended here."[6]

When the Apostle Paul absented the Greek article before νόμος (law) in Romans 3:31 and many other key passages, he knew what he was doing. He was dealing with law as an abstraction, the particular law-way of a society. Such cultural law-ways vary from one society to the next.

Today, we call these different law-ways cultures. When a person or society exercises their faith in Christ, something strange happens to their law-way of living.

The Apostle Paul put it this way: Do we set aside our law-way of life (culture) when we become Christians? Of course not. Instead, we improve our law-way of life.

Romans 3:31 asks, "Do we then make void the law through faith? Certainly not! On the contrary, we establish the law."

CATHOLIC HISTORIAN CHRISTOPHER DAWSON (1989 - 1970) wrote, "Culture is a way of life adapted to a particular environment."[7]

Since νόμος absent the article, represents an abstract noun exhibiting the characteristics and qualities of law, qualities like customs, traditions, beliefs, values, prohibitions, precepts, regulations, entitlements, rules, rights, duties, obligations, commandments, principles, and routines, more than one law-way system existed in a similar sense that there are many kinds of animals, birds, and flowers.

Likewise, many kinds of cultures or law-systems exist from which people need to be redeemed and set free. There is a Pacahuara law-way, a Miccosukee law-way, a Pushtun law-way, a Yaminahua law-way, a Chácobo law-way, and a Pirahã law-way, to name a few.

Each of these cultural laws promotes the values, obligations, allegiance patterns, beliefs, and traditions that are important to each group.

Cultural law-way versus God's law

## CONVICTIONS

- Whenever νόμος (law) occurs without the article, it speaks to a cultural law-way filled with cultural forms that have "no place in the Divine Plan."
- Greek scholar James Moulton wrote, "For exegesis, there are few of the finer points of Greek which need more constant attention than this omission of the article when the writer would lay stress on the quality or character of the object."[8]
- Accordingly, if the meaning and intent of the New Testament writers were to be accurately conveyed, I, as a translator, was obligated to convey the semantic content of "absence."
- American translators ignore this rule.
- A society's law-way will improve when it recognizes that the Bible is the Word of God.

# CHAPTER 35
# FROM BABEL TO THE AMAZON
## CONFUSION OF LANGUAGES BEGAN BY SCRAMBLING WORD ORDERS

### MANY DIVERSE LANGUAGES EMERGED OUT OF ONE UNIVERSAL GRAMMAR

It is worth noting that theoretical linguists like Noam Chomsky believe:

> Children must innately be equipped with a plan common to the grammars of all languages, a Universal Grammar, that tells them how to distill the syntactic patterns out of the speech patterns of their parents.[1]

While the original surface form of the spoken language was lost at the Tower of Babel, the Universal Rules of Grammar, embedded in the subconscious, remained as the underlying foundational framework for all languages.

For example, there clearly occurred the scrambling of the sentence order of *Subject-Object-Verb* among the languages of the world.

My first task as an SIL linguist was to create grammar rules for the Chácobo language,[2] which, when it was published in 1965, was spoken by 145 people. For me the question was: Of the following six possible sentence types, SVO, SOV, VSO, VOS, OVS and OSV, which one were the Chácobo using?

While the order was scrambled at Babel, the functions of subject, objects, and verbs were not lost.[3]

I discovered the Chácobo were assigned a very rare sentence order. It was object-verb-subject. It was like learning to speak English backwards.

For example, the sequence *cama aqui joni* (tiger-kills-man) in Chácobo actually means the man killed the tiger.

In English, the subject man occurs first in the sentence; in Chácobo, the object *joni* (man) appears first.

Despite the change in word order, the same meaning is conveyed in both sentence types.

After confusing the languages, the Lord compelled these diverse language groups to do the very thing they were determined not to do; that is, "to fill the earth." The Bible makes it clear that their thoughts and plans were not His.

> *"For My thoughts are not your thoughts, Nor are your ways My ways," says the LORD. (Isaiah 55:8)*

> *So the LORD scattered them abroad from there over the face of all the earth, and they ceased building the city. (Genesis 11:8)*

But in doing so, He did not erase the Universal Meta-Script for living that existed "within them."

## MANKIND'S REFUSAL TO "FILL THE EARTH"

The God-given task for mankind was to fill the earth and gain mastery over it. Gaining mastery over it meant arranging perceptions under concepts and concepts under categories and then naming them. Those who name the species also write the rules. Only man has the mental capacity to do this task.

"Ruling" meant naming. But instead of becoming classifiers and namers of the earth's species, humans chose to urbanize, make a name for themselves, by attempting to do the "impossible." As a homogenous society sharing one religious, political law-system, nothing would be beyond their capacity to provide for themselves.

But then, Yahweh brought their grand scheme for human development to a halt by "confusing their language." This task was not too difficult. Yahweh simply scrambled the surface rules of grammar while retaining the fundamental Universal Grammatical Framework for all languages residing in the subconscious.

In addition, as He let them "go their own way," their ability to come together in political unity became increasingly more difficult. But this dream of a one-world political-religious-economic law-system designed to do "the impossible" is alive and well today.

Not only was the earth "formed to be inhabited," it was also formed to be managed, used, and cared for by humankind. What began in the garden when Adam was given the task of naming the animals after their kind was not to end there.

To the extent that God gave Adam the honor to manage His creation and to name the animals according to their kind, it was incumbent upon him to pass on the task to his descendants.

He clearly failed. They went no further than the Fertile Crescent and stopped, making Babel its capital.

> Then God blessed them, and God said to them, "Be fruitful and multiply; fill the earth and subdue it; have dominion over the fish of the sea, over the birds of the

air, and over every living thing that moves on the earth" (Genesis 1:28).

Instead of moving out and filling the earth, subduing it, and taking authority over it as commanded, the inhabitants settled down and said:

> "Come, let us build ourselves a city, and a tower whose top is *in the heavens; let us make a name for ourselves, lest we be scattered abroad over the face of the whole earth*" (Genesis 11:4).

They knew it was God's desire that the whole earth be inhabited, but the people refused to budge. If they were not going to disperse and begin naming and classifying the species of God's creation willingly, it would be done under compulsion. God wanted to make sure humankind never again organized themselves against Him as a totalitarian whole.

It began with the confusion of the languages. After the scattering of language groups, the Panoan family of languages crossed the Bering Straits into North America, down the West Coast of North America into South America, then down the West Coast of South America where they crossed the Andes Mountains and split into 34 distinct language groups, spreading throughout the Amazonian Rainforest.

Of the 34 original language groups, 18 are extinct. The "confusion" of the languages began by scrambling word orders as illustrated in the examples below.

- Cama aqui joni
- tiger is killing man = The man is killing the tiger
- Joni camanó aquë
- man tiger killed = The tiger killed the man
- Cama joní aquë

- tiger man killed = The man killed the tiger

As one can see, the OVS and OSV word orders listed in the chart are rare, and both occur in the Chácobo language.

In addition to the rarity of word order, there is the rarity of syllable subtraction. Whenever a three-syllable noun is the object of a sentence, one subtracts the last syllable. But the scrambling does not end there. Whenever a noun is the subject of a transitive verb past tense, it takes an accent. After the scrambling, it reads, "the Lord dispersed them over all the earth" for "the earth was formed to be inhabited."

As the Prophet Isaiah points out:

> *For thus says the LORD, who created the heavens (he is God!), who formed the earth and made it (he established it; he did not create it a chaos, he formed it to be inhabited!): "I am the LORD, and there is no other" (Isaiah 45:18, RSV).*

However, for mankind to meaningfully use the earth's vast resources in the service of God and his fellowman, the earth first had to be classified. In this regard, the first task given to Adam was to be a meaning-giver. This meant everything had to be classified according to their kind.

However, if humans did not know what qualities made up the genera of animals, birds, and trees, the classification of the earth's species would not be possible. When assigned the task of naming the animals, Adam did not ask God, "What is an animal?" or "What is a bird?" He already knew what the qualities of each genus was.

# CREATED IN THE IMAGE OF GOD

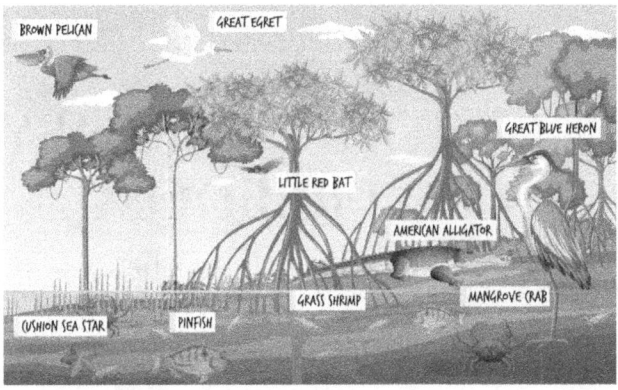

Adam gave names to God's creations

## CONVICTIONS

- Naming indicated "You [God] gave them charge of everything you [God] made, putting all things under their authority—" (Psalm 8:6, New Living Translation).
- To "govern" implies man has the capacity to classify, name, organize, and take care of everything according to their kind.
- This capacity to classify, name, and organize provides us with deductive evidence that there exists within man an innate Universal data base or Lexicon of conceptual constants.

# CHAPTER 36
# COMMODITY, MONEY AND FREEDOM
## CHÁCOBO OF BOLIVIA

Toucan

## CREATED IN THE IMAGE OF GOD

To my surprise, I discovered that the "primitive" Chácobo, who couldn't count past two, had a monetary form that promoted economic freedom. The world's central banks have rejected it. Yet, it's a form from which no central bank can escape.

To understand real money, one must know the qualities of "commodity money." It is limited in quantity, fungible, portable, and has inherent value—in contrast to currency. Toucan feathers, because they were a commodity, were treated as money.

In America, examples of "commodity money" would be tobacco, cigarettes, gold, and silver.

When the Chácobo traded amongst themselves for a "hard-to-obtain" item, they used a "hard-to-obtain" commodity. Unlike the currency in my wallet, which the government calls money (fiat money), the Chácobo traded using a commodity in the form of a toucan feather.

Money has inherent value—in contrast to currency. For safekeeping, it was the custom of every Chácobo male to tie his small basket of "money" to the ridge pole holding up his roof. To get to the basket, he would not only need to climb the pole holding up the roof but also get to the basket hanging in the center of the ridge pole several meters away.

On one occasion, an elder of the village brought me his "money" in a small basket and asked me to take care of it while he was visiting another town with his family. His "money," tied to the ridge pole that held up his roof, was taken down and put in our care.

My language informant explained that Caco wanted me to protect his "money" lest someone in the village stole it. Caco didn't trust his neighbors.

For the Chácobo, "commodity money" was toucan feathers. They were limited in quantity, portable, fungible, and divisible. A single toucan feather, a hard-to-get commodity, was equivalent to any other toucan just like a silver dollar in my pocket has the same value as the silver dollar in your pocket.

When visiting another village, men and women made sure they entered the village properly adorned. Men used the toucan feathers to make headdresses. Women used them to make circular headpieces and armlets.

Another feature of "commodity money" is it has to be divisible and durable. While Chácobo's "money" was long-lasting, it was not imperishable like gold, which fire can't destroy.

As an Amazonian tribe, the Chácobo lifeway was outside the economic sphere of the Bolivian peso. Whenever they had the opportunity to obtain metal things like machetes, axes, knives, pots, and pans, they bartered. In exchange for jaguar skins, manioc, and, at times, labor, they could obtain these desired goods.

Instead of using gold, which is real money, to carry out business transactions, we use currency. My wallet's treasury bills are classified as "fiat money."

However, the U.S. government declares them to be real money. We're deceived if we believe those green paperbacks are real money.

According to economist Arthur Kemp (1919 - 1981), declaring it to be money: "Permits nations to proceed their individual ways with their own particular political and ideological programs without regard to their effects on relationships among individuals in an increasingly interdependent world."[1]

In June 2020, the World Economic Forum (WEF) brought together the world's top academicians, politicians, business leaders, economists, and central bank directors to launch the Great Reset, an initiative to build back better the foundations of our economic and social system in a post-COVID future. The quotes from the meeting are eye-opening.[2]

Because the link between a form common to all and its inherent meaning cannot be broken despite what humanity does, any attempt by society to separate the two will produce adverse effects.

Before 1971, the dollars in my wallet represented gold with inherent value. In contrast, the Bolivian peso was tethered to the government's capacity to collect taxes to pay for its socialistic policies of spreading the wealth.

President Nixon delinked the meaning of currency from gold in 1971 when he removed us from the "gold standard." Since then, I can no longer say my dollars are as "good as gold" since they no longer represent a Universal. In 1971, the meaning of my dollars changed to "floating currency."

In 1978, Russian economist A. V. Anikin wrote a book decrying the idea that currency functions as money "only in its capacity as a representative of gold."[3] Only when a currency represents gold, which has inherent value, does it function as real money. Delinking currency from gold, which he called the Yellow Devil for some unknown reason, seemed impossible.

While convinced gold couldn't be the basis of the modern monetary system, he concluded, "There can hardly be any doubt that the future evolution of the system will be linked to gold in some way or other."[4]

I agree. The link between form (gold) and meaning-content (money) cannot be broken despite what man does. There will be adverse effects whenever man and society attempt to separate inherent meaning from form.

Possessing "sound money" means having a medium of exchange that can't be taxed for capital gains. If, for example, one buys a one-ounce Gold Eagle coin for $1,000 and sells it at a future date for $1,800, the government will declare that one has experienced a capital gain that needs to be taxed.

The spread between the two does not manifest a gain but rather a drop in the buying power of the government-issued dollar bills, which are declared real money when they aren't.

I observed that this is what happened in Bolivia in the late 1950s. When schoolteachers were paid, they went to the streets begging us Americans to exchange our dollars for their Bolivian pesos. The purchasing power of the American dollar at that time was constant because it was linked to gold; the Bolivian peso was not. As each day passed, the Bolivian peso purchased less and less. The exchange rate eventually exceeded 10,000 Bolivian pesos to the dollar.

Modern states, for example, have defrauded the people by declaring their currency to be real money when it isn't. The currency we hold in our purses and wallets is "fiat" money. Deceived by the government, most people believe it to be real until it loses its purchasing power and no one wants it.

The point is this: Until 1971, the dollar represented something with inherent value. Not so today. No currency represents gold, a scarce commodity that has intrinsic value. Like every other nation, the American dollar is merely a "fiat currency," printed paper declared to be money. Instead of representing something with inherent value, namely gold, today it represents debt.

The effects of this national divergence from a "fixed" and constant standard are (a) "unpayable debt," an "external debt with interest that exceeds what the country's politicians think they can collect from taxpayers," and (b) a worldwide currency.

The Chácobo used what some economists call "commodity money" when they made a transaction. I thought this was amazing. A people group that could neither count to two nor understand a seven-day week and thought I had married my father's sister's daughter actually used "commodity money" when transacting among themselves. So what constitutes "commodity money"?

Alasdair MacLeod states:

> Just as there has been an attack on "sound words," there has also been an attack on sound money. They [central bankers] have been motivated to deny gold's fundamental role as sound money because it is superior to their unsound money.[5]

Instead, world governments and leaders declare that real money consists of banknotes in one's wallet and digital currency held by one's bank. The governments of the world have tricked us into thinking we possess real money when we don't. Real money is a commodity.

Today, world bankers maintain hoards of this yellow metal. But why are they holding it if it isn't real money? One would think that central bankers would use gold as currency because it is limited in quantity, difficult to obtain, fungible, and does not corrode. But for political reasons, they do not.

## COMMODITY, MONEY AND FREEDOM

To understand what commodity money is, one must know what the qualities of commodity money are.

Today's economic battle is over meaning. It is over the meaning of sound money versus declared-to-be money.

In the words of Charles Rist (1874 - 1955), a French economist: "We shall have sound money, or we shall cease to be free;"[6] and I would add: "We must have sound words to which inherent meanings are attached, or we shall cease to be free."

"Fiat" money

## CONVICTIONS

- Commodity money is limited in quantity. Toucan feathers were limited in quantity and difficult to obtain. The Chácobo accepted them as money.
- Commodity money must be durable. Toucan feathers do not rot or decay. While durable, they are not imperishable like gold, which fire can't destroy.
- Commodity money must be fungible. Toucan feathers were fungible; that is, a single toucan feather, in the eyes of the Chácobo, was of equal value to a toucan feather in someone else's basket. Likewise, a silver dollar in my pocket has the same value as the silver dollar in your pocket.
- Commodity money must be portable. Toucan feathers were portable. Because they were portable, they could be hidden, stolen, and used as a medium of exchange. Calvinist philosopher-historian Rousas John Rushdoony said, "Modern economics, by 'freeing' money from an objective norm and weight, has transferred rigidity and controls to man. The closer we get to purely fiat money, the more rigid and pervasive the controls."[7]

## CHAPTER 37
# THE PACAHUARA
### BOLIVIA

One of the dying tribes of the Bolivians was the Pacahuara. They lived a couple of hundred miles north of the Chácobo on the Rio Negro near the Brazilian border. They belonged to the same language group as the Chácobo, and that meant there was a good chance I could communicate with them.

We decided to contact them. Once contact was made, we would try to convince them that life would be better if they moved and began life with their linguistic cousins.

In July of 1969, when the rains had stopped, Perry Priest and I flew to the Brazilian town of Fortaleza and hired a boat captain familiar with the area to take us where he had seen them. We traveled a day up the Abuna River, on the border between Bolivia and Brazil, and then up the Rio Negro. After navigating through several heart-thumping rapids on the Rio Negro, we finally arrived where the river captain had seen them fishing.

After unloading our camping gear on the opposite side of the river, we crossed over to spy out the land, taking the captain with us. We only had to walk twenty feet when we came across a trail. We followed the trail inland for twenty minutes until we came to a barrier of palm leaves pulled across the path. The implied message was, "Go no further."

Hoping I could communicate with them speaking Chácobo, we walked around the barrier and continued inland. After following the trail for another twenty minutes, a pack of barking dogs broke the silence, followed by the appearance of a Pacahuara warrior armed with a bow and arrow—signaling us to leave.

I shouted back in Chácobo, "*Shina jiaxëni ca joni bo xo noa. Shishohi no joquë ra.*" (We're good guys. We come to visit.)

Seeing they were in no mood to entertain visitors, we left with their dogs growling behind us. In the morning, we broke camp and returned to Fortaleza. As we returned home the following day, we flew over the area to see if we could see some signs of life—a house, banana grove, or clearing. We could see nothing. They had no axes.

The following year, different families volunteered to camp on the opposite side of the river in hopes of drawing them out. Still, there was no response.

A year later, I took Caco Pistia, the first Chácobo Christian, Guy East, who was on the high school faculty, and my dog, Snoopy. This time, we set up camp on their side of the river. When Snoopy growled at night, we knew they were watching us. After camping for several weeks, we gave up.

Guy and Jeanne East, teachers at our missionary school, volunteered to take on the project. Guy, with the help of various support personnel members, cleared an acre of land and built a more permanent dwelling. Then they constructed a small house on the cleared land and planted manioc.

One morning, they noticed their axe for cutting firewood was missing. Someone had come into the camp at night and stole it.

Later, Lloyd Deister, our radio and computer tech operator, and I volunteered to spend time with Guy. To keep himself busy as we waited, Lloyd had brought a puzzle he said no one could solve. After a few days of trying, he handed it to me. After a morning of shuffling the pieces around, I handed him the puzzle back. To his surprise, I had solved it.

Then, one morning, when Guy and Lloyd were bathing at the river, the Pacahuara showed up. I blew my whistle to let them know we had company. Before I knew it, the male in the group was attempting to pry open the screen door to our outdoor kitchen with the axe he had stolen the week before. Speaking in Chácobo, which he understood to some degree, I told him to stop. I informed him that the axe he held was not his, and he should give it back. But he didn't, and I understood why.

They had watched us go in and out but had no idea there was a handle on the screen door you pulled to open it. In the meantime, his two wives were busy digging up the manioc Guy had planted the year before. As they were leaving, loaded with manioc and a few bananas Guy gave them, Guy indicated he wanted to go with them. They signaled that he was welcomed. I decided to tag along.

When we came to a small creek, the only way to cross was to walk across a fallen tree trunk. When it was my turn, Yaquë jumped up and down on the log, attempting to make me lose my balance and fall in. It didn't work, but the message was clear. I wasn't welcomed.

It must have been a temporary site when we arrived at their camp. There was only one shelter, which one would need to stoop down to enter. They invited Guy, and, of course, he declined.

As nightfall approached, Guy and I cut down some palm leaves on which to sleep and spent the night warding off the women who wanted to sleep next to us. It was a long night. Yaquë, we discovered, was the only male adult among them. They numbered ten.

At the break of dawn, I informed them that Guy and I were returning. They were happy to see me leave, but not Guy. Holding on to his arms, they signaled me to return alone. When I told them *"Ëmë cayamaquia rá"* (I'm not going alone), they finally released Guy, and we walked back to camp together. I was probably the tallest guy they had ever encountered. Lloyd welcomed us back with open arms. A few days later, the Pacahuara returned to our camp.

The idea of doing a translation for a tribe of ten people was out of the question. The obvious solution was to see if the Chácobo would adopt them. After conversing with the Chácobo by radio, they expressed, with the help of Caco, their willingness to live among them. The problem was how to get them there.

To make such a visit possible, Lloyd built a model airplane, which he held in his hand, and circled the clearing, indicating this would be the means of getting them there. The moment he landed the model, Yaquë picked it up and went through the same motions, and after landing the seaplane, he sat on it. What did that mean? We had no idea. Nevertheless, they agreed to move.

The following day, the three of us set off to cut out of the jungle an airstrip long enough for Bill Key to land his Helio Courier. After clearing the underbrush and cutting down the trees, I informed Yaquë that we were leaving but that we would return in a couple of months to set fire to the rubble, clear the debris, and level the land.

After a few weeks at *Tumi Chucua*, Marian and I, along with our two children, Laurel and Jim, flew to *Alto Ivon* to await the grand event. In the meantime, Guy mustered together a small team to finish the airstrip. This time, he took along his family.

When the day arrived for their flight to Alto Avon, most of the Chácobo tribe were there to welcome them to their new home. Uniting two tribes that were members of the Panoan family of languages would be a historic event.

They camped out a few feet from our house in the weeks ahead, where they constructed a small shelter. Then, one of "my kids," who had now become the de facto leader of the Chácobo, convinced them that they would be better off if they settled downstream from *Alto Ivon*. With his help, they moved. It took a little more than an hour to get there on foot.

Pacahuara move to Chácobo

## CONVICTIONS

- "Go therefore and make disciples of all the nations, baptizing them in the name of the Father and of the Son and of the Holy Spirit, teaching them to observe all that I have commanded you; and lo, I am with you always, *even* to the end of the age" Amen. (Matthew 28: 19-20).

# CHAPTER 38
# WAR AGAINST POSITIVE UNIVERSALS
## "ACQUIRED" VS "LEARNED"

Death of a Nuclear Family

When linguist Kenneth Pike penned the words, "A person may distort Innate Positive Universals into negative particular actions,"[1] he was addressing a problem common to all societies: The issue of what is real.

Is there another world beyond the phenomenal world, a world of Ideas (forms) familiar to all with real and constant attached Divine meanings?

Before Plato founded the first institute of higher learning in the Western world, Chinese philosophers living at the time of Abraham proposed, as documented by Wing-Tsit Chan:

> There existed a structure of unlearned innate knowledge ... rooted in the heart of all men, a knowledge which can be demonstrated by the fact that children all know how to love their parents, and that, when men suddenly fall into a well, a sense of mercy and alarm is inevitably aroused in their hearts.[2]

They called this unlearned Meta-Script "rooted in the hearts of all men," The Mandate of Heaven.

In other words, does the unconscious mind possess, as proposed by Plato in the Western World and Chinese sages in the Asian world, *a priori* ideas (forms) common to all to which inherent or Divine meanings are attached?

In addition, is there also structured in the unconscious mind a Universal-Lexicon containing these unlearned Universal ideas which contribute to the psychic unity of mankind?

As stated by Christian philosopher Gordon Clark, while "we cannot know the form without the content,"[3] when exactly, we must ask, were Universal forms and meaning-content linked together?

From a theistic perspective, when God created man in the "image and likeness of Himself," form and meaning-content were linked. The Divine meanings and Universal forms were "fixed at that precise moment."

The naturalists, as well as contextualizers, strongly disagree. In the words of contextualizing missiologist Charles Kraft, "meaning is the structuring of information in the minds [also known as brains] of people."[4]

French anthropologist Claude Lévi-Strauss wrote: "Language was born all at once ... a change has taken place, from a stage where nothing had meaning to a stage where everything has [meaning]."[5]

According to Lévi-Strauss, all that existed before language was "born" was invisible Universal "forms common to all" structured in the brain awaiting the precise moment when meanings imported from the outside would be attached to the appropriate forms.

At the moment when the appropriate forms and the particular meanings imported from the outside were magically connected, language, mind, selfhood, consciousness, and a particular worldview came into existence.

In the words of philosophy professor J. F. Moreland:

> Prior to this level of complexity, matter contained the potential for mind [as well as language and selfhood] to emerge—and at the right moment these potentials were activated, consciousness was

sparked into existence ... it is a view that matter is not just inert physical stuff, but that it also contains proto-mental states in it ... the world began not just with matter, but with stuff that is mental and physical at the same time.[6]

## REJECTION OF AN INNATE DIVINE UNIVERSAL-LEXICON

If Universal forms have "fixed" and constant meanings attached to them, it would imply the existence of a Divine Universal-Lexicon structured in the mind. However, it also intimates that these meanings could be "triggered" and brought to consciousness in a sociolinguistic situation. In this case, such meanings are "acquired" by every child rather than "learned."

The late American psychologist Jerome Brunner (1915 - 2016) supported this view. He stated:

> There exist "certain classes of meaning to which human beings are innately tuned and for which they actively search. Before language, these exist in primitive form as protolinguistic representations of the world whose full realization depends upon the cultural tool of language."[7]

When these meanings are brought to consciousness, the child will "actively begin searching" for the correct symbol to attach to the proper concept.

"Such [acquired] knowledge," according to Peter Carruthers, "will make its appearance at some particular stage in normal cognitive development."[8]

As linguist researcher Melissa Bowerman (1942 - 2011) elaborates, "The child is now commonly viewed as coming to the language-learning task well equipped with a basic stock of concepts."[9]

So instead of Divine meanings being attached to Universal forms when Adam, the first man, was formed in his Creator's image, for the naturalist, the meanings must first be created by social existence. After coming into existence, these created meanings, according to Lévi-Strauss and Kraft, are imported to the mind-brain where they are attached to the correct form. The brain contains proto-mental forms or ideas which lack meaning-content.

However, one must ask, how is this possible? To believe that before language and culture were "born," inert matter called the "brain" contained empty mental forms or concepts awaiting the day they would be filled with the appropriate meaning-content, that implies a belief in the powers of magic and Natural Selection.

In the beginning ...

## CONVICTIONS

- If meanings "belong to the people," as Kraft promotes, then no word has a constant "true" meaning. Verbal inspiration is a theological myth.
- Since innate knowledge of meanings attached to forms common to all people is not "learned" but "acquired," the acquisition of this knowledge begins when the child is exposed to the relevant stimuli in a linguistic-social

environment in which the child is searching for the correct symbol to attach to the form.
- Universal forms having positive meanings promote order.
- Forms having meanings that "belong to the people" increase disorder and illogical thinking.

## CHAPTER 39
# ETIC DIVERGENCE
### REJECTING THE DIVINE PLAN

As previously documented, the Chácobo restructured the nuclear family at some point in their history. From the perspective of a concept-innatist, they replaced the *husband-wife* dyad with that of mother-daughter. In effect, they replaced a Positive Universal with a negative particular, which, according to the Apostle Paul, "sneaked in," having no primary place in the Divine Plan (Romans 5:20).[1]

My perspective as a concept-innatist is supported by Chácobo sages who created stories like the *Dying Raisi* (chapter 8) and *The Story of Pai as a Raisi and Escaping Mother-in-Law Control* (chapter 4, "Chácobo Satire") informing their fellow tribespeople that turning the Chácobo cultural operating system over to mothers-in-law was a bad idea. Their warnings were ignored.

But the existence of such stories implies the existence of innate mental knowledge. This means, for example, that a representation of the nuclear family structured in the unconscious mind can be "triggered" and brought to consciousness.

Sadly, missiologists reject the existence of such innate knowledge, telling us we "must accept and work within structures and processes of others that are different from one's own social game."[2]

I faced these pressures when attending an SIL Community Development Seminar in Quito, Ecuador. The structures I was encouraged to accept and work with were the same structures Chácobo sages of another era had condemned. Their message was that no form has an inherent meaning.

But if no form has an inherent meaning and if all meanings "belong to the people," then humankind has no transcendent standard for judging the behavior of madmen like Stalin, Hitler, and Mao, and the Bible is not the Word of God.

When the Chácobo replaced the *husband-wife* dyad with that of mother-daughter, we have an example of a society replacing a Positive Innate Universal with a negative particular. What "sneaked into" history that had "no place in the Divine Plan" were forms that emphasized biological relationships over bilateral and covenantal.

Romans 5:20 says, "Moreover, the law entered that the offense might abound. But when sin abounded, grace abounded much more."

Instead of accepting the covenantal one-flesh principle of *husband-wife* as the dominant dyad of the nuclear family, what "sneaked in" were biological forms that separated husbands from their wives and wives from their husbands. What replaced the *husband-wife* dyad for the Chácobo was that of mother-daughter.

Throughout the world, the covenantal one-flesh principle of *husband-wife* stated in Genesis 2:23-24 has been replaced by a biological dyad selected by material forces described by the Apostle Paul as the "elemental forces of the world." He warned the philosophically-minded Greeks to:

> *Beware lest anyone cheat you through philosophy and empty deceit, according to the tradition of men, according to the basic principles of the world, and not according to Christ. (Colossians 2:8)*

One such philosophy, promoted by the late Mao Zedong, based its theory on "the elemental forces of the world." When asked where correct ideas come from, he answered: "They come from social practice, and from it alone ... it is man's social being that determines his thinking."[3]

He was parroting and echoing the sentiments of Karl Marx. In answering the same question, the late anthropologist Marvin Harris wrote, "When infrastructural conditions are ripe, they will occur, not once, but again and again."[4]

According to Harris, appropriate ideas will arise when the "elementary forces of the world" coalesce and produce correct thinking. But whenever such need-based ideas arise in the collective mind, the Apostle Paul says they aren't based on Christ, but "having a form of godliness but denying its power. And from such people turn away" (II Timothy 3:5)!

In answering the same question, where do correct ideas come from, the late anthropologist Marvin Mayers, an evangelical Christian, declared that correct ideas come from "culture."

> Culture can be defined in hundreds of ways, but the point is that every thought a person thinks, every hope he has, every step he takes, every belief he holds, and every interaction he takes is controlled by his culture. Every move he makes is programmed into him by his culture.[5]

While it is true that culture shapes human life and can give meaning to human existence, man's behavior need not "be controlled by his culture." The Word of God warns believers to be aware of that happening:

> *And do not be conformed to this world [culture], but be transformed by the renewing of your mind, that you may prove what is that good and acceptable and perfect will of God. (Romans 12:2)*

For Mayers, a former member of Wycliffe Bible Translators, his interpretative system excluded innate knowledge. Mayers reduced man to a programmed robot, declaring, "Every move he makes is programmed into him by his culture."[6]

Pike called such rejection of absolutes *etic* divergence.

Then, there is the interpretative perspective of evangelical anthropologist Charles Kraft: "Each cultural analyst must ask, does the cultural form in question 'fit' the environment, and does it adequately satisfy a need?"[7]

One of the primary forces that shape the behavior and type of social structure a society constructs is that of needs. The types of needs humanity seeks to satisfy are endless. The Chácobo's basic needs were (1) a daily supply of manioc beer and (2) a daily supply of food.

The cultural forms they created to satisfy these primary needs were "adequate," but they were forms that suppressed human freedom. They were forms that demanded Rabi and Carmelo give up their roles as bilingual schoolteachers.

However, for Kraft, "There are no such things as an absolute set of cultural forms … that would imply the existence of some absolute cultural structure and is so misleading that they must be abandoned."[8]

According to Kraft, what must be abandoned is:

The conviction that the nuclear family "is the simplest and smallest unit of society and the real foundation of culture."[9]

The conviction that the status positions of mother, father, brother, sister, son, and daughter are mutually exclusive and that their meanings are "fixed" and absolute.

The idea that "knowledge of the good is innate since man is born to know and practice good … the chief duty of man … consists in loving the people."[10]

CREATED IN THE IMAGE OF GOD

*Husband-Wife* "one flesh"

## CONVICTIONS

- *Etic* divergence describes how Divine meanings attached to forms common to all are rejected and replaced with meanings shaped by the "elemental forces of the world," and they have "no place in the Divine Plan."
- As Dooyeweerd noted, "As soon as the symbolic respect for the husband as head of the community is lost in the internal marital union, we are confronted with a subjective infringement of the internal law of marriage." [11]
- When "respect for the Chácobo husband as head of the community was lost," the Chácobo became a leaderless, goalless, dying society. The internal law of marriage was infringed upon when their law-way of doing things, which they call their *jabi*, prohibited a married couple from leaving the father and mother (Genesis 2:24) and setting up an independent household.
- Diverging from God's standard, the Chácobo changed the structure of the nuclear family. First, they replaced the

dominant dyad of *husband-wife* with that of mother-daughter; and, second, they merged the mutually exclusive status positions of parallel cousins and siblings.
- Merging mutually exclusive status positions is a declaration of war against the Author of Meanings.

## CHAPTER 40
# THE RIGHT TIME
### THE CHÁCOBO OF BOLIVIA, THE IÑUPIAT ESKIMOS OF ALASKA, AND THE SHARANAHUA OF PERU

### HOUSEHOLD-OF-FIVE AMONG THE CHÁCOBO

During our second term (1962 - 1967), I discovered that biblical Israel and the Chácobo had similar family constructs. Each family or household had five members. My awareness of the similarities began when I had to translate two specific passages in the Gospels, Matthew 10:34-36 and Luke 12:51-53:

> "Do not think that I have come to bring peace on earth; I have not come to bring peace, but a sword.
> For I have come to set a man against his father, and a daughter against her mother, and a daughter-in-law against her mother-in-law;
> and a man's foes will be those of his own household"
> (Matthew 10:34-36, RSV).

> "Do you think that I have come to give peace on earth? No, I tell you, but rather division;

*for henceforth in one house there will be five divided, three against two and two against three;*
*they will be divided, father against son and son against father, mother against daughter and daughter against her mother, mother-in-law against her daughter-in-law and daughter-in-law against her mother-in-law" (Luke 12:51-53, RSV).*

I noticed the fifth member of the Jewish household-of-five was the incoming daughter-in-law; for the Chácobo, it was the incoming son-in-law. Having read Francis L. K. Hsu's hypothesis that all cultural lifeways are tethered to one of eight dyads, seven of which are biological and the eighth one being covenantal, it was obvious that the Jewish family was tethered to the dominant, biological dyad of father-son.

Unlike the weak father-son dyad of the Nyakyusa, which linked only three families together, the Jewish father-son dyad linked a limitless number of families together using a type of patrilocal residence rule.

A patrilocal residence rule sets up a social system where married couples live in the household of the husband's parents or somewhere nearby. The Nyakyusa rejected this rule.

In the context of biblical times, it was because of this patrilocal residence rule that Jewish fathers intentionally kept their sons at home.

The practice, however, violated the Universal as stated in Genesis 2:24 and Ephesians 5:31, namely, a "son should leave father and mother" at marriage.

*Therefore a man shall leave his father and mother and be joined to his wife, and they shall become one flesh. (Genesis 2:24)*

> For this reason, a man shall leave his father and mother and be joined to his wife, and the two shall become one flesh. *(Ephesians 5:31)*

Jewish society, for reasons of insecurity, replaced the Universal with a patrilocal residence rule grounded in environmental "fitness."

The new rule: Because fathers need sons to tend the flocks, mend nets, and support the family business, sons remain home after marriage, and daughters-in-law move in.

In the Amazonian Rainforest, where the ecology was different, the Chácobo rule was that daughters remain home after marriage to help their mothers make the manioc beer. Their husbands move in to supply the family with food.

A Jewish father traditionally kept his son home. Jacob, for example, kept ten of his sons at home. Two sons left, Judah and Joseph. Joseph was sold into slavery, and Judah left on his own accord Genesis 38:1 (NLT): "About this time, Judah left home [father and mother] and moved to Adullam, where he stayed with a man named Hiram."

Neither Jacob nor Joseph would have become great leaders if they had remained home.[1]

The same residential principle was held in New Testament times. When Jesus told James and John, who were mending fishing nets with their father to "Follow me, and I will make you fishers of men" (Matthew 4:19), Jesus was bringing a "sword" to the traditional Jewish household-of-five.

To leave one's father meant a rejection of a cultural norm upon which the entire Jewish lifeway had been tethered for over two thousand years.

Their response to the words of Jesus broke the Jewish norm of what it meant to be a good Jewish son. "They immediately left *their* [father and his] nets and followed Him" (Matthew 4:20).

If James and John had been raised as Chácobo sons rather than

Jewish sons, leaving "immediately" would have presented no problem. All Chácobo sons eventually left home. One Chácobo family was shocked when they discovered their teenage son had secretly left and run off to a village on the Yata River where he married and took on the status position of *raisi*.

Their son was not breaking any norm of society. What Jesus asked James and John to do was revolutionary. He declared that the patrilocal residential rule that shaped Jewish society fundamentally opposed His purposes.

∽

## HOUSEHOLD-OF-FIVE IN THE OLD TESTAMENT

Seven hundred years before Jesus arrived on the scene, Yahweh, through Micah, proclaimed that the "sword" was coming to the traditional Jewish household-of-five which was foundational to Jewish society. All the worldly goods each household-of-five had accumulated during the economic boom years, Yahweh declared, "I will give over to the sword [i.e., their enemy, the Assyrians]" (Micah 6:14).

The Jewish family was reshaped under the hands of the Assyrians (734 - 732 B.C.). It was when no consanguineal or affinal relationships could be trusted. According to Micah 7:6 (New Living Translation), it was a time when:

> ... the son despises his father.
> The daughter defies her mother.
> The daughter-in-law defies her mother-in-law.
> Your enemies are right in your own household!

What surprised me was that no Bible commentator questioned the validity of the Jewish household-of-five. No commentator pointed out that when Jesus said, "Come, follow me," He was asking

James and John to violate a cultural rule that could be stated as: "Fishermen fathers need sons to mend the nets, bring in the catch, and carry on the business, so sons must remain home after marriage."

All commentators assume that the Jewish household-of-five is a valid form of "family." Jesus did not, and neither do I.

At the end of our second missionary term in Bolivia, I seriously questioned the validity of such family structures. I visited a Christian bookstore in Chicago when we were home on our second furlough. I saw two volumes of *A New Critique of Theoretical Thought* by Christian philosopher Herman Dooyeweerd.

Since Dooyeweerd addressed issues like the structure of marriage, family, and society, I bought the set, thinking it might be helpful. While struggling with Dooyeweerd's terminology and concepts, I found the following statement about the Creation order significant. He wrote:

> According to the order of creation, marriage pre-supposes that man takes his life companion in an inter-individual societal relation, and not based on any blood-relationship so the conjugal bond might be formed. The view that the natural family and kinship community, founded in blood-relationship, had entirely absorbed temporal existence at least in the first generation of mankind, not only lacks a biblical foundation but is fundamentally contrary to the Scripture.[2]

I understand Dooyeweerd's comments to mean the following: The one-flesh principle stated in the Creation Mandate was not to be based on a "blood-relationship" like that of father-son [Jewish] or mother-daughter [Chácobo].

I agree. If it were, then its dominance would destroy the "interindividual" nature of the marital bond or the one-flesh principle of husband and wife. The result would be a new kind of family, a family which would absorb into itself the nuclear family.

This is what happened to Israel and the Chácobo. For economic and security reasons, the household-of-five had replaced the nuclear family. In doing so, it set limits on human freedom. As a cultural form, it would also constrain evangelism and church growth.

If the nuclear family was to be foundational to a society's cultural operating system, then the natural family demanded that the one-flesh principle be manifested in a dominant *husband-wife* bond of spirit and mind:

> *For this reason, a man shall leave his father and his mother, and be joined to his wife; and they shall become one flesh. (Genesis 2:24, NASB)*

For Dooyeweerd, there existed an internal law structure to marriage that was opposed to "marriages contracted from utilitarian motives."[3]

Interestingly, Chácobo satirists understood that the "inter-individual" nature of the conjugal bond was suppressed and created satire pointing out that it needed restoration.

Among the Sharanahua and Chácobo, the function of marriage was to acquire sons-in-law who would meet the survival needs of a mechanized kind of family grounded in ascribed functions. Likewise, Jacob and Zebedee kept their sons at home to help with the family business. What is significant about leaving one's natal home is that those who left their father and mother all became great leaders; namely, Joseph, Jacob, James, and John.

I eventually concluded that neither the traditional Jewish nor Chácobo household structures were valid. Neither allowed the one-flesh principle of *husband-wife* to become a reality. Jesus said to them:

> *"Have you not read that He who made* them *at the beginning* 'made them male [husband] and female [wife],'

> *"and said, 'For this reason a man shall leave his father and mother and be joined to his wife, and the two shall become one flesh'?*
> *So then, they are no longer two but one flesh. Therefore what God has joined together, let not man separate"* (Matthew 19:4-6).

They had surrendered to environmental pressures that shaped the internal structure of the nuclear family, replacing the covenantal with the biological. Israel was guilty—"They do not know the LORD's laws" (Jeremiah 8:7b, NLT).

∼

## THE MEANING OF SWORD

Lastly, I questioned what Jesus meant when He said He would bring the "sword" to the household-of-five. Did the "sword" symbolize an effect like war, conflict, or division? "Do *you* suppose that I came to give peace on earth? I tell you, not at all, but rather division" (Luke 12:51).

Or, was it a symbol of some compelling force like the Assyrian army of Micah's day: "You shall eat, but not be satisfied; Hunger *shall be* in your midst" (Micah 6:14).

Or an instrument like: "... the sword of the Spirit which is the word of God" (Ephesians 6:17b).

When, for example, Chácobo satirists of another era advocated a return to the Universal one-flesh principle of *husband-wife*, was not this the "Word of God" speaking?

When Jesus told James and John, "Follow me," was he not bringing the "sword" to the traditional Jewish household-of-five?

The Chácobo satirists' satire did not destroy a social construct tethered to the mother-daughter dyad. Its dominance continued until about 1965 when outside social and economic forces began to compel the Chácobo to replace biological and functional material cultural forms shaped by the environment with covenantal forms that promoted freedom.

The first challenge for reform came from married bilingual schoolteachers that SIL had trained without knowing that the new status position of village schoolteacher that we had created was in fundamental opposition to the ascribed function of being a *raisi* (Chácobo son-in-law).

While the Chácobo *raisi*-based lifeway satisfied their need for food, manioc beer, and security in the Amazonian Rainforest, it also rendered the Chácobo leaderless, incapable of resisting the pressures of the new world economic order that was pressing closer each day.

The Chácobo socio-economic operating system shaped by the environment had put power into the hands of women who did not have the authority to issue verbal directives. Nevertheless, directives were issued. They disguised them as desires and complaints.

But not so with the Jewish household-of-five. Fathers and husbands controlled wives, sons, daughters, and daughters-in-law in such households. Unlike the Nyakyusa of Tanzania and Malawi, the father-son dyad's dominance promoted an autocratic, authoritarian, inflexible family leadership style, which no Chácobo would tolerate.

The leadership style that reigned in Bolivia and throughout the Amazonian Rainforest was called the "patron" system. In such a system, the rubber tappers are tied to patrons by debt peonage.

In exchange for using a stand of rubber trees, the tappers buy the industrialized goods necessary for the process. At the end of the season, they must sell any rubber produced to the patron. The amount earned by the rubber tapper is usually less than the debt owed to the patron, resulting in permanent indebtedness.[4]

There existed no way for these rubber tappers to file bankruptcy and have their debt erased. Like the present world order, they were locked into permanent indebtedness. When the Chácobo fled their ranch patrons, they were in debt. If not, why were they hiding on the Benicito River when we arrived?

Surrounded by expanding political and economic forces, I now asked: Had the "appropriate time arrived" in history for the Chácobo to be redeemed not only from an operating system that had enslaved them but also from an external, foreign, cultural operating system grounded in "permanent indebtedness"?

Just as Isaiah spoke of a "right time" when Yahweh would act, I now believe Marian and I had arrived at the "right time."

In this regard, the Apostle Paul notes in Galatians 4:4-6:

> *But when the fullness of the time had come, God sent forth*
> *His Son, born of a woman, born under the law,*
> *to redeem those who were under the law, that we might*
> *receive the adoption as sons.*
> *And because you are sons, God has sent forth the Spirit of*
> *His Son into your hearts, crying out, "Abba, Father."*

What were some of the "right time" features for Jesus to come? The Bible tells us that the nation of Israel expected a Liberator, a Savior, a Messiah to deliver them from the oppressive Roman rule. Luke 3:15 tell us "the people were in expectation, and all reasoned in their hearts about John, whether he was the Christ *or* not ..."

Throughout the Roman Empire, there were Jewish synagogues. When the Gospel spread via those synagogues, they served as one of God's instruments in bringing the Gospel to the ends of the earth.

When the Apostle Paul entered a new Roman city, he immediately went to the Jewish synagogue where he preached the Kingdom of God. But then a time would come when, in the words of Jesus:

> *"They will put you [followers of me] out of the synagogues;*
> *yes, the time is coming that whoever kills you will*
> *think that he offers God service" (John 16:2).*

When Jesus commissioned His disciples to: "Go therefore and make disciples of all the nations (Matthew 28:19a)," a network of roads crisscrossed the empire, and a common lingua franca made the first stage of this evangelistic process possible.

The Apostle Paul intended to use the network of roads to walk from Rome to Spain, for he wrote to the church in Rome:

> *But now no longer having a place in these parts, and having a great desire these many years to come to you, whenever I journey to Spain, I shall come to you. For I hope to see you on my journey, and to be helped on my way there by you, if first I may enjoy your company for a while"* (Romans 15:23-24).

## CENTURIES LATER

Taking the Gospel to the ends of the earth would require more than roads. It would require steamships, planes, radios, jeeps, trucks, Bible translators, linguists, pilots, ham radio techs, satellites, TVs, and the worldwide web.

Reaching the Chácobo in their mother tongue in the 1950s necessitated that Marian and I learn skills that would enable us to reduce a language to written form, entailing uncovering the rules of complex grammar.

In addition, we needed transportation in and out of the tribe by JAARS (Jungle Aviation and Radio Service). The nearest road was hundreds of miles away. JAARS radio technician, Lloyd Deister, supplied us with our first two-way radio which we set up on the corner of our porch.

The Center provided us with a means for communicating daily. It meant they could fly us out quickly if an emergency arose. If JAARS didn't exist, the task would have been far too difficult for us to accomplish.

## A "RIGHT TIME" FOR THE IÑUPIAT ESKIMOS OF ALASKA, THE SHARANAHUA, AND THE CHÁCOBO

According to anthropologist Ernest Burch (1938 - 2010), "In 1890, there probably was not a single Christian Iñupiat (sing.) Eskimo. Twenty years later, there was scarcely an Iñupiat who was not a Christian."

On the surface, the success of this cultural transformation could be attributed to a saturation of various missionary agencies that inundated the vast area. First came Mission Covenant missionaries from Sweden in 1887. In 1890 the Congregationalists, Episcopalians, and Presbyterians arrived. Later came the Friends (Quakers).

Burch writes, "The transformation of the Artic Iñupiat population from zero to nearly 100 percent Christian in less than a generation requires an explanation."[5] Burch's explanation may surprise missionaries who subscribe to the doctrine of social-cultural adequacy.

Before missionaries arrived, cultural forms damaging to evangelism and church growth were upset, scuttled, and abandoned. Had the "right time" come?

Burch writes: "Part of my explanation of prompt conversion in Arctic Alaska is that *the time was right*" [Emphasis added].[6] His explanation is similar to the Apostle Paul's statement in Galatians 4:4-5 (International Standard Version):

> *But when the appropriate time had come, God sent his Son, born by a woman, born under the Law, in order to redeem those who were under the Law, and thus to adopt them as his children.*

Likewise, when the "appropriate time had come," God sent

messengers of the Good News to the Iñupiat, who gladly received the message.

According to Burch, "If the missionaries had appeared 50 or 100 years earlier, they would have been either driven out or killed."[7]

In our case, if the Chácobo were to be reached, it had to be in their language, which meant Marian and I had to study linguistics. In addition, some means other than river travel had to enable us to live among them for twenty-five years.

In 1934, SIL International (then known as the Summer Institute of Linguistics) came into being as a summer training program with only two students attending.

The course was repeated in 1935 with five students. Among these students was Kenneth L. Pike, who eventually became the first president of SIL. If SIL and WBT as institutions had not come on the scene, there would have been no training program for the indigenous tribes of Bolivia to prepare them for the future.

Any attempt to evangelize the Iñupiat would have probably failed before 1850. To understand why they would have been driven out or killed, one must understand how the Iñupiat socio-economic operating system functioned around 1850.

What happened to the Iñupiat between 1850 and 1890 is comparable to what happened to some of the Panoan tribes in Brazil and Peru from 1879 to 1912. Those living in rubber-rich areas became victims of a thirty-three-year rubber boom that swept across Amazonia.[8]

Margarethe Sparing-Chávez shares in her book, *People of Peru*, how the Amazonian basin changed. The boom resulted in a large expansion of European colonization in the area, attracting immigrant workers, generating wealth, and causing cultural and social transformations.

Rubber hunters along the main rivers of Brazil conscripted natives for labor. In some instances, they even attempted to capture and enslave them.

The Sharanahua resisted and fought back, not only to defend

themselves but also to avenge their deaths and to obtain some of the goods the intruders possessed, such as knives, machetes, and firearms.

The Sharanahua say they were numerous when living in Brazil [before migrating to Peru]. Still, the cruel treatment of the intruders and exposure to many diseases at the time of the rubber boom depleted their numbers.[9]

During the first half of the 20th century, experts estimate over 50 percent of the group died from measles, flu, yellow fever, whooping cough, tuberculous, and other diseases which raged through the area for decades.[10]

Compare this with the environmental pressures the Iñupiat experienced between 1850 and 1880. According to anthropologist Ernest Burch, "the ecological foundations of the traditional social systems in Arctic Alaska were largely destroyed. While American whalers drastically reduced the bowhead whale and walrus populations, the Iñupiat all but exterminated the caribou population, and epidemic diseases were introduced."[11]

The result was the decimation of the human population. Population loss, in turn, destroyed the political basis of the traditional social system because the several societies that comprised it no longer had enough members for collective self-defense.

Because of these developments, which were particularly acute in the early 1880s, the first missionaries arrived among people in extremis, people whose traditions, beliefs, and practices failed them. Given those circumstances, they must have been more willing to consider alternatives to their traditional beliefs than they had ever been.

In 1958, the time was ripe for Gene and Marie Scott, married at our SIL Center in Bolivia, to settle among the Sharanahua. Like Marian and I, they discovered the rules of Sharanahua grammar, made an alphabet, created primers, trained a core of Sharanahua individuals to become approved school teachers by the Peruvian government, and finally, they translated the Word of God into the Sharanahua language.

The New Testament was dedicated in 1996. Today, several villages have a congregation of believers led by Sharanahua pastors.

The right time to receive the Gospel

## CONVICTIONS

- Without the services of WBT, SIL, and JAARS, the above life-transforming events would have never happened.

# CHAPTER 41
# IÑUPIAT ESKIMOS
## ALASKA AND ARCTIC SLOPE

The Iñupiat crossed the Bearing Straits into North America around 1000 BC. Also known as the "authentic people," they settled in Northwest Alaska. Today, they number around 9,300.

Instead of breaking into distinct tribal groups like the Panoan (Chácobo, Shipibo, Conibo, Cashibo, Marubo, Sharanahua, Chitonahua, Yaminahua, and Pacahuara), the Iñupiat Eskimos split into twenty different "societies," each one speaking a different dialect of the same language. The tribes were identified by the particular region in which they lived—Colville River, Upper Noatak, King Island, etc.

From the Bearing Straits in the West, crossing over 3,400 miles to Greenland in the East, 10,050 Iñupiat Eskimos resided. What happened in 1850 that made them ripe for missionaries to share the Good News?

Before the missionaries arrived, I would suggest that new forms "written on the heart" replaced social forms that their environment had shaped. In this case, the acceptance of "new wineskins" preceded Christianity.

Because they lived in small, isolated villages, survival depended on the kinsmen who lived close by and whom one could count on for support. Traveling outside of one's kinsmen's territorial sphere, represented by the various territorial shapes of each band, was like entering enemy territory, even though one could communicate with them.

## THE PRIMARY DISTRIBUTION OF IÑUPIAT SOCIETIES

A feature of these 20 bands is they were all endogamous. That is, they didn't "marry out" of their territorial group of 200 to 900 individuals.

While Chácobo villages were separated by territorial space in the Amazonian Rainforest, they were not enemies. A Chácobo could walk into another Chácobo village, where he had no kin, and they would welcome and help him in his time of need.

They knew that being "human" meant helping each other, a principle stated in the *Myth of Nahuapaxahua* (chapter 2, "Discovering an Innate Moral Imperative"). Not so for the Iñupiat Eskimos living in Northwest Alaska. The rule of helping non-kin in need had been suppressed. Killing one's non-kin meant more food for one's family and kin.

For the Chácobo, their desire for manioc beer shaped their cultural operating system. For the Sharanahua, it was wild game. For the Iñupiat, it was the scarcity of food that shaped, to a large degree, their sociocultural operating system. Anthropologist Norman A. Chance describes the seasonal availability of food as follows:

> Inter-territorial hostilities closely followed the seasonal round of subsistence activities. They observed a truce from late spring through the fall. This coincided with the period of greatest productivity and most extensive inter-territorial trading.

Then, in late fall, hostilities commenced when darkness began setting in. Any stranger observed in a given territory at this time was assumed to be either a spy or a member of an opposing group of warriors unless proven otherwise. Exceptions included journeys to or from a Messenger Feast, a ceremonial gathering, or local families from different localities whose leaders were either trading partners or linked by co-marriage. Strangers who could not provide such justification were beaten or killed.[1]

According to anthropologist Ernest Burch, a person without multiple spouses, sons, and daughters was considered to be "a social freak toward whom the other members of society had no acceptable way of behaving."[2]

The classic case is that of a seal hunter who accidentally went adrift on the sea due to wind and current action. If conditions were unfavorable, he might drift for days, weeks, or even months before returning to shore again, if he did at all, and his landfall might be tens or hundreds of miles from his home.

If he landed near a village (as often happened since drifting ice frequently runs aground near points where larger villages are located) and was observed by one of its inhabitants, he was in trouble.

Psychiatrist Silvano Arieti shares: "Unless he could identify himself—which to the Eskimo meant proving he was [biologically] related to people known by the inquisitors—he was probably beaten to death in short order."[3]

His crime? Stealing their seals.

To increase the size of the social world in which one could safely operate, he needed a more extensive network of family members, and therein lies the missiological problem. How does one increase the size of the area in which one can travel, hunt, fish, trade, and share the Good News across "fixed" territorial boundaries if one doesn't have family members living in those territories? Should appropriate evangelism and church planting be determined by how well a cultural form "fits" the environment and satisfies a need?

Under the pressures of an ecologic, economic, and social environment charged with food scarcity, they created an unusual functional, cultural form or custom called *italiuqtuq,* designed to satisfy the need for inter-territorial communication and hunting rights. Its function was to connect a single individual across territorial borders in a society in which he had no family members.

This cultural form, *italiuqtuq,* literally means "to make (someone) a relative [i.e., family member] through a voluntary act," in the same way one makes a house or makes an item of clothing.

"Through the act, a man and woman become spouses, and any children either of them ever had before or after become siblings. [For the Iñupiat Eskimos], sexual intercourse was the only way that kinship could be extended."[4]

The way the Iñupiat increased the size of their family was very innovative. Why didn't they classify fathers' brothers and their male parallel cousins as fathers like the Nyakyusa of Tanzania? Or classify all parallel and cross-cousins as siblings like the Apache did? This is how nearly every society on earth increases its family size, but they chose not to.

I would suggest they were very rational people. They chose not to violate the Laws of Logic. They clearly understood the Law of Non-Contradiction and refused to merge and classify cousins as brothers and sisters, for example. For them, as well as for Americans, a cousin is not a sibling. The concepts were mutually exclusive and should not be merged to satisfy a need.

So instead of expanding the size of their family by classifying uncles and aunts as fathers and mothers, nephews and nieces as brothers and sisters, and the children of nephews and nieces as sons and daughters as many other tribes in the world have done, they chose instead to do so through sexual intercourse and co-spouses. Of course, they produced half-brothers and half-sisters that shared only one parent.

Like the rest of humankind, they faced the same needs for food, shelter, and security but responded in a different but rational way. The Iñupiat, unlike the tribes that surrounded them, refused to violate the Law of Non-Contradiction. They simply refused to merge A (siblings) with B (cousins), thereby rejecting the classificatory kinship system used by many other societies. In doing so, they refused to think paleologically.

According to psychologist Silvano Arieti (1914 - 1981):

> A world paleologically-interpreted corresponds in many ways to the mythical world of ancient people and many cultural repertories of various aboriginal societies today ... and some anthropologists have at various times reported that in some aboriginal cultures, paleo-logic thinking prevails over other types, and that, in general, it is much more common in primitive societies than in Western cultures. A life regulated according to paleologic thinking is not sufficiently equipped to deal with reality.[5]

Many who subscribe to a bottom-up, outside-in approach to concept formation assume that before the Law of Non-Contradiction, primitive man thought paleologically. That is, he used faulty logic.

He believed, for example, that just because A, a son-in-law, shared a property with B, a jaguar, then A and B are considered to be identical.

For the Sharanahua of Peru, a son-in-law could be a dangerous jaguar appearing in human form because they shared a common predicate. Both hunted for the same game: wild pigs, tapirs, deer, monkeys, etc.

By refusing to merge the concepts of siblings and cousins because they shared the same predicate, namely, the same grandparents, the Iñupiat were equipped to deal with reality logically. However, even though they could think logically, they nevertheless, like the Romans, chose "to suppress the truth by their immoral living" (Romans 1:18, GOD'S WORD Translation).

Through sexual intercourse with a spouse from another territory, they created a biological linkage between hostile communities. Its function was to increase one's chances for survival in a dangerous world where food could be scarce and non-kin could not be trusted. The goal in life was to survive, and to survive, one needed family members.

One can only trust family members. A covenantal relationship with a non-kin is suspect and can't be trusted. Regardless of what missionaries and governmental officials thought about *italiuqtuq*, such sexual activity was not motivated by lust. According to anthropologist Ernest Burch, "In the chaotic circumstances of the time, this was not promiscuity but a rational means for dealing with a difficult situation."[6] The cultural form of *italiuqtuq* satisfied a need.

Instead of creating family members by the classificatory method, which meant rejecting the Laws of Logic, the Iñupiat chose to do so biologically, creating, not fiat or "declared to be" sons, daughters, brothers, sisters, fathers, and mothers, but actual biological sons and daughters, brother and sisters, and fathers and mothers whose moral duty was to aid each other in time of trouble.

When entering hostile territory, one could say, "So and so is bone of my bone and flesh of my flesh." But for those who subscribe to the doctrine of sociocultural adequacy, the custom of *italiuqtuq* presents a serious missiological problem.

Is the custom of *italiuqtuq*, which clearly satisfied a need for food, shelter, security, and interaction with outsiders, the kind of cultural form God would want missionaries to use in evangelism and church planting?

∼

It appears the time had come for the "sword" of ecological and economic pressures to destroy a lifeway that was inimical, ill-disposed, and hostile to both the Gospel and the Creation Mandate, which the Chinese called The Mandate of Heaven. Anthropologist Ernest Burch explained why the Iñupiat were receptive to the Gospel: the time was right. Some of the key events that preceded the reception of the Gospel by the Iñupiat, as suggested by anthropologist Ernest Burch, were:

- The ecological foundations [that shaped] the traditional social systems in Arctic Alaska were largely destroyed. American whalers drastically reduced the bowhead whale and walrus populations, the Inupiat all but exterminated the caribou population, and visitors introduced epidemic diseases. The result was the decimation of the human population. Population loss, in turn, destroyed the political basis of the traditional social system because the several societies that comprised it no longer had enough members for collective self-defense.
- Because these developments were particularly acute in the early 1880s, the first missionaries arrived among people in extremis, people whose traditional beliefs and practices had failed them. Given those circumstances, they must have been more willing to consider alternatives to their traditional beliefs than they ever had been previously.[7]

During this time of stress, when the world around them was collapsing, what perhaps confused the Iñupiat the most was the irrational behavior of the "white" missionaries who came into the territory. It was obvious to them that "the welfare of natives was a major concern; the Iñupiat had never seen that before."[8]

According to their belief system, non-kin were not to be concerned about the welfare of non-kin. Yet, these non-kin missionaries wanted to help them in their time of need.

The same is true wherever the Gospel is preached. The initial contact the Chácobo had with the outside world was with the patron system, which they did not understand. As a different kind of *carayana* (rubber-collecting people), we were soon addressed as *Cai* (mom) and *Papa* (father). It was obvious to them that we were not concerned about *carama* (rubber) but rather their welfare.

A significant challenge was how they related to nature. The Iñupiat were animists. They believed everything in nature, personal and impersonal, had a spirit. Every rock, tree, stream, animal, bird, and human being had a spirit.

In this regard, missionaries who disparaged and ridiculed those holding such beliefs were less successful than native converts who "simply declared them to be agents of the devil. This made them evil, but also vulnerable to Christianity."[9]

While missionaries and native evangelists believed Yahweh transcended nature, a difference surfaced. The idea that evil spirits could animate things, as put forth by native evangelists, made it possible for the Iñupiat to become Christians without altogether abandoning their view that spirits can inhabit nature.

Moses records an unusual spirit-filled, naturalistic event from his life in Exodus 3:2-5:

> *And the Angel of the LORD appeared to him in a flame of fire from the midst of a bush. So he looked, and behold, the bush was burning with fire, but the bush was not consumed.*
> *Then Moses said, "I will now turn aside and see this great sight, why the bush does not burn."*
> *So when the LORD saw that he turned aside to look, God called to him from the midst of the bush and said, "Moses, Moses!"*
> *And he said, "Here I am."*
> *Then He said, "Do not draw near this place. Take your*

*sandals off your feet, for the place where you stand is holy ground."*

If Yahweh could speak from a bush, and if Yahweh could lead Israel by a cloud on their wilderness journey, and if Jesus could cast out evil spirits and compel them to inhabit a herd of pigs (Mark 5:1-20), the Gospel made more sense to them than to some Westerners who put more faith in rational thought and scientific method.

The approach of native evangelist Terry Uyaraq "was deliberately to break taboos and to ridicule shamans while holding up a Bible. He did so while proclaiming that the Book represented a spirit far more powerful than anything in the entire Iñupiat pantheon and that this powerful spirit is what protected him."[10]

Anthropologist Ernest Burch concludes by saying: "Facing an uncertain future in which the ancient social and environmental foundations had fallen apart and that offered relief from the crushing burden of taboos that had controlled their lives for so long, it is no wonder that so many Iñupiat accepted the new religion with enthusiasm."

Colville River, region of the Iñupiat Eskimos

## CONVICTIONS

- When the biological dominant dyad of father-son began to be replaced with that of *husband-wife,* the "sword of destruction" came to Iñupiat men's *gazgi* (houses). Since Christian husbands and wives were becoming more intimate, the *gazgi,* whose function was to separate husbands from their wives, was no longer needed.

# CHAPTER 42
# THE LIFE NEEDS NEW FORMS
## OLD WINE SKINS VS NEW ONES

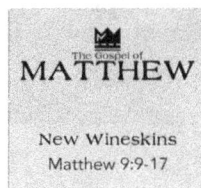

In the spring of 1971, our lives were turned upside down. I was elected to replace Ron Olson as the Associate Director of Tribal Affairs. To fulfill my duties as ADFO, I had to lay aside finishing the New Testament and limit my time spent with the Chácobo.

One responsibility I could not lay aside was preparing "my kids" to take over the roles Marian and I were filling. Someday, Marian and I would no longer be there to help them.

However, there was no urgency to finish the translation until we could produce readers and a generation of young people who could count past two. In fact, how we were going to make readers of the New Testament was not only a Chácobo problem but also a Bolivian Branch problem. This problem landed in my area of responsibility. How, I pondered, were we going to produce readers of the New Testament?

Then, a "miracle" happened. Shortly after I became the new ADFO, we had an unexpected visitor from Canada come to our out-of-the-way SIL Center in Northern Bolivia. He stayed about a week. Only he and God know what motivated him to visit our Center in Northern Bolivia. It was unusual. I don't even remember his name.

Nevertheless, every afternoon, I would spend a half-hour or so with this stranger, trying to explain to him the problems I was facing as the new ADFO. At the top of the list was the problem of producing readers for the New Testament we hoped to publish. There were very few readers in the tribes to which the Bolivian SIL Branch had assigned translators.

While the Branch had produced a purpose statement that emphasized seeing the Scriptures used by the Bolivian tribes, it didn't address the problem of readership. The Branch's Purpose Statement read as follows: "To see in each language group in Bolivia in which we are working the translated Scriptures used by a growing body of believers with indigenous leadership and relating to other believers."

If the Scriptures were to be used, the Branch had to figure out how to produce readers. I explained to our unexpected visitor that we were also dealing, in some cases, with tribal social structures, allegiance patterns, and cultural forms that suppressed the emergence of indigenous leaders.

"Was it possible to have a church without leaders," I asked, "when, in fact, no village had a real leader, and no husband was the 'head' of his household?" Of course, the answer was a resounding no.

I also shared with him some of the satire Chácobo sages had created, stories like *The Dying Raisi* (chapter 8) and *The Story of Pai as a Raisi and Escaping Mother-in-Law Control* (chapter 4, "Chácobo Satire"). Each story implies the rejection of a Positive Universal for a negative cultural particular designed to satisfy some existential need. Before we arrived on the scene, I explained to our guest that Chácobo sages existed who, through satire, expressed their opposition to how their ancestors had structured the nuclear family.

I explained that the Chácobo had replaced the covenantal *husband-wife* dyad with the biological mother-daughter dyad. The cultural operating system they had created had, in my opinion, maimed them. It suppressed the emergence of male leaders. They were, in my opinion, a dying culture.

Finally, I explained to our visiting stranger my vision for an indigenous training school that could address these problems. Some of these Bible-less tribes were not only illiterate, they were neither conversant in Spanish nor familiar with or knowledgeable about the political ways of Bolivian society.

More importantly, within their cultural operating system existed cultural forms that, in my opinion, maimed them. These forms had "no place in the Divine Plan." He was intrigued.

AFTER AN SIL ANTHROPOLOGIST informed me that it was my duty to close the village bilingual school and replace it with a schoolteacher for every Chácobo family-of-five, the message I heard was, "Don't introduce conflict [new forms] unnecessarily into a setting of basic equilibrium."[1]

I was speechless. Nevertheless, the message to me personally was, "Don't attempt to strengthen the *husband-wife* bond, for in doing so, you will be 'introducing conflict unnecessarily into a setting of basic equilibrium.'"[2] I was informed that the Chácobo's structure of the nuclear family was valid because the selected forms "adequately" met the people's needs.

But when translating the Gospel of Matthew, I discovered Jesus had given answers to the problem forms. I found the answer in an old commentary on Matthew, which I had purchased in a second-hand bookstore in Chicago when I was on leave in 1966. Bringing the volumes back to Bolivia was providential! German scholar Heinrich Meyer wrote the commentary, which was published in 1894 and translated into English. Since it was 77 years old, I had it rebound.

Heinrich Meyer paraphrased Matthew 9:16-17 of Jesus' declaration concerning the incompatibility of Jewish cultural forms with the forms needed for the new community, implying a return to the Genesis 2:4 Creation Order.

> The old forms are not suited to the new religious life emanating from me. To try to embody the latter in the former is to proceed in a manner as much calculated to defeat its purpose as when one tries to patch an old garment with a piece of unfilled clothe, which, instead of mending it, as it is intended to do, only makes the rent greater than ever; or as when one seeks to fill old bottles with new wine and ends up losing wine and bottles together. The new life needs new forms.[3] (See Mathew 9:16-17).

After reading Meyer's paraphrase of Jesus' declaration, I concluded that the Chácobo, like the Jews, needed "new forms" that complemented their new life in Christ.

"A Revolution without Guns" that we had initiated had Divine support. What appeared to be "new forms" to the present generation were, in fact, Divine forms that their ancestors, at some point in history, had rejected and replaced with forms designed to satisfy specific existential needs, especially their need for "daily bread" and manioc beer.

From their perspective, their demand for manioc beer necessitated keeping their daughters at home when they married. If they didn't keep daughters at home to help their mothers make the manioc beer, then who would make it? Thus, a residence rule was born stating that all grooms must leave their fathers and mothers and become the fifth member of their in-laws' household.

The result? The restructuring of the nuclear family and the elevation of the mother-daughter dyad to its dominant position within the nuclear family. However, there was a cost.

One of the negative attributes of a dominant mother-daughter dyad was the suppression of male leadership roles and the creation of a new status position called *raisi*. Instead of the groom becoming a "daughter's husband," he became a *raisi*, one whose duty was to be the food supplier for his wife's parents.

In addition to the above, I also noticed that when pressures from the outside world began to increase, their modus operandi was to retreat. They were a leaderless society, a ship without a captain.

As shown in a previous chapter, the biggest threat to their lifeway occurred in the early 1960s. Outside rubber patrons began moving into the area to extract rubber from the very land the Chácobo were occupying. During these pressure-cooked times, no one came forward to lead a discussion as to what action they, as a group, should take.

I noticed that reaching a village consensus on what to do took days, weeks, and sometimes even months. Projecting our observations into the future, we asked ourselves: Can a tribe with less than 140 members survive without leaders familiar with the new kind of economy that was now at their doorsteps and threatening their lifeway?

A few of my SIL colleagues had similar misgivings, some even suggesting the translation we had come to do would never be used. Powerful economic and political forces from the outside would figuratively swallow up this small tribe, and they would disappear from the earth like thirteen other Panoan tribes before them. Their observations made sense.

Nevertheless, though the future for the Chácobo looked bleak, I figured there had to be a solution to the centuries-old, self-inflicted cultural maiming. In the meantime, our presence, no doubt, temporarily halted the downward slide to self-extinction. But when we left, then what?

I feared the minute we left, the slide into cultural extinction would continue unless something was done. What I did was heed the advice of our Lord, who declared: "The old forms [of the Chácobo operating system] are not suited to the new religious life emanating from me" (Matthew 9:16, Prost translation).

My task as a Bible translator was obvious: I was to help them replace the old forms with new ones.

The old forms were replaced with the young men who had escaped the stultifying effects of mothers-in-law who monitored their behavior. They had become heads of their families and the leaders of the new religious life that replaced their allegiance to the *Bird Above*.

However, one old form still needed to be replaced. The old form did not permit women to partake in the communion service to the *Bird Above*. In like manner, the infant Chácobo church started modeling the old. Men sat inside; women looked in from the outside.

When they finally built a building devoted to the Lord, the women moved inside but sat separated from the men. For the first time, Chácobo women were no longer outsiders. They were finally permitted to partake in the breaking of the bread.

At the end of the week, the visiting stranger surprised me by saying, "I think I can help you. I have a friend working for the Canadian Development Agency who might be interested in helping. I'll have him send you a form to fill out. You must describe the project, its goals, and the amount of money you think you'll need."

Since we had to build facilities like classrooms and housing and purchase items like typewriters, blackboards, pencils, desks, etc., I asked for $60,000. We projected it as a two-year project.

## THE LORD PROVIDES

I received word that the project was approved a few months later. After building housing for the students, a large assembly building, and several classrooms, along with desks and blackboards, by September of 1972, we had the project up and running, thanks to an unknown visiting stranger.

But who would direct the school? Again, the Lord provided. Teaching at our SIL base in *Tumi Chucua* was a high school teacher with a Master's in Education. Instead of teaching the children of SIL members, including my daughter, she volunteered to direct the school. She was a fantastic director. Her name was Barbara Hoch.

A year later, as the new Associate Director of Field Operations, I called for a special meeting of everyone living at the SIL Center. I presented a paper at that meeting, the "Scheme for Completing the TASK in Bolivia."

In it, I proposed that January 1, 1984, the date Ron Olson had selected, was realistic, but only if we addressed the problem of leaderless tribes and tribes lacking individuals who had the authority to issue a command that would be carried out. If we were to achieve our primary goal stated in the Branch's Purpose Statement, we could not ignore the problem.

Instead of limiting our goals to linguistics, literacy, and translation, the Bolivian Branch added a fourth goal: Producing indigenous leaders with the authority, skills, and know-how to lead their people into the future.

Since the fourth goal was based on the assumption that SIL-Bolivia was dealing with societies using cultural forms that suppressed the emergence of leaders with the authority to lead, it would have been unconscionable for us not to address the problem.

I proposed that the problem could be traced to how each tribe had structured the nuclear family and whether or not the *husband-wife* dyad was the dominant dyad. If not, what replaced it? In addition, there was the epistemological question: Did forms common to all exist to which there were attached inherent meanings? Had these meanings been replaced with meanings shaped by social existence and "that belonged to the people"?

I eventually discovered that no evangelical anthropologists were aware that the nuclear family could be restructured to satisfy needs. None appeared troubled by the fact that new family types were created simply by merging mutually exclusive status positions.

The idea that a form common to all could have an inherent or Divine meaning was soon rejected by both theists and naturalists.

For such, meaning "belongs to the people."[4] The meaning was a product of social existence.

From their bottom-up, outside-in epistemological perspective, God approves of cultural diversity and the multiplication of forms "that have no place in the Divine Plan." According to one "evangelical" anthropologist (Kraft), "Human biology provides the backdrop for all that we need to know as humans."[5]

According to another (Lingenfelter), "We would be distorting the diversity of God's creation by forcing upon people the idea that ideal forms had inherent meanings."[6]

Such an epistemology declares the Apostle Paul was mistaken when he warned Timothy:

> *Whoever teaches false doctrine and doesn't agree with the accurate words of our LORD Jesus Christ and godly teachings is a conceited person. He shows that he doesn't understand anything" (I Timothy 6:3-4a, GOD'S WORD Translation).*

I agree. The only words with true, sound, and accurate meanings are those with inherent meanings.

As a Bible translator who had graduated from seminary, it became apparent that I was caught in the crossfire of two academic disciplines: Theology and thinking logically versus anthropology and thinking illogically.

Illogical thinking manifested itself in the merging of mutually exclusive status positions, called cultural diversity, and the production of forms having "no place in the Divine Plan" demanded thinking that was irrational.

While Professor Francis L. K. Hsu made it clear that one dominant dyad existed within every nuclear family, he refused to acknowledge, as a cultural relativist, that only one dyad was special, that of *husband-wife*, and that it was the only dyad that promoted freedom over security.

Under the one-flesh principle, the husband and wife take on each other's bilateral kinship identity when they marry, thus excluding the idea that a cousin could be a sibling, an uncle a father, an aunt a mother, a nephew a son, and a niece a sister. Since cousins, uncles, aunts, nephews, and nieces are relatives of the second degree, they should not be categorized as being first-degree.

For the theologian, an ideal type of family exists, and it is called the nuclear family. For most anthropologists, Claude Lévi-Strauss says, "there is no more dangerous idea, the idea ... according to which the biological [nuclear] family constitutes the starting point from which every society elaborates its system of kinship."[7]

As the Associate Director of Field Operations (ADFO), my missiological perspective was based on the words of Jesus, who declared:

> "No one puts a piece of unshrunk cloth on an old garment; for the patch pulls away from the garment, and the tear is made worse" (Matthew 9:16).

> "The old forms are not suited to the new religious life emanating from me" (Prost translation of Matthew 9:16).

The nuclear family has an ideal form that I, as a Bible translator, could not ignore. There was no doubt that these lowland Amazonian tribes had cultural forms that were "not suited for the religious life emanating from Christ." But how these forms came into existence remained a mystery.

Nevertheless, my goal was to show the students who attended our bilingual teacher-leadership training course the importance of investigating the possibility that their ancestors had replaced the *husband-wife* dyad with a biological dyad.

If a biological dyad had replaced the covenantal dyad of *husband-wife*, the nuclear family was defective and malfunctioning. Such family types were designed to meet basic human needs over freedom and human creativity.

Chácobo church/school

## CONVICTIONS

- When evangelical anthropologists insist that the old forms are adequate for evangelism, church planting, and positive community development, don't be tricked. Jesus declared in Matthew 9:16: "No one puts a piece off unshrunk cloth on an old garment; for the patch pulls away from the garment, and the tear is made worse." (See chapter 67, "Requires New Forms").

# CHAPTER 43
# THE RULE OF EXOGAMY - PART II
## THE CONCEPT OF FAMILY AROUND THE WORLD

*exogamy*

The Rule of Exogamy informs every individual to "move out" when getting married, lest they commit incest. According to French anthropologist Claude Lévi-Strauss, "The rule provides the only means of maintaining the group as a group."[1]

The prophet Isaiah writes that the world was not to remain in a state of *tohu* (a perpetual disorganized state of chaos). Instead, the Lord's intent was for the content of planet earth—every animal, bird, plant, vertebrate, and invertebrate—to be categorized, named, and "ruled over."

Anthropologists who have rejected the Creation account in Genesis—which are most of them—have nevertheless asked: What was "the first rule" and the first sin?

Most Christians would be surprised to hear the naturalist's answer to this critical question. According to his interpretation, "the first rule" is that one should not marry a member of one's own family. One must "marry out." The Universal Rule to "marry out" is the Rule of Exogamy.

According to naturalists, the first sin occurred after the evolutionary transition from animalness to human-ness. Someone broke the rule and had sexual relations with a member of his "family," as defined by the group.

For the naturalist, the first sin was incest. The sin is so vile that in some societies, the punishment is death, even today, among some ethnic groups.

The reason the Universal Rule of Exogamy is so important to both the naturalist and to me, a theist, is that the prohibition, in the words of Lévi-Strauss, "sets in motion the creation of social and cultural systems."[2]

While it is true the Rule of Exogamy serves as the starting point for the creation of social and cultural systems, the question naturalists and theists must answer is: Is it possible that the particular socio-economic-cultural-system that the Rule of Exogamy is protecting shouldn't be protected because it is in fundamental opposition to a Divine Universal, the nuclear family, and its internal structure?

For the concept-innatist, the answer is yes!

For the naturalist, the question is an absurdity. There is no Order of Creation.

However, the Universal Rule implies a Rule Maker, and for this Rule Maker, the rule must serve a purpose that anthropologists should be able to explain. Why does the Universal Rule exist?

## THE PURPOSE OF THE RULE

For this concept-innatist, who believes the rule's purpose is to protect the nuclear family and its internal structure, its existence raises some serious questions, especially for a Bible translator who treats Genesis as history and not as allegory.

When the biblical text says, "Cain knew his wife" (Genesis 4:17,

ESV), it assumes she accompanied him into exile, that she was a daughter of Adam, and consequently, a sister of Cain. The marriage of brothers and sisters was inevitable in the case of the children of men if the human race was actually to descend from a single pair.[3]

Assuming that Cain married his sister and his sons married their sisters, which I do, we must ask, "Did they commit incest?" I propose that Cain and his offspring did not commit incest.

While Cain's sons married their sisters, they couldn't commit incest because they could not "marry out." For over 200 years, there were no "outsiders" to marry.

Though the Rule of Exogamy had been "written on the heart," the rule of marrying out had to become conscious knowledge. This means the rule, which existed in the subconscious, first had to be "triggered" and brought to consciousness in a socio-linguist situation.

However, we must ask: Can the concept of marrying out be "triggered" and brought to consciousness when Cain's sons and daughters couldn't marry outside the family? The rule to "marry out" is dependent on the existence of collateral relatives, someone who is not a father, mother, brother, sister, son, or daughter.

For over 200 years, Cain's offspring intermarried. Every brother married a sister, and every sister married a brother. It wasn't until the birth of Enosh, Cain's nephew, that a new era began.

Not only was it a time that people began to worship the Lord, but it was also when new status positions came into existence, such as uncles, aunts, cousins, nephews, and nieces. With the birth of Seth, marrying out became a possibility.

> *And as for Seth, to him also a son was born; and he named him Enosh. Then* men *began to call on the name of the LORD. (Genesis 4:26)*

## THE IMPORTANCE OF THE RULE OF EXOGAMY

How important is an unlearned social rule that requires an individual to "marry out" of his intimate group called "family"? In the field of missiology, it is essential. No rule in life defines who we are as individuals and as a society more than this rule.

From a top-down, inside-out epistemology, the function of this Universal Divine Rule of Exogamy is to protect the nuclear family and the integrity of its internal structure. Since man exists as a transcendent being positioned to live above nature in the sphere of freedom, he can misuse his liberty to rearrange the internal structure of the nuclear family and create new kinds of "families" shaped to "fit" the environment.

Whereas the Universal Divine Rule of Exogamy was given to man to protect the nuclear family alone, it has been used to preserve and maintain whatever form of family fallen man and society have created. According to Lévi-Strauss, anthropologists are correct when they say: "The Rule of Exogamy provides the only means of maintaining the group as a group."[4]

The Great Trickster has convinced most humans that the deviant form needs to be protected because it can better provide for society's needs than the Universal.

However, anthropologists and contextualizing missiologists have failed to recognize that the family types produced by social existence in a particular environment are deviant forms. These forms reduce people to mechanized people-things with ascribed functions.

Whenever a society uses its freedom to deviate from the Divine norm, as stated in Genesis 2:23-24, it is also dependent on using the Rule of Exogamy to protect its own deviant construct of the family. This represents a demonic misuse of the rule.

Such deviant forms exist whenever a society declares "outsiders," like collateral relatives, as insiders, showing they have rejected the Law of Identity, which states an uncle cannot be a father or an aunt a mother. The inherent qualities that make up collateral relatives are not the same as those that comprise nuclear family members.

Finally, the demonic misuse of the Rule of Exogamy has "multiplied sin" and cultural diversity, creating systems or new family types that are in fundamental opposition to the Order of Creation.

## THE CONCEPT OF FAMILY

For the materialist, the idea that there exists a natural family grounded in a covenantal relationship between *husband-wife* and limited to eight status positions, that of *husband-wife,* father, mother, sons, daughters, brothers, and sisters, is rejected, even by evangelical missiologists.

Like the meaning of marriage, for the materialist, the meaning of family must be defined in terms of biology, environmental "fitness," and functionality. The idea is that every individual has a specific function within the family in the same way every body part has a specific function.

The notion that there is a Divine internal structure, the nuclear family, that humans and society can reject and replace with new family structures is firmly rejected by a concept-innatist. However, Jesus, a descendant of David, was aware that his ancestors had restructured the nuclear family to satisfy an existential need.

Jacob, for example, had replaced the covenantal dyad of *husband-wife* with the biological dyad of father-son. Instead of "leaving father and mother" when the sons married, they remained at home. Because it served a need, in time, the dominant dyad of the nuclear family became father-son.

Jesus called the divergent form in Israel "the family-of-five." The form misrepresented the Ideal. Recognizing it to be a divergent form, "All things were created through Him and for Him" (Colossians 1:16b), Jesus prophetically declared:

> "Do you think that I have come to give peace on earth?
> No, I tell you, but rather division;
> for henceforth in one house there will be five divided, three against two and two against three;
> they will be divided, father against son and son against father, mother against daughter and daughter against her mother, mother-in-law against her daughter-in-law and daughter-in-law against her mother-in-law" *(Luke 12:51-53, RSV).*

> "Do not think that I have come to bring peace on earth; I have not come to bring peace, but a sword.
> For I have come to set a man against his father, and a daughter against her mother, and a daughter-in-law against her mother-in-law;
> and a man's foes will be those of his own household" *(Matthew 10:34-36, RSV).*

What biblical commentators have failed to recognize is that in the above passage, Jesus was declaring the beginning of a new dispensation, "From now on." Jesus, in this passage, is specifically foretelling what is going to happen to the family-of-five, both the matrilineal and patrilineal.

Within the patrilineal family, fathers will become angry at sons because they insist on leaving "father" and "mother" at marriage in order to establish independent households. Mothers-in-law will be angry with daughters-in-law because they refused to become the fifth member of the patrilineal household. And mothers will be angry with daughters for their refusal to become the fifth member of their husband's parent's household.

These were revolutionary statements. Any divergence from the Divine norm demanded a response. His response was the eventual destruction of the deviant form, the extended family-of-five, and the restoration of the Universal, the nuclear family, not only among His people but among all people.

## PROPHECY FULFILLMENT

Unknown to most, a worldwide phenomenon is trending, and the nuclear family is replacing the extended family-of-five as the basic unity of society. To the consternation of many, the real foundation of culture, the nuclear family, is slowly replacing the deviant forms.

## SOUTH KOREA

Without this social shift from "extended families" to "one-generation families" or nuclear families, South Korea would not have become a creative economic superpower or have a church that sends missionaries to India, Japan, China, Pakistan, Afghanistan, and elsewhere.

According to sociologist Kweon Sug-In: "From 1920-1995, extended families decreased by two-thirds; one-generation families [nuclear family], on the other hand, increased about three times during the same period."[5]

I consider this a positive move for church growth and economic development. They are one of the great missionary-sending organizations in the world.

## CHINA

The same phenomenon occurred in China under Mao Zedong. After reading Morton Fried's (1923 - 1986) evaluation of Mao's revolution in 1976, I immediately knew that Mao had let a tiger out of the bag. In one stroke, China was launched into the 21st century.

We propose that China became a superpower because the nuclear family and the *husband-wife* dyad were temporarily elevated to their rightful place.

But then things changed: "For the message of the cross is foolishness [absurd and illogical] to those who are perishing *and* spiritually dead [because they reject it], but to us who are being saved [by God's grace] it is [the manifestation of] the power of God" (I Corinthians 1:18, Amplified Bible).

Of course, the materialist and contextualizing evangelical would deny a link exists between a higher living standard and how the nuclear family is structured.

Only when people have the freedom to discover, think, and create does the standard of living ever increase. There is only one dyad that promotes freedom, individualism, and creativity. It is the covenantal relationship of *husband-wife*. Every other dyad promotes some kind of collectivism.

In the words of science writer David Nabhan:

> There is nothing to take the place of an excellent set of parents to assure the superlative success of children. So, there won't be any new and improved authoritarian heavy-handedness aimed at the nuclear family and dreamed up by far-leftist collectivists to supplant it—not now, not ever.[6]

Whatever type of family the collectivist creates, it will not raise the Chinese standard of living. When the biological dyad of father-son was replaced with that of *husband-wife*, the first expressions of this freedom was an explosion of church growth followed by economic growth.

The phenomenon of church growth was no doubt unexpected because, according to Mao's philosophy of life, "They [ideas] come from social practice and from it alone."[7] For Mao, existence preceded ideas.

According to Chinahighlights.com, today, "China holds the record for the fastest developing major country in the history of the world, with no signs of a slowdown at present."[8] But according to some economists, the trend has now reversed itself.

While there will be many reasons to explain this economic downturn, which is not over, I would suggest it has everything to do with the State's rejection of the covenantal one-flesh principle of *husband-wife* and the husband's rejection as the head of the household.

~

## CHÁCOBO

The same can be said of the Chácobo. Today, the dominant form is the nuclear family, not the family-of-five. By replacing the family-of-five with the family of four, they transformed themselves from a dying centripetal society anxious about who was going to provide the food and beer to a creative centrifugal society that spins off its members into the world.

The leaderless society of the Chácobo became a society in which husbands assumed a headship role in the family. This occurred when the "sword" came to the Chácobo family-of-five, a form that denied husbands that headship role.

~

## MIDDLE EAST

And finally, there is Israel. According to the Jewish Agency for Israel, today, "Israel is an extremely family-oriented society and sees the [nuclear] family as its basic unit,"[9] not the extended family-of-five. They are the most creative and innovative nation in the world.

According to writer and sociologist Hakim Barakat, surrounding them are millions of Arabs who, unlike Israel, "socializes its children into dependency,"[10] and the extended patrilineal family is dominant. The present-day Arab family is not usually extended in the strict sense. It is rare for three or more generations to live together in the same household.

Recent studies show a continuing trend toward the nuclear family. Urbanization, industrialization, government employment, education, exposure to the developed world, and the emergence of a middle class have had some impact.

According to data on the Arab Middle East collected by E. T. Prothro and L. N. Diab, the majority of wives interviewed who had married in the 1960s had never lived with their in-laws. A more recent study of family and kinship ties in Iraq shows that the percentage of extended families changed from 82 percent in the 1940s to 34 percent in 1975.

Anthropologist Raphael Patai shares: The primary feature of the Arab family is it is "extended, patriarchal, patrilineal, patrilocal, endogamous, and occasionally polygynous."[11]

Thus, when an Arab girl marries, "she will pass over from her mother's home to that of her mother-in-law."[12] who, like Chácobo's mother-in-law, will prevent her from establishing a strong bond with her son.

Yet despite the reduced prevalence of the extended family, relatives generally remain closely interlocked in a web of intimate relationships that leaves limited room for independence and privacy. They continue to live in the same neighborhood, to intermarry, to group together on a kinship basis, and to expect a great deal from one another.

For example, the global Islamic population is approximately 1,200,000,000, or 20% of the world's population. The global Jewish population is approximately 14,000,000, or about 0.02 % of the world population. While four Muslims have won the Nobel Prize, 129 Jews have clinched the prize. The question becomes, is the nuclear family "the real foundation of culture"?

If the *husband-wife* dyad became dominant, their kinship-based lifeway would collapse.

How IMPORTANT IS the social Rule of Exogamy, which requires an individual to marry outside the family? I can hardly think of a rule that more determines and shapes who we are as individuals than the Rule of Exogamy.

The Universal Rule not only determines what constitutes a family; Lévi-Strauss correctly points out, the Rule of Exogamy "provides the only means for maintaining the group as a group."[13]

For the postmodern materialist, as well as the existentialist, cultural materialist, and contextualizer (i.e., Karl Marx),[14] no form—a form like the concept of family—has an inherent meaning that is "fixed" and absolute. Instead, social existence alone determines what is called a family.

According to Marx, Mao, Sartre, Harris, and others, social existence within a particular ecosystem alone determines how one thinks about duties, obligations, and rights vis-a-vis lineal and collateral kin. They believe the unlearned Rule of Exogamy will protect whatever family type emerges from the shaping and molding, and the "elemental spiritual forces of this world" (Colossians 2:8, NIV).

However, the kind of family it protects clearly will not accord with Christ. II Corinthians 6:15 states: "And what accord has Christ with Belial? Or what part has a believer with an unbeliever?"

For example, missionaries assigned to the Vaupés area of Colombia and Brazil would be, unknown to them, assigned to an area that would classify Joseph and Mary as brother and sister because they spoke the same language.

## THE WANANO TRIBE

Colombia and Brazil prohibited the marriage of a Wanano to a Wanano because they spoke the same language. Strange as it may be, those who spoke the same language were classified as brothers and sisters.

To avoid committing incest, one had to "marry out," that is, marry someone who spoke a different language. Anyone who failed to "marry out" would be guilty of committing incest.

At some point in history, the Wanano, along with approximately sixteen other diverse tribes, collectively decided that the best way to stop inter-tribal warfare over fishing rights was to redefine the meaning of family.

So, they replaced the inherent or Divine meaning attached to the form called "family" with a divergent meaning; namely, "those who speak the same language."

For the postmodern contextualizer who believes no concept has an inherent meaning that is "fixed" and constant, social existence within a particular ecosystem—in this case, those living in the Vaupés Rainforest of Colombia and Brazil—determines what meaning should be attached to the Universal forms called family, father, mother, brother, sister, et al.

Thus, the Rule of Linguistic-Tribal Exogamy emerged. The Wanano concept of the family included four other tribes that belonged to the same language family,

## EASTERN TUCANO

Since these four tribes, the Pira-Tapuya, Arapaho, Siriano, and Tuyuca, all belonged, they had to marry someone who spoke a non-Eastern Tucano language.

For those who believe no inherent or Divine meaning is attached to the concept of family, father, mother, brother, sister, etc., it means environmental pressures determine all meanings, and, according to missiologist Charles Kraft, "belong to the people."

However, if missiologist Charles Kraft is correct when he states: "A cultural form does not have inherent meaning, only perceived meaning, and this meaning is context-specific,"[15] then a translation problem exists that cannot be ignored by every missiologist who agrees with Kraft.

The problem is this: According to the Wanano and the other tribes of the Vaupés, Jesus is a "bastard." The moment the Wanano hear that Joseph and Mary spoke the same language, from their collective perspective, Joseph and Mary committed incest because they were guilty of marrying someone who spoke the same language.

The Wanano and the other tribes of the area would immediately think: Why would this kind and compassionate missionary be proclaiming that Jesus, a "bastard," could save them?

Chácobo men

## CONVICTIONS

- In proclaiming that Jesus was an "exact representation" of God on earth, the missionary cannot avoid the Rule of Village Exogamy and how it negates His essence as the "Son of God."
- When the people of Northern India finally hear and read the Gospel of Luke and discover that Mary and Joseph lived in Nazareth and that Jesus was a "Nazarene," they will immediately wonder why the elders of the village did not put Mary and Joseph to death. After all, the relationship was incestuous because they were classified as being brother and sister.
- To prevent intertribal warfare over land and fishing rights, tribes of the Vaupés compelled their young people to "marry out." This meant marrying someone who spoke a different language.
- Whenever a Wanano bachelor is compelled to marry someone who speaks a different language to prevent inter-tribal warfare, the new family type is being "defectively realized because of sin."[16]

- When tribes of the Vaupés replaced the inherent meaning of family with "those who spoke the same language," a spiritual divergence away from a Positive Universal took place. The divergence made it impossible for husband and wife in one village to become "one flesh" because they spoke the same language.
- The biological principle of brother-brother replaced the covenantal one-flesh principle of *husband-wife*
- Because the Rule of Exogamy, when misapplied, distorts reality and suppresses human freedom rather than promoting it, it is incumbent upon the missionary to attempt to understand, to some degree, how their target group has applied this life-changing rule. It will inform them regarding what society thinks the "family" is, as well as what their anxieties are. The Vaupés tribes were anxious about who controlled the fishing rights.
- At some point in their history, Vaupés tribes permitted a new meaning to be attached to the form called "family." The new meaning "had no place in the Divine Plan."[17]
- Understanding who Jesus is depends on a spiritual return to the Universal, the nuclear family.
- Whenever a form like the "family" begins to represent the Universal, a decrease in ascribing functions to individuals occurs to maximize their freedom. It will be a spiritual move from disorder to order. This will be positive for church growth and economic development.
- According to theologian Henry Van Til, "The [nuclear] family is the simplest and smallest unit of society and the real foundation of culture. If this foundation remains pure, man's culture has promise; but if it becomes polluted, all the rest will turn to dust and ashes."[18]
- Whenever a form like the "family" begins to represent the Divine Ideal, there will occur a decrease in ascribing functions to individuals to maximize their freedom. It

will be a spiritual move from disorder to order. This will be positive for church growth and economic development.

# CHAPTER 44
# FORMS HAVING NO PLACE IN THE DIVINE PLAN
## EXOGAMY IN NORTHERN INDIA

*"I must marry someone who lives in a different village lest I commit incest."*

Hundreds of villages are scattered throughout the province of Uttar Pradesh in Northern India. Members of the same village do not marry. To do so would be an incestuous act worthy of death because, in their minds, the village and the family are the same. The function of such a rule is to suppress inter-village warfare.

Since Joseph and Mary lived in the same town, according to Uttar Pradesh custom, they were "brother" and "sister." Again, the idea that contextualization is the "Scripturally-endorsed approach to taking the Gospel to the world" must be rejected.

How would contextualizing missionaries who believe all meanings "belong to the people" convince the people living in these villages that Jesus was not a "bastard"?

Unlike the Miccosukee of South Florida, who ground their security system in clan exogamy, villages in Northern India ground their security in village exogamy. They classify each village as a family in the same way the Miccosukee classify the matrilineal clans as a kind of family.

Mahatma Gandhi is often quoted as saying, "Real India lives in its villages." In Uttar Pradesh, the average size of the village is 1,224 people.

Members of the same village do not intermarry. People of a village consider themselves brothers and sisters. Therefore, people of one community take a bride from another village.

For example, in Rani Khera, a town in the Aligarh District of Uttar Pradesh, 266 married women came from 200 different villages, averaging between twelve and twenty-four miles away; 220 local women had gone to 200 other villages to marry. As a result of these exogamous marriages, Rani Khera, a village of 150 households, was linked to 400 other nearby towns."[1]

The question is: Why does this area of Northern India, which comprises more than 400 mountainous villages, compel its young people to find spouses in other towns?

The answer appears to be either a) the more villages with whom one can exchange sons and daughters in marriage, the better one's chances of preventing inter-village warfare, or b) alliances are formed between two or more villages to counter a common adversary.

Since the Rule of Village Exogamy serves as part of their defense system against anxiety, a time must have existed when the villages of Uttar Pradesh lived in constant strife and warfare over boundaries and land usage. Social existence demanded a solution. Their solution? They formed alliances symbolized by the interchange of sons and daughters through marriage to stave off and prevent inter-village warfare.

By classifying all people in each village as brothers and sisters, the local authorities of the Uttar Pradesh District could compel the young people to find spouses in other villages. Marrying, for example, an unrelated schoolmate would be classified as an "incestuous act" worthy of death.

This is no empty threat, as evidenced by an "honor killing" in May 2008. Two unrelated schoolmates were put to death. Their crime was incest. They failed to "marry out." Village sentiment was: "We believe people who commit incest should be killed."[2]

## A MISSIOLOGICAL PROBLEM

Suppose social existence is the medium for determining what constitutes a family. In that case, the contextualizers correctly say that the missionary "must accept and work within structures and processes of others that are different from one's own social game."[3]

But any contextualizing missionary working in an area that practices village exogamy rather than nuclear family exogamy will have trouble explaining to his hearers why Jesus, the Son of God, should not be classified as a "bastard."

How does one "accept social structures and processes" that, according to their "social game," classify Jesus as an "illegitimate" child of an incestuous relationship because Joseph and Mary had failed to find a spouse in another village?

According to their "social game," Jesus' parents were brother and sister, and the villagers should have put Mary and Joseph to death. And by playing their "social game," the missionary has no Good News to proclaim.

Woman in Northern India

## CONVICTIONS

- By classifying the village as being a family, society has, in the words of Christian philosopher Herman Dooyeweerd, created a family type that is "defectively realized because of sin."[4]
- When the people of Northern India finally hear and read the Gospel of Luke and discover that Mary and Joseph both lived in the village of Nazareth and that Jesus was a "Nazarene," they will immediately wonder why the elders of the town did not put Mary and Joseph to death. After all, the relationship was incestuous because Uttar Pradesh would classify them as "brother" and "sister."
- According to the Apostle Paul, such forms "sneaked in having no place in the Divine Plan" (Romans 5:20).

# CHAPTER 45
# THE JÍVARO PEOPLE
## EQUADOR AND PERU

In the Equadorian and Peruvian jungles live the Jívaro people. According to American anthropologist Michael Harner, the marriage rule of the polygny-practicing, head-shrinking Jívaro on the Eastern slopes of the Andes is this:

> Thou shall not marry a parallel cousin. She is your sister. Instead, thou shall marry your cross-cousin, your mother's brother's daughter or your father's sister's daughter, and no one else. [1]

It is a marriage rule which the Chácobo rejected. According to anthropologist Michael Harner: "The only kinswoman with whom marriage is formally sanctioned is a *wahë* (cross-cousin) from either parent's side of the family."[2]

Accompanying this rule is the practice of sororal (sisterly) polygyny—the practice of marrying sisters, thereby producing a lack of marriageable Jívaro women and an excess of bachelors who have no hope of marrying and raising a family unless they violate the rule. The restrictive marriage rule created a society at war with itself.

According to Softpedia editor Stefan Anitel, to protect themselves against a fellow brother who felt his rights to a wife were violated, they built fortified longhouses. They were "made of strong wooden planks which cannot be penetrated by javelins, surrounded by a palisade. The path going to the village is carefully hidden and filled with traps meant to impede the advance of the enemies."[3]

But if such thoughts are appropriate, is the following statement by evangelical anthropologist Lingenfelter valid?

> By denying the validity of others' structures we then force upon people our standards and structure of relationships to accomplish the work and purpose of God ... we would then distort the diversity of God's creation ...[4]

~

## THOU SHALL MARRY A CROSS-COUSIN

The acquisition of a *wahë*, also known as an ascribed wife-to-be, was fraught with danger. By restricting marriage to a mother's brother's daughter and a father's sister's daughter, the rule multiplied jealousy, envy, and strife among brothers, real or classified.

Regardless of culture or tribe, all humankind has knowledge of a Universal Rule that says: Marry out! This Universal Rule of Exogamy, as Lévi-Strauss points out, provides "the only means for maintaining the group as a group."[5]

In the Jívaro case, the Universal Rule protected a "kind" of family which did not represent a Universal; rather, it represented a negative particular, a form which has "no place in the Divine Plan."

In this case, the Rule of Exogamy protects a family form which pits siblings against siblings, parallel cousins against parallel cousins, and families against families. Add to the mixture the practice of sororal polygyny, and the Jívaro have simply increased the controversy and strife between brothers, real and fictive. Such practices cannot help but produce shortages of *wahë*, or ascribed wives-to-be.

To guarantee that their ascribed wife-to-be would not be given to another brother, there was also the "practice of 'reserving' a prepuberty girl as a future bride by giving gifts of leatherwork and trade goods to her parents."[6] In effect, *wahë* (daughters) were up for sale to a desired son-in-law, also known as a nephew.

According to anthropologist Michael Harner, after obtaining one's wife, "a man normally hopes that his father-in-law eventually will give him all the latter's daughters as wives."[7] But this practice only exacerbates the problem. It reduces the number of females who can marry.

Their law-way permits them to declare: "There are no marriageable women left, and I expect you to help me administer justice on the one who illegally married my cross-cousin (my real wife to be)."[8]

## CONTRASTING APPLICATIONS OF THE CROSS-COUSIN MARRIAGE RULE

Like the Jívaro, the ideal marriage among the Chácobo was that of marrying a cross-cousin. One day when talking about such matters, a Chácobo asked if Marian was my *wahë* (cross cousin of parent). When I said she wasn't, they asked if she was my *yaya* (aunt). To marry someone you didn't know since childhood didn't make sense. One day it would.

While the Chácobo and the Jívaro shared a similar family type, unlike the Jívaro, the Chácobo did not merge the status positions of mother and mother's sister (aunt) and father and father's brother (uncle).

This is significant because it reduced the number of *wahe* (Jívaro) or *wahë* (Chácobo) available for marriage. For the Jívaro, however, to meet this demand for marriageable cross-cousins, the *wahe* at some point in history merged the status positions of mother and mother's sister and father and father's brother. However, it didn't solve the problem. There was still a shortage.

While actual cross-cousin marriages were preferred among the Chácobo, it was not obligatory. If a non-kinsman married one's cross-cousin, the act was not classified as a violation of a rule written on stone. In fact, I am not aware of any cross-cousin marriages among the Chácobo whereas over 50% of Jívaro marriages are between cross-cousins.

While their definitions of what constituted a family were almost identical, their lifeways or behavioral patterns were extremely different. The Chácobo were pacifists and lived in villages; the Jívaro were headhunters for whom village living was fraught with danger. Very few Chácobo men had two wives. While the cultural ideal for the Jívaro was being married to sisters, the cultural norm for the Chácobo was monogamy.

Because the ideal for the Jívaro was having more than one wife, all of whom were sisters, to meet this ideal, the relationship between ego and his maternal uncles became closer and more important than the father-son relationship.

The reason for this shift in allegiance from father to father-in-law was because one's maternal uncle is the one who supplies ego not only with his first wife, but hopefully wife two or three.

For the Jívaro, the typical household was "one man, two wives, and seven children; or a man, one wife, and three children."[9] The typical household for the Chácobo was one man, one wife, his daughters, and incoming son-in-law whose ascribed task was the fish-and-meat supplier for the wife's family.

In addition, while they shared a matrilocal residence rule, when Chácobo *raisis* (sons-in-law) moved into the households of their in-laws, their stay was not temporary. They were forbidden to leave because their ascribed function was to supply the household with food.

In contrast, the residence rule for Jívaro sons-in-law was temporary. According to Harner, Jívaro sons-in-law generally "remained until the birth of the wife's first son. Thereafter, according to the norm, the son-in-law and his family dwelt in a new house nearby."[10]

A rule which allowed Jivaro sons-in-law to set up an independent household after the birth of the first child gave their bilateral kinship system what Harner calls "a slight patrilineal tendency;"[11] that is, "the man is formally head of the household and also informally seems generally to dominate his family."[12]

For the Chácobo, failure of the daughter to move out and establish a new independent household with her husband clearly suppressed the natural husband leadership role in the nuclear family from emerging. The effect of the married daughter not moving out created an egalitarian society devoid of superordinate-subordiate (S-s) structures.

No Chácobo husband was the head of his family. Instead, the behavior of every son-in-law was watched, monitored, and covertly directed by his mother-in-law.

The positive effects for the Jívaro husbands as heads of their families were manifested whenever the tribe was threatened from the outside. On such occasions, a Jívaro male would take on the role of war chief and unite all the neighborhoods together to resist the threat to their existence. This "ability of the Jívaro to ally against outside invaders"[13] was positive.

Such was not the case among the Chácobo. When their lifeway was threatened by an incoming outsider, no one came forward to take on the role of war chief to unite all the families to resist this obvious threat to their existence. They simply retreated further into the forest.

HOW THE RULE of Exogamy is applied depends on a society's definition of family. And this in turn is influenced in most cases by ecological pressures But, the concept-innatist asks: Is the Jívaro concept of a family, one shaped and determined by social existence in a particular environment, valid?

And does a law of the family exist which declares, as proposed by theologian-philosopher Dooyeweerd, "Membership is absolutely restricted to the parents and their offspring in the first degree,"[14] thereby excluding the merging of the status positions of parallel cousins and siblings.

Quoting Encyclopedia.com, "One must build a wall around one's house to prevent being killed by an angry brother (who biologically was one's parallel cousin)."[15]

For the Jívaro, their defensive system was not against the powerful Incas who lived to the West, nor against the Canelos-Quichua who lived to the North, nor against the Achuar who lived to the East, nor against the Huambisa and Aguaruna to the South, but against their own kin.

The war between fictive classificatory "brothers" and ego began when a fictive brother married ego's ascribed wife-to-be. Customary law declared it to be the ideal marriage. However, from ego's perspective, when the fictive brother or parallel cousin stole his bride-to-be, he had to protect himself.

The "wife stealer" did this by clearing acres of jungle. In the center of the cleared area, he built a longhouse. Then he encircled the long house with a wall.

How this defensive system against anxiety came into existence takes some explaining. It begins with the Jívaro family concept and their misuse of the Universal Rule of Exogamy that says to "marry out." To "marry out" meant something very different to a Jívaro than it did to the tribes living on the Great Plains or those living in Northern India.

Again, according to Harner, for the Jívaro bachelor to "marry out" specifically meant:

> Thou shall not marry a parallel cousin. She is your sister. Instead, thou shall marry your cross-cousin, either your mother's brother's

daughter or your father's sister's daughter, and no one else. She is not your sister.[16]

Their deviation from the Creation Order produced social disorder and multiplied jealousy and envy, adding to the cultural diversity we see in the world today.

Regardless of culture or tribe, all humankind has innate knowledge of the rule which says "marry out." This Universal Rule of Exogamy, as anthropologist Lévi-Strauss points out, provides "the only means for maintaining the group as a group."[17]

Any intimate relationship with a member of one's family as defined by society would be classified as being a sinful, incestuous, act. The Jívaro concept of family prohibited parallel cousin marriages because they were classified as siblings while requiring them to marry cross-cousins.

The concept-innatist asks: Is the Jívaro concept of a family shaped and determined by social existence in a particular environment valid? And is there a law of the family that declares, as proposed by theologian-philosopher Dooyeweerd, "Membership is absolutely restricted to the parents and their offspring in the first degree,"[18] thereby excluding collateral relatives like uncles, aunts, and cousins?

If the meaning of family is "fixed," unchanging, constant, and represents an Order of Creation, then applying the Rule of Exogamy to protect a family form which is relative would be a sinful act that "multiplies trespasses" (Romans 5:20).

By absolutizing the relative, the Jívaro have created a society whose mission in life is to defend a law-script that produces cultural forms "that belong to the people" as described by Dooyeweerd: "The common practice [is to] 'reserve' a pre-puberty girl as a future bride by giving gifts of feather work and trade goods to her parents."[19]

If, as proposed, the purpose of the rule is to protect an Order of Creation, that is, the nuclear family and its internal structure, the effect of applying the rule will be positive. The Universal Rule of Exogamy exists to protect the absolute, not the relative.

If, however, the rule protects a definition of family "which belongs to the people," a definition that emerges from contextual social existence, then application of the rule will increase cultural diversity and disorder.

Equadorian Rainforest

## CONVICTIONS

- The cultural script of the Jívaro declared to all bachelors: You are to marry your cross-cousin because she has been classified as "your legal wife to be." Anyone who violates the script has "sinned" against society's law-way and needs to be punished.
- A primary feature of the Jívaro behavioral script inherited from parents was that it permitted the Jívaro to manipulate their social world to satisfy personal needs and objectives. For example, the classification permitted them to say to their brothers, real and fictive, "There are no marriageable women left, and I expect you to help me

administer justice on the one who illegally married my cross-cousin (my real wife to be)."[20]

- The Jívaro concept of the family canceled the Rules of Logic by merging the mutually exclusive status positions of parallel cousins with siblings, father's brother with father, and mother's sister with mother. Coupled with the marriage rule: "Thou shall marry a cross-cousin and no one else," any intimate relationship with a member of one's family as defined by society would be classified as being a sinful, incestuous act.

# CHAPTER 46
# SHARANAHUA
## PERU

*"When I marry, I will live with my wife's family, and my assigned task will be wildlife supplier."*
*~Sharanahua of Peru*

Among the Peruvian Sharanahua, the covenantal one-flesh principle of husband and wife has been applied to the biological father-daughter dyad. Fathers treasure and value their daughter, for they gain a meat provider only with daughters.

Like their linguistic cousins, the Chácobo, "The crucial reality of Sharanahua life is the necessity for ensuring a secure food supply, and this fact shapes the interactions between men and women, old and young, kinsmen and affinals."[1]

Anthropologist Janet Siskind points out that "This [father-daughter dyad] is the nonsexual relationship that is the building block of the household and a prerequisite for cooperation between men and women."[2] According to the norms of Sharanahua society, men must live in their father-in-law's house.[3]

Sadly, one of the primary attributes of such a living arrangement is a jealousy triangle consisting of two men and a woman. Both father-in-law and son-in-law are competing for the allegiance of the same woman, the conflicted daughter-wife.

Within the same household exists psychological and spiritual warfare regarding which dyad should be dominant—the cultural particular of father-daughter or the Universal *husband-wife* dyad.

Without daughters, a man cannot create an extended household consisting of a father, mother, sons, daughters, and incoming sons-in-law. He will have no security in his later years of life.

This compels one to ask the question: Should missionaries accept the father-daughter as the dominant dyad of the nuclear family?

## THOU SHALL BECOME A PROTEIN SUPPLIER

The existential question of the Sharanahua of Peru (linguistic cousins of the Chácobo) is: Who will provide the meat for the household-of-five, the fifth member being the son-in-law?

Anthropologist Janet Siskind states, "The crucial reality of Sharanahua life is the necessity for ensuring a secure food supply, which shapes the interactions between men and women, old and young, kinsmen and affinals."[4]

Just as the psychological need for securing a steady supply of manioc beer compelled the Chácobo to restructure the nuclear family, the psychological need for a constant supply of meat compelled the Sharanahua to do the same.

The Sharanahua did this by replacing the covenantal one-flesh principle of *husband-wife* outlined in Genesis 2:23-24 with the biological father-daughter dyad. Without daughters, there would be no household-of-five and no security for the father in the later years of his life.

From a Sharanahua perspective, pity the father who has no daughters. He would lack the means to acquire a meat supplier. But it is a form that "sneaked in" that had "no place in the Divine Plan."

In this regard, anthropologist Francis L. K. Hsu points out:

> The total effect of the dominance of the attributes of one structural dyad leads to a particular kind of kinship content which in turn strongly conditions the pattern of thought and behavior of the individuals reared in the kinship system in the society at large.[5]

The "structural dyad" selected was father-daughter; the structural dyad selected by their linguistic cousin living in Bolivia was mother-daughter.

To support their perspective, unlike Chácobo sages of the past who created satire condemning the selection of the mother-daughter dyad, Sharanahua sages created legends that reinforced their selection. Such is the story of a careless Sharanahua father whose daughter's crying angered him.

In his anger, the father threw the infant daughter out of the house and then later realizes the consequences of his action. His irrational behavior destroyed all chances of gaining a son-in-law who could feed his family daily meat.

The following legend supports the cultural idea that the most crucial relationship in Sharanahua society is that of father-daughter, and jaguars appear among them as people who will remove the daughter and set up an independent household.

## A FATHER RETRIEVES HIS DAUGHTER

A jaguar seized the baby daughter, and her father wept, believing the jaguar had eaten her. The jaguar, however, took care of her and married her when she became a woman. She gave birth to three jaguar babies.

One day, the father came to the house when the jaguar went hunting. The woman cried and asked, "Father, why did you throw me out? Now, I am a jaguar's wife."

The jaguar returned from hunting with five peccaries [wild pigs] in a tiny basket and started to growl at his wife's father.

"Don't be angry," she said, "It's my father."

They ate the meat and then slept.

In the morning, the father started to leave and said, "I'm going to take my daughter."

The jaguar was angry and threatening, but the father blew on his hands, and the jaguar, along with his children, died.

The father and daughter went to the father's house, where the daughter got a new husband. This time, she bore a human child.[6]

FOR THE SHARANAHUA, the greatest threat to their mode of living is the man who marries a daughter. He might remove the daughter he married and set up an independent household where, according to Genesis 2:24, the two become "one flesh."

When a bachelor marries, he knows the rule: "[Married] men must live in their fathers-in-law's house." The rule for their linguistic cousins, the Chácobo, was that married men must sleep together in a men's communal house.

But, sadly, in each case, a jealousy triangle is created. For the Sharanahua, it consists of two men (father and husband) and a woman (daughter and wife).

The Chácobo consisted of two women and a man, manifested in the roles of mother and mother-in-law, daughter and wife, and husband and son-in-law.

Among the Sharanahua, the father and the husband compete for the allegiance of the same woman, the conflicted daughter-wife. The legend supports the cultural ideal that a good daughter gives her primary allegiance to her father, not her husband.

For the cultural relativist, the selection "fits" the environment. "Therefore, what God has joined together, let not man separate" (Mark 10:9).

For the theist, the legend represents a psychological and spiritual war regarding which dyad should be dominant: The cultural Universal and one-flesh principle of *husband-wife* or the cultural particular of father-daughter?

From a Sharanahua perspective, the covenantal one-flesh principle of *husband-wife* is dangerous because it undermines the Sharanahua economic security system constructed on the biological one-flesh principle of father-daughter.

Siskind says, "The myth suggests that a woman who marries outside her father's house lives with a dangerous stranger,"[7] one who lives by a different set of cultural rules. Anyone who separates a daughter from her father violates normative standards of Sharanahua behavior.

While the legend supports the Sharanahua cultural operating system, which has made the father-daughter the dominant dyad of the nuclear family, such a legend would not exist if removing daughters from a Sharanahua household and setting up an independent household was not a problem.

As a symbol of the ultimate provider, the jaguar, also known as the son-in-law, is putting into action the one-flesh principle of Genesis 2:24. Whenever a society rejects the one-flesh principle of *husband-wife*, it must restructure the nuclear family and replace the Universal with a negative cultural particular.

In the above legend, any child born to a son-in-law who refuses to be reduced to a "meat provider" for the Sharanahua household-of-five and sets up an independent household will, according to the myth, sire non-human children.

For the Sharanahua, being human means accepting the duties and obligations that go along with marrying someone's daughter. A human son-in-law hunts for his father-in-law, who gives him conjugal rights to his daughter, a place to live, and a mother-in-law who will cook for him. To be inhuman is to be a jaguar who rejects the norms of Sharanahua allegiance patterns generated by contextual pressures.

The legend's message is clear: Any son-in-law contemplating an independent household is a jaguar. Jaguars must be destroyed and eliminated because they are a real threat to a cultural operating system designed to reduce food anxieties over existence.

The dominance of the father-daughter dyad must be maintained at all costs. By a magical clap of the hands, the jaguar is made to disappear, and a Universal Principle "written on the heart" is magically erased. Or is it?

Thou shall become a protein supplier

## CONVICTIONS

- At some point in history, cultural forms that "had no place in the Divine Plan" secretly crept in and became part of the Sharanahua lifeway.
- Human culture is about creating defensive systems against anxieties. The number of defensive systems

created is equal to the number of diverse environments that exist in the world.
- Anxious about who would provide the meat, the Sharanahua ascribed this function to sons-in-law. As a cultural form, it secretly crept into the Sharanahua lifeway and "had no place in the Divine Plan."
- The legend serves as a warning to fathers who fail to inform their daughters that their primary allegiance is to them, not the husband.
- Universal Principles for living have "been woven into the fabric of our existence," and they cannot be deleted from the subconscious.
- For the contextualizer (like Karl Marx), no concept or form has an inherent meaning. Instead, social existence alone determines the ideal dyad and how the nuclear family should be structured.[8]

# CHAPTER 47
# MICCOSUKEE (MIKASUKI)
## FLORIDA, NORTH AMERICA

"It is your moral duty to provide sperm for my family."

> "When I marry and become a father, my biological children will not belong to me."
> ~Miccosukee father

When a Miccosukee father produces children, the children belong to his wife and her family, a family type called the matrilineal clan.

When assigned to the Miccosukee tribe in South Florida after finishing our task among the Chácobo in the Amazonian Rainforest (1955-1980), a missiological problem confronted me that remains to this day—the Miccosukee concept of marriage and family.

Unlike the American kinship system, which is biblical, the Miccosukee kinship system is shaped by what missiologist-anthropologist Charles Kraft calls contextual interaction.

Kraft believes: "Words [like marriage and family]...derive their meanings from their interaction with the contexts in which they participate."[1] According to Kraft, no word has a Divine meaning attached to it. This writer strongly disagrees.

At some point in their history, the Miccosukee tribe rearranged the nuclear family structure, and what "sneaked in" had "no place in the Divine Plan" (Romans 5:20).

It was a new kind of family whose meaning was shaped by contextual interaction. Anthropologists call it the matrilineal clan. Women are in charge.

Restructuring the nuclear family involved replacing the covenantal one-flesh principle of *husband-wife* (Genesis 2:24) with the biological one-flesh principle of sister-sister. After creating the new family type, the daughters of Eve got together and created a myth: "Only two sisters [existed] at the beginning" (Belmont 1985).[2]

To protect the new form, which had "no place in the Divine Plan," they put their hope in a Universal Rule: "Thou shall not marry a family member lest thou commit incest." In doing so, they not only replaced the nuclear family as the basis of society, they refined the meaning of family.

Assuming that the Miccosukee definitions of marriage and family were the same as his, Scandinavian-American Justin Johnson married Rebecca Sanders of the Miccosukee tribe.

As a non-Miccosukee, Johnson had no idea what the consequences would be when his Miccosukee wife gave birth to their first child, Ingrid, as reported in the local news in March 2018.[3]

> Following a public outcry and a demand from U.S. Sen. Marco Rubio, R-Fla., Ingrid was returned a few days later.
>
> But Johnson said the emotional damage was done. Now, he's filing a civil lawsuit naming several members of the tribe, including the child's grandmother, Baptist Hospital, and its employees.
>
> "We are making a call for action," Johnson's attorney, Richard Wolfe, said.
>
> According to the lawsuit, on March 18, 2018, Miccosukee Tribal Police, accompanied by Miami-Dade Police, went into the hospital and took the baby.
>
> "They abducted their child. It's a kidnapping," Wolfe said.
>
> Wolfe said the tribal officer who came to take the baby had his hand on his gun, escalating an already emotional experience.
>
> "If you were in the hospital with your child and someone came in at gunpoint and took your child away from you, you would be outraged," Wolfe said. "We are outraged."[4]

THE ABOVE INCIDENT occurred on March 18, 2018, after a couple of generations of Bible teaching in the Miccosukee Baptist Church. The church members had not been taught that society's basic unit is the nuclear family, not the matrilineal clan. Though the Rule of Exogamy protected the form, the form did not accord with Christ (Colossians 2:8).

The spiritual principles that separated Justin from Rebecca are also grounded in grammar. When I analyzed the Miccosukee posessive pronoun system, I unexpectedly discovered they had an innate knowledge of the one-flesh principle of *husband-wife* stated in Genesis 2:24.

The covenantal one-flesh principle of *husband-wife* surfaced when I asked my language informant, Daniel Tommy, "How do you say, 'my wife?'"

"He replied, '*Cha halke.*'"

The syllable *cha* did not mean "my." It meant "part of someone."

Unlike most languages, the Miccosukee language has no posessive pronouns. For the Miccosukee, life is all about relationships, of which there are two kinds: "The part of someone" kind of relationship and "it exists for someone" kind of relationship. Note the following.

Part of someone: *Cha nooti* my teeth—literally, teeth part of me.

It exists for someone: *Am if chi* my gun— literally, for-me the gun exists.

Every Miccosukee husband considers his wife to be part of his being. It is the same one-flesh perspective that the shocked Johnson no doubt believed to be a Universal, and his Miccosukee wife, his mother-in-law, and the Miccosukee police did not.

Amazingly, before Columbus and the Puritans arrived on the continent, the Miccosukee of South Florida knew the one-flesh principle of *husband-wife*. The principle was not learned. It was "woven into the very fabric of our creation" (Romans 2:15, The Message).

Unfortunately, it was a meaning accepted by Miccosukee husbands but rejected by their wives and their families, known as the matrilineal clan, of which no husband was a member.

After discovering Miccosukee husbands innately knew the one-flesh principle of *husband-wife*, I immediately followed up by asking what a wife says when asked, "How does one say, 'my husband'"?

The answer was, "*Am nankeen.*"

When back-translated into English, it means: "For-me *(dative)* existing husband-thing." Johnson failed to realize that he had been reduced to a mere "thing" like a broom, car, or dog. He was a needed sperm donor.

From a Miccosukee perspective, Justin's primary function as a husband was to serve as a sperm donor who produced children for his wife's family, known as the matrilineal clan. From a Miccosukee perspective, this meant Johnson had no legal rights to his daughter, Ingrid.

Sadly, even today, Miccosukee wives reject the covenantal one-flesh principle of *husband-wife*. Choosing "to go their own way," they replaced the covenantal *husband-wife* dyad with the biological dyad of sister-sister. Wives and their sisters took control of the Miccosukee cultural operating system. Miccosukee women rule.

In doing so, the Miccosukee are guilty of replacing a Positive Universal with a negative particular, thereby creating a new family type, one that slipped into history and has "no place in the Divine Plan" (Romans 5:20).

In this case, a grammatical analysis uncovered the existence of a Universal Form common to all with an inherent Divine meaning, a meaning Miccosukee husbands approve of and subscribe to but which their wives and mothers-in-law, like Eve, rejected.

Unknown to Justin Johnson, the Miccosukee had, at some point in history, rearranged the internal structure of the nuclear family, replacing the *husband-wife* dyad with that of sister-sister and the nuclear family with the matrilineal clan. In the process, they "multiplied sin" [disorder] (Romans 5:20) and increased cultural diversity.

When Miccosukee wives replaced husband headship with wife headship, they created a form that had "no place in the Divine Plan."

> *A law-way which had "no place in the Divine Plan"*
> *slipped into history, increasing sinning.*
> *But as sinning increased, God's grace increased even*
>   *more.*
> *(Romans 5:20, Prost translation)*

Florida Miccosukee Indian tribe

## CONVICTIONS

- Before Columbus and the Pilgrims arrived in North America, the Miccosukee knew the covenantal one-flesh principle of *husband-wife*. The principle is "woven into the very fabric of our creation" (Romans 2:15).
- When compelled by contextual interaction, Miccosukee's wives added cultural diversity, disorder, and chaos to the world. They restructured the nuclear family, replacing the dominant *husband-wife* dyad with a sister-sister dyad.
- If Justin Johnson had known what becoming a Miccosukee husband meant, he would never have married Rebecca Sanders. For the Miccosukee, marriage for the husband means being reduced to a *dative* (for-wife husband-thing), also known as a sperm donor.

# CHAPTER 48
# THE TROBRIAND ISLANDERS
## PAPUA, NEW GUINEA

"Address me as 'husband of my mother,' never as 'father.'"

## A SOCIETY OF FATHERLESS FAMILIES

*"When I marry, I will be addressed by my biological children as 'husband of mother' rather than as their father because my children have been raised to believe no father is a genitor."*

# GILBERT R. PROST

### ~Trobriand father

One of the most unusual socio-cultural operating systems ever created by humankind is that of the Trobriand Islanders of the South Pacific.

I came to this conclusion after reading Polish-British anthropologist Bronislaw Malinowski's *The Sexual Life of Savages* and then reading *Trobriand* by George Fathauer. The latter was an attempt to bring together and systemize all of Malinowski's research data with the goal of presenting to the public a "comprehensible model of Trobriand social structure."[1]

Viewed from my top-down, inside-out frame of reference, which starts with man "created in the image of God" and therefore, endowed with constant and true Universal Principles for living "written on the heart," it became clear that the Trobriand lifeway represented the extreme as to how much a society could diverge from the Divine Meta-Script "within" and still function as a society.

This divergence and its maiming effects are manifest in many ways. They begin with the denial that fathers have a role both socially and biologically as fathers. If Trobriand fathers were to assume their natural roles as fathers, the entire social structure or socio-economic operating system would collapse.

Becoming a Trobriand husband means several things, many very strange to a Westerner and most world cultures. One significant difference is their firm belief that no husband can be a father and that every birth is a virgin birth.

This means that when a woman marries, her brother becomes the head of her family; in other words, a Trobriand brother becomes the head of his sister's family. As head of his sister's family, he has been ascribed the task of planting a garden that provides food for his sister's children.

His brother-in-law, on the other hand, has the moral duty to feed his sister's children, not his biological children, a category Trobriand society denies exists because no husband is a father.

Rejecting the Universal Principle of Fatherhood "written on the heart," they constructed a socio-cultural operating system that "fit" the material environment of the South Pacific. This law-system attempted to suppress and hold back the qualities of fatherhood from coming to consciousness.

WHEN THE TROBRIAND Islanders declared that every birth was a virgin birth, they had to devise a plan of action that would prevent the concept of biological fatherhood, structured in the unconscious mind, from being "triggered" and brought to consciousness—and they did this.

To prevent the concept of fatherhood from naturally developing in their children's minds, the Trobriand developed a spiritual weapon. That weapon is called *teknonymy*.

Its spiritual function is to prevent society from acquiring a Divine perspective on how the nuclear family should be structured. The function of the *teknonym* is to prevent linking the inherent qualities of fatherhood in a Universal-Lexicon embedded in the subconscious with the symbol for father that exists in the language, namely, *tama*.

Every *teknonym* consists of (a) a status position, plus (b) the dative "of." At an early age, Trobriand children are instructed to address their biological fathers with the *teknonym* (husband of my mother.) They are taught never to address or speak of their fathers using the word *tama* (father).

The suppression worked. They were able to prevent the transfer of the concept of fatherhood existing in a Universal-Lexicon structured in the unconscious mind from being "triggered" and thus becoming part of their Lexicon. It was an amazing achievement!

If the word *tama* were uttered in a family context, it would "trigger" the term's meaning, thus destroying their law-way of living. Amazingly, the Trobriand figured this out.

If "husbands of mothers" were to be recognized as biological and social fathers, it would threaten their social defensive construct against anxiety and their need for magic to control events. Thus, using the *teknonym* "husband of mother" became a semantic weapon for protecting the Trobriand's interpretative system.

To be on the safe side, the Trobriand added the myth of an ogre named Dokonikan who would destroy any individual or family who deviated from the Trobriand interpretive script, which denied the existence of the status position of the biological father.

Both the *teknonym* and myth have a shared function. That function is to suppress the "truth of God" (Romans 1:18) concerning fatherhood from being "triggered" and brought to consciousness while preventing *husband-wife* intimacy from developing.

The existence of the *teknonym* "husband of mother" provides proof that structured in the unconscious mind of every Trobriand is *etic* data declaring every child born has a biological father. The Great Trickster pulled off the greatest deception in human history—the idea that every birth is a virgin birth.

If the child had heard the word *tama* in an everyday linguistic-social context, the linkage between the form and Divine meaning would have occurred, and the child would have known the qualities of fatherhood.

In the same way, every child innately knows what the qualities of a tree or animal are. To a large degree, they succeeded in suppressing the truth within them.

Second, since fatherhood qualities are needed in raising children, the Trobriands were compelled to transfer the moral duties of fatherhood to the maternal uncle, who, according to Malinowski, was now "head of the family." The maternal uncle thus became responsible for feeding his sister's children, disciplining them, and instructing them in what it meant to be a Trobriand.

The uncle who masqueraded as "father," the wife's brother, lived in another house. According to anthropologist George Fathauer, despite the distance:

A sister should always respect her brother, bending down when he approaches and obeying his commands in all matters. A woman should regard her brother as her guardian and the legal head of her family of procreation.[2]

But such behavior is in fundamental opposition to what the Word of God teaches:

> *For in the past, the holy women who put their hope in God also beautified themselves in this way, submitting to their own husbands, just as Sarah obeyed Abraham, calling him lord. You have become her children when you do what is good and are not frightened by anything alarming. (I Peter 3:5-6, Holman Christian Standard Bible)*

Sadly, the true meaning of *tama* was never "triggered" and brought to consciousness where it could be linked with the correct symbol. The *teknonym* had maimed them.

Finally, they instill fear in every member of society, the fear of the great ogre, Dokonikan, who had "several rows of teeth and could not speak properly,"[3] as reported by Malinowski. If the Trobriand fatherless kind of family was to survive, then the ogre Dokonikan needed to be slain.

The mother's son slays Dokonikan, the threat to the Trobriand lifeway, through magic. This means that the real enemy of Trobriand society, the spiritual idea of fatherhood, existed as a mental concept in the subconscious that needed to be suppressed. In addition, the *Myth of Dokonikan* was created to protect the divergent form, the fatherless family.

This divergence from the Divine Meta-Script began at some point in history when they collectively rejected the covenantal one-flesh principle of *husband-wife*. They rejected the Order of Creation as stated by Jesus:

> "*But from the beginning of the creation, God* 'made them male and female.
> For this reason, a man shall leave his father and mother and be joined to his wife,
> and the two shall become one-flesh'; *so then they are no longer two, but one flesh.*
> *Therefore what God has joined together, let not man separate*" (Mark 10:6-9).

Then, the Trobriand replaced the Universal Principle with the biological dyad of brother-sister.

∽

## FACED WITH A DILEMMA

Unlike the matrilineal Miccosukee, who replaced the *husband-wife* dyad with that of sister-sister and then created a supporting myth that declared: "In the beginning, life began with two sisters," the matrilineal Trobriands replaced the *husband-wife* dyad with brother-sister:

> In mythology, a brother and sister emerged together from the underworld, the sister to establish a sub-clan and the brother to act as her guardian ... there should be no intimacy between them.[4]

As moral beings, they recognized that becoming intimate with one's siblings would constitute an incestuous relationship and must be avoided.

However, this left the Trobriands with an ontological problem. They had to explain how sisters became pregnant without breaking the Universal Rule of Incest, which classified brother-sister marriages as "sinful."

To their credit, they chose to obey a Moral Rule. They did not have to be taught this rule because the Universal Rule of Incest is innate. Figuratively, it is "written on the heart." Their solution? They declared that every birth was a virgin birth brought about by *baloma* (spirit).

Anthropologists suggest they were mistaken because of biological ignorance. Instead of being ignorant, we propose that Trobriand society innately knew the Universal Rule of Incest. As moral beings they refused to "engage in evil."[5] They did not want to be known as an incestuous, sinful society.

They had to explain how sisters became pregnant because Trobriand life did not begin with Adam and Eve, who became intimate as husband and wife living in the garden. Instead, it started with a brother-sister emerging from the underworld who innately knew that becoming intimate was sinful.

Because culture is a spiritual phenomenon rather than a material one, the Great Trickster, who masquerades as an angel of light, explained how sisters became pregnant. "And no wonder! For Satan himself transforms himself into an angel of light" (II Corinthians 11:14).

∼

## REJECTING THE CREATION ORDER

To relieve their anxieties over existence, the Trobriand constructed a socio-economic operating law-system that attempted to eliminate the biological and social role of the father while promising them economic security. They assumed they could free themselves from Universal "fixed" standards for living and "go their own way" (Acts 14:16) without suffering the stultifying consequences.

This meant the rejection of the Divine meaning of the status position of fatherhood and the Creation Order, which establishes the nuclear family as the foundational norm for all humanity.

So when a Trobriand woman married, according to Malinowski,

her brother became "the head of her family,"[6] not as a father but as a "guardian." As "guardian," his ascribed function was to protect the Trobriand construct of a fatherless family. If the Trobiands were to have appropriate ideas about how to live, the ideas of fatherhood, marriage, and what constituted a family had to be deleted from consciousness.

Rejecting the dual role of father in the nuclear family, they created a new kind of family that not only replaced the covenantal dyad of *husband-wife* with that of sister-brother but also attempted to suppress the concept of father that existed in the mind from being "triggered" and brought to consciousness.

This shift from the spiritual to the biological, from culture to nature, prayer to magic, and from the Creation Order of nuclear families to fatherless families is one example of *etic* divergence.

Rejecting the Divine Meta-Script for living "written on the heart," a design grounded in Conceptual Constants (*etic* data), they created a design for living that promised them security as long as they had the right magic (like the power to control the weather), and each person fulfilled their ascribed function.

In this design for living, according to anthropologist George Fathauer, "Biological fathers are regarded as outsiders since the children belong to the [matrilineal] lineage and sub-clan of his wife, their mother."[7]

But the Trobriand Islander's socio-economic operating law-system was grounded on a biological lie, namely, that no father was a genitor. The lie meant jural rights over the father's children had to be transferred to his wife's brother, who had now become the "head of the family."

Maternal uncles had become the new "guardians." As "guardians," maternal uncles masqueraded as "fathers." This meant assuming many moral duties of fatherhood, such as providing yams to feed his sister's children.

In addition, "the brother responsible for his sister's food is the one who plays the main role of disciplinarian and tutor of her children."[8] Of course, such behavior is in fundamental opposition to biblical teaching that the role of the father is to discipline his children. "The LORD disciplines everyone he loves. He severely disciplines everyone he accepts as his child" (Hebrews 12:6, Names of God Bible).

No Trobriand father has the right to discipline the son he dearly loves because, according to Trobriand law, no son has a biological father.

## FEATURES OF ETIC DIVERGENCE AMONG THE TROBRIANDS

The Trobriand rejection of a Divine Meta-Script "with a script of their own making" is manifested primarily in how they restructured the nuclear family.

First, the internal structure of the nuclear family, consisting of a biological father and mother with their sons and daughters, was replaced with the husband of mother, mother, and virgin-born sons and daughters.

Second, this new kind of family was constructed on a lie; that is, no child has a biological father. Biological fathers were perceived as being "outsiders" since their children, according to the laws of the Trobriand, did not belong to them.

Third, rejecting the Order of Creation, of necessity, the Trobriand were compelled to create misrepresentations of the Universal Concepts of family, fatherhood, and the meaning of marriage. Marriage had nothing to do with becoming "one flesh."

According to Allan Darrah:

> Instead, "marriage among the Trobriand means for political alliance and tributary obligations; it is not surprising that adultery—(wife

stealing) has political overtones. A man's prestige depends on his marriage, as is much of his income."[9]

Rejection of these Universal Truths of marriage, family, and fatherhood led to a transfer of power away from fathers and the nuclear family to a new kind of family, one I would classify as a "fake family."

## CULTURAL DIVERSITY AND THE MULTIPLICATION OF SIN

With the creation of fatherless families, a new cultural law-system for living "slipped in" or "sneaked in" (Romans 5:20) after the Tower of Babel.

When the Apostle Paul used the verb "sneaked in," usually mistranslated as "entered" or "came in" in most translations, he was informing his readers that the kinds of law-systems that "sneaked in" were dangerous. Not only did they create cultural diversity, they "multiplied sin."

Romans 5:20 states: "Moreover the law entered that the offense might abound. But where sin abounded, grace abounded much more ..."

For the Trobriand, it began when they declared (a) "reproduction results from entry into the body of a woman by the *baloma* (spirit) of a dead ancestor," and (b) "the father is not genetically related to the child."[10]

Its principles not only created a new kind of family, it also created a new type of law-system (*nomos* absent article),[11] A law-system that not only increased cultural diversity and multiplied sin but also spiritually and psychologically maimed its members.

## CONTEXTUALIZATION

How does this new design for living affect the preaching of the Gospel to the Trobriands? As stated by Malinowski, it means any missionary who preaches John 3:16: "For God [the Father] so loved the world that He gave His only begotten Son, that whoever believes in Him should not perish but have everlasting life," would immediately be classified by the Trobriands as a liar. When "they [the missionaries] talk that seminal fluid makes a child, lie! The spirit indeed brings [children] at night time."[12]

Incoming missionaries who preached the spiritual and biological truth about paternity were now the enemies of a lifeway that denied the existence of an Order of Creation, the one-flesh principle of husband and wife. They had become representations in the flesh of the mythical ogre Dokonikan.

At this point, the contextualizer faces a severe problem if there exists no Universal concept of fatherhood that is part of a Lexicon of Universal meanings.[13]

According to Malinowski, contextualization means:

> We must realize that the cardinal dogma of God the Father and God the Son, the sacrifice of the only Son and the filial love of the Maker, would completely misfire in a matrilineal society, where the relation is decreed by tribal law to be that of two strangers, where all personal unity between them is denied, and where all family obligations are associated with the mother-line.
>
> We cannot then wonder that paternity must be among the principal truths to be taught by the proselytizing Christians. Otherwise, the dogma of the Trinity would have to be translated into matrilineal terms, and we would have to speak of a God-*kadala* (mother's brother), a God-sister's son, and a Divine *baloma* (spirit).[14]

In addition, contextualization would mean denying both verbal inspiration of the Scripture and the doctrine of man created in the "image of God," a doctrine that implies the existence of an innate interpretative system and Universal-Lexicon for determining what is true and what is false.

One feature of the Rule of Exogamy is how it affects a Trobriand bachelor's choice of mates. The more sisters a potential wife has, the more gardens he must make. Bachelors prefer marrying someone with no sisters to avoid making multiple gardens.

There is also the Law of Non-Contradiction. The Law of Non-Contradiction would say there can be only one kind of Trinity, not two.

Here we have a clear example of what Pike calls *etic* divergence, a rejection and movement away from Universal Truth "written on the heart." If the missionary contextualizes the Gospel, it ceases to be the Gospel!

This moral divergence from the Divine Meta-Script implies that man and society have the freedom and the capacity to "distort innate positive [mental] Universals into negative particular actions"[15] or concepts.

Those who reject the Apostle Paul's declaration that there exist "commandments written on the heart" (Romans 2:15) will also reject the Biblical principle of *etic* divergence, the fact that a society can choose to "go its own way" (Acts 14:16).

What is unusual in this case is this: The Trobriand's attempt to prevent the father's role from being "triggered" and brought to consciousness reveals that they were aware that such a role had been "written on their hearts."

While they possessed the symbol for father, namely, *tama*[16] in their language, they attempted to suppress the true qualities of fatherhood from being linked with the symbol *tama*. It would be analogous to possessing words for trees, birds, and animals without knowing the qualities that constituted each kind. The qualities of the kind must be linked to the correct symbol.

# CREATED IN THE IMAGE OF GOD

## AN INTERPRETIVE SYSTEM WITHIN HUMANS

This "triggering [of innate concepts]," according to psychologist Jerome Brunner, is brought about by:

> The acts and expressions of others and by certain basic social contexts in which human beings interact. In a word, we come equipped ... with a set of predispositions to construe the social world in a particular way.[17]

The Trobriand attempted to suppress this interpretative system but were only partially successful.

We know this when we observe the behavior of "husbands of mothers" toward their biological children. In this regard, I agree with linguist Noam Chomsky's statement that "behavior simply provides evidence for the possession of [innate] knowledge."[18]

In this case, it is knowledge of how a father should treat his children. Despite not being recognized as biological fathers, Trobriand fathers are great fathers, and Trobriand children love their "fathers."

We must ask why "husbands of mothers" would exhibit the natural qualities of fatherhood. Could the caretaker role of fatherhood "written on the heart" not be suppressed?

Anthropologist Fauther points out that the most intimate bond among the Trobriand is that of a father and his son. They reject their own self-imposed cultural law-system, which states that the heir to his property is his sister's child, and "a father [still] tries to give his son as many advantages as he can."[19]

Contrary to the Trobriand customary law, fathers secretly pass on to their sons as much of their estate as they can. But in doing so, they are merely doing what is natural. They are, in fact, acting biblically. They innately know the rights to one's inheritance. In doing so, however, they are rebelling against a cultural law-system that declares fathers have no role in life.

While no Trobriand husband is recognized as the father of his children, he is, according to anthropologist Bronislaw Malinowski, "the head of his sister's family,"[20] of which he's a member.

His brother-in-law, on the other hand, has the moral duty to feed his sister's children, not his biological children, a category the Trobriand tribe denies exists because no husband is a father.

By denying that fathers can have sons, Trobiand society has rejected the Good News that our heavenly Father (God) sent His Son into the world to be our Savior. Missionaries are perceived as being liars.

At some point in Trobriand's history, it is proposed that a collective rebellion occurred against what it meant to be "created in the image and likeness of God," a concept found in a Universal-Lexicon structured in the unconscious mind. This means that attached to forms common to all are Divine meanings which are "fixed" and constant.

The Trobriand rebelled against the inherent meaning attached to the Universal concept of fatherhood. They rejected the Divine meaning and replaced it with the concept of fatherless families.

While missiologist Kraft asserts, "Human biology provides the backdrop for all that we need to know as humans,"[21] the Trobriand would strongly disagree. For them, no child has a biological father.

In addition, the Trobriand would wholeheartedly agree with cognitive psychologist Jerome Bruner:

> Man's biological inheritance ... does not direct or shape human action and experience, does not serve as the Universal cause. Rather, it imposes constraints on human action, constraints whose effects are modifiable ... it is culture, not biology, that shapes human life and the human mind, that gives meaning to human action by situating its underlying intentional states in an interpretative system.[22]

However, the interpretative system of the Trobriand excludes the concept of biological fathers. For the Trobriand, every child is a virgin birth.

Developmental psychologist Paul Bloom supports the thesis that every child comes equipped with a culture-free, interpretative script that compels every child to interpret existence from what we deem to be a Divine perspective. He reports:

> In the last few years, an emerging body of research has explored children's grasp of certain Universal religious ideas. Some recent findings suggest that two foundational aspects of religious belief—belief in Divine agents and belief in mind-body dualism—come naturally to young children.[23]

Sadly, the missiological dogma of contextualization rejects this idea, that structured in the unconscious mind exists mental *etic* data that informs one how to live, innate instructions that a society rejects when it "goes its own way" (Acts 14:16).

For the contextualizer, there exists no culture-free *etic* data from which a society may diverge, basically saying the Apostle Paul was mistaken.

The missionary must refrain from informing the Trobriand that God the Father had a Son. He would be forcing upon the Trobriands "his standard."

Lingenfelter stresses, according to the dogma of contextualization, one's failure to contextualize would mean one is opposing and "distorting the diversity of God's creation ... forcing upon people our standards."[24]

The message of contextualization is clear: There exist no cultural Universals to which are attached "fixed" and constant Divine meanings, only negative cultural particulars since meanings "belong to the people."

In the words of existentialist Jean-Paul Sartre, "Life has no meaning *a priori* ... it is up to you to give it a meaning, and value is nothing but the meaning that you choose."[25]

Contextualizing missiologists would agree. It is up to each society to create its own interpretative system because, in the words of Kraft, "It is people who attach meanings ... to the forms of culture they use."[26] He does not accept that there are forms common to all to which inherent or Divine meanings are attached. Put another way, Kraft does not believe *a priori* culture-free *etic* data exists in the unconscious mind that contributes to man's psychic unity. Instead, he advocates that every society writes its own script.

The Trobriand script declared it was the moral duty of every husband of a mother to "fully share in the care of the children"[27] that did not belong to him.

According to Malinowski, husbands of mothers "will fondle and carry the baby, clean and wash it, and give it mashed vegetable food which it receives in addition to the mother's milk almost from birth. Nursing the baby in the arms or holding it on one's knees, described by the native word *kapo'i*, is the special role or duty of the [biological] father."[28]

However, Malinowski was mistaken when he classified *kapo'i* as a "role." The Trobriand word *kapok* represents a status position, not a natural role. It replaces the term for "father."

Just as Chácobo sons-in-law were ascribed the status position of *raisi*, i.e., food providers for the Chácobo household-of-five, and just as Miccosukee husbands were ascribed the status position of functional sperm donor for the wife's family, the matrilineal clan, Trobriand fathers were ascribed the functional status position of *kapo'i*, i.e., wife's child's nursemaid.

It was a status position every husband of a mother relinquished at puberty, at which point his brother-in-law began to exercise authority over his wife's child.

As sons grow and mature, unlike sisters, they begin to realize they are "outsiders" in the very household in which they were raised. They recognize they are not members of the same clan as the *kapo'i* who nursed them. At puberty, the Rule of Residential Endogamy kicks in.

In Malinowski's words, "Another man appears on the horizon and is called by the child *kadugu* (my mother's brother). The child also learns that where his *kadugu* (mother's brother) resides, he has legal standing."[29] The Rule of Residential Endogamy demands that every son return to his matrilineal family roots.

Unless the biological father has the political power to override the Residential Rule of Endogamy, declaring every son must return to his family or clan or village where his future career awaits him, where his natural allies and associates are to be found,[30] it means walking away from the *kapo'i* who raised him to live with an uncle he barely knows but whose ascribed task is feeding his sister's child with yams from his garden until puberty.

To do appropriate missiology, every contextualizing missionary must evaluate the validity of the Trobriand interpretative system. They must ask: Does their matrilineal design for living—that rejects the concept of fatherhood and says every child is born of a virgin birth—affect the preaching of the Gospel and establishing a church among the Trobriand?

Malinowski recognized that it did. Recognizing the missiological problem, he wrote: "We must realize that the cardinal dogma of God the Father and God the Son, the sacrifice of the only Son and the filial love of the Maker, would completely misfire in a matrilineal society, where the relation is decreed by tribal law to be that of two strangers, where all personal unity between them is denied, and where all family obligations are associated with the mother-line.

According to American anthropologist Elman Service (1915 - 1996):

> From the Trobriand's perspective, missionaries were not bringing Good News; instead, they were liars because, from their perspective, no father had a son. They found the dogma of the Fatherhood of God "to be an absurdity." Unwilling to accept the idea of Fatherhood, the natives strongly disliked the missionaries because of their "lies."[31]

Incoming missionaries who mentioned the biological truth

about paternity were viewed as enemies of the Trobriand lifeway. This lifeway denied the existence of *etic* data structured in the unconscious mind. Their script for living demanded a rejection of a Universal for a negative cultural, a restructuring of the nuclear family that made the brother-sister dyad the dominant dyad.

From a concept-innatist's perspective, the constituents of knowledge—namely, form and meaning-context—were linked together from the beginning. At creation, every form had attached to it a Divine meaning. Man and society had the freedom to reject and the freedom to replace with a meaning "that belonged to the people."

Trobriand village

## CONVICTIONS

- At some point in history, the Trobriand rejected the meaning attached to the form "father" and replaced it with the form *kapo'i* and the form "husband of mother."
- By training children at an early age to address biological fathers as "husbands of mothers," they are able to suppress the truth of father from being "triggered" and brought to consciousness.

- Since no husband of the mother is the father of the daughters living in his household, according to their script, the husband of the mother would not be committing incest if his wife died and he married one of her daughters. But Malinowski points out that "marriage between the two is viewed with definite repugnance."[32] We contend it is repugnant for a reason. It is abhorrent because structured in the unconscious mind is a rule that says, "One shall not have intercourse with a daughter."
- Marriage between a husband of a mother and the virgin-born daughters living under his roof was "viewed with definite repugnance" because the concept of fatherhood could not be deleted from consciousness. Conscience was informing them that sexual intimacy between father and daughter was incestuous.
- For the two to become intimate would violate a Divine Interpretative Script which says "marry out," an innate Interpretative Script that empiricists, materialists, and functionalists like Malinowski all refuse to recognize, despite the empirical evidence.
- According to psycholinguistics researcher Gunter Senft, "Because the Trobriand rejected the concept of fatherhood, planting a church made them one of the most challenging societies to evangelize. Their use of the *teknonym* (husband of mother) continues."[33]
- When Trobriand society replaced the *husband-wife* dyad with that of brother-sister, it introduced chaos and confusion into its lifeway.

# CHAPTER 49
# KIOWA - APACHE
## THE GREAT PLAINS, NORTH AMERICA

*"When I marry, I will never call my wife by her name; she is not important. The one who will be important to me is my brother."*
~eligible bachelor

Such would be the thoughts of tribal bachelors living on the Great Plains. As anthropologist Marvin Harris points out, such thoughts are an effect produced by infrastructural pressures; but we must ask, are such thoughts appropriate?

For those holding a top-down, inside-out epistemology, the answer that the unconscious mind is structured with knowledge is an emphatic yes.

The answer for those who hold to a bottom-up, outside-in epistemology is an emphatic no. The social existence on the Great Plains compelled the Kiowa-Apache to construct a family type known as a band. Their defensive scheme against anxiety was shaped by infrastructural pressures to "fit" the environment.

Survival on the Great Plains, where hunting buffalo was a way of life, compelled them to create a new type of family, a super-family. Each member was given a specific function. Excluding grandparents and grandchildren, the Kiowa-Apache "web of kinship" comprised thirty-six members, thirty more than the biblical family of six. The super-family the Kiowa-Apache constructed depended on rejecting the Law of Identity and merging mutually exclusive status positions.

The Kiowa-Apache "super-family" construct represented a 400% increase in rights, duties, and ascribed obligations. It was also followed by a complementary decrease in voluntary action and the freedom to have an intimate relationship with one's spouse.

Under the pressure of the elementary forces of the Great Plains or what anthropologist Marvin Harris calls infrastructure, the Kiowa-Apache made the brother-brother dyad the dominant dyad of the nuclear family.

> *Beware lest anyone cheat you through philosophy and empty deceit, according to the tradition of men, according to the basic principles of the world, and not according to Christ. (Colossians 2:8)*

According to American anthropologist Fred Eggan (1906 - 1991), the replacement meant: "The most intimate behavior, the closest feelings of unity, is between siblings of the same sex. This loyalty on the part of brothers is cited as a reason for loving a brother more than a wife."[1]

~

## THE KIOWA-APACHE SCHEME FOR LIFE ON THE GREAT PLAINS

Ecological pressures on the Great Plains compelled tribes like the Kiowa-Apache to create similar defensive systems against existential anxieties. Tribes moving West into the Great Plains were also obligated to hunt buffalo. The defensive system had to provide the necessities of life in a harsh environment filled with herds of buffalo.

For example, when horticultural tribes in the East moved into the Great Plains, they all changed family types to hunt buffalo. The super-family band became the dominant social unit of tribes living on the Great Plains.

North American tribes like the Kiowa-Apache, Cheyenne, and Arapaho believed that a super-family band that gave specific functions to their members could better reduce their existential anxieties than a group of independent nuclear families choosing to work together. In other words, social existence preceded and ruled over the "law of God in their inner being."

Eggan supported the position that social existence and environmental pressures did indeed shape the lifeways of the Great Plains' tribes. He states the following:

> Tribes coming into the Plains with different backgrounds and social systems ended up with similar kinship systems ... this is in large measure an internal adjustment to the uncertain and unchanging conditions of the Plains environment—ecological and social—rather than a result of borrowing and diffusion.[2]

It was a great insight into explaining the phenomenon of cultural diversity.

American linguist and anthropologist Roger Keesing (1935 - 1993) points out, for tribes of the Great Plains, "Kinship is [was] the idiom in which political interests are advanced and economic goals are maximized."[3] Economic goals were maximized by restructuring the nuclear family, followed by the creation of a new, intimate group or type of family known as the "band."

Whatever kind of family these tribes from the East had before they entered the Plains, they were all replaced by a new type of structure. This construct merged the status positions of father, mother, sons, daughters, brothers, and sisters with the status positions of collateral relatives: uncles, aunts, cousins, nephews, and nieces. The merging of mutually exclusive status positions satisfied a need and "fit" the environment. However, merging mutually exclusive status positions "had no place in the Divine Plan."

No longer anxious about planting crops, protecting land, or transmitting property, as in the case of the matrilineal Miccosukee living in the Everglades, they now became anxious about how they were going to survive hunting buffalo, collecting buffalo chips for fuel, tanning buffalo hides, and making teepees, leather clothing, and moccasins.

The larger one's family, the more functions they could ascribe to family members. For these Plains tribes, the issue was not freedom but survival in a very harsh environment. Their key to survival as a band depended on:

- Restructuring the nuclear family.
- Under the pressures of the "elements of the Great Plains" (Colossians 2:8), the Kiowa-Apache made the brother-brother dyad the dominant dyad of the nuclear family.
- The suppression of *husband-wife* intimacy.
- The accumulation and stealing of horses. According to whitewolfpack.com, "Horses forever changed life on the Great Plains. They tipped the balance of power in favor of mounted warriors, and they became prized as wealth."[4]
- The existence of a social rule that protected the scheme. It was called the Rule of Exogamy. Quoting Lévi-Strauss, "The Rule of Exogamy provides the only means of maintaining the group as a group."[5] Such a rule is necessary for there to be a super-family.
- Classifying uncles as fathers, aunts as mothers, cousins as siblings, and nephews and nieces as brothers and sisters meant one could obligate uncles and aunts to behave like fathers and mothers, cousins to act like brothers and sisters, and nephews and nieces to act like sons and daughters.

- The Kiowa-Apache rejected logic and declared that *A* (cousins) = *B* (siblings), etc.

Excluding the second ascending generation, namely, FaFaBrSo, FaFaSiSo, FaMoSiSo, FaMoBrSo, and MoMoSiDa, MoMoBrDa, MoFaSiDa, MoFaBrDa which were not charted, anthropologist McAllister lists thirty collateral relatives which were classified as family members. They are:

- Five collateral relatives called "father," *ace*: FaBr, FaFaBrSo, FaFaSiSo, FaMoSiSo, FaMoBrSo.
- Five collateral relatives called "mother," *made*: MoSi (MoMoSiDa, MoMoBrDa, MoFaSiDa, MoFaBrDa).
- Five collateral relatives called "older brother," *daran*: MoBrSo, MoSiSo, FaBrSo, FaSiSo. (The same for *tlaan*, "younger brother").
- Five collateral relatives called "older sister," *dadan*: MoBrDa, MoSiDa, FaBrDa, FaSiDa. (The same for *detcan*, "younger sister").
- Five collateral relatives called "sons," *jaan*: BrSo, FaBrSoSo, FaSiSoSo, MoSiSoSo, MoBrSoSo.
- Five collateral relatives called "daughters," *tceyan*: BrDa, FaBrSoDa, FaSiSoDa, MoSiSoDa, MoBrSoDa.

A socio-economic cost happens whenever a society diverges from God's truth and goes its own way. Some of the social costs of diverging from the law of God in our inner being are:

- A lifeway that destroys parent-child intimacy. McAllister states, "A child usually loves and respects his parents but is not intimate with them."[6]
- A lifeway that replaces father-son intimacy with mother's brother-nephew intimacy. According to McAllister, "The relationship between a mother's brother

and sister's child is one of friendly intimacy ... the mother's brother takes a great deal of interest in the training of a sister's son, teaching him to shoot and taking him hunting ... if a child is in trouble, he is more likely to go to his mother's brother than to his parents, for he knows that his uncle will not refuse him."[7]

- A lifeway in which a man never uses his wife's name, and she never uses his. One husband exclaimed: "Life would be short if I called my wife by her name."[8] The rule existed to prevent *husband-wife* intimacy from developing.
- A lifeway in which the Kiowa-Apache "all say that they love their grandparents more than they love their parents."
- This is a lifeway that demands complete mother-in-law avoidance. "A man would never touch his mother-in-law, look at her, talk to her, call her name, or be alone with her in a teepee."[9]
- The rule suggests a jealousy triangle in which mothers-in-law and sons-in-law compete for the allegiance of the conflicted daughter-wife.

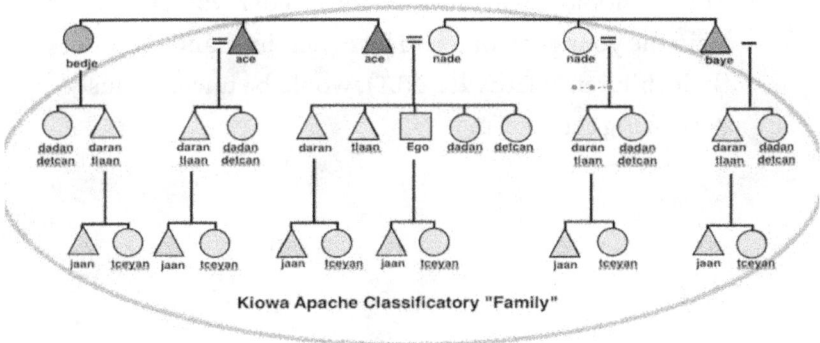

Kiowa - Apache super family

## CONVICTIONS

- Whenever man and society replace God as the Provider to relieve their existential anxieties, they must also replace God's design for living with a man-made defensive system shaped by social existence in a particular environment.
- According to Dooyeweerd, a Kiowa-Apache family construct represents a deviant family form in which membership is not "restricted to the parents and their offspring in the first degree."[10]
- Whenever a new family type exists, it will be protected by the Universal Rule of Exogamy, which instructs members to "marry out." Marrying a classificatory sibling (cousin) would constitute incest, but not so in the biblical kinship system.
- If the Kiowa-Apache defensive lifeway was to survive, then the Kiowa-Apache had to create cultural forms that would prevent *husband-wife* intimacy from developing. A strong *husband-wife* bond would eventually destroy their defensive system against anxiety.
- Any missionary who taught: "These older women must train the younger women to love their husbands and their children" (Titus 2:4, NLT), would be unconsciously destroying the system.

# CHAPTER 50
# DO SOUND WORDS EXIST

## TAKING THE GOSPEL TO THE WORLD NEEDS SOUND WORDS

## Do Strong Words Exist?

"Don't listen to him... He believes sound words exist."

Among the more questionable concepts advanced by evangelical anthropologists is the one presented by Charles Kraft. He unequivocally states, "'Contextualization' is the scripturally-endorsed approach to taking the Gospel to the world."[1]

Really? By promoting the idea that meanings derived from context are attached to forms common to all, Kraft has relativized the meaning of words.

For Kraft, no "sound words" exist—that is, words with meanings that are "fixed," true, and constant. Instead, all meanings are derived from social existence, and they "belong to the people."[2]

But according to the Apostle Paul, "taking the Gospel to the world" meant using "sound words," those of our Lord Jesus Christ.

> *If anyone teaches otherwise and does not consent to wholesome words,* even *the words of our Lord Jesus Christ, and to the doctrine which accords with godliness,*
> *he is proud, knowing nothing, but is obsessed with disputes and arguments over words, from which come envy, strife, reviling, evil suspicions ... (I Timothy 6:3-4)*

Paul was aware that any divergence from using "sound words" when preaching the Gospel was, as New Testament Greek scholar R. C. H. Lenski points out, the first "stepping stone from truth into falsehood."[3] Understanding the Gospel was contingent on the messenger's use of "sound words."

For this reason, the Apostle Paul admonished Timothy: "Hold fast the pattern of sound words which you have heard from me, in faith and love which are in Christ Jesus" (II Timothy 1:13).

The *Good News* translation renders "strong words" as "true words." Another translation renders it as "healthy words." For Jesus and Paul, a "sound word" was a word with a "fixed," constant, and true meaning.

Disagreeing are the contextualizers (i.e., Kraft) for whom there must exist an "appropriate 'fit' between form and content,"[4] and the "fit" must be "context specific."[5] This means no word spoken by Jesus or Paul can have a "fixed" and unchanging meaning. Meanings must "fit" the context. They "belong to the people."

For example, in our postmodern world, two words that are no longer sound and have meanings that "belong to the people" are male and female. What matters today is one's perceived meaning. If a male perceives he is a female, or a female perceives she is a male, it's one's perception that determines one's gender, not biology.

With the rejection of "sound words," Professor Christopher Yuan at the Moody Bible Institute points out that the tenor of our time is to force one to accept one's perceptions of the truth.

> At present, this psychological concept of "gender" is essentially being enforced linguistically, with demands to use preferred pronouns and newly chosen names to match self-perception rather than objective truth. But this is how minds are changed—by first changing language.[6]

We live in a world that rejects what Jesus said when He declared: "But from the beginning of creation, God *'made them male and female'*" (Mark 10:6).

The Bible is clear. The meanings of male and female "do not belong to the people." They belong to God. In today's political climate, anyone believing this may be prosecuted by the government. In 2019, a British court ruled:

> Belief in Genesis 1:27, lack of belief in transgenderism, and conscientious objection to transgenderism in our judgment are incompatible with human dignity and conflict with the fundamental rights of others.[7]

Sadly, the contextualized meanings we attach to cultural forms now taught in our schools and universities will lead to social chaos, the stultification of society, and eventually the persecution of Christians.

The postmodern idea that "meanings belong to the people" is not new. Long before the Puritans landed in the New World, the tribes of North America attached meanings to the concept of family determined solely by environmental "fitness" and human necessity.

For example, the Great Plains tribes decided the nuclear family was not large enough to hunt buffalo in the West. As discussed in chapter 49, "The Great Plains - The Kiowa - Apache Super Family," the creation of a band as a family type demanded the classification of aunts and uncles as mothers and fathers, cousins as siblings, and nephews as sons and nieces as daughters. This merging of lineal and collateral status positions was considered appropriate because it satisfied a need.

However, such thinking represented a spiritual rejection of concepts having inherent (God-given) meanings and they replaced those meanings with perceptions belonging to the people (*etic divergence*).

For the contextualizer, the meaning must be found in experience. The result is cultural diversity and the relativizing of meaning.

Sadly, those who teach contextualization in our seminaries cannot adhere to the biblical standard of "sound words" when they adhere to the empiricist's idea that meanings "belong to the people." Meanings that, in the words of Mao Zedong, "originate in direct experience."[8]

In my opinion, the meanings the Chácobo attached to the concepts of family, father, mother, sons, and daughters needed to be corrected because they represented meanings that "belonged to the people."

As a concept-innatist, and as pointed out by R. J. Rushdoony, I view contextualization of meanings as a product of a postmodern world. It rejects: "A [law] framework [that] is rigid and constant in order to provide man freedom within that framework."[9]

In this regard, note the words of missiologist Charles Kraft as he categorizes those who work in pioneer situations.

> We who teach contextualization are dealing primarily with those whose major concern will have to be on how to bring about change in already existing situations rather than how to plant culturally appropriate churches.[10]

If Kraft is correct, "planting a culturally appropriate church" among the Chácobo meant planting a leaderless church without elders. After all, they were a leaderless society.

However, our missiological strategy grounded in the biblical proposition that new life demands new forms (with inherent meanings) begot the following effects: The Chácobo are no longer a leaderless, dying tribe. Our "Revolution without Guns" was a huge success.

In the words of Christian philosopher Cornelius Plantinga, these concepts annoy the postmodern for whom there are no "sound words" or words having "fixed" and unchanging meanings. He goes on to say:

> Of course, such ideas annoy certain people. The idea of a design to which all of us must conform ourselves, whether we like it or not, appears to be absurd or even offensive to many. People who believe in naturalistic evolution, for example, think that human concepts, values, desires, and religious beliefs are, like human life itself, metaphysically untethered to any transcendent purpose. Our lives and values are rather the product of such blind mechanisms as random genetic mutation and natural selection.[11]

According to Kraft, who rejects the idea that there exists a Universal design or set of concepts having inherent meanings "to which we must all conform ourselves, whether we like it or not," the "planting of a culturally appropriate church"[12] meant planting a leaderless church for the Chácobo.

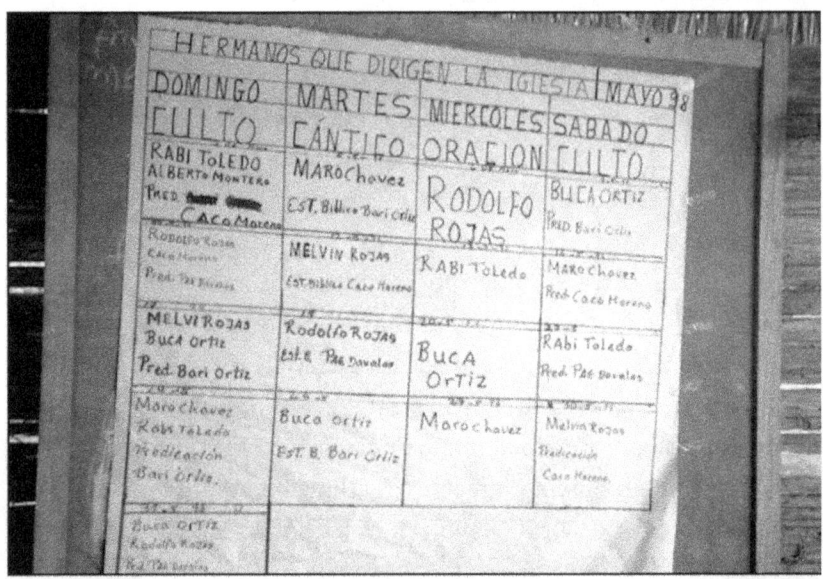

Assignments for the elders of the Chácobo church

## CONVICTIONS

- A "sound word" is a word whose meaning is "fixed," constant, and true.
- The meanings of "sound words" are "not learned." They are "acquired" by being "triggered" and brought to consciousness in a socio-linguistic context.
- The rejection of "sound words" leads to cultural diversity, chaos, and the rejection of logic. The phenomenon is called *etic* divergence.

# CHAPTER 51
# NATURALIZING SINGING AND DANCING
## AGUARUNA AND JÍVARO OF PERU

### I SING AND DANCE TO HELP THE CROPS GROW

Among the Aguaruna and Jívaro of Peru, a belief exists that living deep underground is a goddess named *Nunguí* who emerges at night to dance in the women's gardens. Jívaro women sing to *Nunguí*, believing their songs to *Nunguí* will increase production. Faith in their ability to increase food production is illustrated in the following song:

> "I am a woman of Nunguí.
> Therefore, I sing so that the manioc will grow well.
> For when I do not sing there is not much production.
> I am a woman of Nunguí.
> Therefore, I harvest faster than others."[1]

North American Indians also sing and dance to compel nature to achieve desired results. They sing and dance to grow crops, bring rain, heal the sick, and bring animals within killing range.

As illustrated in the verb chart at the end of this chapter, among the Miccosukee, singing and dancing do not represent actions in culture but in nature. This shift from culture to nature is reflected semantically in replacing *-ek* verb margins with *-ak* verb margins. It also reveals that singing and dancing serve a material function using forms that have "no place in the Divine Plan."

## MICCOSUKEE TRANSLATION PROJECT

When assigned to the Miccosukee Translation Project, I was surprised the Miccosukee language provided proof of the existence of two scripts for living. Linguistic analysis revealed a Divine Plan and a people's plan.

Each script is designed to handle the human problem of existential anxiety. Each plan, God's or humankind's, addresses the issue differently.

In Matthew 6:26, the Divine Plan rhetorically asks:

> "Look at the birds of the air, for they neither sow nor reap nor gather into barns; yet your heavenly Father feeds them. Are you not of more value than they?"

The Miccosukee plan decreed: The only way to relieve your existential anxieties is to create a cultural operating system that reduces husbands to person-things, gives women control of assets, and relies on magic to control nature.

To my surprise, this spiritual struggle—the psychological, physical, and material needs of society—was made linguistically explicit in their language.

These two plans surfaced when I asked my Miccosukee informant, "What is your word for sing followed by the word for dance?"

I discovered they had naturalized singing and dancing. Instead of classifying them as a cultural event, they classified them as a material event.

This shift from singers and dancers in the sphere of culture to performers of magic in the sphere of nature manifested itself linguistically in replacing the *-ek* culture verb margins with *-ak* nature verb margins.

By reducing transcendent acts in the sphere of culture represented by the syllable *-ek* to compelled behavior in the sphere of necessity represented by the syllable *-ak,* the Miccosukee were guilty of replacing Divine meanings attached to the cultural forms of singing and dancing with meanings "that belonged to the people."

The " law of sin" now directed the body and its parts. They now served a function, and that function was magic. They did so by using their bodies, physical members—arms, legs, feet, mouth, and vocal cords—to wage "war" against the law of God.

By linking a verb margin, either *-ek* or *-ak,* to the forms called singing and dancing, the speaker could inform his listeners why they were singing and dancing.

If it was out of pleasure and joyfulness, the speaker would use the *-ek* verb margin; if it was out of necessity and self-preservation, the *-ak* verb margin was used.

This reductionism from culture to nature was a clear manifestation of their rejection of God as Provider. Linguistic analysis revealed the Miccosukee were using the material laws of necessity described by the Apostle Paul as the "law in my members" to overthrow the "law of the mind," also known as God's Law, "written on the heart" (Romans 2:15), and as stated by the Apostle Paul in Romans 7:23:

> *But I see another law in my members, warring against the law of my mind, and bringing me into captivity to the law of sin which is in my members.*

Canceling Providence, they used the Universal singing and dancing forms to prod and compel nature to be their provider.

By reducing transcendent acts in the sphere of culture represented by the syllable *-ek* to compelled behavior in the sphere of necessity represented by the syllable *-ak,* the Miccosukee were guilty of replacing Divine meanings attached to the cultural forms of singing and dancing with meanings "that belonged to the people."

Replacing an *-ek* margin with an *-ak* margin, as illustrated in the chart at the end of this chapter, informed me that the Miccosukee, like the Hopi and other North American tribes, did not dance for pleasure.

Sociologist Leo W. Simmons describes in his book, *Sun Chief - The Autobiography of a Hopi Indian,* like the Hopi chief who declared, "I knew I was not dancing for pleasure, but to help with the crops,"[2] the Miccosukee sang and danced not for pleasure but because they believed singing and dancing were part of a natural order through which their corporeal existence was maintained and enhanced.

Before every hunt, they would sing and dance to compel the deer to appear. Before a ballgame, they would sing and dance to make the pitched ball invisible. Then there were songs for success in childbirth and for treating the sick, etc.[3] It represented a mechanized version of the Christian concept of prayer.

Miccosukee singing and dancing must be interpreted as material events in nature rather than cultural events in freedom as manifested by the presence of *-ak* verb margins in the words *talw-ak* (dancing) and *hopaan-ak* (singing).

This shift from *-ek* to *-ak* provides empirical linguistic evidence that the "naturalization of human actions—the treatment of certain human actions as if they were an integral part of physical determinism"[4]—is real.

# CREATED IN THE IMAGE OF GOD

| Culture vb rt + ek (culture margin) | Nature vb rt +ak (nature margin) |
|---|---|
| hakl-**ek**, listening | hakl-**ak**, can hear |
| heech-**ek**, looking | heech-**ak**, can see |
| akom-**ek**, desiring something | baan-**ak**, needing something to exist |
| shahaay-**ek**, teaching | atääƐ-**ak**, learning (a response) |
| nööh-**ek**, cooking something | etb-**ak**, lukewarm |
| hööp-**ek**, planting | Ɛaneey-**ak**, sprouting |
| apöft-**ek**, thinking | ewan-**ak**, tired |
| achan-**ek**, praising | hafëëb-**ak**, yawning |
| ~~hopaan-ek, singing~~ (becomes) >>>> | hopaan-**ak**, singing as a function |
| ~~talw-ek, dancing~~ (becomes) >>>> | talw-**ak**, dancing as a function |

Naturalizing singing and dancing

## CONVICTIONS

- Replacing a Positive Universal with a negative cultural action is called *etic* divergence. Such a spiritual phenomenon is real, and missiologists and social scientists of every type have ignored it.
- If a Bible translator were to translate the word "sing" in the phrase "one will sing, another will teach …" (I Corinthians. 14:26, NLT) as *hopaan-ak* rather than as *hopaan-ek*, the Miccosukee reader would conclude that the Apostle Paul was advocating the use of magic rather than prayer because God could not provide.

# CHAPTER 52
# WAR AGAINST THE LAW OF THE MIND

## WINNEBAGO SATIRE - THE WAR BETWEEN THE RIGHT AND LEFT ARMS

### DISCOVERING WINNEBAGO SATIRE

Before the Puritans arrived and long before emigrants populated the Great Plains, Indian tribes known as the Winnebago lived in Wisconsin, Nebraska, Minnesota, Iowa, and Illinois. Before the missionaries shared the Gospel, these sages recognized their need for a Savior. As native philosophers, they also believed that every human possessed a set of unlearned transcendent principles structured in the mind that could be "triggered" and brought to consciousness.

They knew humanity possessed a set of learned principles derived from social existence "that belong to the people." Such principles fundamentally oppose what the mind is telling one to do.

Browsing through a used bookstore in Gainesville, Florida, I came across a book that supported my conviction sages of the past must exist who, like the Chácobo, created satire critical of the beliefs, practices, and cultural forms of their fellow tribespeople. Such stories I found in a paperback: *The Trickster: A Study in American Mythology*.

In American mythology, a trickster is a character who breaks the rules, confounds expectations, and overturns conventional behavior. He represents a struggle that all humans face every day: A struggle between transcendent ethical principles that are innate versus learned behavioral patterns and customs that "belong to the people."

Through satire, Winnebago's sages attempted to express this mental battle. The Apostle Paul describes it as a battle between the law of the mind and the law of sin. The Winnebago satirist describes it as a spiritual battle between the left arm representing what is innate and the right arm representing what is learned.

It is a battle between two meaning systems, portrayed as the battle between Trickster's left arm and his right arm to skin a buffalo.

In the story which follows, Trickster, impersonating a human, finds his right and left arms fighting over how to skin a buffalo.

Every time the left arm tries to prevent the right arm from performing an unethical act, the left arm responds by grabbing the right arm, attempting to prevent the right arm from acting unethically. In the process, the knife wounds the left arm wielded by the right arm.

Today, this ethical battle, common in all societies, is front and center. In America, we speak in such terms as pro-abortion versus pro-life, socialism versus capitalism, naturalism versus creationism, atheism versus theism, state versus parents, material versus immaterial, ascribed duties versus freedom, and so forth.

GILBERT R. PROST

## LESSON: IF ONE SEEKS TO PREVENT UNETHICAL BEHAVIOR, EXPECT TO GET HURT.

## THE WAR BETWEEN THE LEFT AND RIGHT ARMS

As Trickster walked along, suddenly, he sighted a knoll. To his surprise, he saw an old buffalo near it as he approached.

"My, my, what a pity. If I hadn't thrown away my bundle of arrows, I could have killed and eaten this animal!"

Thereupon, he took a knife, cut down the hay, and fashioned it into figures of men. These he placed in a circle, leaving an opening at one end. The place was very muddy. Having constructed this enclosure, he returned to where he had seen the buffalo.

Trickster shouted, "O, ho, my younger brother, here he is eating without having anything to worry about. Indeed, let nothing prey upon his mind. I will keep watch for him against intruders."

Thus, he spoke to the buffalo who was feeding to his heart's content.

He said, "Listen, Younger Brother. People surround this place. Over there, however, is an opening through which you might escape."

The buffalo raised its head unsuspiciously, and, to Trickster's surprise, it seemed ready to be surrounded by people. At the place Trickster designated, an opening appeared.

The buffalo ran in that direction. Soon, he sank into the mire, and Trickster was immediately upon him with his knife and killed him. He dragged the buffalo over to a cluster of trees and skinned him. Throughout all these operations, he used his right arm only.

During these operations, suddenly, his left arm grabbed the buffalo. "Give that back to me; it is mine."

"Stop that, or I will cut you into pieces. That's what I'll do to you," his right arm said.

The left arm released its hold. Afterward, however, the left arm grabbed the right arm. This time, it snatched his wrist when the right arm began to skin the buffalo. This happened again and again.

In this manner, Trickster made his arms quarrel. That quarrel soon turned into a vicious fight, and the right arm cut up the left arm badly.

"Oh, oh. Why did I do this? Why have I done this? I have made myself suffer!"

The left arm, indeed, was bleeding profusely.

Then he dressed the buffalo. When he finished, he started again.

As he walked, the birds exclaimed, "Look, look. There is Trickster!" Thus, they would cry and fly away.

"Ah, you naughty little birds. I wonder what they're saying."

Every bird he met would chirp, "Look, look; there is Trickster. There he is, aimlessly walking about."

～

## TWO INTERPRETATIONS OF THE CONFLICT

The task of the Winnebago hearer is to decode the hidden messages. What is the author of this story saying, and who are his tribal members? The story is not meaningless.

Anthropologist Paul Radon (1883 - 1959) suggests the storyteller is attempting to explain to his fellow tribespeople that he has solved the riddle concerning how pre-humans became humans with ethical values. Those who hold to such an interpretation also believe that ethical values emerged out of inert matter. Out of nature emerged a new state of being called culture.

Those who believe man is a spiritual being existing in a material body are inclined to believe the storyteller is describing a spiritual war familiar to all people: a war between what one is inclined to do because of particular personal needs and desires and what one ought to do because it serves a greater good.

The story implies the existence of a moral law "written on the heart" (Romans 2:15), a law that is not learned.

In addressing the people of Israel, Jeremiah, speaking on behalf of God, is more explicit. Instead of talking through satire, God speaks through Jeremiah in Jeremiah 16:12, who declares:

> *'And you have done worse than your fathers, for behold, each one follows the dictates of his own evil heart, so that no one listens to Me' (Jeremiah 16:12).*

Just as there were social consequences for refusing to listen to what the left arm was saying, there were social consequences when Israel refused to listen to what God was saying through the prophets.

> *'Therefore I will cast you out of this land into a land that you do not know, neither you nor your fathers; and there you shall serve other gods day and night, where I will not show you favor' (Jeremiah 16:13).*

For anthropologist Paul Radin, a committed naturalist, no law "written on the heart" informs one how to live. The butchering of the buffalo with the right hand represents an evolutionary explanation of how sub-humans without ethical standards became ethical beings, as symbolized by the emergence of the left hand.

For the naturalist, the story represents humankind emerging from nature into culture. With the birth of culture and personhood came the birth of an ethical code illustrated by the left hand, which disagrees with what the right hand is doing. Radin describes his bottom-up, outside-in perspective as:

No ethical values exist for him. And how does he kill and butcher the buffalo? With only one hand, his right. The incident shows he only used one hand.

He is still living in his unconscious, mentally a child, symbolized by the struggle between his right and left hand. His left hand is badly cut up by the right hand, but he is hardly aware of why this has occurred.[1]

The problem with such an interpretation is how an impersonal, amoral nature gives birth to a moral self that knows right from wrong. Radin, as a committed materialist, has no explanation.

In contrast, an innatist's starting point is the Word of God, which declares that within every person is a "law of the mind," also known as the law of God in our inner being.

> *For I delight in the law of God according to the inward man.*
> *But I see another law in my members, warring against the law of my mind, and bringing me into captivity to the law of sin which is in my members.*
> *O wretched man that I am! Who will deliver me from this body of death? (Romans 7:22-24)*

This law informs all humankind how to live. If such a law of God in our inner being did not exist, there would be no Winnebago story describing a battle between the right arm and left nor Chácobo satire like *The Story of Pai as a Raisi and Escaping Mother-in-law Control* (chapter 4, "Chácobo Satire") and *The Dying Raisi* (chapter 8).

The Winnebago story of *The War Between the Left and Right Arms* states two distinct meaning systems within humans. As the Apostle Paul discovered, when he wanted to do what was right, he often did what was wrong. No doubt the storyteller found this to be true of his own behavior, portraying it in the life of Trickster.

As a miserable representative of humankind, Trickster cries out: "Oh, oh. Why did I do this? I have made myself suffer!"

The satirist points out that whenever the right arm of cultural particulars determines and shapes the narrative, the left arm, which represents the Universal, will be wounded. The Universal is rejected because there exist those Jesus describes in John 3:19b: "... and men loved darkness rather than light, because their deeds were evil."

While Trickster was seen "wandering around" and asking, "Why have I made myself suffer!" the Apostle Paul recognized, though tainted and corrupted by the "law of sin" (Romans 7:22), the Good News of Romans 8:1: *"There is* therefore now no condemnation to those who are in Christ Jesus..."

The Winnebago satirist was looking for a way out.

Two doors - two choices

## CONVICTIONS

- The Winnebago storyteller informs his listeners that life is a struggle between two meaning systems: A transcendent meaning system embedded in the "law of

the mind" (Romans 7: 22) and a meaning system belonging to the Winnebago.
- At some point in their history, the Winnebago replaced Divine meanings attached to forms common to all with meanings "that belonged to the people."

## CHAPTER 53
# EAT ME, AND YOU WILL DEFECATE
### WINNEBAGO SATIRE

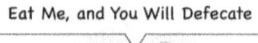

Before the early settlers and Puritans arrived in the Winnebago lands of the Northwest, bringing the Gospel with them, the Winnebago wrestled with the problem of sin and the need for cleansing. Their myth, *Eat Me, and You Will Defecate*, expresses that need.

When reading the following story,[1] I asked, what is the satirist's real message? What is he attempting to convey to his listeners?

EAT ME, AND YOU WILL DEFECATE

As Trickster wandered aimlessly, he suddenly heard someone speak. He listened very carefully, and the voice said, "He who eats me will defecate."

"He will defecate—that's what he said. Why is this person talking in this manner?"

Trickster walked in the direction that he heard the voice, and again, he heard someone say, "He who eats me will defecate."

Trickster asked. "Why does this person talk in this fashion?"

He walked to the other side. Then, right at his very side, a voice said again, "He who eats me will defecate."

"Well, I wonder who is speaking. I know very well that if I eat it, I will not defecate," Trickster muttered.

But he kept looking around for the speaker and finally discovered, much to his astonishment, that it was a bulb on a bush. The bulb is what was speaking. So he seized it, put it in his mouth, ate it, swallowed it, and went on.

Trickster continued to mutter to himself. "Well, where is that bulb that talked so much? Why, indeed, should I defecate? When I feel like defecating, then I shall defecate. No sooner. How could such an object make me defecate?"

Thus, Trickster spoke.

Even as he spoke, however, he began to break wind. "Well, this, I suppose, is what it meant. Yet, the bulb said I would defecate, and I am merely expelling gas. In any case, I am a great man even if I do expel gas." Thus, he spoke.

As he was talking, he again broke wind. This time, it was strong. "Well, what a foolish one I am. This is why I'm called Foolish One."

He broke wind again and again. "So this is why the bulb spoke as it did, I suppose," Trickster muttered.

Again, he broke wind. It was deafening this time, and his rectum began to smart.

"Well, it surely is a great thing!" he muttered.

He broke wind again, and the force propelled him forward this time. "Well, well, it may even make me give another push, but it won't make me defecate!" he defiantly exclaimed.

The next time, he broke wind, the force of the expulsion lifted his hind part so much that he landed on his hands and knees.

"Well, go ahead and do it again. Go ahead and do it again!" he roared.

He broke wind again. This time, the force of the expulsion shot him up in the air, and he landed on his stomach.

The next time Trickster broke wind, he had to hold onto a log because he was thrown so high. However, he raised himself up, and after a while, he landed on the ground with the log on top of him.

The next time Trickster broke wind, he reached for a nearby poplar tree and held on with all his might. Nevertheless, even then, his feet billowed in the air.

He broke wind again, and Trickster held on to the poplar tree with everything he had, and he pulled up the tree by its roots.

To protect himself, the man continued until he reached a large oak tree. He wrapped both arms around its trunk. Yet, when Trickster caught wind, his legs swung up, and his toes struck the tree. But he held on for dear life.

After that, he ran to a place where people lived. When he arrived, he shouted, "Hurry up and take down your lodge, for a big war party is upon you, and they will surely kill you. Come, let us get away!"

He scared them so much that they quickly took down their lodge, piled it on top of Trickster, and scrambled on top of him. They likewise placed all the little dogs on top of Trickster.

Then Trickster broke wind, and the force of the explosion scattered everything on top of him in all directions. The people stood around and shouted, and the dogs scattered here and there and howled at one another. Trickster stood laughing until he ached.

He proceeded onward, thinking he had gotten over his troubles.

"This bulb did a lot of talking," he muttered, "yet it could not make me defecate."

But, even as he spoke, he began to have the desire to defecate again. Trickster said, "What a braggart it was. I suppose this is why it said this."

Even as he spoke, however, he began to have a desire to defecate, even if it was just a little.

"Well, this is what it meant. It certainly bragged a good deal."

Even as he spoke, he defecated again. "What a braggart it was! I suppose this is why it said this."

As Trickster spoke these last words, he defecated a lot. After a while, as he was sitting, his body touched the excrement. So, he got on top of the log to sit, but he felt the excrement even then.

He decided to climb up on a log leaning against a tree, but his body still brushed against it. He kept climbing higher and higher.

However, he couldn't stop defecating. He kept climbing until he reached the treetop. It was small and quite uncomfortable. Nevertheless, the excrement clawed its way up to him.

So he climbed even higher. Higher and higher he went, and the excrement found its way to him. As he sat on the limb, he defecated again. He decided to try a different position.

However, since the limb was very slippery, he fell into the excrement. Down he fell, down into the dung. He disappeared in it, and it was only with great difficulty that he could escape it.

Filth covered his raccoon-skin blanket, and he came out dragging it after him. Still blinded by the filth, he started to run. He could not see anything, and as he ran, he ran into a tree.

The old man cried out in pain. He reached out, felt it was a tree, and sang, "Tree, what kind of tree are you? Tell me something about yourself."

The tree answered, "What kind of tree do you think I am? I am an oak tree. I am the forked oak tree that used to stand in the middle of the valley. I am that one."

"Oh, my. Is it possible there might be water around here?" Trickster asked.

The tree answered, "Go straight on." This is what the tree told him.

As he went along, he bumped against another tree and was knocked backward by the collision.

Again, he sang, "Tree, what kind of tree are you? Tell me something about yourself."

"What kind of tree do you think I am? The red oak tree that used to stand at the edge of the valley, I am that one."

"Oh, my. Is it possible there is water around here?" Trickster asked.

The tree answered, "Keep straight on," so he went again.

Soon, he knocked against another tree. He spoke to the tree and sang, "What kind of tree are you? Tell me something about yourself."

"What kind of tree do you think I am? The slippery elm that used to stand among the others, I am that one."

Trickster asked, "Oh, my. Is it possible there would be some water near here?"

The tree answered, "Keep straight on."

On and on he went, and soon he bumped into another tree. He touched it and sang, "Tree, what kind of tree are you? Tell me something about yourself."

"What kind of tree do you think I am? I am the basswood tree that used to stand on the water's edge. That is the one I am."

"Oh, my, it is good," Trickster said.

He jumped and lay in the water, washing himself thoroughly.

It is said the old man almost died that time, for it was only with the greatest difficulty that he found the water.

He certainly would have died if the trees had not spoken to him. He cleaned himself after a long time and only after great exertion, for the dung had been on him a long time and had dried. After he had cleansed himself, he washed his raccoon-skin blanket.

When he realized what he had done, he muttered, "Oh, my, what a stupid fellow I must be. I should have recognized this. Here, I have caused myself great pain."

# CREATED IN THE IMAGE OF GOD

Isaiah 53:6: All we like sheep have gone astray; We have turned, everyone, to his own way ..."

## CONVICTIONS

- When Isaiah compared humankind to "sheep," he was not comparing sheep to their good qualities but to their foolishness, stupidity, and lack of sense. Sheep are prone to go astray from the shepherd. For these Winnebago sages, Trickster manifested the same qualities. He rejected the voice of conscience saying, "There are consequences to eating forbidden fruit."

# CHAPTER 54
# "HELP! I NEED TO BE CLEANSED!" AN ANALYSIS OF A WINNEBAGO STORY
## PERSONAL TESTIMONY OF A WINNEBAGO

Unknown to most, the Winnebago were dualists. That is, they viewed existence in terms of what was moral and what was material. This dual view of existence was manifested in a dual exogamous social structure called moieties.

A moiety is one of two functioning groups into which a society allocates its members at birth. One was either a member of the Above People, whose function was to maintain the spiritual health of the tribe, or a member of the Below People, whose function was to preserve the tribe's material well-being.

Since the Universal Rule of Exogamy proclaimed that anyone marrying someone from the same moiety would be guilty of committing incest, the nuclear family was rendered meaningless. What replaced the nuclear family was a new type of "family" called the moiety. Marrying out meant marrying someone from another moiety. They innately knew that existence was dual, spiritual and material.

Because the story is about the moral consequences of eating the forbidden fruit, the storyteller most likely was a member of the Above People. As a member of the Above People, it was his moral duty to inform his people that they were all rule breakers. They had all been defiled by figuratively eating the forbidden fruit in the garden and needed cleansing.

This propensity for man to break the rules is revealed in the life of a Winnebago mythical hero Trickster. He could easily be tricked because he lived a life without boundaries.

In the myth, *Eat Me, and You Will Defecate,* as told in chapter 53, the storyteller is attempting to inform his hearers that they, as a people, all have a moral problem: Ignoring boundaries and eating forbidden fruit.

Suppose the story represents an evolutionary bottom-up, outside-in explanation of how pre-humans became moral beings. In that case, the story ceases to be satire and is specifically aimed at exposing the human condition. It becomes a story attempting to explain how naked apes moved from a state of nature to becoming cultural beings knowing right from wrong.

In contrast, Winnebago sages, for the analyst who believes in a historical fall, declared long before any missionary arrived on the scene, that every Winnebago was aware of a sin problem that defiled the soul. The satirist, in this case, declares: "We live in a moral universe in which all mankind breaks the rules and then suffers the consequences."

*Eat Me, and You Will Defecate* is the personal testimony of one Winnebago who declared, "So we are Winnebago. We like all that is forbidden. We are like Blow-Himself-Away (Trickster) who did not heed the warning."[1] And as he went along, life became more intolerable.

The LORD is my shepherd.

## CONVICTIONS

- In the words of psychiatrist Carl Jung, "Only out of disaster can the longing for a savior arise."[2] Like the Winnebago who testified, "Like Trickster, we like all that is forbidden," the Bible's description of the human condition is similar: "All we like sheep, have gone astray; We have turned, every one, to his own way ..." (Isaiah 53:6).
- The satirist longs for a savior.

# CHAPTER 55
# THE CONTEXTUAL SHAPING OF MEANING
## BEWARE LEST ANYONE CHEAT YOU THROUGH PHILOSOPHY AND EMPTY DECEIT, ACCORDING TO THE TRADITION OF MEN

"Beware lest anyone cheat you through philosophy and empty deceit, according to the tradition of men, according to the basic principles of the world, and not according to Christ."
**Colossians 2:8**

## THE FORMATION OF CULTURE

The infrastructural pressures that produced distinct Kiowa-Apache, Trobriand, Yaminahua, Winnebago, and Chácobo cultures are all different. While differing environments produce different forms or ways of living, the forms they adopted had "no place in the Divine Plan" (Romans 5:20).

This ability to critique a particular cultural form was made possible because, in their unconscious minds, a Universal Plan or Universal-Lexicon existed which enabled them to critique their own cultural forms.

The postmodern says all meaning and truth are derived from context and social existence. Pastor and author Jim Leffel shares on his website, "We do not exist or think independently of the community that we identify with. No one can have independent or autonomous access to reality. All of our thinking is both communal and contextual."[1]

As a Bible translator, anthropologist, and researcher, I discovered much truth in the idea that context can shape the meanings attached to concepts common to all. But are context and social existence the only "authors" of meaning?

The Apostle Paul knew that external contextual forces and social existence shaped Greek traditions and behavior. Aware of the problem, he warned the Colossians in 2:8: "Beware lest anyone cheat you through philosophy and empty deceit, according to the tradition of men, according to the basic principles of the world, and not according to Christ."

In time, I realized that many of the Chácobo and Miccosukee ideas were shaped by contextual and environmental forces.

For the Chácobo, as a result of the pressures of the Amazonian Rainforest, they restructured the nuclear family, replacing the covenantal *husband-wife* dyad with the biological dyad of mother-daughter.

Thirty years later, when assigned to the Miccosukee of South

Florida, I observed that the South Florida Everglades' contextual and environmental pressures compelled the Miccosukee to classify singing and dancing as events in nature rather than in culture. To survive, one had to sing and dance to make the rains come and the crops grow. In addition, contextual anxieties over existence compelled them to replace the *husband-wife* dyad with that of sister-sister.

I examined some defensive schemes among tribes living on the Great Plains. Again, anthropological data supported the theory that external forces in every environment shape behavior, institutions, and lifeways in negative ways.

Anthropologist Fred Eggan notes that tribes entering the Great Plains to hunt buffalo ended up with similar kinship or family types. Both he and Marvin Harris have attempted to explain how contextual environmental pressures can shape a society's lifeway and people's thoughts.

However, as committed materialists, they have been unable to explain why there were satirists who were critical of the forms that society had imposed upon them.

Today, missionaries face an ontological and an epistemological problem that shouldn't be ignored. Social scientists, psychologists, anthropologists, and missiologists, for the most part, are committed to a methodological naturalism that must explain the contextual shaping of meaning in terms of biological and material forces. For them, no form has an inherent meaning.

They advocate a bottom-up, outside-in materialistic epistemology, which basically says that all meanings attached to cultural forms are created outside the mind. Once created and shaped by contextual pressures and social existence, they are imported into the mind where they are miraculously linked, through some undiscovered process, to the correct Universal form that the mind created. The existence of forms common to all structured in the mind implies a miracle.

Nevertheless, according to anthropologist Claude Lévi Strauss,

"It is only forms and not contents that can be common. If there are common contents, they must be sought outside the mind."[2] But from where did the forms common to all come?

In addition, every person has an unlearned taxonomic system that gives all humans the capacity to classify perceptions under concepts and arrange those concepts into their proper categories. We must ask:

- From where did this innate taxonomic system come?
- Who or what created the natural categories under which the concepts are arranged?

Without concepts, categories, and an innate taxonomic system, humans could not exist as thinking, language-speaking cultural beings. As linguist Pike points out, "It is our categorization of elements of our universe [that] allows us to have a particular understanding of the universe."

This innate ability to understand the universe is linked to man's capacity to categorize his perceptions and create knowledge and understanding of the world in which he lives.

The ontological starting point for the materialist and theist are radically different. For the materialist, there is the problem of pre-humans passing from nature to culture. They must explain in materialistic terms how pre-humans became thinking people or how homo sapiens were equipped with an inborn taxonomic system that compelled them to think of themselves as "other than nature."

This is not a problem for the theist who maintains that Adam innately knew that he was "other than" nature. For the first human, there was no transition from nature to culture.

As manifested in the Miccosukee language, the existential categories of culture and nature always existed. For the theist, culture did not emerge from nature.

For anthropologist Edmund Leach, however, the existential question is: "How is it and why is it that men, who are a part of nature, manage to see themselves as 'other than' nature even though, to subsist, they must constantly maintain relations with nature?"³

The answer is simple for those holding a top-down, inside-out epistemology. Within every person's psyche, an existential culture-nature binary exists that compels everyone to think of themselves as "other than" nature.

For those holding to a bottom-up, outside-in epistemology, an existential culture-nature binary always existing in the psyche is denied. Therefore, for them, the reason humans continue to see themselves as "other than" nature remains a mystery.

Lima, Peru - culture

## CONVICTIONS

- Man did not become a language-speaking being; he was created as a being capable of speaking with God in language.
- Whenever a society rejects God and goes its own way, it will create a new family form or type that will replace the covenantal dyad of *husband-wife* with a biological dyad.

# CHAPTER 56
# THE MYSTERY OF THE ONE-FLESH PRINCIPLE
## JAPANESE FAMILY

The mystery

Professor Francis L. K. Hsu proposed that from each of the seven consanguineal relationships, father-son, father-daughter. mother-son, mother-daughter, brother-sister, brother-brother, and sister-sister, an assortment of dissimilar lifeways would emerge. Quoting:

> His hypothesis presupposes that each structural dyad [both consanguineal and non-consanguineal based] possesses inherent and distinctive attributes. When one dyad is elevated over other dyads in each kinship system [or cultural operating system], the attributes of the dominant dyad tend to modify, eliminate, or at least reduce the importance of the attributes of other structural dyads.
>
> The hypothesis further states that the total effect of the dominance of the attributes of one structural dyad leads to a particular kind of kinship content, which in turn strongly conditions the pattern of thought and behavior of the individuals reared in the kinship system [or lifeway] in the society at large.[1]

In addition, it is proposed that the function of each of these "one-flesh" biological dyads is to eliminate existential anxieties produced by the stresses and pressures of living in a particular ecological, economic, social, and technological environment. The attributes of each dyad are then transmuted into specific "patterns of thought and behavior" and ways of living that contrast with those of other societies.

∼

## JAPANESE FAMILY-OF-FIVE

One of the most contrastive lifeways is that of the Japanese. For the missionary, it makes an interesting case study because, as a nation, the Japanese culture has been resistant to the Gospel, not because of their pride, as Kraft suggests, but because of the attribute of a cultural form called "matriarchy" that still exists after thousands of years.

## MOTHER AND FIRST-BORN OF THE JAPANESE

Even though outwardly, the Japanese are classified as a patrilineal society, the dominant dyad of Japanese culture is that of mother and first-born son. For a long time, this puzzled me. How could households that emphasize patrilineal descent be controlled by a matriarch rather than a patriarch?

I found the answer rooted in Japanese history. We need to go back in history 2,000 years. Before 250 AD, the Japanese social operating system was vastly different. During that pre-Confucian and pre-Buddha time, the Japanese were matriarchal, a rarity in operating systems.

In describing the effect of a first-son marriage, anthropologist George De Vos notes:

> In marrying the eldest son, the young bride coming into a new household [of five] was in a sense entering into her second apprenticeship, under the severe and sometimes jealous tutelage of her husband's mother. If she failed in any way to meet the exacting requirement or showed herself to be inept, she could be sent back to her family as a failure.[2]

While all children are trained to achieve and succeed in life, the burden falls upon the first-born son to achieve success and prosperity. He is responsible for managing the family estate or enterprise and carrying on the family traditions and lineage. It is the first-born sons who inherit the estate.

First-born sons in Japan and their wives who have been "trained in the particular traditions and values of her husband's lineage," live under unique social pressures. Unlike their younger brothers, they are not exempt from the residence rule and must remain at home. This often leads to a loss of initiative and psychological stultification, contrasting with the more independent lifestyles of their younger siblings.³

Second and third-born sons can set up independent households somewhat free of parental and in-law control.

We note that Japanese inheritance rules contrast with Jewish inheritance rules.

∼

## PARABLE OF THE TWO SONS - LUKE 15: 11-32

> *Then He said, "A certain man had two sons. And the younger of them said to his father, 'Father, give me the portion of goods that falls to me.' So he divided to them his livelihood.*
>
> *"And not many days after, the younger son gathered all together, journeyed to a far country, and there wasted his possessions with prodigal living. But when he had spent all, there arose a severe famine in that land, and he began to be in want.*
>
> *"Then he went and joined himself to a citizen of that country, and he sent him into his fields to feed swine. And he would gladly have filled his stomach with the pods that the swine ate, and no one gave him anything.*
>
> *"But when he came to himself, he said, 'How many of my father's hired servants have bread enough and to spare, and I perish with hunger! I will arise and go to my father, and will say to him, 'Father, I have sinned against heaven and before you, and I am no longer worthy to be called your son. Make me like one of your hired servants.'*
>
> *"And he arose and came to his father.*

"But when he was still a great way off, his father saw him and had compassion, and ran and fell on his neck and kissed him.

"And the son said to him, 'Father, I have sinned against heaven and in your sight, and am no longer worthy to be called your son.'

"But the father said to his servants, 'Bring out the best robe and put it on him, and put a ring on his hand and sandals on his feet.

"'And bring the fatted calf here and kill it and let us eat and be merry; for this my son was dead and is alive again; he was lost and is found.'

"And they began to be merry.

"Now his older son was in the field. And as he came and drew near to the house, he heard music and dancing. So he called one of the servants and asked what these things meant.

"And he said to him, 'Your brother has come, and because he has received him safe and sound, your father has killed the fatted calf.'

"But he was angry and would not go in. Therefore his father came out and pleaded with him.

"So he answered and said to his father, 'Lo, these many years I have been serving you; I never transgressed your commandment at any time; and yet you never gave me a young goat, that I might make merry with my friends.'

"'But as soon as this son of yours came, who has devoured your livelihood with harlots, you killed the fatted calf for him.'

"And he said to him, 'Son, you are always with me, and all that I have is yours. It was right that we should make merry and be glad, for your brother was dead and is alive again, and was lost and is found.'"

# CREATED IN THE IMAGE OF GOD

∼

Luke 15: 11-32 would seem odd to a Japanese reader. In the parable of the older and younger brother, both sons are entitled to a share of the inheritance.

It is not so in the minds of Japanese people who have learned the rules of a different operating system. No younger son of a Japanese family would ever ask his father for his share of the inheritance. His share of the inheritance is zero.

The Rule of Primogeniture puts the entire inheritance under the control of the oldest son to keep the family fortune intact.

Knowing this, Japanese younger sons usually leave to look for jobs in the city or migrate to look for jobs elsewhere, to the islands surrounding Japan, and then to Latin American countries like Peru, Brazil, Mexico, Hawaii, and the West Coast of the U.S.

Women who marry first-born sons, unlike women who marry second and third-born sons, find themselves in a situation like Miccosukee husbands, who, upon marriage, move into their wives' matrilineal-based camp. The Japanese women married men, like the Miccosukee men married women, and lost their freedom.

A Japanese farm woman who married a first-born son complained, "Other women get married. I went as a daughter-in-law. I had a husband and his [younger] brothers and sisters. Other women can come and go as they please, free to do all they please."[4]

Anthropologist Gail Bernstein explains that "the Japanese household traditionally has only one housewife: Only when the mother-in-law retires from family affairs or dies can the wife give up the status of daughter-in-law and become the woman of the house."[5]

While today's "sword" of global economic pressures is slowly replacing this residence rule, forcing young married couples to set up independent households in the cities where the jobs are, the traditional rules, standards, and values that held up the household-of-five as normative and ideal for centuries are slow to change. The tradition that first-born sons and their wives are to exist under the control of their mothers-in-law continues to exist even though many couples no longer live with their husbands' parents.

A grandmother who lived under the old rules testified, "I didn't mind working hard. I just hated the way my mother-in-law treated me."[6]

Another complained about her arranged marriage and said, "I was this man's fourth bride. The first three had run away because his mother was so hard on them. The first ran away after a year, the second after a month, and the third after six months. My husband's mother didn't like me either."[7] Matriarchy still exists in Japan.

## ORIGIN OF CULTURAL DIVERSITY

This is how a "bottom-up" Maslow/Kraft need-satisfaction approach to human existence affects one's interpretation of Scripture.

For this Bible translator, there are some serious problems with this naturalistic, bottom-up biological-contextual approach to meaning and human existence. However, it certainly has great explanatory power when understanding the origin of cultural diversity.

First, the contextual approach means the Bible must be interpreted through the lens of environmental determinism. This would mean the Apostle Paul was in error when he spoke of "laws written on the heart" (Romans 2:15) because all laws are derived from social context and then "constructed" in the mind.

Niebuhr states no Universal Moral Code exists, which "is part of one's real self." Instead of "their moral actions giving proof of commandments written on the tablets of the heart," their moral actions reveal only a relative environmental-derived standard, implying that God, "the Righteous Judge," must judge the world regarding each society's context-derived morality.

Sin, in this case, is defined in terms of environmental "fitness" and how well one fulfills one's ascribed duty. This is how Hinduism and Transcendental Meditation define sin. Similarly, today's environmentalists define sin as "producing $CO_2$," not as violating a transcendent law "written on the heart."

Second, if Kraft is correct, then clearly Jesus was in error when He declared, "What God has joined together, let not man separate" (Matthew 19:6).

Beginning in the Garden of Eden, humankind's goals and desires have been at work throughout history to undo, invalidate, and nullify what God has "joined together" by transferring the spiritual one-flesh principle to a biological dyad.

If the bottom-up, naturalistic approach to human existence is valid, Jesus had to be in error. If all "meaning is the structuring of information in the minds of persons," and this meaning is "context-specific,"[8] as Kraft insists, there can be no Universal Truth. If Kraft is correct, then Bible translation is meaningless because it implies a change of "wineskins," i.e., cultural forms.

But humans, we contend, are more than physical things that respond to the impulses and pressures of nature. They are also men and women who believe and put their faith in first principles, whatever those first principles may be.

If his principles include the Creation Mandate of Genesis 2:23, his "psychological mindset" will not be determined by his environment.

Suppose his first principles exclude the spiritual one-flesh principle of *husband-wife*. In that case, life will be lived on the plane of cultural relativity, and no Universal Transcendent Principles will exist that apply to all men everywhere.

In this case, no *epignosis* or "precise and correct knowledge" exists that is "fixed," unchanging, and not derived from context. Yet the writers of Scripture distinguish between *gnosis* (knowledge skewed by culture) and culture-free *epignosis* (knowledge that comes to humanity from the outside). The one-flesh spiritual principle represents the latter. It is not derived from context.

We conclude that whenever a society grounds its cultural operating system in *gnosis* and some dominant one-flesh biological dyad like sister-sister (Miccosukee), mother-daughter (Chácobo), brother-sister (Aymara), or mother and first-born son (Japanese), the cultural operating system will lack Universality because it "remains continuously open to each concrete situation in life [context] in which it finds itself placed."[9] In this case, there exists no Universal, culture-free ideal one-flesh dyad. All is relative.

On the other hand, if one begins with the premise that humankind is a spiritual being gifted with cultural-free, "outside-knowledge" that represents Universal Relational Principles and concepts with inherent meanings applicable to all societies, then one escapes the meaningless cycles of nature. Only then does the spiritual one-flesh principle of husband and wife begin to make sense.

The Apostle Paul called this relationship "a mystery" in Ephesians 5:31-33:

> For this reason a man shall leave his father and mother and be joined to his wife, and the two shall become one flesh.
> *This is a great mystery, but I speak concerning Christ and the church. Nevertheless let each one of you in particular so love his own wife as himself, and let the wife see* that she respects *her* husband.

How can two people from two biological descent lines or kinds of families, each having its own goals, needs, and objectives, become "one flesh"?

# CREATED IN THE IMAGE OF GOD

Gil and Marian, June 13, 1953

## CONVICTIONS

- When intimacy and unity of thought and action occur between husband and wife, marriage shifts from being a contract grounded in need satisfaction to a covenantal relationship in which each partner exists for the other in the sphere of freedom and love rather than the bondage of ascribed duties and functions.

# CHAPTER 57
# CULTURAL DIVERSITY
## THE TWO BECOME ONE FLESH

Cultural diversity is a spiritual phenomenon rather than a material one. It occurs whenever a society rejects and replaces a Positive Universal with a negative cultural particular.

When one attempts to explain the problem of cultural diversity and why we have such a multiplicity of dissimilar lifeways or worldviews, we eventually end up with the mysterious one-flesh principle of *husband-wife* first mentioned in Genesis 2:23:

> *"This is now bone of my bones*
> *And flesh of my flesh;*
> *She shall be called Woman,*
> *Because she was taken out of Man."*

HUMANS, alienated from their Creator, tend to diverge from the Divine Plan and create a new family form. Cultural diversity starts with replacing the covenantal *husband-wife* dyad with one of the following biological dyads: father-son, father-daughter, mother-son, mother-daughter, brother-sister, brother-brother, or sister-sister.

The kind of family a society creates will seek security in a particular biological dyad rather than a covenantal relationship transcending biology.

Such societies create what Francis L. K. Hsu calls "deep-seated centripetal tendencies ... the place of the individual in the "web of kinship" is inalienable and perpetual."[1]

In such societies, individuals are not likely to leave their families and run off to follow some charismatic leader. The web of interrelated ascribed functions is a powerful force that constrains such behavior.

As long as one spouse is compelled to remain home and the other spouse moves in, the kind of family that comes into existence has centripetal tendencies which lock its members into an "inalienable and perpetual" way of living. Establishing a bilateral family in which relatives on the father's and mother's sides are of equal importance will be difficult, if not impossible.

When missiologist-anthropologist Charles Kraft declared: "Human biology provides the backdrop for all that we need to know as humans,"[2] he is talking like a materialist rather than a theist.

Is the biological dyad (father-son, father-daughter, mother-son, mother-daughter, brother-brother, brother-sister, sister-sister) more important than the covenantal *husband-wife*?

When the one-flesh principle is applied spiritually, it is specifically applied to the *husband-wife* dyad in the context of a biblical worldview that states: Upon marriage, husband and wife, both of whom come from different natal families, should leave their natal homes, pledge themselves to each other, have children, and love each other as much as they love themselves. In the process, the two become "one flesh." It is a relationship that has nothing to do with biology.

In becoming "one flesh," they also create a very different kind of family structure than one in which the dominant dyad is biological.

As a representation of the Universal, the nuclear family will reject the merging of mutually exclusive status positions, a phenomenon which states A (brother) can be B (cousin). Members promote logical thinking.

When one attempts to explain cultural diversity and why we have such a multiplicity of dissimilar lifeways or worldviews, one eventually ends up with the mysterious principle of "one flesh," first mentioned in Genesis 2:24. Because it is a spiritual principle rather than a biological one, this principle transcends the laws of nature and biology.

However, as humans seek to find security in biological relationships, real or fictive, it is the spiritual aspect of human existence that humans and society reject, distort, cast off, and suppress.

It is then replaced with a one-flesh biological dyad, of which there are seven: father-son, father-daughter, mother-son, mother-daughter, brother-sister, brother-brother, and sister-sister.

Metaphorically, the principle is applied to fictive categories such as brotherhoods, fraternities, and secret societies. In the case of Jonathan, "he loved him [David] as he loved his own soul" (I Samuel 20:17b).

## THE TWO BECOME ONE FLESH

First, this kind of family is discontinuous. After the children leave and the parents die, the family ceases to exist.

Second, it is the kind of family structure that spins off its children into the world. They become explorers, risk-takers, entrepreneurs, Nobel Prize winners, and missionaries.

When the first Chácobo extracted himself from the Chácobo matrix of ascribed functions/duties that had locked him into an "inalienable and perpetual" way of living, it wasn't without a struggle.

Breathing the fresh air of freedom, he was now free to move out and exist for the entire Chácobo community and not just his wife's family. This was revolutionary. It eventually cost him his wife, who left with her parents and moved to another river.

When the Bible says that a "man shall leave his father and mother and be joined to his wife, and they shall become one flesh" (Genesis. 2:24), "the reference is not only to sexual relations but also, and more importantly, to the spiritual relationship."[3]

This is the interpretation that the Apostle Paul gives to this passage in I Corinthians 6:16:

> *Or do you not know that he who is joined to a harlot is one body* with her? For *"the two,"* He says, *"shall become one flesh."*

Like most people, the church at Corinth interpreted sexual union to be merely a physical act that did not affect a person spiritually.

But it is God, not humans, who determines the structure of marriage and the meaning of the sexual union. Ignored by man and woman is that marriage takes place under the decree of the Creator. Jesus said, "Therefore, what God has joined together, let not man separate" (Matthew 19:6b). Divorce is no trivial matter.

When the Apostle Paul corrects the Corinthian church regarding immoral sexual behavior, he defines the one-flesh principle of Genesis 2:23-24 in terms of a spiritual union that even the pagan Corinthians who did not have the Scriptures should have known. Paul's statement suggests that sexual intercourse itself should have "triggered" the principle and brought to consciousness its spiritual meaning.

For example, Chácobo satirists who had never heard of the one-flesh principle of Scripture nevertheless believed that upon marriage, husband and wife should "leave and cleave," become "one flesh," and establish a new social unit that we call the nuclear family.

For economic and security reasons, Chácobo society rejected the notion that they would be better off if their married sons and daughters would "leave and cleave," and trust God for their security. Giving political and economic power to the nuclear family was anathema. It would destroy their defensive social operating system against anxiety, which they had created and which Jesus called "the family-of-five."

Because the family-of-five had reduced some of its members to a person-thing, thereby refusing its offspring the opportunity to set up independent households, Jesus declared that He would apply the "sword" to it.

> "Do not think that I came to bring peace on earth. I did not come to bring peace but a sword.
> "For I have come to 'set a man against his father, a daughter against her mother, and a daughter-in-law against her mother-in-law';
> "and 'a man's enemies will be those of his own household'"
> (Matthew 10:34-36).

But this was not God's purpose in marriage. It is fundamental because it maximizes human freedom. It prevents segments of society from being reduced to person-things.

Making the *husband-wife* dyad and the nuclear family the dominant building blocks of society is risky business because it involves trust in God rather than trust in mechanical, ascribed functions. Replacing this spiritual covenantal dyad with a negative cultural particular is an abomination. It manifests a perverted will that seeks to operate independently of its Creator.

Therefore, church-planting missionaries must consider the family type they will likely encounter and the potentiality of a non-biblical internal structure. Because they will probably be working in a non-centrifugal societal order that has ascribed long-term functions or duties to its members, it would be foolish not to recognize the existence of such deep-seated constraints in Scripture, church planting, and community development.

CREATED IN THE IMAGE OF GOD

The great mystery, the sword

## CONVICTIONS

- The concept of marriage was instituted and ordained by God. His instruction to Adam was that "a man shall leave his father and mother and be joined to his wife, and they shall become one flesh" (Genesis 2:24).
- Gay marriage is unnatural; it fails to procreate. This form of marriage fundamentally opposes what the Lord said to Adam and Eve, "Be fruitful and multiply; fill the earth and subdue it ..." (Genesis 1:28a).

# CHAPTER 58
# DEMOLITION OF DIVINE MEANINGS IN PROGRESS
## UNIVERSAL VS RELATIVE IN ANTHROPOLOGY

Adam, the first man, was mentally equipped to converse with God. So was his wife, Eve. If form and meaning-content were not linked when God breathed life into Adam and Eve, then how could they have been human beings created in the image of God?

While the materialist insists existence precedes meaning, the theist insists that meaning precedes existence.

When one begins to analyze how meanings are attached to forms, one can't ignore the materialistic bottom-up, outside-in explanation set forth by Claude Lévi-Strauss. As a Jewish anthropologist instructed in the Torah, he ignores the problem of using the term "mind" and states, "It is only forms and not contents that can be common. If there are common contents, they must be sought ... outside the mind."[1]

Webster points out that he was not proclaiming a "fresh theory of human nature but Judaeo-Christian orthodoxies which have been reconstructed in a secular form, safe from the attacks of science precisely because they are presented as science."[2]

Rejecting Plato's hypothesis that forms plus meaning-content are "tied together" in the unconscious mind as the source of Universal ideas, Lévi-Strauss and missiologist-anthropologist Charles Kraft untied the two and declared: "Meaning-content must be sought outside the mind." The result? A biological-mental explanation as to how contextual social existence precedes meaning.

Lévi-Strauss and Robert Kraft's explanations regarding the source of all knowledge fails to explain how meaning-content derived from contextual social existence was imported into the brain and then, without error, attached to the correct forms that were "structured" in the brain. Is such a linkage mathematically possible?

As a non-contextualizing theist, I find it more rational to believe form and meaning-content were "packaged right" when the Lord breathed mental data into an inert bodily form, and the form became a living, cultural, language-speaking person possessing a mind filled with *etic* data.

The consequence of detaching inherent meanings from forms or ideas common to all created two kinds of data. The first kind consisted of invisible forms structured in the brain. The second kind consisted of meaning-content imported from "outside the brain," also known as the "mind."

To be a true materialist, as neo-Darwinist Richard Webster says, we must "think with our bodies."[3] For the materialist, the mind is, in effect, an illusion produced by our failure to understand the evolutionary history and the neurophysiological complexity of the human organism."[4]

What troubled materialist Lévi-Strauss the most was the origin of language and meaning. He finally concluded:

> Language was born all at once. Whatever the moment and the circumstances of its appearing in the range of animal life, language has necessarily appeared all at once ... a change has taken place, from a stage where nothing had meaning to a stage where everything had meaning.[5]

For the materialist, the birth of language and self-consciousness remains a mystery. For them, a time existed when form and meaning-content were not connected. It wasn't until the two were magically connected that "naked apes" became language-speaking people. At that magical moment, language was born.

As a theist, I agree with theologian and philosopher, Bill Roach: "Humanity was fashioned so that human beings could speak from the moment of creation. There is an internal connection between thought, language, and the Logos of God."[6]

When God breathed the breath of life into an inert form called man, He created a language-speaking being who could converse meaningfully with others.

Materialist Lévi-Strauss believes form and meaning-content were initially separated, and then, after billions of years, magically connected. All at once a new species, homo sapiens, came into existence.

In addition, the brain, rather than the mind, was "structured." Lévi-Strauss believes the brain was "structured" with meaningless forms that would eventually be connected with meanings derived from social existence. "It is only forms and not contents that can be common. If there are common contents, they must be sought ... outside the mind."[7]

Another "son of Abraham," linguist Ray Jackendoff (1945-) agrees. He says, "Input from the environment is needed."[8] In other words, social existence provides the necessary meaning-content for language to be born.

Surprisingly, evangelical anthropologist Charles Kraft agrees with Levi-Strauss and Jackendoff. Kraft wrote: "A cultural form does not have inherent meaning, only perceived meaning. And this meaning is context-specific."

For the Bible-believing theist, there is a problem with such an interpretation. The idea that all meanings come from sense perceptions negates II Timothy 3:16a (ESV): "All Scripture is breathed out by God ..."

Kraft rejects such an interpretation. He believes the Scriptures contain "an accurate record of the spirit-guided perceptions of human beings who were committed to God."[9]

However, perceived meanings derived from experience "cannot give us Universal judgments."[10] Instead, they give us relative judgments shaped by a particular context. Otherwise, the Scriptures become nothing more than a collection of perceptions and experiences of men who thought they were speaking for God.

The mentalist, like myself, believes learning a language depends on both the form and its inherent meaning being "triggered" and brought to consciousness.

The materialist believes there can be no misrepresentations of the "law written on the heart" because there is no "law written on the heart." So no Universal meaning-content can be "triggered" and brought to consciousness. Kraft believes words like father, mother, and family "derive their meanings from their interaction with the contexts in which they participate."[11] Man and society create meaning, not God.

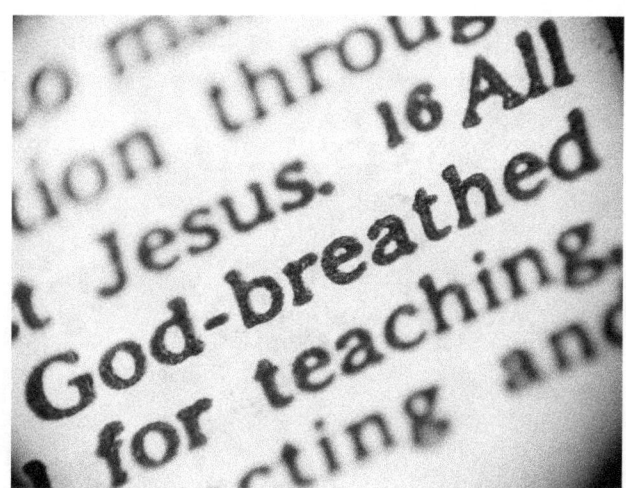

God-breathed

## CONVICTIONS

- Throughout history, the inherent positive "fixed" meanings of concepts, categories, and rules "written on the heart" have been constantly under attack.
- While God's truth can be suppressed and distorted, Divine meanings cannot be detached from Universal forms. God has not ceased to speak; God is not dead.
- When the Lord breathed life into an inert form called "man," He "breathed" into man a Meta-Script that informed man how to live as a human being.
- The materialist's doctrine of environmental "fitness" and Natural Selection, which states that correct meanings should be connected to the proper form "structured" in the brain, represents a form of magic.
- Replacing Divine meanings attached to Universal forms with forms created by man has negative consequences.

# CHAPTER 59
# THE PIRAHÃ OF BRAZIL
## TRICKSTER STORY - DON'T TRUST YOUR PERCEPTIONS

Long before Scottish philosopher David Hume (1711 - 1776) argued "that the total content of the mind can be reduced to data produced by sensory experiences or perceptions,"[1] Winnebago philosophers of another age warned their listeners through satire, "Don't trust your perceptions! If you do, you will cause yourself great pain."

### THE COMPLEX CASE OF THE PIRAHÃ

According to linguist Daniel Everett, Pirahã tribe history stands outside the sphere of "immediacy of experience" and therefore cannot be talked about. Since nothing can be more certain than what happens to our senses, the Pirahã think of themselves as being *Hiatíihi* (Straight Ones), those whose minds have not been corrupted when in reality their minds have been highly corrupted.

One thing is clear: Before the Pirahã can talk about events in history, they must come to realize that their senses cannot provide them with true knowledge. At this point, we are dealing with the constituents of knowledge, form, and meaning-content.

The two were linked together when God "breathed spiritual stuff" into "material stuff" and created a being who could understand what his Creator said. According to Job (Job 32:8), it is "... the breath of the Almighty [which] gives him [man] understand[ing]."

In contrast, Everett postulates that forms common to all were linked to primitive meaning-content two million years ago when naked apes invented language and became people.

According to SIL missionary Daniel Everett, Pike's idea that Innate Positive Universals are structured in the unconscious mind and a society can reject and replace those Universals with negative particular actions made no sense.

Such a statement implied that societies like the Pirahã had replaced Innate Positive Universals with negative particular actions, thus becoming a people whom God had given over to corrupt minds so that they did things they ought not to do.

According to Romans 1:18, "... the wrath of God is revealed from heaven against all ungodliness and unrighteousness of men, who suppress the truth in unrighteousness ..."

As documented by cognitive scientist Philip Lieberman (1934 - 2022), according to Everett, two million years ago a miracle took place. Homo erectus developed the ability to:

> ... formulate thoughts about what is to be said; then recall the appropriate words that express these thoughts; then order the words in a grammatically correct sequence; then perform unbelievable "acrobatic maneuvers" with the lungs, mouth, tongue, lips, teeth, velum, larynx, pharynx, and other speech organs that most of us don't even know we have.
>
> We must control nasality, volume, pitch, stress, intonation, and speed. We perform this complex task in one or two seconds for an average sentence. As if this were not enough, we are constantly thinking ahead to the next sentence and the one after that. The listener meanwhile must perform this same operation in reverse,

trying to make sense out of what is really nothing more than a continuous stream of noise.²

The idea that language was an invention of pre-humans, as proposed by Everett, doesn't make sense.

According to Everett, "One of the most important values in Pirahã culture is immediacy of experience." Evidence, starting with the five senses—sight, hearing taste, smell, and touch—is very important to them. "[They are] the ultimate empiricists."³ Empiricism (the theory that all knowledge originates in experience) made the Pirahã the author of reality.

Because of the Pirahã's empiricism, SIL missionary Daniel Everett claimed the Pirahã lost interest in Jesus when they discovered he [Daniel] had never seen him.

AGREEING WITH SCOTTISH PHILOSOPHER, David Hume, were men like Chairman Mao Zedong and missiologist Charles Kraft. As an empiricist, Mao declared: "At first, knowledge is perceptual. The leap to conceptual knowledge, i.e., to ideas, occurs when sufficient perceptual knowledge is accumulated."⁴

Kraft, wrote, "Theologizing is a dynamic discovery process engaged by human beings according to human [sense] perception."⁵

THROUGH SATIRE, Winnebago philosophers of another age warned their listeners not to be tricked. This warning, which is especially relevant today, is embedded in the following Trickster story.

## DON'T TRUST YOUR PERCEPTIONS

As Trickster was engaged in cleaning himself, he happened to look into the water. Much to his surprise, he saw many plums there. The man carefully surveyed them and dove into the water to get some. But only stones did he bring back in his hands.

Again, he dove into the water. But this time, he knocked himself unconscious against a rock at the bottom.

After a while, he floated up and gradually came to. He was lying flat on his back in the water. Opening his eyes, he saw many plums on top of the bank. What he had seen in the water was only a reflection.

Then he realized what he had done. "Oh, my, what a stupid fellow I must be! I should have recognized this. Here, I have caused myself great pain."[6]

AS AN EMPIRICIST, Trickster assumes that nothing could be more certain than what his five senses told him. He believes what he sees in the water is the real thing. Perceptions are reality. So he dives into the water to get some plums and gets rocks instead. Repeating the process, he finally knocks himself unconscious. When Trickster comes to and opens his eyes, he realizes what he saw in the water were misrepresentations of the real thing.

The Winnebago wisemen warned against the idea that all true knowledge originates in perceptions. A concept-innatist would agree with the wisemen because, in the words of Gordon Clark, "If all knowledge is based on experience [perceptions] alone, then there can be no knowledge of any necessary truth."[7]

I would also add, there can also be no absolute truth.

Clark goes on to say, "Knowledge requires the combination of *a priori* forms and *a posteriori* experience."[8]

Before one's perceptions can be converted into knowledge, they must be classified under concepts, and then concepts under categories. This can only be done with a set of unlearned *a priori* concepts that are independent of empirical data.

Only people, created in the "image of God," have this *a priori* set of concepts that enable them to classify their perceptions and create knowledge. In the words of the late philosopher R. C. Sproul, "The best the senses can do is to awaken the consciousness to what it already knows."[9]

## GOD-BREATHED WORDS

When God revealed Himself in the Scriptures, He did so by using "God-breathed words" rather than "spirit-guided perception," as proposed by anthropologist-missiologist Charles Kraft. Kraft proposed that instead of being "God-breathed," the words of the Bible give us "an accurate record of the spirit-guided perceptions of human beings who were committed to God."[10]

The problem with relying on sense perceptions, as theologian and apologist Edward J. Carnell (1919 - 1967) notes, is that "sense perceptions cannot report to us anything meaningful,"[11] even when they are spirit-guided.

As theologian Cornelius Van Til points out, "Unless as sinners we have an inspired Bible [having words whose meanings are "God-breathed"], we have no God interpreting reality for us. There is no true interpretation at all."[12]

God-breathed words

## CONVICTIONS

- "If all knowledge is based on experience [perceptions] alone, then there can be no knowledge of any necessary truth" (Clark, 2004).[13]
- "Knowledge requires the combination of *a priori* forms and *a posteriori* experience" (Clark, 2004).[14]
- Like Trickster, empiricists tend to be tricked into thinking that true knowledge is perceptional.
- The *Pirahã* people have been tricked.
- Missiologist Charles Kraft said, "The Bible is an accurate record of the spirit-guided perceptions of human beings who are committed to God,"[15] rather than " sound words" whose meanings "belong to God."
- "Sense perceptions cannot report to us anything meaningful" (Carnell, 1952),[16] even if spirit-guided.

# CHAPTER 60
# THE NATURE OF ETIC DIVERGENCE
## WHAT IT MEANS TO BE CREATED IN THE IMAGE OF GOD

Upon discovering that the Chácobo had restructured the nuclear family, the first questions that came to mind were:

- Does evil exist that arises from structures within human society rather than from individual wickedness?
- Did the Chácobo satire I collected reveal the existence of such evil, a divergence from God's truth?

How one answers the above questions will determine the kind of strategy a missionary will use in evangelism, church planting, and community development. In this regard, the evangelical community offers two perspectives.

The first perspective is from Christian philosopher Cornelius Plantinga:

> Moral evil is social and structural as well as personal; it comprises a vast historical and cultural matrix that includes traditions, old patterns of relationship and behavior, atmospheres of expectations, [and] social habits.[1]

Christian anthropologists Charles Kraft and Sherwood Lingenfelter offer a second perspective:

> Structures ... due to the sinfulness of the human creators of the structures, are tipped (as with an uneven playing field), but are not evil in and of themselves (Kraft, 2005).[2]

> We must accept and work within structures and processes of others that are different from one's own social game (Lingenfelter, 2005).[3]

If structural sin exists, as Plantings proposes, should we blindly "accept and work with structures that are different from ours"? Or should we seek to reestablish the inherent meanings of forms that were rejected and replaced with meanings shaped by what Karl Marx called social existence that "belong to the people"?

When one begins to examine the cultural form of "kinship structures," one will note they all share the same irrational kind of thinking, with one exception: They all believe that *A* can be *B* under specific contextual pressures. For example, a cousin can be a sibling, an uncle a father, an aunt a mother, a nephew a brother, and a niece a sister.

In this regard, Plantinga notes: "Contexts strain and constrain people if social and cultural dynamics exert their pressures regularly and powerfully enough to make certain behaviors predictable."[4]

If there are external "pressures that make certain behaviors predictable," it seems reasonable to conclude my task was to discover what the environmental pressures of the Amazonian Rainforest were which compelled Chácobo men to live in a men's communal house that separated them from their wives and mothers-in-law. After all, did not Jesus declare that nothing should separate the "one-flesh" union of *husband-wife*?

Historically, when Israel was about to enter the "Promised Land," Jehovah explicitly warned Moses in Leviticus 18:3 (Common English Bible):

> *"'You must not do things like they are done in the land of Egypt, where you used to live. And you must not do things like they are done in the land of Canaan, where I am bringing you. You must not follow the practices of those places.'"*

What were these Egyptian and Canaanite practices that Jehovah warned against?

In this case, the context tells us what constitutes a family, and the Rule of Exogamy will reveal what constitutes a "family" for society. It knows what constitutes an incestuous relationship, and what constitutes an incestuous relationship will vary from one society to the next.

As a result, different types of families, different kinds of residence rules, different kinds of marriage rules, different kinds of kinship systems, and so forth, will emerge.

For the Chácobo, marrying a cross-cousin was permitted; marrying a parallel cousin was not. If one did, one would be marrying a "brother" or "sister." Such a marriage would be classified as being "incestuous."

For economic reasons, they ignored the Rules of Logic and classified parallel cousins as brothers and sisters. By merging mutually exclusive status positions, they diverged from a "fixed" Divine order and increased disorder in the world.

According to sociologist Bernard Farber, "In kinship systems that emphasize the unity of the nuclear family, such as the biblical kinship system, first-cousin marriages seem to be permitted and perhaps preferred."[5]

In this regard, Mary's father was Eli, and Joseph's father was Jacob. Eli and Jacob were brothers, and Joseph and Mary were first cousins. Marriage to a first cousin was not prohibited.

Instead, Jehovah's command in Leviticus 18:8-10 (NIV) was:

> *"'Do not have sexual relations with your father's wife;
> that would dishonor your father.*
> *"'Do not have sexual relations with your sister, either your
> father's daughter or your mother's daughter, whether
> she was born in the same home or elsewhere.*
> *"'Do not have sexual relations with your son's daughter or
> your daughter's daughter; that would dishonor you.'"*

Unlike others, the biblical kinship system did not violate the Rules of Logic by merging mutually exclusive status positions.

Whenever a society merges mutually exclusive status positions to meet specific needs, not only has that society rejected God as Provider, but it has also created a structure that is inherently evil.

THE EXISTENCE of spiritual phenomena is totally rejected by all naturalists because it opens the door to a theist's explanation of certain phenomena, like allegiance patterns, classificatory kinship systems, residence rules, totems, and the fact that man, as an "image bearer" of his Creator, has been equipped with knowledge that makes every man a taxonomist.

Nevertheless, I propose that the spiritual phenomenon of diverging from innate Universal semantic and cultural constants is open to analysis when one understands the nature of *etic* divergence and what it means to be created "in the image and likeness of God."

In this anthropologist's search for constants, I note a constant of human existence: Humankind is prone to diverge from God's truth, resulting in the maiming of society.

Strangely, and to my dismay, I found myself working in an environment in which "contextualization" had become, in the eyes of my colleagues, "the scripturally-endorsed approach for taking the Gospel to the world ... postulating that God recognizes and employs

the sociocultural adequacy principle of cultural forms (Kraft, 2005)."
6

Accepting this new doctrine makes one a cultural relativist, a status position I reject as unbiblical. For me, the "doctrine of sociocultural adequacy of cultural forms" shaped by the "material elements of the world" does not "accord with Christ" (Colossians 2:8).

Structural evil

## CONVICTIONS

- Whenever a society merges mutually exclusive status positions to meet certain needs, not only has that society rejected God as Provider, but it has also created an inherently evil structure, a structure that has "no place in the Divine Plan."
- Whenever a society violates the Rules of Logic and declares that a male can be a wife, a female can be a husband, a cousin can be a sibling, a male can be a female, a female can be a male, a shaman can be a jaguar, and a someone can be a something, it has not only violated the Rules of Logic that say $A \neq B$, but it has also created an evil structure.
- *Etic* divergence occurs when an inherent concept representing a Positive Universal that belongs to God is rejected and replaced with a meaning "that belongs to the people."

## CHAPTER 61
# THE GLEANING OF MEANINGS
### PERCEPTIONS, CONCEPTS, CATEGORIES, AND LANGUAGE

Philosopher-theologian R. C. Sproul wrote: "He [Socrates] sought the Universals from an examination of the particulars."[1] This is a great insight, but gleaning Positive Universals from an "examination of the particulars," which I believe should be the task of every linguist, anthropologist, and missiologist is not easy.

The task is more difficult because forms common to all may share two kinds of meanings: (1) inherent meanings that belong to God; and (2) learned meanings that belong to humans and that are derived from social existence.

The meanings that belong to God are "fixed," exact, and absolute. They are brought to consciousness by being "triggered" in a socio-linguistic environment.

The meanings that belong to man are relative. They misrepresent the kinds of meanings that belong to God. Instead of being "acquired," they are "learned."

Theoretical linguist John Lyons expressed this inside-out, non-materialist perspective this way: "The vocabularies of all human languages can be analyzed, either totally or partially, in terms of a finite set of semantic components which are themselves independent of the particular semantic structure of a given language."[2]

In other words, if true, an innate Divine "interpretive system" exists within humans free from cultural contamination. Lyons, the materialist, believes that if "there is a 'fixed' set of components, [then they must be] lexicalized in all languages."

The fact that a "fixed" set of Universals has not been lexicalized in all languages supports his belief that no Universal-Lexicon exists and that *etic* divergence is a religious myth linked to the fall.

However, Lyon's materialistic perspective underestimates man and society's spiritual capacity to suppress the truth from being lexicalized. The Chácobo, for example, had no word for thanksgiving.

In my Chácobo lexicon, I had no entry for thanksgiving. But this did not mean the concept did not exist in the subconscious. In time, I discovered that it did. Chácobo society had suppressed the idea from coming to consciousness, thereby preventing the innate-concept from being lexicalized.

This innate Universal-Lexicon, along with an innate categorizing concept, is the kind of information that not only capacitates all humankind to arrange perceptions under concepts and concepts under the appropriate categories, but without this mental *etic* data encoded in the subconscious, there would be no thinking, no spoken language, no knowledge of the world in which we live, and no sphere of existence called culture. All that would exist would be unrelated things existing in nature.

The content of this Universal-Lexicon and categorizing concepts is neither learned nor inherited; instead, each concept, with its inherent meaning, is "acquired" and brought to consciousness in a socio-linguistic situation by "triggering."

When we move to the sphere of semantics, different kinds of concepts exist. First are unlearned classificatory concepts, which are necessary for learning to be possible. As philosopher Gordon Clark points out, before our perceptions can become knowledge, they must first be classified. "Unless we had concepts or categories of quality, quantity, and relations, we could not think of botany, baseball, or anything else."[3]

The semantic contents of this Universal-Lexicon that one already possesses exist independent of one's particular language. It is culture-free. Their meanings have not been invented by society nor created and shaped by the material "elements" of the environment.

∽

## CATEGORIZING AND NAMING

> *"So Adam gave names to all cattle, to the birds of the air, and to every beast of the field" (Genesis 2:20a).*

The Bible makes it clear that when the Lord God brought the animals to Adam, he innately knew their qualities. There was no need for him to ask, "What is an animal?" Adam knew what features constituted an animal. He knew that monkeys, tigers, wild boars, and deer were different animals.

Likewise, he innately knew the features that made a bird and what qualities were bird-like. He recognized those qualities, like feathers, wings, and beaks. He innately knew that sparrows, parrots, ducks, and hawks represented birds.

He classified creatures having the qualities of animal-ness as animals and creatures having the qualities of bird-ness as birds. Knowledge as to what qualities constituted a kind, a genus, and a species was innate and not learned.

Adam could name the birds and animals "according to their kind." Because Adam knew the inherent qualities of each kind, he was up to the task. One thing is clear: Physical phenomena, in this case, the inherent qualities of animals and birds, reveal the existence of an "interpretative system" residing within Adam.

When the Chácobo arrived in the Amazonian Rainforest, they, like the Miccosukee, named the birds, animals, plants, and trees according to their kind. They did not invent the categories. The spiritual nature that positioned them above nature allowed them to arrange their perceptions under concepts and concepts under the proper categories so they could be named.

Classificatory concepts consist of concepts like part of, kind of, same-different, big-small, few-many, male-female, and cause-and-effect. Without these classificatory tools, the earth's species would never have been classified according to their kind.

According to linguist Noam Chomsky, human beings are born with a set of grammatical rules hard-wired into their brains, which he calls Universal Grammar. Whereas Chomsky locates the Universal Grammar in the brain, the theist locates it in the mind. The mind is not a blank slate. The materialist must merge the two.

When Kraft says, "Words and all other cultural symbols derive their meanings only from their participation in the cultural context of which they are a part," he is saying all meaning exists outside of man in his material environment. There exists no unchanging, "fixed" definition within man that can be "triggered" and brought to consciousness in a linguistic-social environment.

For the contextualizer, there exists no uncontaminated culture-free meanings, no representations of the truth within from which all humanity can diverge.

I disagree. Besides a Universal Grammar, there exists structured in the unconscious mind a Universal-Lexicon containing forms or concepts common to all to which are attached Divine or inherent meanings. Societies can reject these Divine meanings and replace them with meanings shaped by societal influences within a particular environment.

## ACQUIRING MEANING

A search-and-find faculty exists in the mind analogous to Google search. Every child's mind, regardless of language, knows how to extract from their parents' speech patterns syntactic categories like subject, object, verb, and the order in which they occur. The child discovers how time, action, cause, and effect are expressed in language.

Cognitive scientist Jerome Bruner quotes from Anna Wierzbicka in *Semantics, Primes and Universals*, "Children must be basically acquiring labels for concepts they already have."[4]

When a child acquires word labels for these innate concepts which are brought to consciousness by "triggering," the child is provided with a Divine, uncontaminated, culture-free, semantically "fixed" framework for interpreting the world in which he or she lives.

The materialist would strongly disagree. For the materialist, all meanings, concepts, and categories are either invented by man, manufactured by the cerebral cortex, or exist as derivatives of social existence within an environment that is in continual flux.

The materialist believes there are no words with meanings that represent "fixed" and unchanging concepts. Neither are there meanings that misrepresent the Universal or the Divine Ideal. He thinks each society creates its own ideal, script, and truth, and these are open to change because of the ever-changing environment.

In contrast, two kinds of meanings exist for a non-contextualizer like myself. First, there are Divine meanings. They are culture-free. They are not learned but reside within humans and are brought to consciousness by "triggering."

Second, meanings are imported into the mind from outside humans through the interaction of humanity and society with their environment.

The latter derive their meanings from the mind-shaping powers of the "basic material elements of the world" (Colossians 2:8) and

Galatians 4:3: "Even so we, when we were children, were in bondage under the elements of the world."[5]

It is a perspective that has "secretly crept" into missions. According to the Apostle Paul, such meanings do not "accord with Christ" (Colossians 2:8).

## EVIDENCE OF A DIVINE INTERPRETATIVE SYSTEM WITHIN MAN

Besides the child's capacity to acquire the correct symbol or word for the meaningful concepts that exist within the subconscious, Bruner goes on to say: "It is culture, not biology, that shapes human life and the human mind, that gives meaning to human action by situating its underlying intentional states in an interpretative system."[6]

For the concept-innatist, culture is a spiritual phenomenon. For the contextualizing materialist, it is not.

Kraft believes: "Human biology provides the backdrop for all we need to know as humans."[7] This means an "interpretative system" must first be created.

For the concept-innatist, it already exists within humans. Evidence of this Divine "interpretive system" existing within humans is found in humankind's innate capacity to arrange perceptions under concepts and concepts under the proper categories. This is a spiritual phenomenon, not a biological one.

It is also revealed phenomenally in man's capacity to discover new categories that serve as constituent parts of a society's "interpretative system." This ability to discover new categories is significant.

An enlightening example would be the discovery of what constitutes light. Physicists assumed that light was made of particles until the eighteenth century. Then, in 1865, James Maxwell proposed that light consisted of particles and waves. He later discovered that the actual constituents of light were, indeed, particles and waves, as he had earlier proposed.

When I was assigned to help the Miccosukee translation team in the mid-80s, I assumed that the project had stalled because the translation team had failed to uncover the real grammatical categories in the language. The normal semantic-linguistic categories they used did not "fit" the data.

In response to the paper I gave, Pike sent me an unexpected postcard congratulating me on discovering "new categories." I did not "invent" the dual culture-nature semantic categories of the Miccosukee language, nor did the Miccosukee. They remained to be discovered.

God gave Adam and all of humankind the innate ability to classify and categorize

Eventually, they were discovered by a Bible translator who believed man had been positioned above nature to categorize the world in which he lived. Interestingly, my biblical worldview provided the analytic framework for making the discovery.

I was also surprised to discover, along with the semantic verb categories of culture and nature, that the Miccosukee language had a dual pronoun system that complemented the dual verb system.

One set of subject pronouns (*-ele*) positioned man outside nature in the sphere of culture; the other set (*cha-*) positioned man in nature.

These dual semantic unlearned categories pointed to an innate "interpretive system" within the subconscious that gives all humans the capacity to classify in a language their sense experiences and gain knowledge of the world in which they live.

The Miccosukee were endowed with an "interpretative system" to classify the material environment of Florida.

~

## LANGUAGE AND RULES OF CULTURE

For a child to learn a language and the rules of culture, the child needs to be raised in a social environment. Even though the child's unconscious mind is structured with a Universal Grammar, a Universal-Lexicon, and a search-and-find faculty, the faculty only works in an environment where language is spoken.

Deprive the child of such an environment, and the child will become an adult with severe handicaps, making it difficult to function as a normal human being.

Consider the following example. Oxana Malaya was born on November 4, 1983, in Southern Ukraine.[8] When she was three, her alcoholic parents abandoned her. Five years later, she was found curled up inside the family kennel with the mongrels to keep warm.

After years of not being near a human, she adapted all the traits of a dog. She walked on all fours, ate raw meat, growled, whiffed, barked, and even showed her teeth when approached.

This is a tragic example of what can happen to a child when not raised in a caring language-social environment. But Oxana is not the only case.

For a child to acquire language and the rules of culture, the child needs to be raised in an environment in which both the Universal

Grammar and the Universal-Lexicon structured in the mind are permitted to interact in a social-linguist environment. Without this interaction between the two, the child will grow up handicapped and impaired intellectually.

Screen shot from this Youtube video:
https://www.youtube.com/watch?v=UkX47t2QaRs

# CONVICTIONS

- God created man to exercise dominion over nature.
- Psalm 8:4-8 (Names of God Bible).

   *... what is a mortal that you remember him or the Son of Man that you take care of him?*
   *You have made him a little lower than yourself.*
   *You have crowned him with glory and honor.*
   *You have made him rule what your hands created.*
   *You have put everything under his control: all the sheep and cattle, the wild animals, the birds, the fish, whatever swims in the currents of the seas.*

- Cultural and language Universals are not "learned;" they are "acquired" and brought to consciousness by being

"triggered."
- Structured in the unconscious mind exists a search-and-find faculty without which learning a language would not be possible.

## CHAPTER 62
# INNATE UNIVERSALS FROM THE FIELD OF PARTICULARS
## CONSTITUENTS OF KNOWLEDGE—FORM AND MEANING

### ETIC DATA PROVIDED ACCESS INTO THE SYSTEM

What constitutes *etic* data? According to Kenneth Pike, "*etic* data provides access into the system—the starting point of analysis."[1]

We also get a clue what he means when we realize the term *etic* is abstracted from phon-*etic*. On a phonetic chart, *etic* data consists of "fixed," constant, unchanging sound data.

The same principle Pike proposed could be applied to the field of anthropology. What was needed was a similar *etic* framework, a framework consisting of concepts, values, and structures whose attached meanings were "fixed," constant, and unchanging—the kind of scheme or framework every anthropologist needs to judge the validity of a cultural form.

∼

With a culture-free *etic* framework, it becomes possible for the analyst to judge the validity of a society's customs, social structures, and values. I soon discovered that the SIL Branch administrators where I had become a member were not interested in identifying the negative forms that suppressed human freedom and positive creativity. They informed me that they had rejected Pike's idea that the unconscious mind is structured with innate knowledge that a society can reject.

Instead, the position of the Branch administration was that advocated by Eugene Nida of the American Bible Society, who acknowledged:

> There is a tendency to regard a word's "true meaning" as somehow related to some central core that is said to exist (in some Universal-Lexicon), either implicitly or explicitly, in each of the different meanings of a word or a linguistic unit. All the different meanings are supposed to be derivable from this central core of meaning.[2]

I, for one, believed there existed a Universal-Lexicon structured in the unconscious mind. The entries of this Universal-Lexicon consisted of "forms common to all" to which there were attached "inherent meanings."

Such a perspective, which Pike called *etic*, proposed that "form" and meaning-content should never be separated. Nida and evangelical anthropologists rejected this perspective.

For a few who agreed with Pike, two lexicons existed: a Universal-Lexicon and a people's lexicon. For those who agreed with Nida, only one lexicon existed, one whose meanings were shaped by social existence and that "belonged to the people."

In contrast, the Universal-Lexicon structured in the unconscious mind contained "fixed" meanings that belonged to God. The meanings attached to these Universal forms were brought to consciousness by being "triggered" in a social-linguistic situation.

For example, the Trobriand Islanders knew of a Universal-

Lexicon structured in the unconscious mind. Lest they "trigger" the meaning of father and bring it to consciousness, destroying their cultural operating system, they instructed every child to address the man who lived with their mother as "husband of mother" and never as *tama* (father).

For a society that believed every birth was a virgin birth, they knew the meaning of father could be "triggered" and brought to consciousness. Their solution—replace the word *tama* (father) with the *teknonym* (husband of mother), and it worked.

Upon review, my discovery of Chácobo satire, which is critical of the Chácobo lifeway, convinced me of social structures that were misrepresentations of the Universal.

Outwardly, how they had structured the nuclear family appeared normal. Then I discovered they had restructured the nuclear family by replacing the *husband-wife* dyad with that of mother-daughter.

I was now a member of a Branch that rejected Pike's conviction that "a person may distort Innate Positive Universals into negative particular actions."[3] If true, it meant that my task as a budding anthropologist was to uncover the Universal meanings that society had rejected.

AS A THEIST, linguist Kenneth Pike proposed: "*Etic* data provided the starting point of analysis" for both linguistic and cultural phenomena in the same way phon-*etic* data provided the phonologist "the starting point of analysis" for a society's sound system. He echoed the sentiments of Socrates, who "sought the Universals gleaned from an examination of the particulars."[4]

However, the cultural relativist has rejected the idea that one can glean the Universals from an examination of the particulars. For such, the cultural analyst has no culture-free *etic* frame of reference for judging the validity of cultural forms like the following:

- One must marry someone who speaks a different language lest thou commit incest.
- Thou shall become the food supplier of one's in-laws when one marries.
- One is free to select one's gender and disregard the biological fact that those who have xx chromosomes are female and those who have xy chromosomes are male.

For Pike, a culture-free standard existed for judging the validity of the above statements. Cognitive anthropologist Ward Goodenough agreed with Pike, noting: "[*etc* data] provide the frame of reference, the conceptual constants, through which to examine the similarities and differences among different behavioral systems."[5] The truth is, among academicians, no accepted *etic* frame of reference exists for judging what ought to be.

Nevertheless, as a theist, Pike's goal as a linguist was to see the procedure used in phonology applied to linguistic and cultural phenomena. He theorized an analysis of cultural and semantic phenomena should lead to a "gleaning" of cultural and linguistic Universals whose meanings were "fixed," constant, and absolute.

For concept-innatists like Pike, linguistic and cultural forms structured in the unconscious mind have meanings brought to consciousness by being "triggered." Such meanings are "acquired." Returning to British philosopher Peter Carruthers' position, "Most of our concepts are 'triggered' rather than learned."[6]

Linguistic and cultural forms also exist with meanings that are learned, "that belong to the people," and, according to Karl Marx, derived from social existence. It is "social existence [that] determines consciousness."[7] For such, social existence precedes and determines meaning.

In contrast, Pike believed cultural and linguist forms exist with meanings that "do not belong to the people." These meanings are neither learned nor determined by social existence. To be explicit, these meanings "belong to God." When environment and social existence change, their meanings will remain "fixed" and constant regardless of how a society lives.

Philosopher Peter Carruthers: "Most of our concepts are "triggered" rather than learned."[8] They are not derived from social existence. They "do not belong to the people."

For example, every Chácobo knew his moral duty was to help those in need. They didn't learn this principle from family, missionaries, or Bolivian nationals. The Universal Principle of helping one in need was innate. The fact they had *a priori* knowledge of the Universal Principle was revealed in the *Myth of Nahuapaxahua* (chapter 2, "Discovering an Innate Moral Imperative").

According to Chinese philosopher Wing-Tsit Chan, "Knowledge of the good is innate in us ... since man is born to know and practice the good ... the chief duty of man ... consists in loving the people."[9] Chan provides an example of the task of a gleaner.

For one to glean the Universals that exist in every cultural operating system, the gleaner must recognize, like Chan, that he is dealing with the constituents of knowledge—form and meaning. Knowing how the two should be packaged is crucial to understanding and interpreting linguistic and cultural phenomena. In the words of Pike, "Matter and mind—tie them up tight, package them right."[10]

For example, I observed a Chácobo woman bring a gift of freshly roasted manioc flour to another lady in the village, but she never said "thank you." Instead, she filled her basket with the identical fresh manioc flour she was making. I immediately made a mental note: They do not understand the meaning of "gift."

They have replaced a Divine meaning with one that belonged to the Chácobo. I needed to help them restore the Universal. A true gift need not be reciprocated.

Eventually, the Christians attached the proper meaning to it, but it took years. They had to learn it was impossible to pay God back for His gift of salvation.

As a theist, Pike knew humankind, estranged from God, could

detach from forms held in common by their inherent meanings and replace them with relative meanings derived from social existence; i.e., the rejection and replacement of a Positive Universal with a negative cultural particular (*etic* divergence).

The first Universal I "gleaned" from examining the cultural particulars occurred when collecting Chácobo stories. Long after we moved to *Biiyá* , I discovered Chácobo satirists who rejected the Chácobo definition of marriage.

The definition their ancestors attached to the form of marriage had reduced each son-in-law to a person-thing whose function was to provide his wife's parents their daily bread in exchange for conjugal rights to their daughter. Then, lest husband and wife figuratively become "one flesh," no Chácobo husband was permitted to live in the same house or room with his wife.

I concluded the only way these Chácobo sages could have known that the one-flesh principle of *husband-wife* represented the Universal was because the principle had been "written on their hearts," just as Chinese sages knew that "knowledge of the good" was "written on their hearts."

The existence of satire critical of the Chácobo concept of marriage and how they had structured the nuclear family implied that, at some point in history, the Chácobo had detached from the form or concept of marriage and its inherent Divine meaning and replaced it with a meaning derived from social existence in the Amazonian Rainforest.

Contrary to what Karl Marx and contextualizing missiologists think, "Marriage was not 'figured out' by man; God instituted it from the beginning. And it is God's definition that matters, not later attempts by man to redefine it."[11]

When I explained my discoveries and convictions to Pike, his response was positive.

CREATED IN THE IMAGE OF GOD

Chácobo church

## CONVICTIONS

- "Acquired" meanings are "triggered" and belong to God.
- Meanings derived from social existence and "learned" belong to the people.
- Since there presently exists no frame of reference through which to examine the similarities and differences among different behavioral systems, and since "*etic* data provides access into the system—the starting point of analysis,"[12] the time has come for anthropologists to glean the Universals from the field of particulars and create such a culture-free frame of reference.
- According to Pike, "A person may [choose to] distort Innate Positive Universals into negative particular actions."[13]
- The creation of such an analytical frame of reference would reveal that God's definitions matter, not man's.

# CHAPTER 63
# SPECIES VERSUS KINDS
## CHÁCABO AND CHINESE LAD

When I asked a Chinese lad whose parents attended a biweekly Bible Study we held in our home, "What kind of animal are you?" He immediately replied, "I'm not an animal. I'm a human being."

How did he know he was a human being and not a kind of animal? Embedded in my question was the problem of knowledge: How do we know what we know? How did this lad realize he was not a kind of animal?

THE LATE CHRISTIAN Apologist John W. Robbins put it this way:

> The fundamental crisis of the twentieth century [as well as the 21st] is neither political, nor social, nor economic. It is intellectual, and the primary intellectual problem is neither metaphysical nor ethical: It is epistemological. No attempt to solve the various problems and end the seemingly interminable crises of the twentieth century

will be successful unless it is recognized that the justification of knowledge is always the ultimate problem, and that unless this problem is solved, no other problem can be.[1]

But before the epistemological problem of how we know can be solved, academia must first recognize that "knowledge is always a combination of form and content. As expressed by Christian philosopher Gordon Clark, "We cannot know the form without the content."[2] Recognizing the problem, linguist Kenneth Pike wrote: "Form and meaning [are] tied together."[3]

However, what Pike failed to recognize is that forms, like family, marriage, husband, wife, son, daughter, gift, animal, birds, trees, and so forth, have attached to them (a) meanings selected by one's environment that have "no place in the Divine Plan," and (b) meanings belonging to God that have a place in the Divine Plan.

Meanings derived from context, what anthropologist Kraft called "cultural context," what Mao Zedong called "social practice," and what Karl Marx called "social existence," such meanings are "learned."

In this regard, Charles Kraft wrote, "Words and all other cultural symbols derive their meanings only from their participation in the cultural context of which they are a part."[4]

In contrast to the idea that all meanings "belong to the people" and are "learned," as I've attempted to convince the reader, some meanings are not "learned" but rather "acquired" by being "triggered" and brought to consciousness. Otherwise, culture is reduced to a feature of nature, and being "image bearers of God" who transcend nature must be rejected.

In contrast to meanings that "belong to the people," inherent meanings belong to God. Such meanings are "recorded" in a Universal-Lexicon structured in the unconscious mind in the same way our information-bearing DNA genetic code is structured in the cell.

When I asked the Chácobo the same question I asked the

Chinese lad, "What kind of animal are you?" They were shocked. "We are people," they responded." Not only had I "triggered" the same answer, I had "triggered" a response of unbelief: "Papa doesn't know we are people."

The point is that the answers the Chinese lad and the Chácobo gave to the question, "What kind of animal are you?" were the same. How is that possible? They were brought to consciousness by being "triggered."

In fact, according to philosopher Peter Carruthers, "Most of our concepts are 'triggered' rather than learned."[5] Among them is the concept that man is not a species or a kind of animal.

If man is not a species, then what is man? It is a question that King David asked: "What is man that You are mindful of him, And the son of man that You visit him" (Psalm 8:4)?

Man is unique. He is the only one of its kind. Only man has language. Only man can talk to his Creator. Man is the only being who writes books, cooks food, and walks upright. Only man can create linguistic and cultural forms that have "no place in the Divine Plan" and thereby increase the amount of chaos that exists in the world.

The answer the Chinese lad and the Chácobo gave to the question, "What kind of animal are you?" implies they innately knew that man is unique and one of a kind.

# CREATED IN THE IMAGE OF GOD

God's biodiversity

## CONVICTIONS

- Approximately eight million, seven hundred thousand species exist on planet earth, but man, as one of a kind, is created in God's image. He is not a species!

## CHAPTER 64
# DOES A DIVINE PLAN FOR LIVING EXIST
### A TRANSFORMATION

Jesus admonished in Matthew 10:34: "Do not think that I came to bring peace on earth. I did not come to bring peace but a sword."

The context shows the object of the "sword" was the household-of-five, a social construct that had existed since the time of the Patriarchs. Jesus knew that continued maintenance of the form He called the "household-of-five" would hinder worldwide evangelism.

Two thousand years later, the very same form, the household-of-five, would be condemned by Chairman Mao, who believed the Chinese household-of-five was an obstacle to economic development.

As a revolutionary, Mao rejected the type of family structure his culture imposed on society, namely, the dominance of the father-son dyad within the nuclear family.

Anthropologist Morton Fried pointed out, "When Mao was twenty-four, he was attacking 'three bonds [dyads],' the ties binding ruler and subject, father and son, and husband and wife, declaring that they had to be done away with for the salvation of China."[1]

For the good of China, he pushed Chinese families toward a "modern family form" which was the nuclear family.

Mao fully understood that serving the Chinese people's "heart and soul" would be impossible if the household-of-five, consisting of a dominant father-son relationship and a weak *husband-wife* bond, continued to serve as the primary building blocks of Chinese society.

The old form meant that no son or daughter-in-law would be free to serve the Chinese "people's heart and soul" if the primary allegiance of sons was to their fathers and the primary allegiance of daughters-in-law was to their mothers-in-law. In 1949, God used Mao to bring the "sword" to the Chinese household-of-five.

Providentially, what replaced the household-of-five was the nuclear family. Chinese young people were finally free to leave their father and mother to serve Christ and their people's "heart and soul."

Besides economic growth, there was an unexpected consequence of Mao bringing the "sword" to the Chinese household-of-five. It was an explosive growth in evangelism and church growth, a phenomenon the government is attempting to suppress.

The point is this: Family structures matter regarding economic development and church growth. When a society rejects the Divine Plan, contextual social existence will shape how people relate to God and each other.

At some point in history, the Miccosukee living in South Florida took the first step away from the Divine Plan when they replaced inherent meanings attached to Universal cultural forms with meanings derived from social existence.

The rejection of Providence and their anxieties over survival compelled them to believe that someone, a *nakne* (husband), could be reduced to a something. This turning of a someone into a something occurred when they made *nakne* (husband) the subject of the impersonal existential verb em-££om *nakne* (for-me exists it).

But in doing so, not only was a Universal Rule of Grammar violated, but every husband in Miccosukee society was reduced to a needed something. In this case, a sperm donor, whose function was to produce children for his wife's family, technically called a "matrilineal clan."

At some point in history, a meaning that belonged to God now belonged to the Miccosukee people. *Nakne* (husband) no longer represented its true meaning.

Along with reductionism, the nuclear family was also restructured. The covenantal one-flesh principle of *husband-wife* was exchanged for the biological one-flesh principle of sister-sister, reflected in the myth *In The Beginning There Were Two Sisters*.[2]

But sadly, for those who teach contextualization in our institutions, the concept of the Lord bringing the "sword" to the household-of-five and establishing the nuclear family and the *husband-wife* dyad as the primary building blocks of society doesn't make sense.

They believe meanings "belong to the people," and the meanings the Chinese, Miccosukee, and Chácobo attach to concepts like father, son, husband, wife, and family are valid if the cultural form satisfies a need.

According to Kraft, "The basic appropriate evaluation criterion is the concept of 'fit' or 'fulfillment.' The question is how well this cultural form fulfills such and such a function."[3]

Anyone who believes that such function-based meanings represent a distortion of Positive Innate Universals stands falsely accused of being more interested in Americanizing the cultural forms of society rather than in planting a church directed by indigenous elders.

In this regard, once again, note the words of Charles Kraft as he categorized those who work in pioneer situations:

> We who teach contextualization are dealing primarily with those whose major concern will have to be on how to bring about change in already existing situations rather than how to plant culturally appropriate churches.[4]

Such a statement applied to Marian and me. We lived among a leaderless, monolingual people who could neither read, write, nor count to two. They had no concept of a seven-day week, a weekend, or money. All trade was by barter.

But more importantly, they had a family type Jesus called the "household-of-five." For me, this was disconcerting.

After translating Matthew 10:34 into the Chácobo language and discovering that Chairman Mao had brought the sword to the Chinese "household-of-five," I was convinced that unless the "sword" came to the Chácobo household-of-five, the Chácobo would cease to be a viable culture. They now numbered less than 150 souls.

Eventually, the Chácobo household-of-five was challenged by bachelors who became public school teachers and then married. Becoming a *raisi*, they immediately reacted to what was expected of them.

Rabi, for example, instead of going hunting and fishing, walked two hours to the village of *Alto Ivon* to teach school and then two hours back. Carmelo refused to follow his mother-in-law when she decided to retire to the Benicito River, taking his wife with her. For the Chácobo, the time had come for the household-of-five to be dissolved.

So, the existential question became: Did a Divine design exist for living that humans and society could reject and replace with a plan of their own making?

In the words of Cornelius Plantinga, "Did godlessness spoil the proper relations between human beings and their Maker and Savior?"[5] And did the absence of a superordinate-subordinate structuring of Chácobo society provide proof of such godlessness? Plantinga goes on to say:

> Of course, such ideas annoy certain people. The concept of a design to which we all must conform, whether we like it or not, appears absurd or even offensive to many. People who believe in naturalistic evolution, for example, think that human concepts, values, desires,

and religious beliefs are, like human life itself, metaphysically untethered to any transcendent purpose. Instead, our lives and values are the product of such blind mechanisms as random genetic mutation and natural selection.[6]

According to Kraft, who rejects the notion that such a Universal design for the family exists, the "planting of a culturally appropriate church" meant planting a leaderless church. "Only in marriage can a true subordination and super-ordination be set forth adequately in terms of human relations."[7]

It made no sense, but it made sense to me. To avoid becoming a leaderless church, we needed to teach Chácobo bachelors God's design for marriage: Husbands and wives were to become "one flesh" and the wife was to be her husband's helper rather than her mother's, as was the Chácobo custom.

If accepted, we assumed the superordinate-subordinate structuring would occur naturally. However, this self-structuring of the nuclear family only happened after we left in 1980. It took time.

When I returned eighteen years later in 1998, the Chácobo had an indigenous leadership. This meant the Chácobo church was "not dependent upon any artificial life support," i.e., anything culturally foreign or non-essential, especially money, buildings, and professional clergy.[8] This revolutionary transformation can be seen in the following photos.

Graduating health promoters

Bilingual school at *Tumi Chucua*

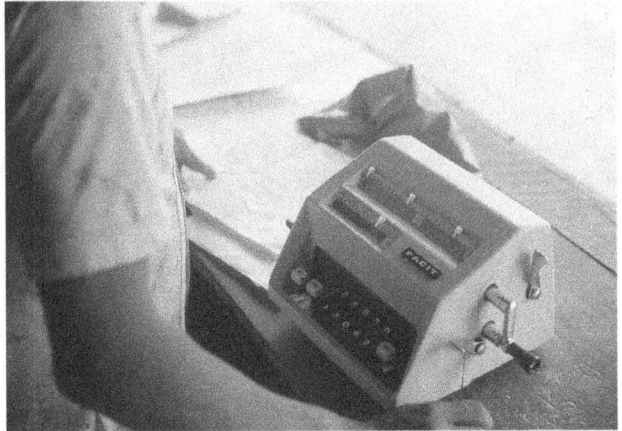

Accounting

New building and satellite dish, 1998

## CONVICTIONS

- A divergence from the Divine Plan is possible because godless humankind has the freedom and capacity to reject God's plan. "For what can be known about God is plain to them, because God himself has made it plain to them" (Romans 1:19, ISV).

- Any divergence from the Divine Plan implies the need for a replacement plan "that belongs to the people."
- If carried out, the replacement of the Divine Plan with a plan "that belongs to the people" will necessitate restructuring the nuclear family and replacing a covenantal dyad with a biological one.
- The emergence of China as a superpower can be attributed to Mao Zedong's introduction of the "sword" to the Chinese household-of-five.
- The emergence of a Chácobo church free of external influence and money can be traced to the "sword" coming to the Chácobo household-of-five.

# CHAPTER 65
# CHÁCOBO LEARN HOW TO PARTICIPATE IN BOLIVIAN SOCIETY
## THE BEGINNING OF THE REVOLUTION WITHOUT GUNS

Since tribal leaders who could relate to government officials without fear was zero, Barbara Hoch brought in government representatives from different departments to explain their functions. The officials told the students as citizens they had the same rights as the nationals.

With the help of SIL nurses and Bolivian doctors, Director Hoch developed a course to train tribal health promoters. I suggested the students also be trained in buying, selling, and property management.

With a grant from the Canadian government, we purchased two dozen Monopoly games in Spanish. Once a week, in the last class before lunch, they played Monopoly. If they wanted to continue playing into the lunch break, they were free to do so.

"My kids" who had graduated from the Norwegian Mission School and who were attending our indigenous training school loved it. Upon completion, they purchased a couple of games to take back to the tribe. They had moved from a people who couldn't count past one to understanding the importance of being able to add, subtract, buy, and sell.

Since large portions of the Bolivian prairie were grasslands, we gave some students the skills and know-how to become ranchers or at least ranch hands. A small cattle farm at the SIL Bolivian Branch could be used to transfer such skills to the indigenous Bolivian people. With my encouragement, the Chácobo acquired a small herd of Brahman cattle, each cow privately owned.

The project was a complete failure. At heart, the Chácobo were individualists rather than collectivists.

Who, for example, owned the pasture land? While each rubber trail was privately owned and maintained, no one owned the pasture.

Who, for example, would pay for the barbed wire and provide the fencing to keep the cattle off public space? Collectivism didn't work, and I should have known better.

In addition, even if one individual owned the herd, it still would have failed because of envy. The rule was: If you have it and I don't have it, you can't have it either.

For example, one industrious Chácobo who had planted orange trees around his house discovered someone trying to kill them. At the base of each tree, someone had driven in rusty nails. The man probably was not generous enough with the oranges his trees produced. After we left in 1980, each cow was individually sold off to Bolivian ranchers.

Aware of the lack of indigenous literature in each tribe, Director Hoch encouraged students to write narratives or stories in the Chácobo language and then have them published using silkscreen. They wrote and published these stories.

After two years, SIL produced several bilingual school teachers whom Barbara Hoch recommended the Bolivian government accept as part of its bilingual educational program. Among them were Cana Alvarez and Rabi Ortiz. Both were students in Marian's first reading class (see photo at end of chapter).

With the government's approval of the appointment of Cana and Rabi as salaried teachers, Marian could give up her task as a village school teacher in *Alto Ivon*. We could also place a teacher in *Nucleo* village. What we needed was a teacher for the *California* village.

However, the funds for continuing the program had run out. If the program which had produced bilingual teachers for several communities was to continue, the Canadian funds needed to be replaced. What had become a bilingual leadership training school designed to produce bilingual school teachers for five lowland tribes, the Adore, Cavineña, Chácobo, Ese Ejja, and Sirionó, was ending unless another miracle occurred.

And then, it happened again. The day before we were to have our closing exercise, Dave Farah, our government representative in *La Paz*, Bolivia, sent me a message saying there was an official from the German government who was looking for Christian projects to fund.

The next day, I flew to *La Paz* and met the government representative, explaining to him that we were having our graduation program that very evening. I said it would give him some idea of what the SIL was trying to do if he were there. He agreed.

That evening, our guest witnessed our bilingual demonstration. Rabi, one of "my kids," was the teacher. He was both bilingual and bicultural and served as a model for the type of "bridge leaders" SIL was trying to produce. Our guest was impressed.

When I said we would like to include all the lowland tribes in Bolivia, including six more tribes, he surprised me by saying, "Ask big."

I submitted a request for $300,000. A month later, I received word that our request had been granted. It meant we could extend our bilingual educational program for several more years. The Lord again was gracious in our time of need. "Let us therefore come boldly to the throne of grace, that we may obtain mercy and find grace to help in time of need" (Hebrews 4:16).

A month after graduation, the Chácobo villages of *Nucleo* and *Alto Ivon* had their first bilingual schools. Working with "my kids" was starting to pay off.

The Bolivian Government appointed both to fill these posts. Cana was appointed to teach in the *Nucleo* village.

According to their "social game," which I did not fully understand at the time, marriage meant every son-in-law lived in the village of his in-laws. Cana's in-laws lived in *Nucleo*.

When Rabi married, I learned there was more to a Chácobo marriage than a change of residence. Rabi was single when he was appointed to teach school in *Alto Ivon*. A few months later, he married. I eventually learned that instead of Rabi becoming a son-in-law when he married, Rabi became a *raisi*. The status position of *raisi* meant being the fish and wildlife provider for his in-laws, whom he also called *raisi*.

Obeying the rules of their game, Rabi moved. But instead of hunting and fishing in the morning as a *raisi*, which in-laws expected, Rabi walked two hours to *Alto Ivon* where he taught school. He returned home around three or four in the afternoon, only to walk back to *Alto Ivon* the following day.

He wasn't going to give up his career as a bilingual schoolteacher. Aware that God "hated divorce" (Malachi 2:16), and while trying to figure out their "social game," we decided to close the school in *Alto Ivon* and opened a school in *California*. Rabi no longer had to travel back and forth each day.

Not understanding their "social game," I was ignorant regarding the pressures Rabi faced when he married and became a *raisi*. I eventually figured out the term *raisi* did not mean son-in-law, but rather "one who provided fish and wildlife for his in-laws in exchange for conjugal rights to their daughter."

One thing was clear. In exchange for sexual rights to someone's daughter, he had lost his freedom to serve the community. It was also clear that such a form had "no place in the Divine Plan." The Chácobo had transferred the one-flesh principle from *husband-wife* to that of mother-daughter.

AFTER WATCHING Rabi travel back and forth for several months, I decided the time for a regime change had come. The next time Rabi came to *Alto Ivon*, I told him we needed to talk about Chácobo's future and adopting me as their "patrón." I shocked him when I told him Marian and I were planning on leaving and someone needed to replace me. Then, I suggested that he was that someone.

If accepted, it meant Rabi giving up his job as a village schoolteacher and assuming the role of a businessman. Instead of coming from the Bolivian Government, his salary would come from the profits the business generated.

For the sake of his people, I told him he needed to make a career change and replace me as the one in charge. This meant he needed to live in the village of *Alto Ivon*, and his in-laws needed to release their daughter to accompany him. He wasn't sure they would.

I offered Rabi the small thatched-roof building, our former home, which was still standing, as their home. This would be the first time he and his wife would share the same living space. It would be revolutionary. Such a move we knew would strengthen the *husband-wife* bond while weakening the mother-daughter bond.

I told him I had figured out their "social game," which prohibited him from becoming "one flesh" with his wife, as commanded in Genesis 2:24.

I followed this up by having him read a satire his ancestors wrote. As a *raisi*, he had experienced first-hand what it was like living with a mother-in-law who was trying to control his every move.

When he returned to *Alto Ivon* a few days later, he showed up with his wife and son. I was surprised. By releasing their daughter, his *raisi* had lost their primary food provider. He and his wife moved into our former dwelling, and I immediately trained him to replace me with every task I had assumed.

Besides buying and selling, he had to learn that the function of every business was to make a profit, and if he gave away the goods in his store to his *raisi*, which they no doubt expected him to do, the business would not survive. Having played Monopoly at our bilingual training course, he knew everything about buying, selling, and trading. If he gave his assets away, he would soon be out of business.

After a few months had passed and his wife's family had not received any store goods, his *raisi* took their daughter and grandson back. From their perspective of how the game of life should be played, their daughter and grandson belonged to them. Since he failed to fulfill his duties as a *raisi*, taking them back was the right thing to do.

The time had also come to replace the monopoly money with Bolivian currency. They knew now that the numbers on each bill represented a value that could be exchanged for store goods. Having told Rabi that the store's function was twofold, to meet social needs and to make a profit, I now had the task of providing him with the financial tools to manage a small business. He needed the tools to determine whether the store was losing or gaining assets.

So, I acquired a textbook on a double ledger accounting system for tracking credits and debits. To my dismay, the principles set forth were far above my ability to transfer to "my kids," Rabi and Paë. How would I help them when I, a linguist, could barely grasp the concepts in the textbook? Nevertheless, I would try.

Because acquiring these financial tools was so important, I flew Rabi and Paë to our Center from *Alto Ivon*. With an accounting textbook before me, as I was writing principles of accounting on the blackboard, I received a call from our DC-3 airplane pilot informing me that they had onboard a passenger wondering why we invited him to our Center in Northern Bolivia. Somebody told them to pick him up in Santa Cruz.

Since the DC-3 airplane was about to land, I hopped on my Honda motorcycle and headed to the hangar to greet this unknown guest. Thinking he was a government official, I asked him what department he represented. He replied, "None." He then said, "I am an accountant."

I was shocked. The Lord had sent me an accountant just when I needed one! I couldn't believe what I heard.

After explaining that I was attempting to teach a couple of Chácobo how to do accounting, I expressed my hope that he could help me.

He hopped on the back of my Honda, and we took off to my office, where Rabi and Paë awaited my return. After I showed him what I was trying to do, he said, "I think I can help you." After taping a few pages together, he set before us a simple double-ledger.

His accounting system would show if the business had made a profit or loss. What I saw unfold amazed me. Before me were the "tools" that Rabi and Paë needed for operating a business. It also gave me the means to ensure no one was cheating. In my time of need, the Lord again provided. The timing was incredible, beyond belief.

I profusely thanked the accountant, saying there was no way I could repay him for his help. He spent the evening with us and then flew back to Santa Cruz in the morning.

Along with checking Rabi's books every month, there was the task of taking the rubber and Brazil nuts to *Riberalta* to sell. During high water, rubber and Brazil nuts were transported to *Riberalta* by boat, where they were sold. I went along to help and give guidance.

During the dry season, when the water in the *arroyo* (river) had dried up, JAARS transported them to *Riberalta*. However, the day was coming when neither I nor JAARS would be there to serve them.

Since I had proposed to the Branch that we would be closing down our Center in Northern Bolivia by 1984, this became a problem in search of an answer. How would they get their products to *Riberalta* once SIL terminated its work in Bolivia?

∼

SHORTLY AFTER THE Pacahuara were settled into their new environment, Dave Farah sent me a message stating the Bolivian Minister of *Asuntos Campesinos* was coming to *Riberalta* to present to the Chácobo title to the land they occupied. Our request was finally being honored.

As the delegation from *La Paz* arrived, a Chácobo elder from the village of *Nucleo* proclaimed to me and all who could hear, "Rabi serves us all! You should not remove him from this position."

If Rabi had not freed himself from the cultural form of *raisi* which enslaved him, he would not have been able to "serve all" by organizing the event.

What this elder from *Nucleo* did not understand was that at some point in history, his ancestors had created a brilliant system to ensure their food needs would be met as they aged. But this system destroyed their freedom and ability to serve others. I was witnessing a spiritual phenomenon in which young married men were not only becoming heads of their families, but they were becoming leaders of the entire community.

When Rabi's mother-in-law took back her daughter (Rabi's wife) because he failed to meet his responsibilities as a *raisi*, at that moment, he was freed from a negative cultural form that had prohibited him from "serving all." It was a form that had "no place in the Divine Plan."

I witnessed the beginning of a society returning to a Universal that their ancestors had rejected but which Chácobo wise men of another era had recommended.

Marian's first class circa 1960

Store

## CONVICTIONS

- The Lord again was gracious in our time of need.
- "A Revolution without Guns" had begun.

# CHAPTER 66
# THE MISSIOLOGICAL CROSSROAD
## "NEW WINE" OF CHRISTIANITY DEMANDED "NEW SKINS"

As we were introducing the "new wine" of the Gospel, it became increasingly apparent that there was tension between the "new wine" and the "old wineskins," that is, the liberating message of the Gospel and some of the particulars of Chácobo culture; i.e., what they thought about sin, gift giving, thanksgiving, and the roles of husbands and wives.

Their men's communal houses, whose function was to constrain and prevent husbands from becoming "one flesh" with their wives, were, in my opinion, contrary to what was revealed in the Scriptures and in particular Genesis 2:23:

> *"This is now bone of my bones*
> *And flesh of my flesh;*
> *She shall be called Woman,*
> *Because she was taken out of Man."*

Rejecting the advice of one missiologist who advocated using the "old wineskins," that is, all the existing cultural forms, I chose to follow Jesus and take the revolutionary approach. After fifteen years of observing the Chácobo way of doing things and convinced that a leaderless tribe could not survive in the economic, political, and cultural world now encroaching upon their lifeway, I took out a folder. I wrote on the front of it, "A Revolution without Guns."

In the folder, I began to outline my revolutionary strategy for social change, starting with the Chácobo "family-of-five" (father, mother, sons, daughters, and incoming sons-in-law) to which Jesus prophesied He would bring a "sword."[1]

If Jesus condemned this socio-economic arrangement called the "family-of-five," which I was convinced was the case, then the form could not possibly be valid no matter how high it ranked on the contextualizer's "needs satisfaction test." My hope was to replace the dominant dyad of mother-daughter with that of *husband-wife*.

Of course, in doing so, I was aware that some missiologists would accuse me of introducing to the Chácobo my American way of doing things rather than a revealed way as stated in the Bible, namely, in the Creation Mandate of Genesis 2:23-24.

To me, the choice was clear. It was either the Creation Mandate that Jesus reinforced in Matthew 19:4-6 or the Chácobo way that would lead them to cultural extinction.

> *And He answered and said to them, "Have you not read that He who made them at the beginning 'made them male and female,'*
> *"and said, 'For this reason a man shall leave his father and mother and be joined to his wife, and the two shall become one flesh'?*
> *"So then, they are no longer two but one flesh. Therefore what God has joined together, let no man separate."*

Eventually, the accusation against me was that I had introduced them to my "American" way rather than God's way. According to Kenneth McElhanon:

"The residence pattern [Prost] introduced was neolocal—the same as [his] native American—rather than patrilocal, characteristic of the biblical era."[2]

But why should I have introduced a patrilocal residence rule characteristic of the biblical era when it, too, violated the Creation Mandate stated in Genesis 2:23-24 and was reiterated and reinforced by Jesus in Matthew 19:4-6?

Second, we didn't introduce a rule grounded in our American way of life but in Scripture. For me, God blessed America based on the behavior of the Bible-believing Puritans who attempted to incorporate biblical principles into their lives. In this case, a residence rule promoted the freedom that accounts for America's greatness and productivity. If this rule had not been incorporated into the American way of life, America, in my opinion, would not have become known for its creativity, innovation, and freedom.

## THE STRATEGY

The strategy for introducing a Universal residence rule was simple. No outward condemnation, criticism, or denunciation of Chácobo cultural forms. In this case, the Chácobo family-of-five, Chácobo men's communal houses, and the matrilocal residence rule. Though the forms constrained, prevented, and obstructed *husband-wife* intimacy from taking place, thereby preventing the two from becoming "one flesh" (Genesis 2:24), I would remain silent on this crucial issue.

I decided it would take just one young Christian married man convinced that the primary building block of the Chácobo family and society should be that of *husband-wife* rather than the mother-daughter. It would be a young man whom we had been preparing for this role for fifteen years. We had trained him to be a bilingual schoolteacher, and he served as a bilingual schoolteacher in another village. As was the custom, this potential leader lived with his in-laws, who controlled his wife's movements and, to some degree, his own through their daughter.

It would be a test to see if the dominant mother-daughter dyad could be replaced with that of *husband-wife*. In our opinion, the negative consequence of an institutionalized cultural form that intentionally separated husbands from their wives suppressed the emergence of superordinate-subordinate status positions that the tribe desperately needed to survive. If we were right, their solution for removing the dialectical tension between mothers-in-law and sons-in-law using men's communal houses had to be the wrong solution.

The correct solution was to return to the Universal, which they had suppressed for hundreds or thousands of years. The solution was for both to "leave father and mother," as stated in the Creation Mandate (Genesis 2:23-24).

Leaving and cleaving was God's solution to the problem. It was more than a material problem. It was a spiritual problem.

Leaving and cleaving would mean trusting God's promises as ultimate Provider, not in their social construct, which Jesus called the "family-of-five" in Luke 12:52-53, a construct to which he would bring a "sword."

> *"For from now on, five in one house will be divided: three against two, and two against three.*
> *"Father will be divided against son and son against father, mother against daughter and daughter against mother, mother-in-law against her daughter-in-law and daughter-in-law against her mother-in-law."*

## DIALECTICAL THINKING IN MISSIONS

What does this dialectical, evolutionary thinking have to do with missions today, especially for the missionary who thinks "contextualization" is the appropriate way to do evangelism and church planting?

First, contextualizers would accept the Chácobo solution to the dialectical tension between mothers-in-law and sons-in-law. Put all husbands in a men's communal house.

Second, contextualizers would say that whatever tensions arise between the "new wine" of the Gospel and the relational forms of the culture, using the old forms is appropriate. Give them new meaning, or use the old forms, as Kraft suggested, in a non-sinful way, if possible. Kraft's solution is a "slow transformation [yeast-like] change."[3]

Third, any notion that the "new wine" of Christianity demands "new skins," i.e., new cultural forms, as Jesus made clear, is unacceptable. Why? As mentioned, the old forms served specific functions in meeting society's basic needs. Man's solution to existential anxieties, discontent, and survival apparently is more appropriate than God's solution.

Providentially, I discovered the real solution to our problem in a New Testament commentary published in 1884, which I thought would be helpful in our translation project.

Heinrich Meyer's exegesis of Matthew 9:16-17 gave me answers on how to resolve this tension. The solution was to introduce new cultural forms that represented the Universals. Is this not what Jesus advocated:

> "No one puts a piece of unshrunk cloth on an old garment;
> for the patch pulls away from the garment, and the
> tear is made worse.
> "Nor do they put new wine into old wineskins, or else the
> wineskins break, the wine is spilled, and the wineskins

> *are ruined. But they put new wine into new wineskins, and both are preserved" (Matthew 9:16-17).*

Meyer in his commentary points out that Jesus' comparison shows that the coming wine of Christianity will need new relational forms and allegiance patterns. The old forms will not do.

Meyer paraphrased Jesus' declaration:

> The old forms are not suited to the new religious life emanating from me. To try to embody the latter in the former is to proceed in a manner as much calculated to defeat its purpose as when one tries to patch an old garment with a piece of unfulled clothe, which, instead of mending it, as it is intended to do, only makes the rent greater than ever; or as when one seeks to fill old bottles with new wine, and ends up losing wine and bottles together. The new life needs new forms.[4]

For Chácobo Christians, the new life needed new forms representing the Universal.

Instead of a dialectical synthesis that assumes cultural forms are "neutral," Jesus, we contend, is advocating a revolution by replacing negative cultural forms with Positive Universal forms.

Such positive relational forms that promote human freedom and covenantal relationships exist; yet, contextualizes deny their existence.

This is what the struggle is all about. They claim that all relational forms are "essentially neutral."

I strongly disagree. One does not remove a natural tension between the new wine of the Gospel and the old allegiance patterns or forms that make up the old wineskins by declaring them "neutral."

As Meyer writes, "The new life needs new forms." Slowly, the context of my folder, "A Revolution without Guns," took shape.

Eventually, the seed for revolution was planted. But it wasn't until after we left in 1980 that the superordinate-subordinate structuring of Chácobo society took place. The restructuring turned them from a leaderless tribe to a self-directed tribe free from inside and outside controlling forces that sought to enslave them.

The picture of the young Chácobo man teaching his fellow tribe members the Scriptures was taken in 1978 (see photo at end of chapter). The Sunday services had moved from the men's communal house into the schoolhouse.

Two years later, in 1980, the congregation included women (see photo at end of chapter). The photograph reveals the dominance of the mother-daughter dyad over the *husband-wife* dyad was slowly losing strength. Husbands and wives were coming to church together, which was revolutionary. The "new wine" of Christianity was slowly emerging into new cultural forms.

What I find interesting in all of this is that when checking Kraft's index of biblical references in his highly influential book *Christianity and Culture*, the following essential passages in Scripture dealing with cultural forms are absent: Matthew 9:16-17, Mark 2: 21-22, and Luke 5:36-39.

Such verses and Meyer's interpretation do not support Kraft's theory of contextualization and the neutrality of cultural forms. Jesus did not recommend eliminating the tension between the Gospel and age-old allegiance patterns through a dialectical process in which the "old wineskins" are newly classified as "neutral" rather than negative.

The figurative language speaks of "social revolution."

Instead of attempting to use old cultural forms with the hope that the "old skins" could contain the life-transforming power of the Gospel, we encouraged the use of "new skins," or new forms that would enhance personal freedom and dependence on God.

By God's power and Scripture reading, the Chácobo were transformed from "person-things" to genuine people capable of determining the direction of their lives.

The same is true of David J. Bosch's book *Transforming Missions*.

These important passages should be discussed. In any missiological theory that supports a dialectical approach to missions, these passages concerning the "new wine" needing "new wineskins" are never mentioned regarding church planting, evangelism, and Scripture in strategizing.

Men's communal house

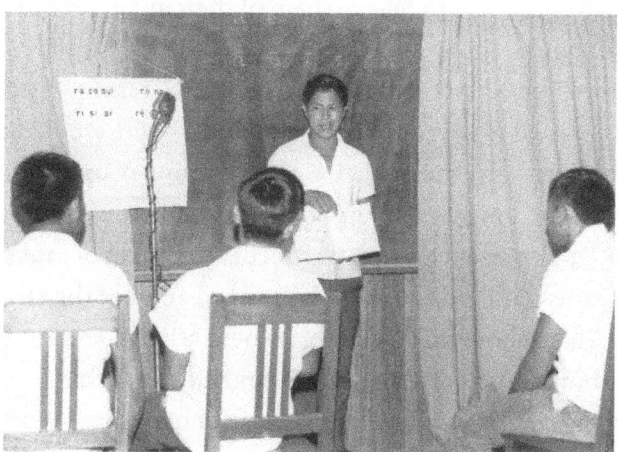

Rabi teaching the men

Church service, 1980, men, women, and children

## CONVICTIONS

- For the first fifteen years, I failed to grasp that the function of the forms which replaced the Positive Universals was to relieve them of their anxieties over existence.
- Once I understood the kind of cultural operating system they created to relieve their anxieties—who would make the beer—my message to a core of young people was: You'll no longer need the Summer Institute of Linguistics and our presence to be your security blanket because:
- "... the LORD will make you the head and not the tail; you shall be above only, and not be beneath, if you heed the commandments of the LORD your God, which I command you today, and are careful to observe *them*" (Deuteronomy 28:13).

# CHAPTER 67
# REQUIRES NEW FORMS
## THE CHÁCOBO MEANING ATTACHED TO THE CONCEPT OF MARRIAGE HAD "NO PLACE IN THE DIVINE PLAN"

DOCUMENTS TALK

A few weeks after receiving title to 43,000 hectares of land, a Bolivian patron immediately tested what the Chácobo would do if he tried to exploit the virgin rubber trees. Upon hearing the bad news, I hiked to their camp, taking Rabi along.

When I arrived, they were connecting the rubber trees to a walking path for the tapper. I showed the patron our land title and pointed to the boundary we had made. The following day, the tappers packed up and left.

The Chácobo who came with me were amazed. Once more, they witnessed that documents "talked." The older generation was starting to realize the importance of their young people learning to read, write, and do arithmetic.

To "self-actualize," not only did they need to learn to read, write, count, and understand the value of Bolivian currency, they needed to know what their rights were as Bolivian citizens. When the course ended, I brought to *Alto Ivon* a couple of lawyers from *La Paz* to explain to Rabi and Paë what their rights were as Bolivian citizens.

In our quest to prepare the Chácobo for life in the new economy they were about to enter, we continued to play Monopoly under the glow of our kerosene lamp. To some degree, playing Monopoly represented the world of commerce they could not escape.

Carmelo, one of the Chácobo "mighty men," graduated from our teacher training course the following year. He was appointed to the teaching post in *Alto Ivon*.

Before he took Rabi's old post, however, unknown to me, he had joined the Bolivian military and became the first Chácobo to do so. The Chácobo no longer feared the Bolivian army as they had. As part of his training assignment, he received an order to reopen the school in *Alto Ivon*, knowing he was a qualified teacher trained by SIL.

After a few months of teaching at *Alto Ivon*, Carmelo married. Since he married someone from the village of *California*, I now had some idea of what he faced. So I closed the school in *Alto Ivon* and reopened the school in *California* where he became the fifth member of the Chácobo household-of-five.

Then we went on a three-month furlough in the U.S.. When we returned, we were surprised to hear his *raisi* was planning to return to the Benicito River where the fishing was better. Suddenly, like Rabi, he faced a problem. He could either keep his government job as a schoolteacher or keep his wife.

He asked me for advice. I responded by saying, "Let me think about it," knowing that God hated divorce but still somewhat ignorant about what it meant to be a *raisi*. However, before I could answer him, I had to squeeze in a trip to Quito, Ecuador, where I attended an SIL Community Development (CD) Seminar directed by anthropologist Dr. Marvin Mayers.

The seminar's purpose was to promote community development among the tribes. According to Mayers, the seminar's director, using existing cultural forms was the most effective. That shocked me. Use forms that had "no place in the Divine Plan"? That didn't make sense.

I was skeptical after reading Francis L. K. Hsu's article on "Kinship and Ways of Life" and witnessing what had happened to Rabi. Using a form that put control of the Chácobo operating system in the hands of mothers-in-law ran counter to what the Scriptures taught and what their sages warned against.

At the conference, no mention was made of the possibility that cultural forms might exist that had "no place in the Divine Plan," which multiplied sinning. Instead, we were being encouraged to be "cultural relativists."[1] The message was God loved cultural diversity.

In such an environment, the last thing I would do was tell Dr. Mayers I had a folder on which I had written the words "A Revolution without Guns." The revolution I was conducting acknowledged the existence of cultural forms that "had no place in the Divine Plan." The function of these forms was to satisfy two needs: Their need for a daily supply of protein and their need for manioc beer.

In exchange for food security, the Chácobo invented a plan to address those needs at some point in the past. In exchange for a heavenly Provider, they had reduced Jehovah to the Bird Above and made husbands-to-be *raisis*. The cost was their freedom.

Since Carmelo had asked me what I thought he should do regarding giving up his job as a village bilingual schoolteacher to follow his in-laws and wife who were relocating to the Benicito River, I decided to see what Dr. Mayers would say.

When I explained Carmelo's situation, Dr. Mayers didn't hesitate. "He should give up his government job as a teacher and tag along with his wife."

The answer revealed he had no objection to using forms that "had no place in the Divine Plan." He had rejected the biblical instruction that "the husband is head of the wife, as also Christ is the head of the church; and He is the Savior of the body" (Ephesians 5:23).

I asked him: "Who is the head of your household"?

He surprised me by saying: "Sometimes my wife; sometimes me. It depends on context."

I was shocked. The context selected the head, not the Word of

God. For Mayers, the context selected which dyad should be the dominant dyad of the nuclear family.

When Mayers said, "Carmelo should go along with his in-laws, and your task is to provide a bilingual schoolteacher for every family," I was aghast. Close down the village school and provide every Chácobo family with a bilingual schoolteacher. It was insane! It was a task no one would be able to fulfill.

His answer confirmed he didn't believe that "the husband is the head of his wife as Christ is the head of the church" nor the idea a Divine Plan existed "hardwired" into the unconscious mind that man could reject.

I discovered I was a member of an organization that had a department that taught that no form has an inherent meaning and that we should be "cultural relativists" rather than concept-innatists.

Since Carmelo had graduated from a Christian boarding mission school, he was probably unaware that when he married a Chácobo, he would become a *raisi* rather than a *yerno* (son-in-law). After all, during those years, he attended a Christian school and church and was undoubtedly taught a biblical perspective on marriage. As a *raisi*, his ascribed task as the fifth member of his in-law's household was to be their daily fish and wildlife supplier.

When I returned from the conference, I learned that Carmelo had decided himself. He had refused to move to the Benicito River with his wife's parents. He refused to be shackled by a freedom-suppressing form that demanded he become the fish and wildlife supplier for his wife's parents. He refused to become a *raisi* and lose his freedom.

Since marriage, according to the Divine Plan, was about husband and wife becoming "one flesh," a "state of affairs" that Chácobo customs and values would never allow, I would classify his marriage as invalid. I concluded the Chácobo meaning attached to marriage had "no place in the Divine Plan."

# CREATED IN THE IMAGE OF GOD

Rabi at the land office with judge circa late 1970s

*Biiyá* circa late 1950s

Land grant ceremony

## CONVICTIONS

- Did Jesus not declare: "The old forms are not suited to the new religious life emanating from me"?

# CHAPTER 68
# CULTURAL RELATIVIST VERSUS CONCEPT-INNATIST
## SIL MISSED THE MARK

A few years later, Carmelo remarried. This time, he became a *yerno*. He married the daughter of a Christian Bolivian family that had become a member of the *Alto Ivon* village. He was now free to set up an independent household and be the head. Because he refused to become his in-law's daily fish and wildlife supplier, he was free to serve his community.

During those stressful years of setting up a bilingual school in each village, it became evident we had a cultural problem that needed to be resolved. No one had prepared me for the reality that Chácobo marriages were all about parents using their daughters as bait for obtaining a daily food supplier

As stated before, every *raisi* had to submit to his mother-in-law's will for the food delivery system to function correctly. He was not allowed to set up an independent household. It would mean the end of a well-conceived plan to meet food needs apart from God.

Suddenly, living in Chácobo society were two former *raisis*, Rabi and Carmelo. Both informed the Chácobo community that new life in Christ demanded new forms. Lest they again get entangled in a system that robbed them of their freedom, Rabi and Carmelo married daughters of a Christian family that had providentially moved to *Alto Ivon*. The Lord had provided a way out, and now Rabi and Carmelo were free to serve the Lord and the community.

In the meantime, to counteract the cultural script Chácobo young people were learning from their parents, I would point out to "my kids" there existed a Meta-Script revealed in Scripture and "written on their hearts." Its principles were "acquired" rather than "learned."

In addition, another script existed, one they inherited from their parents. The script contained forms common to all, like family, that had been restructured to satisfy a particular existential need. It was a script that Chácobo sages of another age rejected and warned against.

Aware that "my kids" might diverge from God's truth when they became adults, during our leadership training course, I would have them memorize the Scriptures in Spanish and Chácobo. If they chose to diverge from God's truth later in life when they were adults, the Scriptures they memorized in their youth would whisper in their ears:

> *"This is the way, walk in it."*
> *Whenever you turn to the right hand Or whenever you*
> *turn to the left" (Isaiah 30:21b).*

Since I miraculously learned how to do simple accounting based on balancing assets against liabilities and equity during our bilingual teacher-leadership training course, I took a student from each tribe to teach them this system. To complement the accounting lessons, we opened a store that sold not only food supplies to the students but also household goods and other in-demand items. Under my supervision, they operated the store.

Instead of setting up a kitchen and dining room for feeding, we provided each student or family with a cooking sheet, pots, and pans, along with a weekly allowance they were free to spend in any way they chose. Once a week, the accounting students took inventory, counted the cash, subtracted the liabilities, and calculated whether or not we had made a profit or a loss.

Along the way, I would point out that if they felt coerced into giving some of the goods to demanding relatives, they would soon be out of business. The "web of kinship" obligations had to end. If they were going to serve the community, they would have to be firm—that they were not "goods providers" for their kin.

Next, we added an electronics course taught by Lloyd Deister, our JAARS radio technician. Lloyd's class was small. For a student to qualify, he had to pass a math test. Of the six students who qualified, two were Chácobo, Coni (see picture at end of chapter) and Maro. Both had graduated from the Norwegian Mission School.

Twenty years later, Coni and Maro were important leaders in the Chácobo community. After leaving the tribe in 1980 and returning 18 years later, to my utter amazement, Maro directed an organization called CIRABO.

He informed me that after SIL pulled out of Bolivia, he, along with Rabi, Carmelo, Coni, and others who had attended our teacher-leadership course, hired a Bolivian lawyer who told them that they needed to form an institution dedicated to reaching shared tribal goals. So they each chipped in and rented a small office in *Riberalta*, and they named the institution CIRABO (Central Indigena de la Región de Bolivia).

Besides adding a course in electronics, I added a course in sociology. Since I had personally confronted firsthand how a society's concept of family and marriage could constrain community development and Scripture, the problem needed addressing. So I set out to warn the students that a "web of kinship" probably existed which could entrap them.

Using Francis L. K. Hsu's theory of the "web of kinship," I developed a simple course explaining that it was highly probable their ancestors had replaced the covenantal *husband-wife* dyad with a biological dyad, which in turn manifested itself as a "web of kinship" duties and obligations that suppressed individual freedom and creativity.

Unlike Professor Francis L. K. Hsu, however, I believed whenever a society elevated a biological dyad above that of *husband-wife*, it had rejected God's design for living with a design of its own making.

The Apostle Paul said in Acts 14:16: "... who in bygone generations allowed all nations to walk in their own ways."

By informing the students that there existed a Divine way for the nuclear family to be structured, I stepped outside the boundaries of what SIL-Anthro was teaching. From Dr. Marvin Mayers' perspective, every translator "should be a cultural relativist."[1] I wasn't.

If no form has an inherent meaning, then why be a Bible translator? Instead of using Divine meanings to express God's truth, missionaries were encouraged to believe that "God seeks to use and to cooperate with human beings in the continued use of relative cultural forms to express absolute supra-cultural meanings."[2]

How is it possible to use a form that rejects the one-flesh principle of *husband-wife* and then use an anti-one-flesh principle to express a Universal of the one-flesh principle of *husband-wife*? It's impossible.

The idea that God would bless a society that diverges from the Universal and restructures the nuclear family to "fit" a particular environment is inconceivable. While God permits a society to diverge from the ideal and "go its own way" (Acts 14:16), such behavior has negative consequences.

Romans 2:8-10 also states:

> *... but to those who are self-seeking and who do not obey*

> *the truth, but obey unrighteousness—indignation and wrath,*
> *tribulation and anguish, on every soul of man who does evil, of the Jew first and also of the Greek;*
> *but glory, honor, and peace to everyone who works what is good, to the Jew first, and also to the Greek.*

As a concept-innatist, I informed the students that the nuclear family had an Ideal internal structure, and undergirding this Ideal structure was the biblical principle: A man shall leave his father and mother and cleave to his wife.

In 1975, an SIL anthropologist unexpectedly arrived at our *Tumi Chucua* Center to critique what we were teaching the students. Marvin Mayers had discovered I had diverged from the department's policy of cultural relativism, which he taught at the conference in Quito, Ecuador, a couple of years earlier.

For me, the height of foolishness was the idea of using cultural forms that suppressed human freedom and creativity by replacing the *husband-wife* dyad with a dyad selected by the people. Our Bolivian Branch goal was to help the students attending to increase individual freedom and creativity, not suppress it.

After evaluating what we were teaching, the SIL anthropologist concluded, "I am afraid the program as now conceived is going to fall far short of its intended goal because it fails to consider implications of social change."

My conclusion was that SIL had completely missed the mark. I told him that we were a Bible translation organization and that what we were teaching should be judged by whether concepts common to all, like family, marriage, husband, and wife, had inherent meanings.

If they did, what could be wrong with pointing out to students the importance of the *husband-wife* dyad? After all, it was the only dyad that promoted freedom to serve one's community.

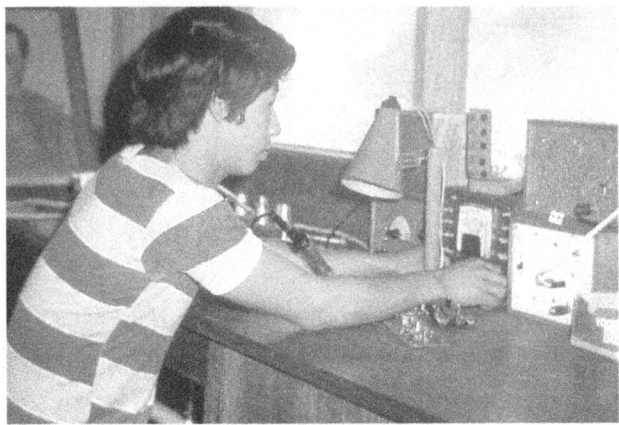

Coni, radio technician

## CONVICTIONS

- My vision of what forms promoted community development and the Scriptures was in fundamental opposition to SIL-Anthro's vision. The idea that the nuclear family should promote freedom didn't match their concept of what doing appropriate missiology was all about.

# CHAPTER 69
# THE "YOKE OF SLAVERY" LONGS TO BE BROKEN
## RETURNING THE HUSBAND-WIFE BOND TO ITS RIGHTFUL PLACE IN GOD'S FAMILY

Among Christian scholars rejecting the idea that the dominant dyad of the nuclear family should be selected by the environment is Christian philosopher and Professor of Law Herman Dooyeweerd.

He believed there was an "Inner Structural Law of the Family"[1] in the unconscious mind which should not be violated. Conscience informs all mankind that "membership is absolutely restricted to the parents and their offspring in the first degree."[2]

When membership includes cousins, uncles, aunts, nephews, and nieces who are also classified as brothers, sisters, fathers, mothers, sons, and daughters, society has violated the "Inner Structural Law of the Family." Such categorizing rejects the Laws of Logic which says A ≠ B. A cousin can't be a brother, an uncle can't be a father, and a person can't be a thing.

As a result of these discoveries, and because each tribal group attending our bilingual teacher-leadership training course had restructured the nuclear family by replacing the Universal *husband-wife* with a particular selected by their environment, the ethical thing to do was to point this out to them.

I worked on the assumption an "Inner Structural Law of the Family" existed whose "membership is absolutely restricted to the parents and their offspring in the first degree."[3]

Since the initial data I had collected declared that meaning precedes existence, the goal was simple: To strengthen the *husband-wife* bond and see it returned to its rightful place in the nuclear family. A return to its rightful place would promote individualism, freedom, logical thinking, and for security, a dependence on God.

In contrast, whenever a society replaces the Universal with a negative particular and the covenantal one-flesh principle with a biological one-flesh principle, it will choose collectivism over individualism, security over freedom, unsound thinking over logic, and a "web of kinship" responsibilities over Providence.

As anthropologist Robin Fox correctly points out, "Kinship systems are responses to various recognizable pressures within a framework of biological, ecological, and social limitations ... they are there because they meet certain needs."[4] "What remains Universal is the need."[5]

Agreeing with Fox are evangelical anthropologists Stephen Grundland and Marvin Mayers who believe: "Need satisfaction forms the foundation step for interpersonal relationships,"[6] rather than the nuclear family providing the foundation step for interpersonal relationships.

Evangelical anthropologist Charles Kraft believes one should ask, "How well does this cultural form 'fit' or 'fulfill' such and such a function [need]?"[7]

As a concept-innatist, perhaps a better question is: "Why does the form of the nuclear family best meet the basic needs of society?"

SOCIETIES GROUNDED in the teaching of God's Word are protected from such material pressures because its teachings inform them that the nuclear family's primary dyad is the *husband-wife* dyad. Reject revelation and demonic forces will arise which will attempt to replace the nuclear family with some other type of family structure.

The idea that such spiritual forces exist has been totally rejected by materialist Marvin Harris. In his tripartite research strategy consisting of infrastructure-structure-superstructure, it is infrastructure alone that ultimately determines what one believes and how one should behave. What Harris omitted from his tripartite plan was revelation.

The idea that the Bible provided our Founding Fathers with a vision of what we could be is revealed in the words of Noah Webster, author of *The American Dictionary of the English Language* (1828), who wrote: "Our liberty, growth, and prosperity was the result of a biblical philosophy of life."[8]

In Marivn Harris' quest to understand how "appropriate thoughts"[9] come into existence, as a son of Abraham, he ignored revelation.

Since we needed to make sure we would have readers for the Chácobo New Testaments we planned to publish in the future, it made sense to give priority to the training and production of bilingual school teachers.

However, there was the sociological problem of what anthropologist Francis L. K. Hsu calls the "web of kinship" relations.[10]

In this regard, once again, anthropologist Francis L. K. Hsu points out:

> "The total effect of the dominance of the attributes of one structural dyad leads to a particular kind of kinship content which in turn strongly conditions the pattern of thought and behavior of the individuals reared in the kinship system in the society at large."[11]

> **IF PARTICULARS ARE TO HAVE MEANING, THERE MUST BE UNIVERSALS.**
> ...Plato

Universal *husband-wife* dyad

## CONVICTIONS

- I believed the "yoke of slavery" caused by the biological mother-daughter dyad longed to be broken, and my goal was to replace it with God's covenantal *husband-wife* dyad.

# CHAPTER 70
# BREAKING THE YOKE OF SLAVERY
## TEARING DOWN STRONGHOLDS

Moses and the parting of the Red Sea

While I was aware that the Chácobo had restructured the nuclear family by replacing the *husband-wife* dyad with that of mother-daughter, I was unaware that the term *raisi* did not mean son-in-law but rather someone who would supply his wife's parents' with food in exchange for conjugal rights to their daughter.

It slowly dawned on me that setting up a bilingual teacher in each village was problematic. I had encountered a cultural operating system which was in fundamental opposition to our efforts to produce village schoolteachers.

In fact, at the Community Development Seminar held in Quito, Ecuador, I was personally informed that my task was not to produce bilingual teachers for the village but rather to provide a bilingual teacher for each Chácobo family-of-five lest I introduce conflict into their scheme for living.

But such a strategy would have legitimized the replacement of the *husband-wife* dyad with that of the mother-daughter dyad. It would have promoted the idea that social existence precedes essence (knowledge) of what ought to be. In addition, such a strategy would never have been supported by the Bolivian government, nor was it a task I could possibly fulfill.

Despite being advised not to bring conflict into the Chácobo scheme for living, as a translator, I was also aware that Jesus declared, "The old forms are not suited to the new religious life emanating from me."[1] Contextually, the old forms for satisfying needs were not suited for the new life in Christ.

Such forms included a marriage rule, a residence rule, and the internal structure of the nuclear family. Until the day Rabi and Carmelo's mothers-in-law took back their daughters, Rabi and Carmelo were not free to fully experience the kind of freedom Christ intended for them to have. Galatians 5:1 states: "Stand fast therefore in the liberty by which Christ has made us free, and do not be entangled again with a yoke of bondage."

# CREATED IN THE IMAGE OF GOD

As I look back over the years, I can report that our "Revolution without Guns" was a great success. When I explained to Kenneth Pike in 1978 what our "Revolution without Guns" was all about, I had no solid evidence to prove that what Marian and I had initiated would be successful. We had to wait eighteen years.

While the Bolivian Branch of SIL was committed to fulfilling its goals in linguistics, literacy, and Bible translation, unlike all other branches, it set out to tackle the problem of what anthropologist Francis L. K. Hsu called the "web of kinship."

The Chácobo web of relationships was real even though small when compared to other societies. Its web was designed to meet two needs: The need for manioc beer and the need for a steady supply of fish and wildlife.

So, in 1978, when on a three-month furlough, I flew out to San Francisco to discuss the "web" with Professor Hsu. He was teaching at the University of San Francisco.

How the nuclear family was structured was extremely important to me. For Hsu, it wasn't, even though the Chinese web of relations had made sons helpmates of their fathers in the same way the Chácobo web had made daughters helpmates of their mothers.

## CHINESE FAMILY-OF-FIVE AND BREAKING GIRLS' TOES AND ARCHES

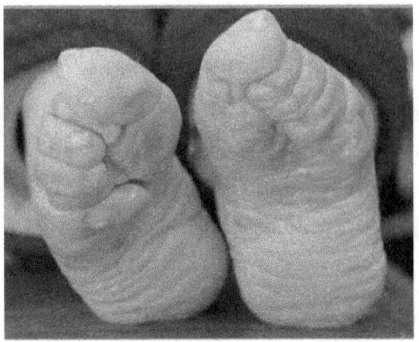

Chinese girl's foot-binding

For over a thousand years, the Chinese had "the custom of breaking girls' toes and arches and binding them to the sole of the foot with cloth—thought to be a passport to a better marriage and a better way of life."[2]

Nothing could be further from the truth. Foot binding persisted because it prevented daughters-in-law from escaping the Chinese household-of-five where their ascribed duty was that of being their mothers-in-law's helper.

According to Anthropologist Laurel Bossen:

> In the conventional view, it [foot-binding] existed to please men. They were thought to be attracted to small feet ... girls who had their feet bound didn't lead a life of idle beauty but rather served a crucial economic purpose, especially in the countryside, where girls as young as seven weaved, spun, and did work by hand.
>
> The feet of daughters were bound by parents to prevent them from running back home, thereby compelling them to return the "bride price."[3]

Like the Chácobo household-of-five, the Chinese household-of-five existed for meeting survival needs. For the brides and grooms who became the fifth member of these households, life became a web of duties and obligations from which they could not escape.

Regarding life in a society where the dominant social unit was the household-of-five, Jesus declared:

> *"For from now on five members in one household will be divided, three against two and two against three.*
> *"They will be divided, father against son and son against father, mother against daughter and daughter against mother, mother-in-law against daughter-in-law and daughter-in-law against mother-in-law"* (Luke 12:52-53, NASB).

Unknown to me, when reading the above verses in 1958, I discovered that the social unit, known as the "household-of-five" was the dominant social unit in Israel during the time of Jesus on earth. I had assumed it was the nuclear family. I was wrong.

Like Israel, this was also the custom of the Chinese. A married daughter went to live with her husband's people where she became her mother-in-law's "helpmate," not her husband's. Since the structure was unnatural, it pitted, in the words of Jesus, "mother-in-law against daughter-in-law and daughter-in-law against mother-in-law."

The Chinese scheme for living was ideologically opposed to a strong conjugal bond. When visiting a Chinese scholar who had landed in the hospital when attending the University of Florida, I asked him if he had let his wife know about his illness. To my surprise, it was his brother that he called, not his wife. He then went on to explain why he did not call his wife. The explanation was expressed in the following Chinese proverb:

> *My head is my father,*
> *My arms are my brothers,*
> *And my wife represents clothes to wear.*

Despite Mao's effort to destroy the dominance of the father-son bond that had existed for thousands of years, it was still alive. His wife, like a piece of clothing, was still considered to be dispensable.

At some point in history, the Chinese rejected the covenantal one-flesh principle of *husband-wife* and replaced it with the biological one-flesh principle of father-son. And now, unknown to Mao, the goal of his cultural revolution was to restore the Universal. He set out to replace a negative particular, the Chinese household-of-five with its custom of foot-binding, with a Positive Universal, the nuclear family.

The two—the residence rule and the foot-binding custom—complemented each other. Change the residence rule and the custom of foot-binding would cease. The dominance of the father-son dyad upon which the Chinese social and economic operating system was constructed would also collapse.

According to anthropologist Morton Fried, "The economic base upon which the extended families and lineages thrive has been almost completely destroyed, but the economic base upon which the nuclear family thrives is probably enhanced."[4]

With the reforms of the 1980s, households were encouraged to be more focused on conjugal loyalties rather than consanguineal loyalties. Perhaps unknown to Mao Zedong, he was replacing the traditional family-of-five and the dominance of the father-son dyad with that of the nuclear family and the *husband-wife* dyad.

Mao Zedong and his government treated women more like equal partners in the revolution. They immediately outlawed foot-binding throughout the country which had significantly diminished women's value as workers.

While the old cultural forms were designed to provide security, the new forms thrived in the new sphere of freedom, free from parental and in-law control. As the nuclear family and the one-flesh principle of *husband-wife* strengthened, so did human freedom, economic development, entrepreneurship, and church growth. These were positive effects.

Under the old system, the married man's duties to his parents and sons took precedence. A son could be made to divorce his wife if she failed to please him. Sons and their wives were not free to act independently.

When I read Hsu's description of the Chinese cultural operating system, it sounded like the reverse of the Chácobo operating system where a married woman's primary allegiance was not to her husband but to her mother. It was sons-in-law rather than daughters-in-laws who left father and mother to live under the control of their in-laws.

While an incoming Chinese daughter-in-law's primary duty was to her mother-in-law, it was now clear to me that the incoming Chácobo son-in-law's primary duty was to his in-laws, not to his wife.

In this regard, Christian philosopher Cornelius Plantinga declared:

> Moral evil is social and structural as well as personal: it comprises a vast historical and cultural matrix that includes traditions, old patterns of relationship and behavior, atmospheres of expectations, [and] social habits.[5]

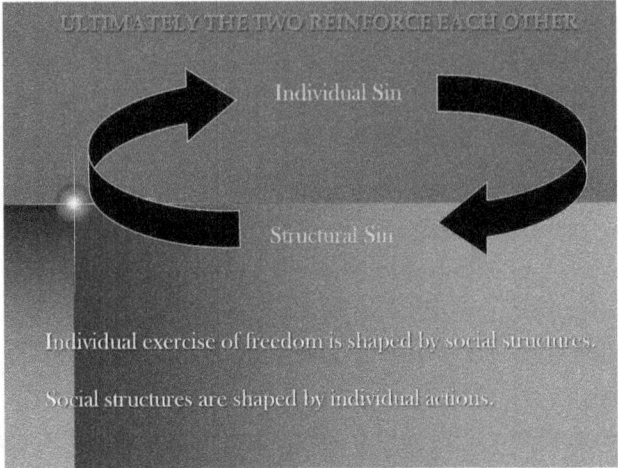

Structural and individual sin

Upsetting the equilibrium of the status quo is not new. The same problems we encountered when confronting a cultural operating system which put power into the hands of mothers-in-law Jesus faced when challenging the cultural forms of Jewish society.

As stated previously, German scholar Heinrich Meyer (1800–1873) paraphrased Jesus' declaration concerning the incompatibility of Jewish cultural forms with the kinds of forms needed for the new community of Christ followers as previously discussed in Matthew 9:16-17.

The present forms which made the mother-daughter dyad the dominant dyad of the family-of-five was not suited for a religion where "the husband is head of the wife, as Christ also is head of the church" (Ephesian 5:23).

If the Chácobo were to flourish, they needed "A Revolution without Guns."

Jesus would never have encouraged his followers to apply the "sociocultural adequacy principle" as presently advocated by missiologists. Because such forms are grounded in environmental "fitness" and are open to being modified "by the elements of the world" (Colossians 2:8), they are replaceable.

# CREATED IN THE IMAGE OF GOD

In the words of German theologian Johann Christian Konrad von Hofmann (1810-1877), such teachers are guilty of "permitting the material things [the elements of the world], of which the world is created, to form its standards."[6]

In doing so, they are following in the steps of Eve to whom God said:

> *"Your desire shall be for your husband,*
> *And he shall rule over you" (Genesis 3:16b).*

Chácobo children in school circa 1998

## CONVICTIONS

- After reading Meyer's paraphrase of Jesus' declaration, a paraphrase which made explicit the spiritual meaning of the parable, I concluded the Chácobo, like the Jews, needed "new forms" if the "new life" in Christ was to have the freedom to be expressed in word and deed.

# CHAPTER 71
# THE BATTLE LINES ARE DRAWN
## WHERE DO THE RULES OF BEHAVIOR COME FROM

1955 – 1980

In 1977, I resigned as Associate Director of Field Operations (ADFO) to complete translating the Chácabo New Testament. A year later, we completed the task with the dedication in the Fall.

Perry Priest, the Director of the Bolivian Branch of the SIL, flew in to encourage those who could read about the importance of reading the Word of God daily. Paë served as his interpreter.

I followed up with a brief message, reading from the Chácobo New Testament. Thirty-three years later, in 2010, unknown to me, the Chácobo New Testament was republished.

Shortly after the dedication of the Chácobo New Testament, Kenneth Pike, the president of SIL, arrived in Bolivia. He was aware that the Branch was making plans to close the Center in a couple of years. He had come to see how the process was working out.

We would be the first SIL Branch to phase out its work. In their report to the Branch Conference, they recommended closing our Center located in Northern Bolivia by July 1, 1981.

# CREATED IN THE IMAGE OF GOD

In that year, the Bolivian SIL Branch turned beautiful *Tumi Chucua* over to the Bolivian government. I wasn't there when the Branch's DC-3 airplane flew out with its last members. At fifty, I was an anthropology student at the University of Florida.

During Pike's visit before we moved to Florida, I made it a point to make known in embryonic form what I had discovered during our 24 years with the Chácobo. I informed him that I had recorded Chácobo satire critical of how their ancestors had structured the nuclear family.

At some point in history, I explained, the Chácobo had replaced the covenantal *husband-wife* dyad with that of mother-daughter. After sharing some of the satire with him that I had recorded, I pulled out my folder, which had written on it, "A Revolution without Guns."

I explained that I was attempting to help the Chácobo restore the *husband-wife* dyad to its rightful place in the nuclear family. For some reason unknown to me then, the Chácobo had replaced the *husband-wife* dyad with that of mother-daughter. It had become the dominant dyad of the nuclear family. I shared my conviction that the creation of satire provided "visible proof of commandments written not on stone but on tablets of the heart."[1]

I explained that without *a priori* information on how the nuclear family should be structured internally, it would have been impossible for these sages to create satire critical of their nuclear family.

When I finished, I waited for his response, knowing fully that SIL anthropologists would have condemned such an experiment.

He responded, "Gil, that's the most significant thing I have heard in the last twenty years. When you finish your work here in Bolivia, you need to study anthropology so that you can write it up for the academic community."

His answer shocked me. I left the meeting eager to explain to Marian what our next move would be after Bolivia.

While Pike approved of our approach to community development and social change, SIL-anthro disapproved. Pike was not a cultural relativist who believed that no forms had inherent meanings attached to them.

~

I HAD PROMISED the Chácobo we wouldn't leave until they had a means to get their rubber and Brazil nuts to market. Of all the projects I tackled, building a 125-mile road through the Amazonian Rainforest had my colleagues scratching their heads, and I didn't blame them.

However, I had promised the Chácobo that Marian and I would not leave until they had a road on which they would be able to transport their rubber and Brazil nuts to *Riberalta*. With Rabi's help, I had rotating weekly teams of Chácobo men flown to *Tumi Chucua*, the start-off point.

While the Chácobo slashed a straight path through the jungle, Bob Wilkinson cleared the trunks with the JAARS bulldozer. When we came to a creek, we put in a trench made from empty gasoline drums that I had welded together.

When we had cleared a twenty-mile trail through the jungle, we quit. Marian, Jim, and I were taking a three-month furlough to the States. It would allow me to check out universities in the Chicago area as a possible place to study. I needed an anthropology department that could explain why the dominant dyad of the Chácobo nuclear family was that of mother-daughter rather than *husband-wife*.

In the morning, we were scheduled to fly to Miami in our JAARS DC-3 airplane. Late in the afternoon, I heard a knock on the screen door while packing our suitcases. The man at the door introduced himself as a surveyor from *La Paz*.

He said, "The Bolivian government wants to build a road from *Riberalta* to *La Paz*. I hear you are building a road and want to see what you have done."

Traveling together on my Honda, I showed him the 20 miles of crude road we had made, and then we returned. He thanked me, and we parted company.

Upon returning three months later, to my amazement, the Bolivian government was building our road. The Lord had provided a road through the wilderness. My last trip to *Alto Ivon* was to bring a load of rubber from *Alto Ivon* to *Riberalta* for sale using what was to be called Highway 8.

Before we left for the States, I made a short trip to visit the Pacahuara. I wanted to inform them that Marian and I were returning to the land where we were born. But I didn't go alone. I took Rabi and one of "my kids" along. While there, I asked Rabi to do an impossible task: To help the Pacahuara to continue to adjust to their new life. It would not be easy. Very few people would have taken on such a task.

Marian and I were now free to leave Bolivia. We turned the work over to Phillip and Alicia Zingg from the *Misión Evangélica Suiza*. They had come to Bolivia to set up a Bible School in *Riberalta* at our urging. They were a God-sent replacement.

IN MY SEARCH for an anthropology department that could explain why the Chácobo had restructured the nuclear family, I enrolled at the University of Florida—a providential enrollment. Unknown to me, the University of Florida was the only university with a professor who could explain why the Chácobo nuclear family's dominant dyad was mother-daughter.

The year before, the Lord had arranged for Professor Marvin Harris to leave Cornell and teach at the University of Florida. I was unaware that he was not only Pike's severest critic but also the only one who had the answer to my burning question.

With Harris came a new way of looking at human existence and man's environment. His magnum opus, *Cultural Materialism: The Struggle for a Science of Culture*, had just been published. In it, he expresses his view of the Bible.

> There is no conflict between the biological and theological version of the species as long as the Bible is regarded as a metaphor. But if fundamentalists insist that the revealed word is more authentic than science as a source of evolution, then the battle lines are necessarily drawn.[2]

As one who believes that science can only discover what is and that only revelation can explain what should be, I entered an environment where "the battle lines were drawn." But to my amazement, Harris, the materialist, raised the same question I asked: "Where do the rules and behavior come from?"[3]

To answer the question, anthropologist Marvin Harris took Ken Pike's *etic* data concept and flipped it upside-down. Instead of the unconscious mind being structured with mental forms to which inherent meanings (*etic* data) are attached, he applied the idea of *etic* data to the material constants existing in one's environment.

The concept of mental constants, or "laws written on the heart," for Harris, the materialist, was absurd and academically unreasonable.

Eventually, to my amazement, I concluded the Apostle Paul had anticipated Harris' question: "Where do the rules and the behavior come from?" What Harris called infrastructure, the Apostle Paul called "the elemental forces of the world" (Colossians 2:8).

According to Harris, "Appropriate thoughts will occur repeatedly when infrastructural conditions are ripe."[4] However, one "appropriate thought" that will never surface in the mind because of infrastructural pressure is how the nuclear family should be structured.

The unconscious mind informs us that the *husband-wife* dyad is the dominant dyad of the nuclear family. How the nuclear family should be structured has already been hardwired in the unconscious mind.

If Harris is correct, the following "thoughts" represent what should be classified as appropriate. But are they "appropriate"?

> "I must marry someone who speaks a different language lest I commit incest."

Seventeen tribes living in the Vaupés area of Colombia believe such a thought is appropriate. The rule's function is to suppress inter-tribal warfare and wife stealing.

However, according to the Apostle Paul, such thinking "does not accord with Christ" (Colossians 2:8).

This also leaves the contextualizing missionary who believes all meanings "belong to the people" with a complex problem. How does one explain to these tribes of the Vaupés jungles that the Savior of the world was not a "bastard"?

After all, according to their "social game," Jesus must be classified as such because Joseph and Mary spoke the same language. The idea that contextualization is the Scripturally-endorsed approach for taking the Gospel to the world doesn't make sense.

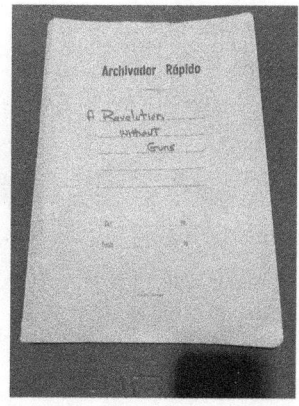

Gii Prost's Notebook, A Revolution without Guns

# GILBERT R. PROST

Gil and Marian with their children Laurel and Jim circa 1963

Chácobo New Testament

CREATED IN THE IMAGE OF GOD

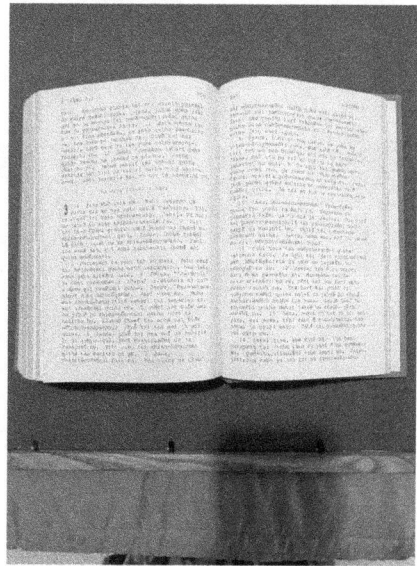

Chácobo New Testament interior

CONVICTIONS

- The rules and behavior of society, what Harris calls "infrastructure," the Apostle Paul calls "the elemental forces of the world" in Colossians 2:8.

# CHAPTER 72
# YEAR 1998 IN GAINESVILLE, FLORIDA
## RETURN TO BOLIVIA AFTER AN EIGHTEEN-YEAR HIATUS

University of Florida is in Gainesville, Florida, where Gil earned his Masters in Anthropology

## CREATED IN THE IMAGE OF GOD

In May of 1998, Guy East and I decided to return to Bolivia to see how the Chácobo and Pacahuara had fared in our 18-year absence. On our flight from Miami to *Riberalta*, we had a stopover visit at *Porto Velho*, the location of one of the SIL-WBT Centers in Brazil. At the Center lived a couple of our former colleagues from Bolivia, among them Lloyd Deister and his wife. Visiting with them after being separated for eighteen years was great.

Since I was the one who had written up the Bolivian Branch's Termination Scheme, Lloyd evidently encouraged the base administrators to hear what was included in our termination plan.

The next morning I was given the opportunity to express what the Bolivian Termination Scheme included. Besides the normal goals in the fields of grammar, literacy, and Bible translation, I shared that we had added a fourth goal that I called "leadership development."

I related from personal experience that the Chácobo had no "leaders" who had the authority to issue a command that would be carried out by others. This absence of leaders was related to how the nuclear family was internally structured.

At some point in history, I pointed out that Chácobo ancestors had replaced the *husband-wife* dyad with the mother-daughter, putting political control into the hands of mothers-in-law. The replacement, in turn, had stirred up the consciousness of Chácobo sages of another era who created satire critical of what their ancestors had done. They were advocating a return to the Universal that their ancestors had rejected.

This ability to create satire and become informed critics of a learned lifeway passed down to them by their parents implied the existence of a Universal Meta-Script, structured in the unconscious mind, that informed them as to what ought to be. This led the existentialists to believe that existence preceded meaning (essence) rather than meaning (essence) preceding existence.[1]

Unknown to me at the Center was one of SIL's most gifted linguists. He was a student of the world-renowned linguist Noam

Chomsky. His name was Daniel Everett (1951 -). He had just arrived from Pittsburgh where he chaired the Linguistics Department of the University of Pittsburgh.

When I met him on my way to Bolivia, he still had not made known to either SIL-WBT nor his family that he no longer believed the Bible was a historical record of God's purposes for humankind, and people had the freedom to reject His Divine Plan and choose a plan of their own making. His tribal experience, he claimed, had compelled him to become an atheist.

> *"Men why are you doing these things? We also are men with the same nature as you, and preach to you that you should turn from these useless things to the living God, who made the heaven, the earth, the sea, and all things that are in them"* (Acts 14:15).

When Professor Everett heard that I believed the unconscious mind was structured with innate knowledge which made language and culture possible, he reprimanded me in front of everyone.

My assignment to the Miccosukee people of South Florida had uncovered grammar which compelled every speaker to view reality from either (a) a material-self perspective, or (b) a transcendent-self perspective. It was this dualistic mind-body perspective which compelled me to declare:

> *"I praise you, for I am fearfully and wonderfully made. Wonderful are your works; my soul knows it very well"* (Psalm 139:14, ESV).

Uncovering linguistic-semantic forms which positioned man above and outside of nature was totally unexpected. The discovery implied the existence of innate forms common to all to which there were attached inherent meanings.

In contrast, Everett's linguistic assignment to the Pirahã people had turned him into a militant atheist who believed, in his words, that "language is a human invention to solve a human problem."[2]

## RIBERALTA

The next morning Guy and I hired a taxi to take us south to the Brazilian town of *Guajará-Mirim* where we had our passports stamped before crossing the Mamoré River to the Bolivian side.

After arriving in *Guayaramerín*, a port of entry, we had our passports stamped again and then hired a taxi to transport us to the town of *Riberalta*.

On our trip, the taxi driver warned us to be careful because in *Riberalta* existed *tigre-gente* (jaguars) posing as people who were looking for people like Guy and myself that they could deceive and rob. When I informed him that I did not believe such creatures existed, he pitied us.

However, I was aware of the existence among some Amazonian tribes of the belief that jaguars posing as humans really existed.

When we arrived in *Riberalta*, we immediately went to *Misión Evangélica Swiza*. We spent a few days there before traveling to *Alto Ivon*.

The next morning, there was a knock on our screen door. When we opened it, a delegation from Peru stood on the porch, consisting of an anthropologist, a sociologist, and a reporter. They wanted me to explain how, in one generation, "primitive" people who at one time couldn't count to two could become so advanced and developed.

They had been to *Alto Ivon*, and whatever they saw impressed them. On the other hand, I had yet to learn what they were discussing.

Nevertheless, I explained that in the 50s, the Chácobo were a leaderless, dying tribe of no more than 133 people. Then, as I was collecting Chácobo stories, I came across Chácobo satire created by Chácobo sages of another era who were critical of how the nuclear family had been structured.

Through satire, these sages of the past were informing their kinsfolk that they needed to make the *husband-wife* dyad the dominant dyad of the nuclear family, not the mother-daughter dyad. In other words, they encouraged their familiar relatives to return to a Positive Universal that their ancestors had rejected when they decided "to go their own way" (Acts 14:16).

I pointed out that not only did the Bible teach the dominant dyad of the nuclear family was that of *husband-wife*, but so did these Chácobo sages of another era. Once I understood why they were a dying tribe, I explained that we set out to help them return the *husband-wife* dyad to its rightful place in the nuclear family.

I explained that their sages couldn't know that the dominant dyad of a nuclear family should be the *husband-wife* unless the idea had been "written on the heart" (Romans 2:15).

Every child born into the world is born with a mind that contains "forms" that can be "triggered" and brought to consciousness in linguistic-social situations.

I shared with them my non-relativistic worldview, beginning with every human being is created in "the image and likeness of God" (Genesis 1:26-27).

I explained that being created in the "image and likeness of God" implied no child came into the world with a blank mind. Instead, the principles of God's Laws were woven into the very fabric of human existence. The unconscious mind was structured with language and cultural forms that had inherent meanings.

It alone explained how Chácobo sages of the past could create satire critical of their cultural OS (operating system). It alone explained how they knew, long before I arrived on the scene, that showing love and kindness to those in need was the ultimate mark of being human. It alone explained why they saw themselves as being *nohiria* (people) rather than a kind of primate.

I also explained that our message to the young people, as irrational as it may have appeared, was as stated by Moses in Deuteronomy 28:13:

> "And the LORD will make you the head and not the tail; you shall be above only, and not be beneath, if you heed the commandments of the LORD your God, which I command you today, and are careful to *observe* them."

Finally, I explained that the starting point for positive social change began with the nuclear family and how it was structured internally.

Of course, this was new information to them. The positive change they witnessed occurred because the Chácobo had, as a society, replaced a negative cultural particular, the mother-daughter dyad, a dyad that suppressed husbands and wives from becoming one-flesh, with a Positive Universal, the *husband-wife* dyad.

The group appreciated the explanation. But if Daniel Everett, the professor of sociology and global studies I had just met on the way to Bolivia, had been there, he would have told the group I was out of my mind,[3] that there were no Universal Principles figuratively "written on the heart" from which society could diverge.

> **IF PARTICULARS ARE TO HAVE MEANING, THERE MUST BE UNIVERSALS.**
> ...Plato

TWENTY-THREE YEARS EARLIER, I had received a letter from an anthropologist sent by Marvin Mayers, head of SIL's anthro department, to specifically check out what our leadership training course was all about.

A copy of his report read: "I am afraid that the program as now conceived is going to fall far short of its intended goal for failing to consider full implications of social change."

Twenty-three years later, I was witnessing firsthand what the effects of restoring the *husband-wife* dyad to its proper place within the nuclear family were. Instead of "falling short of its intended goal," it far exceeded my wildest dreams.

What I saw the next day shocked me as much as it did the academicians from Peru.

- The bilingual school system SIL had helped the Bolivian government implement was a success. They had taken ownership of the project (1972 - 1979). Chácobo teachers taught grades one, two, and three while Bolivian teachers from *Riberalta* were teaching the higher grades. Carmelo, the visionary, was trying to do what SIL had done—produce teachers for the future.

- If these goalless, leaderless tribes were to "relate to others," it implied the need for a core of indigenous "bridge-leaders" who had a basic understanding of Bolivian law, language, and culture. This part of the Branch's ten-year scheme was the responsibility of the bilingual school training program funded by the Canadian government.

- The biblical principles we taught the students produced effects that far exceeded my expectations. I discovered that "my kids" had transformed Chácobo society.

- Mothers-in-law no longer controlled Chácobo society, and bachelors did not have to serve their mothers-in-law when they married. The status position of *raisi* was a dying form.

∼

THE FOLLOWING DAY, Rabi and Paë showed up with a truck filled with goods they were bringing back to *Alto Ivon*. Guy and I jumped into the cab, and a half hour out of *Riberalta*, we found ourselves traveling down the very road we foolishly set out to make nineteen years earlier.

As we drove into the village of *Alto Ivon*, the truck pulled up to Rabi's house. Next to his house was a satellite dish. Inside Rabi's house and outside looking in were over thirty-five young men watching a World Cup soccer match.

Close to Rabi's house was a football field. When I asked him what the buildings at the end of the field were, he replied, "That's our clinic." I was shocked. His younger brother Coni, whom Lloyd Deister had trained in electronics, operated the clinic. The Zinggs of *Misión Evangélica Swiza* had trained him to be the village health promoter.

To the right stood another building, their new school. After visiting the school with more than 100 Chácobo students, seeing Coni operate the Chácobo clinic, which was open to all, and witnessing their connection to the outside world via TV, I began to understand why this team of scholars from Peru was so eager for me to explain the transformation to them.

On Tuesday, they said there was a meeting for the youth. One of "our kids," whom we had taught the Scriptures, gave a Bible lesson that evening. But what caught my attention was the chart tacked to the wall behind him. Across the chart were the words: "Brothers Who Lead the Church." They didn't learn that from me.

I witnessed the positive effects of an experiment I began when I wrote on a folder thirty years earlier the words: "A Revolution without Guns."

## A REVOLUTION WITHOUT GUNS

As young married men were being released from mothers-in-law control and the status position of *raisi* was rejected, they emerged as community leaders.

Instead of life being controlled by mothers-in-law, the Chácobo had become a society directed by young men who now were the heads of their households.

For example, never did I think a Chácobo would be running for public office 25 years later, that *Alto Ivon* would have a clinic operated by one of "my kids," that they would be connected to the outside world via satellite dish, or that more Chácobo children would be attending school than there were Chácobo in 1955.

After we left Bolivia, the *Misión Evangélica Swiza* established a Bible School in *Riberalta*. I would attribute a great deal of the biblical knowledge the Chácobo acquired to the work of Phillip and Alicia Zingg, who replaced us.

The new church they were building received no outside funding. When various denominations offered to build a church for them, they refused. Rabi's answer was: "We will build our own church building."

On Sunday morning, I was greeted and asked to speak a few words, followed by a Bible lesson from Bari, the church leader.

As I was visiting various households, I noticed a political poster glued to the wall. On it was the face of Coni, the village health promotor. The Chácobo had someone running for political office.

Forty years before running for political office, Coni was raised in a community where the Chácobo feared the Bolivian government. They eventually discovered the government was their friend, and the Chácobo now had a tribal member running for public office.

Besides building a new bilingual school and a clinic, the Bolivian government also constructed a water tower and a small power station to provide clean water and street lighting throughout the village. Shamo, a Chácobo, ran the power station.

It was time to visit the Pacahuara, who lived a short distance downstream from *Alto Ivon*. Maro, our faithful friend, left *Alto Ivon* and now lived north of the Pacahuara, where the *arroyo* (river) was wider and filled with more fish. We discovered that they were intermarrying with the Chácobo.

While in *Alto Ivon*, Rabi informed us the Chácobo had an office in *Riberalta*. Rabi said the Bolivian lawyer whom they hired to protect their land rights from being violated told them they needed to organize all the other tribes living in Northern Bolivia and unite their political interests—the Ese-Ejja, Tacaná, Araona, Cavineña, etc. By uniting, they would have more political clout.

That was not too difficult for them to do because they had made friends with members of all these tribes when attending SIL's Bilingual-Teacher Leadership Training Course twenty years before. The Chácobo could contact members from all these tribes, and together, they formed an organization called CIRABO (Central Indigena de la Región Amazonica de Bolivia).

The leaderless, goalless Chácobo were now leading, organizing, and promoting not only their own welfare but the interests of all the tribes of Northern Bolivia. So, the first thing Guy and I did when we returned to *Riberalta* was to visit CIRABO.

When we walked into the CIRABO office that next morning, two Bolivian Army officers were seated before a desk discussing with Cuya Duran, one of "my kids," the problem of having an army base on indigenous land. The army base was causing them trouble. I was witnessing an incredible event. Cuya told them they had to remove their base from Cavineña land. I couldn't believe what I was seeing.

The president of CIRABO was Maro Duran, one of "my kids" and a disciple of Lloyd Deister. I was shocked when he related that he, as a representative of the indigenous people of Bolivia, had been to Europe and the Middle East. On his trip to Europe, he passed through Miami and was shocked to see so many automobiles.

Rabi's school

# CREATED IN THE IMAGE OF GOD

Satellite dish next to Rabi's house

CIRABO, in *Riberalta*, created to provide representation for all the tribes of Northern Bolivia circa 1998

Bolivian army officers seated before desk talking with Cuya Duran, one of Gil's "kids," discussing issue with having a base on indigenous land

## CONVICTIONS

- Eighteen years later, when I returned to visit the tribe Marian and I were assigned to that could neither read, write, count, handle money, or look forward to a weekend, during our absence, they had prospered beyond my wildest dreams.
- When I greeted Marian at the Miami airport upon my return, the first words out of my mouth were, "You will not believe what I saw." Our goal of returning the *husband-wife* dyad to its proper place in the nuclear family had produced results far beyond anything Marian or I could have imagined.

## CHAPTER 73
# DISCOVERING "GOLD" AMONG THE PARTICULARS
### THE MICCOSUKEE TRANSLATION PROJECT

A NEW ASSIGNMENT

The Miccosukee Translation Project began in 1955, the same year we were assigned to the Chácobo. For some unknown reason, it had stalled. The first translation team had been replaced with a second team, which was also floundering. The question was why?

The Bolivian SIL Branch rejected Pike's approach to linguistics and anthropology; I embraced it. They hoped I would resign and go elsewhere; I suggested an assignment to the Miccosukee (Seminole) of South Florida. They agreed.

The new assignment challenged me because of the philosophical divide over the nature of human existence and the problem of concept formation (epistemology). Strangely, and to my dismay, again, I found myself working in an environment in which "contextualization" had become, in the eyes of my colleagues, "the scripturally-endorsed approach for taking the Gospel to the world ... postulating that God recognizes and employs the sociocultural adequacy principle of cultural forms."[1] Acceptance of this doctrine makes one a cultural relativist, a status position I've always rejected as un-Biblical.

As a budding anthropologist my primary question was: What was the dominant dyad of the nuclear family? I hypothesized that it had to be brother-sister. My new assignment provided the opportunity to find out.

It was all about spiritual divergence from a cultural constant, a phenomenon no anthropologist to my knowledge is interested in. I had no doubt that the Miccosukee had diverged from the constant by rearranging the internal structure of the nuclear family.

As a Christian anthropologist and a cultural analyst, I needed to recognize that I was not only dealing with a material phenomenon but also a spiritual phenomenon. It is a phenomenon that missiologists ignore and materialists categorize as being "unscientific" and insane.

It didn't take long before I, for linguistic reasons, was thankful Marian and I had first been assigned to the Chácobo, a member of the Panoan language family[2] located in the South America Amazonia Rainforest rather than a tribe which was a member of the Muskogean language family located in North America.

After poring over two PhD dissertations on the Miccosukee language in the University of Florida library, I concluded that thus far no linguist had figured out the grammatical categories of the language, including our SIL-WBT linguists. How could that be?

In my reports to the Branch, I would share my findings. The idea that three different linguists had failed to figure out the grammatical categories, two having PhDs, I'm sure my reports didn't make sense to them.

As far as I was concerned, the categories still remained to be discovered. Nevertheless, not knowing what these grammatical-semantic categories were, like a prospector looking for gold, I pressed on. There had to be a coherent and rational answer. The reason? They had failed to recognize they were dealing with spiritual categories.

Nevertheless, one cannot avoid dealing with the Universal spiritual phenomenon of restructuring the nuclear family to satisfy a perceived need. I believe it explains to some degree why the third world is poor and is presently attempting to migrate by the hordes to the West. The meanings they had attached to cultural forms common to all, which they were presently leaving, had, unknown to them, failed to deliver the goods and satisfy their needs.

Instead of the *husband-wife* dyad being the dominant dyad in the Miccosukee family, I expected to find that they had replaced a covenantal dyad with a biological. But since the translation project had stalled, my first priority as a linguist had to be the grammar. Why had the translation program stalled?

Then, to my utter surprise, as I shuffled around the stack of Miccosukee grammatical data on my desk, there appeared before me two mutually exclusive semantic categories, a transcendent-self, marked by the subject pronoun –ele, which positioned ego outside of nature, and a material-self, marked by the pronoun, *cha-* which positioned ego in nature. The two semantic categories were part of an unlearned interpretive Script "written on the heart." It could not have been created by social existence.

Next, I discovered that the Miccosukee could create misrepresentations of the Universal. They had, in the words of Pike, the capacity "to distort innate positive Universals into negative particular actions"[3]

## THE FIRST DISCOVERY - THE EXISTENCE OF A DUAL PRONOUN SYSTEM

When I recognized what the grammatical categories were, my discovery whooped, "essence precedes existence." These categories could not have been derived from social existence. They could not have been learned. The discovery was providential.

∽

## PROVIDENCE

In 1998, I moved our home trailer from Big Cypress to Gainesville, Florida, where the Lord provided us a home in the student ghetto. We lived one and a half blocks from campus and a few hundred feet from the TM (Transcendental Meditation Center). From there we carried out a ministry to International students until the year 2000.

Since we had initiated a Bible Study for international students in our home, our Christian mailman began prodding us to invite the director of the Transcendental Meditation Center located at the end of the block to our meetings.

After several months, I finally did, and discovered that the director had a PhD in physical psychology. Wondering who these Christian neighbors were, she accepted the invitation and began to attend regularly. Soon she was joining Marian and I as we went to a prayer meeting on Wednesday and church on Sunday.

In the meantime, I was trying to figure out what TM meant by the term "transcend." In time I figured out that they kept the form or concept, but gave the concept a new meaning.

Instead of it denoting an experience which positioned ego above and outside of nature, it was just the opposite. To "transcend" meant being reduced to a functional cog or person-thing in the universe, performing an ascribed function parading as a "duty" needed for maintaining the universe.

As I pondered the effects of a mechanistic existence in nature in which, according to her guru, the late Maharishi Mahesh Yogi (1918 - 2008), "All actions are performed by the forces of nature. Through ignorance, man takes authorship upon himself and becomes bound by them."⁴ It meant, according to their bottom-up, outside-in epistemology, I was a great "sinner."

I was guilty of "taking authorship" of my actions by acting intentionally. By acting intentionally I was guilty of suppressing the evolutionary forces of nature "where all actions are performed by nature." Such actions Maharishi had classified as being "sinful."

Instead of man and society having the capacity to sin by diverging from a *Divine* Meta-Script "written on the heart," an intentional act resulting in cultural maiming, from a bottom-up, outside-in perspective, "sin," according to Maharishi, "is that through which a man strays from the path of evolution. It results in suffering."⁵

A materialist believes behavior must be explained in terms of a bottom-up, outside-in epistemology. They think everything that exists comes from nature and fails to recognize the reality of spiritual phenomena.

The weakness of such a bottom-up, outside-in epistemology is that it is useless in uncovering the spiritual constants of language and culture, both of which have spiritual underpinnings. For the materialist, the only constants that exist are those grounded in biological needs and the environment in which one lives.

Naturalists reject the existence of spiritual phenomena because it opens the door to a theist's explanation of certain kinds of phenomena—like allegiance patterns, classificatory kinship systems, residence rules, totems, and the notion that humans are "image bearers" of God and equipped with knowledge that makes them a taxonomist.

Nevertheless, I propose the spiritual phenomena of diverging from Innate Universal semantic and cultural constants is open to analysis when one understands the nature of *etic* divergence and what it means to be created in the image and likeness of God. As recorded in Genesis 1:27: "So God created man in His *own* image; in the image of God He created him; male and female He created them."

In the anthropologist's search for constants, we note one constant of human existence that is totally ignored by cultural analysts. It is this: Humankind is prone to diverge from God's truth, go his own way, and, in the process, replace Divine meanings with meanings derived from social context and environmental "fitness." The consequence—the maiming of society.

∾

## SECOND DISCOVERY - REJECTION OF A UNIVERSAL

Since the Miccosukee were a matrilineal society, I immediately assumed that at some point in history they had rearranged the internal structure of the nuclear family by replacing the covenantal one-flesh principle of *husband-wife* with a biological one-flesh principle.

First, I thought it had to be brother-sister. I was mistaken. I was shocked to discover, through grammatical analysis of the "possessive pronouns," that the biological one-flesh dyad was sister-sister.

In doing so, they had rejected the one-flesh principle of *husband-wife* (Gen. 2:24) and reduced husbands to "sperm donors" needed to produce children for their wives' "families."

Upon making this discovery, I immediately visited the University of Florida Library for the Miccosukee tribe. I discovered that the Miccosukee believed "there were only two sisters in the beginning."[6]

As I suspected, they had rearranged the internal structure of the nuclear family and, in the process, rejected the Creation Order that "membership [in the family] is absolutely restricted to parents and their offspring in the first degree." The size of the Miccosukee family far exceeded "parents and offspring in the first degree."

More importantly, the Miccosukee concept of what constituted a family excluded all fathers. No Miccosukee father was the head of his family. Discipline of his biological children had been transferred to his wife's brother. Based on this family structure, how should a Bible translator render Hebrews 12:7b, which says, "for what son is there whom a father does not chasten?"

Should social context determine meaning? It was a clear example of spiritual *etic* divergence, the rejection of a transcendent truth being "suppressed in unrighteousness."

However, that was not the only evidence of spiritual *etic* divergence. To my amazement, the Miccosukee grammar manifested an unlearned biblical dual view of selfhood.

There was a transcendent-self personal pronoun *-ele* which positioned humankind outside and above nature in the sphere of freedom and culture; and a material-self personal pronoun *cha-* which positioned man in nature, the realm of biological necessity and stimulus-response behavior.

Grammatical analysis revealed that no Miccosukee was a sinner. The Universal Truth of Romans 3:23: "... for all have sinned and fall short of the glory of God" was not a constant.

When I asked my informant, "How do you say, 'I sinned?'" his reply was *cha-shapahkom*. He had positioned himself in the sphere of nature with zero accountability. He should have said *shatapahkon-ele*. But he didn't.

Before me was someone who refused to accept that he was a sinner. Whatever unlawful act he committed was reduced to a "mistake that unfortunately happened" over which he had no control. This temptation to avoid accountability can be done by positioning oneself in the field of nature by using the *cha-* pronoun.

∽

## A TRANSLATION PROBLEM

This being the case, then how should a Bible translator render Hebrews 12:7b which says, "For what son is there whom a father does not chasten?" Would it be proper for the translator to replace father with "maternal uncle" and son with "sister's son"?

If one believes social existence precedes essence, then it would be proper to render the rhetorical question as: "What nephew is there that a mother's brother does not discipline"?

This leads to the question: Should social existence or cultural "programming" determine meaning? For me, it was a clear example of a spiritual phenomenon, the rejection of a conceptual constant that was being "suppressed in unrighteousness."

## UNEXPECTED RESPONSE TO MY DISCOVERY

When I sent the Pikes my description of Miccosukee selfhood presented at a linguistic conference at the University of Kansas,[7] their response was, "So you have found new categories - great."

New categories

## CONVICTIONS

OUR ASSIGNMENT to the Miccosukee was providential for the following reasons.

- It provided me with one more example of how the family concept could be "defectively realized" in society by restructuring the nuclear family. At some point in history, the Miccosukee replaced the covenantal one-flesh principle of *husband-wife* with the biological one-flesh principle of sister-sister. Then they created an unbelievable myth to support it.
- The discovery of an unlearned Meta-Script that informed every Miccosukee how to live was providential. The dual semantic categories revealed that man was "other than nature," a transcendent being positioned outside and above nature. To believe these dual categories in culture and nature were invented by the Miccosukee stretches the imagination!
- The discovery that every speaker of Miccosukee could, to some degree, reject innate categories "written on the heart" (Romans 2:15) and "go their own way" (Acts 14:16) provided one more example of the spiritual phenomenon of *etic* divergence, a phenomenon my SIL colleagues did not believe existed.
- The spiritual phenomenon of diverging from a cultural constant is real. Whenever a society decides to "go its own way" (Acts 16:14) as the Miccosukee did, it must replace positive, Divine Universals with negative cultural particulars that belong to the people.
- Human suffering is not an effect of "straying from the path of evolution," but rather an effect of diverging from the "law of God, in my inner being" (Romans 7:22, ESV).
- Divergence from the Meta-Script will compel a society to sin by restructuring the nuclear family.
- There exists a spiritual phenomenon which some theologians call "structural sin."

# CHAPTER 74
# ALLEGORY OF THE CAVE
## FROM PLATO'S REPUBLIC

### LORILYN ROBERTS' NOTES ON ALLEGORY OF THE CAVE

Plato's "Allegory of the Cave" is an insightful parable that focuses on the condition of man in his fallen state.

After anthropologist Prost unraveled the mysteries of the Chácobo, examined dozens of Indian tribes around the world, and drew comparisons to many cultures as highlighted in *Created in the Image of God*, one observation is clear: Man's *etic* divergence (sinfulness) is universal.

I see Plato's classic as a conduit—illustrating missionaries who have brought the Gospel to tribes living in the remotest regions of the planet to the born-again Christian with instant access to knowledge and scientific inquiry. All of humanity live in darkness.

I Corinthians 13: 12 (CSB) says:

> *For now we see only a reflection as in a mirror, but then face to face. Now I know in part, but then I will know fully, as I am fully known.*

Even a classic, non-biblical allegory written by a Greek philosopher thousands of years ago reflects the depravity of humanity and his need for a Savior and Redeemer.

Praise be to God, He has not left us in a dark cave. Matthew 4:16 (CSB):

> *The people who live in darkness have seen a great light,*
> *and for those living in the land of the shadow of death,*
> *a light has dawned.*

Because God created us in His image, if we possess [agape] love, God will reveal "... all mysteries and all knowledge ..." (I Corinthians 13:2b).

The spiritual need in the "Allegory of the Cave," the scientific inquiry to know the truth, and man's search for meaning can only be found in Jesus Christ.

## PLATO'S ALLEGORY OF THE CAVE

This much-discussed [and much-misunderstood] story is a key part of Plato's *Republic*, a work which has the claim to be the first ever literary utopia.[1]

In *The Republic*, Plato and a number of other philosophers discuss the ideal society, focusing on education, political leadership, and the role and responsibility of the individual within society.

"The Allegory of the Cave" represents a number of the core ideas of Plato's thinking in one short, accessible parable.

## EMIC AND ETIC

Emic perspective

Etic perspective

Plato recognized two kinds of ideas or information: Information representing a particular culture's worldview (*gnosis*) and culture-free knowledge that is part of the soul, what Greek philosophers called *epignosis*. Pike later coined these terms *emic* and *etic*.

Plato's "Allegory of the Cave" reveals these two kinds of knowledge: Knowledge that is relative and incomplete, symbolized by the cave (*gnosis*); and knowledge that is "fixed" and "written on the heart," symbolized by the sun outside the cave (*epignosis*).

AN EXCERPT FROM INTERESTINGLITERATURE.COM[2]

"One of the key ideas in *Plato's Republic* is his theory of forms, where 'forms' means much the same as 'ideas.' The 'Allegory of the Cave' represents Plato's approach to ideas.

"We are invited to imagine a group of people sitting in an underground cave, facing the walls. They are chained up and they cannot move their heads. Behind them, a fire is forever burning, and its flames cast shadows onto the cave walls.

"Between the fire and the cave walls, there is a road, and people are walking along this road, carrying various objects: models of animals made of stone and wood, human statuettes, and other things. The people who walk along the road, and the objects they carry, cast shadows on the cave walls.

"The people who are chained in the cave and facing the wall can only see the shadows of the people (and the objects they carry): never the actual people and objects walking past behind them. To the people chained up in the cave, these shadows appear to be reality, because they don't know any better.

"Reality, to these people chained in the cave, is only ever a copy of a copy: the shadows of the original forms which themselves remain beyond our view.

"But someone comes and unchains the people in the cave. Now they're free. Let's say that one of them is set free and encouraged to look toward the fire behind him and his fellow cave-dwellers. He can now see that the things he took for reality until now were merely shadows on the wall.

"But this knowledge isn't, at first, a good thing. The revelation is almost overwhelming. The light of the fire hurts his eyes, and when he is dragged up the slope that leads out of the cave, and he sees the sun outside, he is overwhelmed by its light.

"In time, however, he comes to accept that the sun is the true source of light in the world, the cause of the seasons, and the annual cycle of things. And he would come to feel sorry for those who remain behind in the cave and are content to believe that the shadows on the cave wall are reality. Indeed, the people who remain behind in the cave believe he wasted his time in going outside and simply ruined his eyes for nothing.

"But the man who has been outside knows there is no going back to his old beliefs: his perception of the world has changed forever. He cannot rejoin those prisoners who sit and watch the shadows on the wall. They, for their part, would resist his attempts to free them, and would sooner kill him than be led out of the cave, as he was.

"And so if the man who has seen the sun returns to the cave, his eyes will take time to adjust back to the darkness of the cave and to the shadows on the wall. He will now be at a *disadvantage* to his fellow cave-dwellers, who have never left the cave and seen the light."

> *They show that the work of the law is written on their hearts, while their conscience also bears witness, and their conflicting thoughts accuse or even excuse them on that day when, according to my gospel, God judges the secrets of men by Jesus Christ. (Romans 2:15-16, English Standard Version)*

## GNOSIS AND EPIGNOSIS

In today's world, *gnosis* represents knowledge that we would refer to as "worldview"— a mixture of opinions, beliefs, values, and factual information that is culture-specific.

A more common definition from Wikipedia is, "It refers to the framework of ideas and beliefs through which an individual, group, or culture interprets the world and interacts with it."[3]

*Epignosis* represents the absolute. It is knowledge that comes to us from outside the sphere of human culture (*epi-* "outside" + *gnosis* "knowledge") and represents a Universal set of innate, exact, "fixed," unchanging concepts and ideas that man and society can reject, distort, and replace with negative cultural particulars. It is an important distinction made by the New Testament writers.

Plato and Aristotle made these distinctions between 428 BC and 322 BC (a few hundred years after Buddha). These Greek philosophers/psychologists termed these distinctions which Alexander the Great carried to Israel in his conquest of the known world.

While these distinctions are extra-biblical, the writers of Scripture used them nonetheless, and they were commonly-used terms in their day.

This *etic* versus *emic* distinction, or outsider versus insider approach, was explicitly used by the Apostle Paul to bring the Gospel to the Gentiles. As an "outsider," Paul based his missiological approach to the Gentiles on *etic* knowledge: Culture-free, outside knowledge (*epignosis*), which he called "laws written on the heart."

He knew that negative cultural forms—the "basic principles of the world"— enslaved society. In contrast to his approach, there were the "Judaizers" who insisted on turning the Gentiles into Jews.

Once unbound and set free outside the cave, the prisoners realize their former way of life enveloped them in a corrupted world with a distorted view of reality. The cultural forms were not neutral; they enslaved society. According to Dr. Oliver Tearle of Loughborough University:

> The essential point is that the prisoners in the cave do not see reality, only a shadowy representation of it. The importance of the allegory lies in Plato's belief that invisible truths lie under the apparent surface of things which only the most enlightened can grasp.[4]

Used to the world of illusion in the cave, the prisoners at first resist enlightenment, as students resist education, or people refuse to embrace truth (perhaps because it's too painful), or laziness saps their energy to "rise up" (Newton's first law of motion: "A body at rest remains at rest, or, if in motion, remains in motion at a constant velocity unless acted on by a net external force").[5]

At the end of the passage, Plato expresses another of his favorite ideas: Education is not a process of putting knowledge into empty minds but of making people realize what they already know. This notion that truth is embedded in our minds was powerfully influential for centuries.[6]

~

## THE PRISON-HOUSE IS THE WORLD OF SIGHT

According to certified educator Lori Steinbach, M.A.: "Our argument shows that the power and capacity of learning exists in the soul already."[7]

Every child comes into the world with a Universal-Lexicon that contains functional concepts that give him the capacity to classify his sense experience.

In the cave, he fails to receive a true representation of reality because the Universals of life are distorted by the illusion of realism on the cave walls.

The most disturbing aspect of this classic allegory is the resistance of the people in the cave to embrace the truth. They preferred to live in darkness to light. They preferred the illusion to the real thing because the illusion they saw on the walls was what they knew. So they settled for *gnosis* rather than *epignosis*.

A more recent version of the "Allegory of the Cave" is the movie *The Matrix*. People had the choice to take the red pill, which represented freedom, or the blue pill, which represented bondage.

Unfortunately, the evil one has deceived the masses. Sin enslaves, but the truth sets a person free—to serve God, his family, and his country. Ultimately, there is an even higher freedom that

God gives to His imagers that comes with responsibility—to share the truth. But there is a catch: one can't know the truth unless he surrenders his life to Jesus Christ, dies to self, and is born again. The Gospel of John 3:3-8 records a conversation between Nicodemus and Jesus.

> *Jesus answered and said to him [Nicodemus], "Most assuredly, I say to you, unless one is born again, he cannot see the kingdom of God."*
> *Nicodemus said to Him, "How can a man be born when he is old? Can he enter a second time into his mother's womb and be born?"*
> *Jesus answered, "Most assuredly, I say to you, unless one is born of water and the Spirit, he cannot enter the kingdom of God.*
> *"That which is born of the flesh is flesh, and that which is born of the Spirit is spirit.*
> *"Do not marvel that I said to you, 'You must be born again.'*
> *"The wind blows where it wishes, and you hear the sound of it, but cannot tell where it comes from and where it goes. So is everyone who is born of the Spirit."*

## DECEPTION

Deception is the most powerful tool in Satan's arsenal. It has been this way from the beginning, back to the Garden of Eden. He disguises himself under different names in different cultures.

The following excerpt is taken from Dr. Douglas Hamp's book, *Corrupting the Image 3: Singularity, Superhumans, and the Second Coming of Jesus*.

> After the Flood, he [Satan] gave his power, throne and authority to Nimrod, who became a hybrid, was hailed as Ninurta, son of Enlil

(Satan), and was the Beast who: "was, is not and will ascend out of the abyss."

Satan deceived the ancient world by posing as the god, Enlil (the prince of the power of the air), who usurped the authority of the Creator and dramatized his boast for all to see in the annual spring spectacle called the Akitu Festival.

Here, Satan indoctrinated all stratums of society with the belief that he was god and could make men into gods. He used Ishtar, the woman known as Mystery Babylon, to lure mankind into building a gateway to reach the gods.

Now, in these last days, the deception will be the same, but the lingo will change slightly; the ancient gods are now dubbed advanced extraterrestrial beings who came here long before we did and can help us evolve.[8]

Perhaps, in the anthropological world of academics and syncretism, if Satan can convince most anthropologists there are no spiritual forms and all forms are material, then how much easier the devil's task is. The ignorant will stay in the cave, trusting the illusion that forms on the walls, and remain in bondage to something that is only a shadow of the real thing.

> *For these rules are only shadows of the reality yet to come. And Christ himself is that reality. (Colossians 2:17, NLT)*

# CREATED IN THE IMAGE OF GOD

"Behold, I stand at the door and knock. If anyone hears My voice and opens the door, I will come in to him and dine with him, and he with Me" (Revelation 3:20).

## CONVICTIONS

* One in five people are still waiting for a Bible translation in their native language. Is the method used today getting the job done? I submit that it's not.

* In fact, the work of Bible translation comes up so woefully short that God sends an angel during the Tribulation to reach the unreached with the Good News: "And I saw another angel flying through the sky, carrying the eternal Good News to proclaim to the people who belong to this world—to every nation, tribe, language, and people" (Revelation 14:6, NLT).

* Until humans hear the Good News, repent, and believe in Jesus, they will seek fulfillment in meaningless activities; i.e., drinking manioc beer, worshipping idols, and "sinning" because of their sinful nature.

* Being "born again" awakens God's image within a man and a woman, and only through this "triggering process" can humankind self-actualize and become a "new creature in Christ."

* This side of eternity, without Jesus Christ, humans live in dark-

ness chained and enslaved, but there is hope. "... the people who sat in darkness have seen a great light. And for those who lived in the land where death casts its shadow, a light has shined" (Matthew 4:16, NLT).

# CHAPTER 75

# A REVOLUTION WITHOUT GUNS

## MAKING DISCIPLES OF JESUS CHRIST AMONG ALL NATIONS

If it were not for Kenneth Pike who encouraged me to get a degree in anthropology, I wouldn't be doing what he wanted me to do, which was to write this highly controversial material using the vocabulary and concepts of academia.

As a student of the Bible, Bolivian missionary, anthropologist, and Bible translator, I will ask you to consider "the problem" which few if any want to discuss.

What if Marian and I had not supported "A Revolution without Guns"? Would the Chácobo have become extinct? Would the Scriptures we labored so hard to give them be in use? Would there be a viable Chácobo church? Would the Chácobo have rescued their neighbors, the Pacahuara, from extinction?

What about all the other missionary efforts that never produced lasting fruit? Why don't we talk about them? Do we honestly care about all the wasted resources?

Modern missiology is like a dysfunctional family in denial because no one wants to talk about the elephant in the living room. Why are translations sitting in boxes or on bookshelves unused? Where are the disciples His translated Word was supposed to produce? Where are the thriving church communities discipling believers and reaching the lost? Why have some mission efforts achieved little or nothing, or certainly far less than what was believed possible?

May I suggest it is because no one has come up with the answers to these questions: How does culture affect receptivity to the Good News of repentance and forgiveness of sins, turning from the self-life to Jesus as Lord?

And how does culture impact the establishment of a viable, healthy self-replicating community of believers, the Ecclesia, a "called-out assembly of Christ followers"?

Our first assignment as missionaries to the Chácobo changed my perspective of how one should approach the task of evangelism. Unknown to me, we were entering an era in which missionaries were being told by Charles Kraft—an American anthropologist, linguist, evangelical Christian speaker, and Professor Emeritus of Anthropology and Intercultural Communication in the School of Intercultural Studies at Fuller Theological Seminary in Pasadena, California, as well as other Christian anthropologists—that "God seeks to use and cooperate with human beings in the continued use of relative cultural forms to express absolute supra-cultural meaning."[1]

In this new era, no concept has attached to it an inherent meaning that is "fixed" and absolute. The idea that "relative cultural forms" can express "absolute supra-cultural meaning" exhibits a belief in magic.

In this regard, I believe Marvin K. Mayers' *Christianity Confronts Culture: A Strategy for Crosscultural Evangelism* is not only theologically weak but also dangerous and to be avoided at all costs. It is grounded in the doctrine of cultural relativity, embracing the idea that context alone determines how one should think.

For all his "success," William Carey (1761 - 1834) failed in the latter. He left no viable church legacy in India. In contrast, Adoniram Judson (1788 - 1850), sent to Burma (Myanmar) by Carey, left a great legacy among the *Karen* people.

However, no one asks why. We merely laud Judson's achievement and laud Carey for inspiring the modern missionary movement while ignoring Carey's lack of enduring results.

If Carey in India is not enough of an example, let's look at Japan. Doug Birdsall of the Lausanne Movement wrote, "There is not a country ... where the church has sown the Gospel so generously yet reaped so sparingly."[2]

Yet, has anyone analyzed the Japanese culture to understand what features have blocked the Gospel's success there? I would suggest the mother-first son relationship has eclipsed the *husband-wife* union and male headship.

Further, their concept of "gift," their view of deity, and their view of themselves as the "superior yellow people," the rightful rulers, make the gift of the Christian Creator God in giving His Son as a humble suffering servant who was brutalized and murdered to atone for their sins an unappealing option.

To the Japanese, a gift is a way to obligate others to repay you, a tool for social manipulation (the root meaning of gift being poison). What can be done to change our methods of reaching the Japanese?

In my opinion this problem in present-day missiology has deep roots going back to the 19th century and also modern roots since WW II. The ideas of Freud, Marx, Darwin, and Margaret Meade, coupled with the textual criticism of the supernatural in the Old and New Testament Scriptures by German theologians, challenged the biblical paradigm of man's transcendence over nature, being gloriously created like God, and God's salvific involvement in man's history, especially the life, death and bodily resurrection of Jesus Christ.

Out of this milieu came Nietzsche's philosophy of "God is dead," atheistic Marxism in Lenin's Russia, and Hitler's "Tooth and claw" (survival of the fittest) philosophy of his Third Reich.

More important to my book is the chief modern architect of this problem, Charles H. Kraft, out of Fuller Theological Seminary, whose text, *Christianity in Culture: A Study In Biblical Theologizing In Cross-*

*Cultural Perspective,* now in its 25th edition, has become the handbook of missiology for over 35 years.

Kraft teaches that culture is essentially a gift from God which enables people groups to develop, from the "bottom up," a system of need fulfillment in a particular environmental, economic and political context.

He teaches (and our seminaries and mission schools follow) that culture is not bad. It is not opposed to the Gospel or establishing a viable church, and should be viewed as neutral or even positive by the missionary.

Therefore, no one should try to change culture (pollute it with our values, no matter how Christian or biblical one might think they are). Instead, culture should be used to contextualize the Gospel message in forms better understood by the people.

While this sounds good, there is a huge problem. Kraft rejects the clear teaching of God's Revelation regarding the nature of man, the nature of marriage and family, the activities of Satan and his minions, and the true nature of humanity.

Kraft denies that man, created in God's image, has unique Universal qualities, features in his mind or constitution, independent of culture, which allow him to know (communicate with) God and do His will. These are the qualities of "personhood" of an eternal being.

> "You have made him a little lower than the angels;
> You have crowned him with glory and honor..."
> *(Hebrews 2:7-8)*

Man was created to know God and to serve as His Vice-Regent on the earth. The Apostle Paul refers to some of these qualities in the second chapter of Romans as "laws written on the heart." I have attempted to explain these spiritual themes in some detail in this book.

Kraft almost ignores the mandates of God to Adam and Eve in the garden: That they become "one flesh," leave their families of origin, and be joined together to form a new family unit and have many children.

Kraft virtually ignores the active involvement of Satan and his devils in human society and individuals. With thousands of years to study man and the human condition after the Fall in the Garden, Kraft acts like the cultural systems Satan uses to manipulate man into creating forms "that belong to the people" would not be opposed to belief and trust in a sovereign and loving God.

Kraft does not acknowledge Satan's power and authority as the Prince of the Power of Darkness, the Prince of this World, or the Prince of the Air, or that he would deceptively use that power to institutionalize sin in cultural patterns as opposed to knowing and trusting the truth of God and being set free from the "law," the way of doing things mandated by one's culture.

That law is commonly referred to by anthropologists as the "folkways and morays" of a people group, many of which are incorporated in "positive laws" adopted to govern the whole.

Further, Kraft chooses to ignore, or certainly marginalizes, the clear teachings of Jesus and the Apostle Paul, James, and John about the negative impact of the world's culture on Christ's disciples (followers). Jesus challenged the religious teachings and traditions that governed His world by His own teachings in the *Sermon on the Mount,* and by calling them "old wineskins" that could not contain His message of forgiveness and freedom in knowing Him.

In Romans 12:2, the Apostle Paul told believers not to be pressed into (or conformed into) the world's mold. James warns us:

*Whoever therefore wants to be a friend of the world makes himself an enemy of God. (James 4:4b)*

John instructed us that loving the world and the things of the world would create enmity (conflict) between us and our Lord and Savior, Jesus Christ. These references encapsulate the cultural operating systems that regulate one's beliefs, values, and behavior.

Having so departed from biblical truth, Kraft operates in the Post-Modern zeitgeist of truth being relative—personal to each individual or social setting. He rejects any Universal absolute truth—concepts created by God as part of man's nature which allow humans to receive communications from God and live a life pleasing to Him.

I find it strange that Kraft would suggest that each people group ascribe their own unique meanings to words like father, mother, brother, child, marriage, love, gift, sin, and sacrifice, which would prevent them from grasping the meanings God intended in His Revelation (Holy Scriptures) to man, especially as conveyed by the life and teachings of Jesus Christ.

For Kraft, Jesus would only make sense to Jews whose culture had been shaped by the word meanings from the Old Testament Scriptures because Jesus used only those concepts to convey truth to his hearers. An Amazonian tribe would not and could not have a clue what Jesus was all about.

Contextualizing can be done in degrees. In fact, the chief architect of ways for reaching Muslims has suggested seven levels of contextualization, the final level being syncretism where all truth is lost in the pagan cultural context.

This author is not making a wholesale rejection of any contextualizing, but rather a responsible look at the unbiblical underpinnings of the fundamental teachings of Kraft and others, a bottom-up approach, who have departed from the truth of God's Word.

## POSTSCRIPT

Gil Prost emailed me [Roberts] the following on 12-13-22.
In Re: Daniel Everett

I got held up on writing my story because I am capping it off with an encounter I had with a Bible translator turned atheist on my return trip to the Chácobo after an absence of 18 years. On my trip back, I stopped off at a jungle town in Brazil where some of our Bolivian Branch members had relocated after we terminated our work in Bolivia.

Arriving at the same time was a SIL-WBT member of the Brazilian Branch who was also head of the Linguistic Department at the University of Pittsburgh. He was a student of famous linguist Noam Chomsky. His name was Daniel Everett. He has become famous for his anti-Biblical, materialistic views of language and culture.

When he heard that I believed the unconscious mind was structured with innate knowledge ("laws written on the heart"), he reprimanded me before everyone in the room.

When I returned to Gainesville several weeks later there was a letter from the University of Pittsburgh. In it was a copy of a letter he had sent to SIL denouncing me for my theological position.

Now I am enclosing a copy of his testimony as to how he became an atheist. [Roberts' note: The attachment did not arrive with Gil's email].

Now what is interesting is that many features of the Pirahã

culture were identical to that of the Chácobo who lived around 900 miles southwest of them.

These include:

1. Neither tribe could count and do arithmetic.

2. Neither tribe had a concept of a week

3. The marriage rule for each was identical. One should marry a cross-cousin.

4. Marriage in both cases meant a daily payment of fish to in-laws or those related to ego's wife.

Where both cultures separated was when it came to semantics. The Pirahã had no words for mother, father, husband, wife, mother's sister, mother's brother, father's brother, father's brother's sons and daughters, mother's and mother's sister's sons and daughter. This is unheard of. The question is why?

At some point in history, from my perspective, they decided "to go their own way" (Acts 14:16). But why would they reject the above status position? Any ideas?

I get the impression that they didn't want to be held accountable to anyone other than by those who were the recipients of fish.

Just as Chácobo mothers-in-law were the final judges of their sons-in-law, a similar pattern of behavior appear among the Pirahã. Now I am attempting to write a short chapter explaining why the now famous Daniel Everett is mistaken. Nothing has been written.

Now by examining their behavior, it becomes apparent that the Pirahã are a very anxious people. Whereas the Pirahã were promiscuous, the Chácobo were Puritanical. The Piranha must be one of the most difficult societies on earth to evangelize.

A visit would be great.

~Gil

# CREATED IN THE IMAGE OF GOD

## FOLLOW-UP NOTE BY ROBERTS

Instead of attaching a copy of Everett's testimony, Gil sent me a link to the Freedom From Religion Foundation, ffrf.org. I am not including the link because it's now a broken link.

To my knowledge, Gil never wrote that chapter. I did not find it in the 40-plus gigabytes of information I sorted through in the compilation of his book.

So, I will offer this explanation on Gil's behalf based on my own research and clues that Gil left us:

For the Pirahã to believe something was true, it had to be based in reality. When they asked Daniel Everett if he had ever met Jesus Christ personally and he replied, "No," the Pirahã were no longer interested in learning about Jesus (see chapter 59, "The Pirahã of Brazil" under the subheading, "The Complex Case of the Pirahã."

Every born-again Christian has met Jesus personally and has a personal relationship with Him. The Holy Spirit within us is validation of that relationship.

I [Roberts] would contend that Daniel Everett never met Jesus personally, as he stated when asked by the Pirahã, and therefore, never was a Christian.

# GILBERT R. PROST

King of Kings

## CONVICTIONS

- It is my hope that I have achieved the purpose for which I wrote this book: To analyze these challenges in detail, the unbiblical paradigm of contextualizing, and offer tools for discerning those elements of culture inimitable to God's plan.
- We can make disciples from all nations and build His church. But without this kind of understanding and analysis [as put forth in this book], we can only expect the same underachieving results. I believe our God deserves better. ~Gil Prost

> *"Go therefore and make disciples of all nations, baptizing them in the name of the Father and of the Son and of the Holy Spirit, teaching them to observe all that I have commanded you; and lo, I am with you always, even to the end of the age." Amen. (Matthew 28:19-20)*

# APPENDIX - EMAIL FROM GIL PROST TO ROY [GARREN]

## ROBERTS' NOTES ON GIL PROST'S EMAIL TO ROY [GARREN], DATED APRIL 22, 2022

As I was finishing the compilation of Gil Prost's book, providentially, I came across the email below that I was cc'd on but I didn't remember receiving. I felt like, through the Holy Spirit, Gil was confirming that I had extracted what was most important to him to be included in his upcoming book. I was relieved that I had included everything that Gil would have wanted included if he were here to finish it.

I also tried to validate that the primary recipient on the email was Roy Garren. I contacted him by text and email but never heard back. I also could not find an email, at least that I was cc'd on or that Gil sent to me, where Roy ever responded.

That being said, I felt like this email was important to include because it shows, even as Gil was in his 90s when he wrote it, his commitment to finish the book he had worked on for decades.

My belief is that Gil's book *Created in the Image of God: Missionary to the Chácobo of Bolivia Ignites A Revolution Without*

# APPENDIX - EMAIL FROM GIL PROST TO ROY [GARREN]

*Guns*, is more relevant now than at any time in the past. One only needs to listen to the news, glimpse a recent Hollywood movie, or look at what's streamed on the internet to see how Godless this world has become and the complete depravity that is closing in around us.

My fondest memories with Gil are the times we talked about these very issues. I miss that, but I know in heaven, we will meet again.

∽

# EMAIL

April 22, 2022

Dear Roy [Garren],

I have a personal request. The story I am writing is more than a story of my life. It is also about how one does evangelism, church planting, and community development.

What is presently taught in our Christian Universities, Bible Schools, mission departments, and missionary agencies is a paradigm called "contextualization." I consider it to be immoral, a trick of the Great Trickster.

The leading exponents of this paradigm include: (a) Charles H. Kraft, Professor Emeritus of Anthropology and Intercultural Communication in the School of Intercultural Studies at Fuller Theological Seminary, (b) Sherwood Lingenfelter, Senior Professor of Anthropology at Fuller Theological Seminary, and (c) Marvin K. Mayers, Dean of the School of Intercultural Studies and World Missions at Biola University. He is the author of *Christianity Confronts Culture*. I'm sure there are many more.

Please note the following statements.

Kraft's—

- "A cultural form does not have inherent meaning, only perceived meaning. And this meaning is context-specific." But if no concept has an inherent meaning, then God ceases to speak. And one should never trust one's "perceptions."

- "Words, like all information-bearing vehicles ... derive their meanings from their interaction with the contexts in which they participate." Such a statement supports wokeness. If social existence in a particular context determines the meaning of a word, then we have no fixed standard. No Word from God.
- "Human biology provides the backdrop for all that we need to know as human." What provides the background for what we need to know is knowledge that has been structured in the unconscious mind.

Lingenfelter's—

- "We must accept and work within structures and processes of others that are different from one's own social game." But Jesus said, "the new life needs new forms."
- "By denying the validity of others structures we then force upon people our standards and structure of relationships to accomplish the work and purpose of God ... we would then distort the diversity of God's creation ... forcing upon people our standards."

I personally denied the validity of the biological mother-daughter dyad which had replaced the covenantal dyad of *husband-wife*. Interestingly, so did Chácobo satirists.

Mayer's—

- "Missionaries are emphatically not ethical relativists, but equally emphatically should be cultural relativists." It is impossible to be a cultural relativist and an ethical purist at the same time. I sat in a classroom filled with anthropologists from all over the USA. Mayer, a cultural relativist, began the class saying: "I will end the class by ending a prayer to Mother God." I couldn't believe what I heard.

Providentially, he wasn't given the opportunity because the bell rang and everybody walked out. Now, if he had uttered the prayer, he would have violated what Jesus said: "When you pray, say, "Father, hallowed be Your name, Your kingdom come." Should we teach

## APPENDIX - EMAIL FROM GIL PROST TO ROY [GARREN]

Christians living in matrilineal societies to pray, saying, "Mother, hallowed be thy name"?

When I made my complaint to the directorate of the North American Branch of SIL, of which I became a member after completing our task in Bolivia, I said such classes needed monitoring by some theologian. They never sent me a reply.

Wokeness, I believe, had entered missiology, and no one is pointing it out. That is why what I am writing is so important.

I would like you to send to the Centerites who remember me the following PDF files in order for them to understand what the war is about and how to pray intelligently, and that the Lord provide the health so that I will be able to finish the task. I believe it will be finished in six months. In the book I also quote the above missiologists - anthropologists.

I also have a team of three here in Gainesville who will help me finish and hopefully get it published. Proofreading it will certainly take time. I am forwarding materials to them also. They are probably wondering what happened to me.

The PDF files that I think are important are listed below:

- Chácobo.
- The Chácobo Concept of Marriage: *The Frustrated Raisi.*
- Discovering an Innate Moral Imperative.
- *The Story of the Long Night.*
- Introducing the Seven Day Week.

This is spiritual warfare, and the enemy exists within the body of Christ. I need all the prayer support that I can garner.

Still marveling that He could use a nobody to be a minister of the Good News cross-culturally.

~Gil

# AFTERWORD BY LORILYN ROBERTS

My dear friend, Gibert R. Prost, graduated to glory on November 22, 2023. For almost 80 years, Gil served his Lord and Savior, Jesus Christ.

A moving memorial service was held on January 20, 2024, for his family and friends. The testimonies that people shared about what Gil meant to them were inspiring and, at times, heart-wrenching. Gil touched many lives, including mine.

I promised Gil on his deathbed that I would get his book published. God gave me this task—to finish the work Gil started. At age 93, he came up just short of completion. His work on this book spans decades. Any mistakes herein are mine, not his.

I pray that God will use *Created in the Image of God: Missionary to the Chácobo of Bolivia Ignites A Revolution Without Guns* in ways beyond human comprehension. All proceeds from book sales will be donated to missions organizations and those involved in Bible translation.

I also pray the spiritual fruits of this book will mirror Gil's passion for sharing the Gospel to the ends of the earth. We can indeed ignite *A Revolution Without Guns*, just as Gil and Marian did with the Chácobo.

Please share *Created in the Image of God* with family, friends, churches, pastors, professors, anthropologists, linguists, Bible translators, teachers, current missionaries, former missionaries, future missionaries, leaders, movers, shakers, media, and, most importantly, anyone who loves Jesus.

The time is short before our Lord's return. May Jesus, our Savior, find us busy fulfilling His Great Commission of Bible translation for the Kingdom of God as the Kingdom of Heaven draws near.

~Lorilyn Roberts, April 26, 2024

# ABOUT THE AUTHOR GILBERT R. PROST

Gilbert R. Prost, visit the author's website https://in-the-image-of-god.wixsite.com/gprost

On November 22, 2023, **Gilbert R. Prost** graduated to glory after serving his Lord and Savior, Jesus Christ, for almost 80 years. Gil, as he is affectionately known to family and friends, earned his undergraduate degree from Wheaton College.

He grew up in a Chicago church that birthed several important ministries that have impacted the world, including the Pacific Garden Mission (it's still on the radio today), New Tribes Missions, and AWANA International, a children's program with games and Bible memory. Gil served as one of the first teenage AWANA leaders, and he recruited children from the neighborhood to build a Sunday School class of over 40.

With his beloved wife, Marian, Gil embarked on a 25-year mission with Wycliffe Bible Translators and SIL, serving the Chácobo tribe in the Amazonian Rainforest of Bolivia and translating the Bible into the Chácobo language.

Concerned about the tribe's long-term survival, using AWANA children's curriculum and Scriptural insights regarding cultural transformation, they equipped the Chácobo with the necessary skills to thrive in an encroaching world they did not understand. In the process, they fostered leadership among the Chácobo men and left a lasting Christian legacy among the indigenous people of Bolivia.

After Gil finished his work with the Chácobo, he continued his education at the University of Florida, obtaining a Master's degree in anthropology, including some doctoral work. He also made several important linguistic discoveries in connection with the Miccosukee Translation Project (Seminole Indian Language).

Gil started a ministry for international students at the University of Florida, which spanned almost 25 years. The highlight each year was a Thanksgiving meal at Creekside Community Church for hundreds of international students and their hosts.

Gil was a prolific writer and published most of his research regarding Bible translation, anthropology, and Christian missiology on his website. He also published several articles in anthropology journals.

His book *Created in the Image of God: Missionary to the Chácobo Ignites A Revolution Without Guns* represents a culmination of his work as a Bible translator, anthropologist, and researcher regarding what he considered hindrances to The Great Commission. Gil was a visionary, and much of what he warns the reader of in this book began decades ago in missiology.

Gil is preceded in death by his wife, Marian. He is survived by his daughter, Laurel, his son, James, and two grandsons, Geoffrey and Christopher, and many co-laborers and friends in Christ.

# NOTES

### THE CHÁCOBO INDIAN TRIBE IN BOLIVIA

1. A word "coined" by the late Dr. Michael S. Heiser (1963 - 2023).

### GIL PROST'S NOTE TO READERS

1. Pike, Kenneth. 1993. *Talk, Thought, and Thing: The Emic Road Toward Conscious Knowledge*. Dallas: SIL, 76.
2. Kraft, Charles. 2005. *Christianity in Culture: A Study in Biblical Theologizing in Cross-Cultural Perspective*, 25th edition. Maryknoll, NY: Orbis Books, 27.
3. Unless otherwise noted, the New King James Version (NKJV) is used for all biblical citations.
4. Pinker, Steven. 1997. *How the Mind Works*. New York: W. W. Norton & Co, 129.
5. Kraft, Charles. 2005. *Christianity in Culture: A Study in Biblical Theologizing in Cross-Cultural Perspective*, 25th edition. Maryknoll, NY: Orbis Books, 27.
6. Stack Exchange. Biblical Hermeneutics. 2022. "What is the Meaning of '*theopneustos*' when the Apostle Paul says, 'All scripture is God-breathed.' Did He breathe on/in the scriptures, or did He breathe them out?" Looking at II Timothy 3:16, New International Version. https://hermeneutics.stackexchange.com/questions/73923/what-is-the-meaning-of-theopneustos-when-paul-says-all-scripture-is-god-breat
7. Callow, John, and Beekman, John. 2003. *Translating the Word of God*. Revised 2002 for LinguaLinks. Dallas: SIL International Digital Resources.
8. Wierzbicka, Anna. 1996. *Semantics, Primes and Universals*. Oxford, UK: Oxford University Press, 297.

### 1. CONFRONTING A MISSIOLOGICAL PROBLEM

1. "SIL is a nonprofit organization whose main purpose is to study, develop, and document languages, especially those that are lesser-known, in order to expand linguistic knowledge, promote literacy, translate the Christian Bible into local languages, and aid minority language development." Wikipedia. SIL International. https://en.wikipedia.org/wiki/SIL_International.
2. Kraft, Charles. 2005. *Christianity in Culture: A Study in Biblical Theologizing in Cross-Cultural Perspective*, 25th edition. Maryknoll, NY: Orbis Books, 94.
3. Pike, Kenneth Lee. 1993. *Talk, Thought, and Thing: The Emic Road Toward Conscious Knowledge*. Dallas: SIL, 63.

## NOTES

4. Kraft, Charles. 2005. *Christianity in Culture: A Study in Biblical Theologizing in Cross-Cultural Perspective*, 25th edition. Maryknoll, NY: Orbis Books, 257-258.
5. Dooyeweerd, Herman. 1969. *A New Critique of Theoretical Thought*, Vol. III-IV. The Presbyterian and Reformed Publishing Company, 304.
6. Plantinga Jr., Cornelius. 1995. *Not the Way It's Supposed to Be: A Breviary of Sin*. Grand Rapids: MI: Eerdmans Publishing Company, 16-17.
7. Pike, Kenneth Lee. 1993. *Talk, Thought, and Thing: The Emic Road Toward Conscious Knowledge*. Dallas: SIL. 63.
8. Wozniak, R. H. 1975. "Dialecticism and Structuralism." In *Structure and Transformations*, edited by Klaaus F. Riegek and George C. Rosenwald. New York: John Wiley & Sons, 36.
9. Nida, Eugene A. 1971. "Implications of Contemporary Linguistics for Biblical Scholar." *Journal of Biblical Literature*, 91:73-89.
10. Kraft, Charles H. 2005. "Why Isn't Contextualization Implemented?" *Appropriate Christianity*. Pasadena, CA: William Carey Library, 257-258.
11. Kraft, Charles. 2005. "Meaning Equivalence Contextualization." *Appropriate Christianity*. Pasadena, CA: William Carey Library, 163.

## 2. DISCOVERING AN INNATE MORAL IMPERATIVE

1. JAARS. https://www.jaars.org
2. Instead of adding intonation to mark a sentence, the Chácobo added the syllable *ni*.
3. Blore, Shawn, Shane Christensen, Alexandra de Vries, Eliot Greenspan, Charlie O'Malley, Jisel Perilla, Neil E. Schlecht, & Kristina Schreck. 2008. *Frommer's South America*. Wiley Publishing House: NJ, 227.
4. Róheim, Géza. 1950. *Psychoanalysis and Anthropology: Culture, Personality, and the Unconscious*. New York: International Universities Press, 347.

## 3. DOES THE GAME OF LIFE HAVE AN UMPIRE

1. Goodenough, Ward. 1981, *Culture, Language, and Society*. Menlo Park: Cummings Publishing Co., 17-18.

## 4. CHÁCOBO SATIRE

1. Niebuhr, Reinhold. 1949. *The Nature and Destiny of Man: A Christian Interpretation*. Volume 1. New York: Charles Schribner's Sons, 182.

NOTES

## 5. A MIND STRUCTURED WITH A PRIORI KNOWLEDGE

1. Van Til, Henry R. 1979 (1959). *The Calvinistic Concept of Culture.* Grand Rapids, MI: Baker Book House, 32.
2. Dr. Lisle, Jason. 2018. "The Biblical Basis for the Laws of Logic." April 13, 2018. https://biblicalscienceinstitute.com/logic/the-biblical-basis-for-the-laws-of-logic/#
3. Pike, Kenneth. 1993. *Talk, Thought, and Thing: The Emic Road Toward Conscious Knowledge.* Dallas: SIL, 63.

## 6. THE GREAT DISCOVERY: CHÁCOBO SATIRE

1. Hsu, Francis L. K., 1972. "Kinship and Ways of Life." In *Psychological Anthropology.* edited by Francis L. K. Hsu. Cambridge, MA: Schenkman Publishing Co.
2. Positive self-actualization occurs within the boundaries of God's Laws. God instructed to Moses: "You must obey my rules and my laws, because whoever obeys them will live. I am the LORD" (Leviticus 18:5, Easy-to-Read Version, ERV).
3. Kraft, Charles. 2005. *Christianity in Culture: A Study in Biblical Theologizing in Cross-Cultural Perspective.* Maryknoll, NY: Orbis Books, 53.
4. Róheim Géza. 1950. *Psychoanalysis and Anthropology: Culture, Personality, and the Unconscious.* New York: International Universities Press, 347.
5. Kraft, Charles. 2005. *Christianity in Culture: A Study in Biblical Theologizing in Cross-Cultural Perspective,* 25th Edition. Maryknoll, NY: Orbis Books, 94.

## 7. THE MARRIAGE TRAP: BECOMING A RAISI

1. AWANA. http://awana.org/about.
2. Cassuto, U. 1972. (1944). *A Commentary on the Book of Genesis.* Jerusalem: The Magnes Press, 137.
3. Niebuhr, Reinhold. 1949. *The Nature and Destiny of Man: A Christian Interpretation.* Vol. 1. New York: Charles Scribner's Sons, 182
4. Ibid., 192.
5. παρεισῆλθον. Arndt, William and F. Wilbur Gingrich. 1957. *A Greek-English Lexicon of the New Testament and Other Early Christian Literature.* Chicago: University of Chicago Press, 630.

## 8. THE DYING RAISI

1. Niebuhr, Reinhold. 1949. *The Nature and Destiny of Man: A Christian Interpretation.* Vol 1. New York: Charles Schribner's Sons, 182.
2. Professor Charles Kraft proclaims: "There is no such thing as an absolute set of cultural forms."

NOTES

# 9. A CULTURAL LAW-WAY SNEAKED INTO HISTORY AND HAS NO PLACE IN THE DIVINE PLAN

1. Kraft, Charles. 2005. *Christianity in Culture: A Study in Biblical Theologizing in Cross-Cultural Perspective*, 25th edition. Maryknoll, NY: Orbis Books, 78.
2. Kraft, Charles H. 2005. "Why Isn't Contextualization Implemented?" *Appropriate Christianity*. Pasadena, CA: William Carey Library, 257-258.
3. Machen, J. Gresham. 1949. *New Testament Greek for Beginners*. NY: The MacMillan Co., 23.
4. Moulton, James Hope. Cited by Dana and Mantey.
5. Dana H, E. and Mantey, J. 1950. *A Manual Grammar of the Greek New Testament*. NY: The Macmillian Company, 138.
6. Slaten, Arthur. 1918. *Qualitative Nouns in the Pauline Epistles and Their Translation in the Revised Version*. Chicago: University of Chicago Press.
7. Moo, Douglas J. 1996. *The Epistle to the Romans*. Grand Rapids, MI: Eerdmans Publishing Company, 346.
8. Moule, Handley C. *The Epistle to the Romans*. London: Pickering & Inglis, 155.
9. Murray, John. 1968. "The Epistle to the Romans." *The New International Commentary of the New Testament*. Grand Rapids, MI: Eerdmans Publishing Company.
10. Godet, F. 1956 (1883). *Commentary on the Epistle to the Romans*. Grand Rapids, MI: Zondervan., 227.
11. Hodge, Charles. *A Commentary on the Epistle of Romans*. Grand Rapids, MI: Louis Kregel. A reprint of the 1886 edition.
12. Lenski, R. C. H. 1945. *Interpretation of Romans*. Columbus, OH: Wartburg Press, 384.
13. παρεισῆλθον. Arndt, William and Gingrich, F. Wilbur. 1957. *A Greek-English Lexicon of the New Testament and Other Early Christian Literature*. Chicago: University of Chicago Press, 630.
14. Moulton, James Hope. Cited by Dana and Mantey.

# 10. THE CONCEPT OF CULTURE

1. Kroeber, A. L. and Kluckhohn, Clyde. 1963. *Culture: A Critical Review of Concepts and Definitions*. New York: Vintage Books.
   [2] Sharma, Ashish. English with Ashish. "Abstract Noun Masterclass." https://www.englishwithashish.com/abstract-noun-masterclass/(blog).
2. Ellis, Matt. 10-6-2022 (updated). Grammarly. "What Are Abstract Nouns? Definition and Examples." https://www.grammarly.com/blog/abstract-nouns/
3. Hart, H. L. A. 1961. *The Concept of Law*. Oxford: Clarendon Press, 15.
4. Ladd, George Eldon. 1974. *A Theology of the New Testament*. Grand Rapids, MI: Eerdmans Publishing Co., 504.
5. Clark, Gordon. 2004 (1973). *Christian Philosophy*. Unicoi, TN: The Trinity Foundation, 275.

NOTES

## 11. THE SHAPING OF CULTURE

1. Clark, Gordon. 1993 (1968). *An Introduction to Christian Philosophy*. Jefferson, Maryland: The Trinity Foundation, 229.
2. Carruthers, Peter. 1995. *Human Knowledge and Human Nature*. Oxford, UK: Oxford University Press, 103.
3. Sproul, R. C. 2000. *The Consequences of Ideas*. Wheaton: Crossway Books, 122.
4. Harris, Marvin. 1980. *Cultural Materialism: The Struggle for a Science of Culture*. New York: Vintage Books, 56.
5. Cultural forms represent observable customs, behavioral patterns, institutions, allegiance patterns, marriage rules, residence rules, sleeping rules, taboos, rituals, and all the patterns of living that make up a cultural lifeway.
6. Arndt & Gingrich. 1957. *A Greek-English Lexicon of the New Testament*. Chicago: University of Chicago Press, 290.
7. Norenzayan, Ara. and Steven J. Heine. 2005. "Psychological Universals: What Are They and How Can We Know Them?" In *Psychological Bulletin*, 131 (5): 763-784.
8. Lawless, Robert. 1979. *The Concept of Culture*. Minneapolis: Burgess Publishing Co., 9.
9. Marx, Karl, cited by Afanasyev, V. 1968. *Marxist Philosophy*. Moscow: Progress Publishers, 352.
10. Kraft, Charles H. 2005. "Contextualization and Time: Generational Appropriateness." In *Appropriate Christianity*. Pasadena, CA William Carey Library, 257-258.
11. Ottenheimer, Martin 2001 "Relativism in Kinship Analysis" In *The Cultural Analysis of Kinship, The Legacy of David M. Schneider*, edited by Richard Feinnberg and Martin Ottenheimer. Urbana, Il: University of Illinois Press, 52.
12. Ottenheimer, Martin 2001 "Relativism in Kinship Analysis." In *The Cultural Analysis of Kinship, The Legacy of David M. Schneider*, edited by Richard Feinberg and Martin Ottenheimer. Urbana, Il: University of Illinois Press, 52.
13. Kraft, 27.

## 12. DOES CULTURE DETERMINE WHAT ONE THINKS

1. Zedong, Mao. 1963. Marxists.org. "Where Do Correct Ideas Come From?" *Selected Works of Mao Zedong*. May, *1963*. https://www.marxists.org/reference/archive/mao/selected-works/volume-9/mswv9_01.htm.
2. Marx, Karl. 1970 (1859). *A Contribution of the Political-Economy*. New York: International Publishers, 21.
3. On Practice. 1937. "On the Relation Between Knowledge and Practice, Between Knowing and Doing." *Selected Works of Mao Zedong*, Vol. I, 299-30. July, 1937. https://www.marxists.org/reference/archive/mao/selected-works/volume-1/mswv1_16.htm
4. Ibid.
5. Clark, Gordon, 2004 (1973). *Christian Philosophy*. Unicoi, TN: The Trinity Foundation, 30.

## NOTES

6. Harris, Marvin. 1980. *Cultural Materialism: The Struggle for a Science of Culture*. New York: Vintage Books, 79.
7. Mayers, Marvin K. 1987. *Christianity Confronts Culture: A Strategy for Crosscultural Evangelism*. Grand Rapids, MI. Academie Books, 98.
8. Kraft, Charles. 2005. *Christianity in Culture: A Study in Biblical Theologizing in Cross-Cultural Perspective*. Maryknoll, NY: Orbis Books, 107.
9. Clark, Gordon H. "Special Divine Revelation as Rational." In *Revelation and the Bible*, edited by Carl. F. H. Henry. Grand Rapids, MI: Baker Book House, 147.
10. Clark, 148.
11. Pike, Kenneth. 1993. *Talk, Thought, and Thing: The Emic Road Toward Conscious Knowledge*. Dallas: SIL, 17.
12. Ibid., 63
13. Hsu, Francis L. K.. 1972. "Kinship and Ways of Life." In *Psychological Anthropology*, edited by Francis L. K. Hsu. Cambridge, MA: Schenkman Publishing Co.

## 13. WHERE ARE THE POSITIVE UNIVERSALS

1. Clark, Gordon. 1993 (1968). *An Introduction to Christian Philosophy*. Jefferson, Maryland: The Trinity Foundation, 149.
2. Sil.org. 1996. "K.L. Pike on *Etic* vs. *Emic*: A Review and Interview." Franklin, Karl J. (Interviewer). Summer Institute of Linguistics. November 27, 1996. https://www.sil.org/about/klp/interviews-tributes/karl-franklin-interview
3. Pike, Kenneth. 1993. *Talk, Thought, and Thing: The Emic Road Toward Conscious Knowledge*. Dallas: SIL, 63.
4. Clark, Gordon. 2004 (1973). *Christian Philosophy*. Unicoi, TN: The Trinity Foundation, 198-199.
5. Sil.org. 1996. "K.L. Pike on *Etic* vs. *Emic*: A Review and Interview." Franklin, Karl J. (Interviewer). Summer Institute of Linguistics. November 27, 1996. https://www.sil.org/about/klp/interviews-tributes/karl-franklin-interview
6. Wierzbicka, Anna. 1996. *Semantics, Primes, and Universals*. Oxford, UK: Oxford University Press, 24.
7. Goodenough, Ward H. 1981. *Culture, Language, and Society*. Menlo Park, CA: The Benjamin/Cummings Publishing Company, 17.
8. Kraft, Charles. 2005. *Christianity in Culture: A Study in Biblical Theologizing in Cross-Cultural Perspective*, 25th edition. Maryknoll, NY: Orbis Books, 230.
9. Harris, Marvin. 1980. *Cultural Materialism: The Struggle for a Science of Culture*. New York: Vintage Books, 79.
10. Harris, Marvin. March. 2007. "Cultural Materialism and Behavior Analysis: Common Problems and Radical Solutions." In *The Behavior Analyst / MABA* 30(1), 37- 47.
11. Sproul, R. C. 2000. *The Consequences of Ideas*. Wheaton: Crossway Books, 31.
12. Meyer, Heinrich August Wilhelm. 1885. *Critical and Exegetical Commentary: Philippians, Colossians & Philemon*. New York: Funk and Wagnalls Co., 292-293.
13. Van Til, Cornelius. 1946. *The New Modernism, An Appraisal of the Theology of Barth and Brunner*. Philadelphia, Penn: The Presbyterian and Reformed Publishing House, 166.

NOTES

## 14. THE LONG NIGHT

1. Velikovsky, Immanuel. (1950) 1968. *Worlds In Collision*. New York: Dell, 310.
2. Ibid., 61.
3. Boas, Franz. 1975 (1966). *Kwakiutl Ethnography*, edited by Helen Codere. Chicago: The University of Chicago Press, 306
4. Richard, T., Contributor. Christian Forums. Nov. 18, 2006. https://www.christianforums.com/
5. Grigg, Russell. Creation Ministries International. https://creation.com/joshuas-long-day

## 15. INTRODUCING THE SEVEN-DAY WEEK

1. Zerubavel, Eviatar. 1985. *The Seven Day Circle: The History and Meaning of a Week*. Chicago: University of Chicago Press, 11.
2. Ibid., 11.

## 16. THE CHÁCOBO

1. Harris, Marvin. 1980. *Cultural Materialism: The Struggle for a Science of Culture*. New York: Vintage Books, 59.
2. Dawson, Christopher. 1948. *Religion and Culture*. New York: Sheed & Ward, 47.
3. Dillistone, F. W. 1951. *The Structure of the Divine Society*. Philadelphia: The Westminster Press, 190.
4. Dooyeweerd, Herman. 1969. *A New Critique of Theoretical Thought*, Vol. III-IV. The Presbyterian and Reformed Publishing Company, 271.
5. Kraft, Charles. 2005. *Christianity in Culture: A Study in Biblical Theologizing in Cross-Cultural Perspective*. Maryknoll, NY: Orbis Books, 97.
6. Kraft, 41.
7. Dooyeweerd, Herman. 1969. *A New Critique of Theoretical Thought*, Vol. III-IV. The Presbyterian and Reformed Publishing Company, 271.

## 17. EPIGNOSIS VERSUS GNOSIS

1. Bloom, Alan. 1987. *The Closing of the American Mind*. New York: Simon & Shuster, 56.
2. Hsu, Francis L. K., 1972. "Kinship and Ways of Life." In *Psychological Anthropology*. edited by Francis L. K. Hsu. Cambridge, MA: Schenkman Publishing Co.
3. Carruthers, Peter. 1995. *Human Knowledge and Human Nature*. Oxford, UK: Oxford University Press, 99.

## 18. THE NEED FOR ETIC ANALYSIS

1. Kraft, Charles H. 1978. "Interpreting in Cultural Context." *Journal of the Evangelical Theological Society*, 359.
2. Hsu, Francis L. K.. 1972. "Kinship and Ways of Life." *Psychological Anthropology*, edited by Francis L. K. Hsu. Cambridge, MA: Schenkman Publishing Co.
3. Cultural forms represent observable customs, behavioral patterns, institutions, allegiance patterns, marriage rules, residence rules, sleeping rules, taboos, rituals, and all the patterns of living that make up a cultural lifeway.
4. Norenzayan, Ara. and Steven J. Heine. 2005. "Psychological Universals: What Are They and How Can We Know Them?" In *Psychological Bulletin* 131 (5): 763-784.
5. Lawless, Robert. 1979 *The Concept of Culture*. Minneapolis: Burgess Publishing Co., 9.
6. Franklin, Karl L. Nov. 27, 1996. K.L. Pike on *Etic vs. Emic*, A Review and Interview. Dallas, SIL, 4.
7. Lawless, Robert. 1979. *The Concept of Culture*. Minneapolis, MN: Burgess Publishing Co., 9.

## 19. WHEN DID SOCIETY GO ITS OWN WAY

1. Harris Marvin. 1980. *Cultural Materialism: The Struggle for a Science of Culture*. New York: Vintage Books, 278.
2. Hsu, Francis L. K. 1972. "Kinship and Ways of Life." In *Psychological Anthropology*. Cambridge, MA: Schenkman Publishing Co.
3. Harris, Marvin. 1980. *Cultural Materialism: The Struggle for a Science of Culture*. New York: Vintage Books, 275.
4. Bailey, Derrick S. 1952. *The Mystery of Love and Marriage*. New York: Harper & Brothers, 44.
5. Hsu, Francis L. K. 1972. "Kinship and Ways of Life." In *Psychological Anthropology*. Cambridge, MA: Schenkman Publishing Co., 518.

## 20. THERE IS A WAY THAT SEEMS RIGHT TO A MAN

1. Harris, Marvin. 1980. *Cultural Materialism: The Struggle for a Science of Culture*. New York: Vintage Books, 85.
2. Ibid.
3. Van Til, Cornelius. 1946. *The New Modernism: An Appraisal of the Theology of Barth and Brunner*. Philadelphia, Penn: The Presbyterian and Reformed Publishing House, 166
4. Van Til, Cornelius. 1952. *An Introduction to Systematic Theology*, 152. Cited by Rousas J. Rushdoony. In *By What Standard?* Philadelphia, Penn.: The Presbyterian and Reformed Publishing Co., 146.
5. A theory that all knowledge is derived from sense experience and that the mind is a *tabula rasa* upon which the rules of behavior are written and learned, which denies the existence of innate knowledge.

## NOTES

6. Berry, John W. 1990. "Imposed, *Emics*, and Derived *Etics*: Their Conceptual and Operational Status in Cross-Cultural Psychology." In *Emics and Etics: The Insider/Outsider Debate*, edited by Thomas N. Headland. Newbury Park, CA: Saga Publications, 84-89.
7. Ottenheimer, Martin. 2001. "Relativism in Kinship Analysis." In *The Cultural Analysis of Kinship*, edited by Richard Fienberg and Martin Ottenheimer. Urbana: University of Illinois Press, 123.
8. Wikipedia. "*Emic* and *Etic.*" https://en.wikipedia.org/wiki/Emic_and_etic.
9. Schaeffer, Francis A. 1985. *A Christian View of the West (The Complete Works of Francis A. Schaeffer*, Vol. V*)* Wheaton, ILL: Crossway (The Good News Publishers).
10. Teflpedia. https://teflpedia.com/images/thumb/1/15/IPA_chart_2005.png/1200px-IPA_chart_2005.png
11. Pike, Kenneth L. 1967. *Language in Relation to a Unified Theory of the Structure of Human Behavior*. Second edition. The Hague: Mouton, 38-39.
12. Goodenough, Ward. 1981, *Culture, Language, and Society*. Menlo Park: Cummings Publishing Co., 17.
13. Wierzbicka, Anna, 1996. *Semantics, Primes, and Universals*. New York: Oxford University Press, 297.
14. Kraft, Charles H. 2005. "Contextualization and Time: Generational Appropriateness." In *Appropriate Christianity*. Pasadena, CA: William Carey Library, 257-258.
15. Empiricism: A theory that all knowledge originates in experience.
16. Harris, 78.

## 21. WHICH COMES FIRST

1. Dooyeweerd, Herman. 1969. *A New Critique of Theoretical Thought*, Vol. III. The Presbyterian and Reformed Publishing Company, 304.
2. Pike, Kenneth. 1993. *Talk, Thought, and Thing: The Emic Road Toward Conscious Knowledge*. Dallas: SIL. 63. The quote reveals Linguist Kenneth Pike was an innatist.
3. Tiger, Stephen. The Official Website of Greater Miami and Miami Beach. "Miami's Native American Heritage: History of the Miccosukee Tribe." https://www.miamiandbeaches.com/things-to-do/history-and-heritage/miamis-native-american-heritage.

    For purposes of this book, the author has elected to use "Miccosukee" for both the tribal name and language.
4. Pike, Kenneth. 1993. *Talk, Thought, and Thing: The Emic Road Toward Conscious Knowledge*. Dallas: SIL, 23.
5. Lévi-Strauss, Claude. 1968. *The Savage Mind*. Chicago: The University of Chicago Press, 25.
6. Lewontin, Richard. 1997. "Adaptation." In *Evolution: A Scientific American Book*. San Francisco: Freeman Living "appear to have been carefully and artfully designed ." 114-125. "Billions and Billions of Demons." In the *NY Review of Books*. January 7, 1997. http://hyperphysics.phy-astr.gsu.edu/Nave-html/Faithpathh/lewontin.html

# NOTES

## 22. THE GREAT AWAKENING

1. The Greek word ὑγιαινόντων, usually translated as "sound" or "true," literally means "healthy." The use of healthy words will produce sound doctrine. *A Greek-English Lexicon of the New Testament and Other Early Greek Literature*. William F. Arndt and F. Wilbur Gingrich, 839.
2. Kraft, Charles H. 2005. "Contextualization and Time: Generational Appropriateness." In *Appropriate Christianity*. Pasadena, CA: William Carey Library, 257-258.
3. Lenski, R. C. H. 1946. *The Interpretation of St. Paul's Epistle to the Colossians, to the Thessalonians, to Timothy, to Titus, and to Philemon*. Columbus, Ohio: Wartburg Press.
4. The notion that people can be jaguars is not limited to tribal societies. When I returned to visit the Chácobo in 1998, my taxicab driver warned us about possibly meeting a *tigre-gente* (tiger person) in my dealings with Bolivian nationals. More shockingly, I was surprised to hear a visiting Haitian pastor in my church express the same belief. His concept of personhood had been distorted and replaced with a meaning that belonged to his culture. In academia, especially anthropology, people are a kind of animal.
5. Embraced by Truth. "Innate Knowledge." http://embracedbytruth.com/Man/Crown%20of%20Creation/Innate%20Knowledge.htm [editor's note: No longer a working link].
6. Carnell, Edward J. 1952. *An Introduction to Christian Apologetics*. Fourth Edition. Grand Rapids, MI: Eerdmans Publishing Co., 163.
7. Kraft, Charles. 2005. *Christianity in Culture: A Study in Biblical Theologizing in Cross-Cultural Perspective*, 25th Edition. Maryknoll, NY: Orbis Books, 105.
8. Carnell, Edward J. 1952. *An Introduction to Christian Apologetics*. Fourth Edition. Grand Rapids, MI: Eerdmans Publishing Co., 169.
9. Lenski, R. C. H. 1946. *The Interpretation of St. Paul's Epistle to the Colossians, to the Thessalonians, to Timothy, to Titus, and to Philemon*. Columbus, Ohio: Wartburg Press, 770.
10. Hsu, Francis L. K.. 1972 "Kinship and Ways of Life." In *Psychological Anthropology*, edited by Francis L. K. Hsu. Cambridge, MA: Schenkman Publishing Co., 517.
11. Ibid., 518.

## 23. HEALTHY WORDS

1. Carruthers, Peter. 1995. *Human Knowledge and Human Nature*. Oxford, UK: Oxford University Press, 103.
2. Harner, Michael J. 1989. *The Jívaro*. Berkeley, CA: University of California Press, 70-72.
3. Acevedo, Nicole. 2021. NBC News. "Pete Buttigieg and Husband, Chasten, Welcome Two Children Into Their Family." September 4, 2021. https://www.nbcnews.com/feature/nbc-out/pete-buttigieg-husband-chasten-welcome-two-children-their-family-n1278512.
4. Malinowski, Bronislaw. 1987 (1931). *The Sexual Life of Savages*. Boston: Beacon Press, 161.

# NOTES

5. Pike, Kenneth. 1993. *Talk, Thought, and Thing: The Emic Road Toward Conscious Knowledge*. Dallas: SIL, x.
6. Kraft, Charles H. 2005. "Why Isn't Contextualization Implemented?" In *Appropriate Christianity*. Pasadena, CA: William Carey Library, 257-258.
7. The Greek word ὑγιαινόντων, usually translated as "sound" or "true" literally means "healthy." The use of healthy words will produce sound doctrine. *A Greek-English Lexicon of the New Testament and Other Early Greek Literature*. William F. Arndt and F. Wilbur Gingrich, 839.

## 24. THE NUCLEAR FAMILY

1. Dooyeweerd, Herman. 1969. *A New Critique of Theoretical Thought*, Vol. 1. The Presbyterian and Reformed Publishing Company, 304.
2. Van Til, Henry R. 1979 (1959). *The Calvinistic Concept of Culture*. Grand Rapids, MI: Baker Book House, 32.
3. Lévi-Strauss, Claude. 1968. *The Savage Mind*. Chicago: The University of Chicago Press, 25
4. Povos Indigenas Brasil. Socioambiental.org. Siasi/Sesai 2014. "Pirahã." https://pib.socioambiental.org/en/Povo:Pirahã
5. Dooyeweerd, Herman. 1969. *A New Critique of Theoretical Thought*, Vol. III and IV. The Presbyterian and Reformed Publishing Company, 344.
6. Grunlan, Stephen A. and Marvin K. Mayers. 1979. *Cultural Anthropology: A Christian Perspective*. Grand Rapids, MI: Academie Books, 206.
7. Róheim, Géza. 1950. *Psychoanalysis and Anthropology: Culture, Personality and the Unconscious*. New York: International Universities Press, 81-82.
8. Niebuhr, Reinhold. 1949. *The Nature and Destiny of Man: A Christian Interpretation*. Vol. 1. New York: Charles Scribner's Sons, 182.
9. Dillistone, F. W. 1951. *The Structure of the Divine Society*. Philadelphia: The Westminster Press, 190.
10. Niebuhr, Reinhold. 1949. *The Nature and Destiny of Man: A Christian Interpretation*. Vol. 1. New York: Charles Scribner's Sons, 182

## 25. CENTRIPETAL SOCIETIES

1. Hsu, Francis L. K.. 1972. "Kinship and Ways of Life." In *Psychological Anthropology*, edited by Francis L. K. Hsu. Cambridge, MA: Schenkman Publishing Co., 517.
2. Morris, Desmond. 1967 *The Naked Ape: A Zoologist's Study of the Human Animal*. New York: McGraw-Hill Book, 14.
3. Franz, Alexander (source unknown).
4. Kraft, 2005. *Christianity in Culture: A Study in Biblical Theologizing in Cross-Cultural Perspective*, 25th edition. Maryknoll, NY: Orbis Books, 66.
5. Harris Marvin. 1980. *Cultural Materialism: The Struggle for a Science of Culture*. New York: Vintage Books, 54.

## 26. THE RULE OF EXOGAMY - PART I

1. ] Hsu, Francis. 1972. "Kinship and Ways of Life." *Psychological Anthropology,* edited by Francis L. K. Hsu. Cambridge, MA: Schenkman Publishing Co., 514-515.
2. Lévi-Strauss, Claude. 1969. *The Elementary Structures of Kinship.* Boston: Beacon Press, 479.
3. Kraft, Charles H. 2005. "Why Isn't Contextualization Implemented?" *Appropriate Christianity.* Pasadena, CA: William Carey Library, 257-258.
4. Ibid., 74
5. Lingenfelter, Sherwood. 2005. "Power-Giving Leadership: Transformation for a Missional Church." In *Appropriate Christianity.* edited by Charles H. Kraft. Pasadena, CA, 285.
6. Goodreads.com. https://www.goodreads.com/author/quotes/7084.Karl_Marx
7. Lévi-Strauss, Claude. 1969. *The Elementary Structures of Kinship.* Boston: Beacon Press, 24.
8. Ibid., 8.
9. Clark, Gordon, 2004 (1973). *Christian Philosophy.* Unicoi, TN: The Trinity Foundation, 345.
10. Dooyeweerd, Herman. 1969. *A New Critique of Theoretical Thought,* Vol. III-IV. The Presbyterian and Reformed Publishing Company, 276, 304.
11. Niebuhr, Reinhold. 1949. *The Nature and Destiny of Man: A Christian Interpretation.* Vol 1. New York: Charles Schribner's Sons, 69.
12. Satre, Jean-Paul. enotes.com."What Does Sartre mean by 'existence precedes essence' in 'Existentialism is a Humanism,' and how does it affect morality?" https://www.enotes.com/topics/jean-paul-sartre/questions/existentialism-humanism-sartre-argues-that-1360266

## 27. THE MEANING OF GIFT

1. Benedict, Ruth. 1989. (1946). *The Chrysanthemum and the Sword.* Boston: Houghton Mifflin Co., 116.
2. Ibid.
3. Bernstein, Gail Lee. 1983. *Haruko's World: A Japanese Farm Women and Her Community.* Stanford, CA: Stanford University Press, 126.
4. Kahuashima, Takeyoshi. 1967. "The Individual in Law and Social Order." In *The Japanese Mind,* edited by Charles A. Moore. Honolulu: East-West Center Press, University of Hawaii, 282.
5. Bernstein, Gail Lee. 1983. *Haruko's World: A Japanese Farm Woman and Her Community.* Stanford, CA: Stanford University Press, 105.
6. Spacey, John. Japan Talk. updated July 10, 2012. https://www.japan-talk.com/jt/new/sumimasen
7. Benedict, Ruth. 1989. (1946). *The Chrysanthemum and the Sword.* Boston: Houghton Mifflin Co., 106.
8. Bernstein, Gail Lee. 1983. *Haruko's World: A Japanese Farm Woman and Her Community.* Stanford, CA: Stanford University Press, 126.

9. Kahuashima, Takeyoshi. 1967. "The Individual in Law and Social Order." *The Japanese Mind*. Charles A. Moore, editor. Honolulu: East-West Center Press, University of Hawaii Press, 282.
10. Fruechen, Peter. 1961. *Book of the Eskimos*. New York: The World Publishing Co., 154.
11. Fruechen, 214.
12. Barry Irwin, cited by Wayne Dye in "Toward a Cross-Cultural Definition of Sin." *Missiology* 4:27-41. 1976, 37. Also cited by Kraft in *Christianity in Culture: A Study in Biblical Theologizing in Cross-Cultural Perspective*, 196.
13. Dye, Wayne, cited by Kraft in *Christianity in Culture: A Study in Biblical Theologizing in Cross-Cultural Perspective*, 196.
14. Kraft, Charles. 2005. *Christianity in Culture: A Study in Biblical Theologizing in Cross-Cultural Perspective*, 25th edition. Maryknoll, NY: Orbis Books, 11.
15. Ibid., 163.
16. Goodenough, Ward. 1981, *Culture, Language, and Society*. Menlo Park: Cummings Publishing Co., 11.
17. Wierzbicka, Anna. 1996. *Semantics, Primes, and Universals*. Oxford, UK: Oxford University Press, 297.
18. Lawless, Robert. 1979. *The Concept of Culture*. Minneapolis: Burgess Publishing Co., 9.

## 28. THE BIBLICAL UNDERSTANDING OF GIFT

1. *dorea* = "denotes a free gift, stressing its gratuitous character." It manifests the intention of the giver. *doron* = "of gifts [customarily] given as an expression of honor" as in: "Then they opened their treasures and presented him with gifts of gold, frankincense and myrrh" (Matthew 2:11). It is the custom of all nations for individuals to give gifts to royalty. However, the intention of some gift-givers may be the idea of reciprocity. See: Vine, W. E. 1959. *An Expository Dictionary of the New Testament Words with their Precise Meanings*. London: Oliphant's LTD, 146-147.
2. Lear, Jonathan. 1980. Quoted by Noam Chomsky in *Rules and Representations*. New York: Columbia University Press, 12.
3. Lenski, R. C. H., 1945. *Interpretation of Romans*. Columbus, OH: Wartburg Press, 165.

## 29. THE LAW OF CONTRADICTION AND THE LAW OF IDENTITY

1. Arnn Larry P. December 2020. "Orwell's 1984 and Today." In *Imprimas*, Vol 49, No. 12, Hillsdale College.
2. Kraft, Charles, 2005. *Christianity in Culture: A Study in Biblical Theologizing in Cross-Cultural Perspective*. Maryknoll, NY: Orbis Books, 74.
3. Clark, Gordon, 2004 (1973). *Christian Philosophy*. Unicoi, TN: The Trinity Foundation, 161.

NOTES

4. Niebuhr, Reinhold. 1949. *The Nature and Destiny of Man: A Christian Interpretation.* Vol. 1. New York: Charles Scribner's Sons, 69.

## 30. CULTURE AND NEUROSIS

1. Kroeber, A. L. and Clyde Kluckhohn. 1963. *Culture: A Critical Review of Concepts and Definition.* New York: Vintage Books.
2. Géza Róheim, cited by Kroeber and Kluckhohn, 200.
3. Kraft, Charles. 2005. *Christianity in Culture: A Study in Biblical Theologizing in Cross-Cultural Perspective,* 25th edition. Maryknoll, NY: Orbis Books, 78
4. Géza Róheim. Cited by Kroeber and Kluckhohn, 200.

## 31. CREATING A DEFENSIVE SYSTEM AGAINST ANXIETY

1. Róheim Géza. 1950. *Psychoanalysis and Anthropology: Culture, Personality, and the Unconscious.* New York: International Universities Press, 81.
2. Fox, Robin. 1992 (1967). *Kinship and Marriage.* Cambridge: Cambridge University Press, 25.
3. Campagno, Marcelo P. 2009. "Kinship and Family Relations." eScholarship.org. http://escholarship.org/uc/item/7zh1g7ch
4. Dillistone, F. W. 1951. *The Structure of the Divine Society.* Philadelphia: The Westminster Press, 190.

## 32. LEARNING REQUIRES A PRIORI EQUIPMENT ETIC DATA

1. Pinker, Steven. 1997. *How the Mind Works.* New York: W.W. Norton & Co, 129.
2. Ibid., 243.
3. Clark, Gordon, 2004 (1973). *Christian Philosophy.* Unicoi, TN: The Trinity Foundation, 297.
4. Clark, Gordon. 1993 (1968). *An Introduction to Christian Philosophy.* Jefferson, Maryland: The Trinity Foundation, 30.
5. Ibid., 301.
6. Carruthers, Peter. 1995. *Human Knowledge and Human Nature.* Oxford, UK: Oxford University Press, 50.

## 33. A BIBLE TRANSLATOR'S DILEMMA

1. Some translators render νόμος (law) as the Law.
2. Tenney, Merrill. 1950. *Galatians: The Charter of Christian Liberty.* Grand Rapids, MI: Eerdmans Publishing Co., 129.

# NOTES

3. Dana, H. E. and Julius R. Mantey . 1950. *A Manual Grammar of the Greek New Testament*. New York: The Macmillian Co.
4. Cited by Dana and Mantey, 136.
5. Ibid., 136.
6. Ibid.
7. Moulton, James Hope. Cited by Dana and Mantey.
8. Slaten, Arthur. 1918. *Qualitative Nouns in the Pauline Epistles and Their Translation in the Revised Version*. Chicago, IL: University of Chicago Press, 9.
9. Slaten, Arthur. 1918. *Qualitative Nouns in the Pauline Epistles and Their Translation in the Revised Version*. Chicago, IL: University of Chicago Press, 9.

## 34. THE MANDATE OF HEAVEN

1. The Mandate of Heaven is interpreted to mean the Mandate from God. When the Prodigal Son prayed, he said, "I have sinned against heaven," meaning, "I have sinned against the God who dwells there." Heaven is inserted for God.
2. Chan, Wing-Tsit. 1967. "The Story of Chinese Philosophy." In *The Chinese Mind*, edited by Charles A. Moore. Honolulu: East-West Center Press, 36.
3. Wu, John C. H. 1967. "Chinese Legal and Political Philosophy." In *The Chinese Mind*, edited by Charles A. Moore. Honolulu: East-West Center Press.
4. Wu, John C. H. 1967. "The Individual in Political and Legal Tradition." In *The Chinese Mind*, edited by Charles A. Moore. Honolulu: East-West Center Press, 345.
5. Clark, Gordon. 1993. *Language and Theology*. Jefferson, Maryland: The Trinity Foundation, 141.
6. (1), SDA, 1989:245; (2), Black, 1989; Meyer, 1884; (3), Dodd, 1932; Hunter, 1955; Moo, 1996; Vine, 1948; (4), Barnes, 1966; (5), Best, 1967; Käsmann, 1980; May,1990); (6), Denney; Barrett, 1957; (7), Lenski, 1945; Morris, 1988; (8), Chas Hodge: 1958.
7. Dawson, Christopher. 1948. *Religion and Culture*. New York: Sheed & Ward, 47.
8. Moulton, James Hope. 1906. "Grammar of the New Testament." Vol. 1. *Prolegomena*, 83.

## 35. FROM BABEL TO THE AMAZON

1. A description of Noam Chomsky's position given by Steven Pinker. See: Pinker, Stephen. 1995. *The Language Instinct*. New York: Harper Perennial, 22
2. Prost, Gilbert. 1965. Chácobo. In *Gramaticas Estructurales de Lenguas Bolivianas*. Riberalta, Bolivia: Instituto Lingüístico de Verano.
3. Pinker, Steven. 1995. *The Language Instinct*. New York: Harper Perennial, 234.

NOTES

## 36. COMMODITY, MONEY AND FREEDOM

1. Kemp, Authur. 1975. "Is the Gold Standard Gone Forever?" *Gold is Money*, edited by Hans Sennholz. Westport, CN: Greenwood Press, 177.
2. Schwab, Klaus. World Economic Forum. 2020. "Now is the time for a 'great reset.'" June 3, 2020. https://www.weforum.org/agenda/2020/06/now-is-the-time-for-a-great-reset/
3. Anikin, A. 1978. *Gold the Yellow Devil*. USSR: Progressive Publishers, 11.
4. Ibid., 236
5. MacLeod, Alasdair. 2017. "Central Banks and Gold." 3-12-2017. https://www.goldmoney.com/research/goldmoney-insights/central-banks-and-gold
6. Rist, Charles. 1961. *The Triumph of Gold*. Philip Cortney, translator. New York: Philosophical Library, 2.
7. Rushdoony, Rousas John. 1975. "Hard Money and Society in the Bible." *Gold is Money*, edited by Hans S. Senholz. London: Greenwood Press, 168.

## 38. WAR AGAINST POSITIVE UNIVERSALS

1. Pike, Kenneth. 1993. *Talk, Thought, and Thing: The Emic Road Toward Conscious Knowledge*. Dallas: SIL, 63.
2. Chan, Wing-Tsit. 1967. "The Story of Chinese Philosophy." In *The Chinese Mind*, edited by Charles A. Moore. Honolulu: East-West Center Press, 36.
3. Clark, Gordon. 1993 (1968). *An Introduction to Christian Philosophy*. Jefferson, Maryland: The Trinity Foundation, 149.
4. Kraft, Charles. 2005. *Christianity in Culture: A Study in Biblical Theologizing in Cross-Cultural Perspective*. Maryknoll, NY: Orbis Books, 105.
5. Cited by Jean-Marie Benoist, 1974. "Classicism Revisited: Human Nature and Structure in Lévi-Strauss and Chomsky." In *The Limits of Human Nature*, edited by Jonathan Benthall. New York: E.P. Dutton & Co., 30.
6. Lee Strobel's Interview with J. F. Moreland. *The Case for a Creator*. 2004.
7. Bruner, Jerome. 1990, *Acts of Meaning*. Cambridge, MA: Harvard University Press, 72.
8. Carruthers, Peter. 1995. *Human Knowledge and Human Nature*. Oxford, UK: Oxford University Press, 50.
9. Bowerman, Melissa. 1973. *Early Syntactic Development: A Cross-Linguistic Study with Special Reference to Finnish*. (Cambridge Studies in Linguistics, Series Number 11) Cambridge, England: Cambridge University Press, 112-13.

## 39. ETIC DIVERGENCE

1. According to Greek scholars Arndt and Gingrich, what slipped into history, "having no primary place in the Divine Plan," was a kind of law-way (νόμος absent the article). Also, the word παρεισῆλθεν in Romans 5:20, translated as "entered" in most translations should be translated as "to slip in," "come in as a side issue," or "sneak in." Paul uses the same word again in Galatians 2:4: The

# NOTES

   law did not "sneak in" at Mount Sinai. What "sneaked in" were diverse cultural law-ways. Arndt, William and F. Wilbur Gingrich. 1957. *A Greek-English Lexicon of the New Testament and Other Early Christian Literature*. Chicago: University of Chicago Press, 630.
2. Lingenfelter, Sherwood. 2005. "Power-Giving Leadership: Transformation for a Missional Church." In *Appropriate Christianity*, edited by Charles H. Kraft. Pasadena, CA.: 285.
3. Mao Zedong. 1938. *Dialectical Materialism. Selected Works of Mao Zedong*. April-June 1938. http://www.marxists.org/reference/archive/mao/selected-works/volume-6/mswv6_30.htm
4. Harris, Marvin, 1980. *Cultural Materialism: The Struggle for a Science of Culture*. New York: Vintage Books, 59.
5. Mayers, Marvin K. 1987. *Christianity Confronts Culture: A Strategy for Crosscultural Evangelism*. Grand Rapids, MI: Academie Books, 98.
6. Mayers, Marvin K. 1987. *Christianity Confronts Culture: A Strategy for Crosscultural Evangelism*. Grand Rapids, MI: Academie Books, 98.
7. Ibid., 74.
8. Kraft, 94.
9. Van Til, Cornelius. 1952. *An Introduction to Systematic Theology*, 32.
10. Chan, Wing-Tsit. 1967. "The Story of Chinese Philosophy." In *The Chinese Mind*, edited by Charles A. Moore. Honolulu: East-West Center Press, 63
11. Dooyeweerd, Herman. 1969. *A New Critique of Theoretical Thought*, Vol. 1. The Presbyterian and Reformed Publishing Company, 328.

## 40. THE RIGHT TIME

1. When Jacob prophesied about what was to happen to each of his sons in the future, concerning Judah, he said, "Judah, you *are he* whom your brothers shall praise; Your hand *shall be* on the neck of your enemies; Your father's children shall bow down before you. Judah *is* a lion's whelp. From the prey, my son, you have gone up. He bows down, he lies down as a lion; And as a lion, who shall rouse him? The scepter shall not depart from Judah" (Genesis 49: 8-10). Joseph became a great leader in Egypt. If they had not left "father and mother," neither would have had the freedom to exercise their leadership skill.
2. Dooyeweerd, Herman. 1969. *A New Critique of Theoretical Thought*, Vol. III & IV. The Presbyterian and Reformed Publishing Company, 657.
3. Ibid., 310
4. Our present economic world order is grounded n the idea of permanent indebtedness. Debts are rolled over and never canceled.
5. Burch, Ernest R. 1994. "The Iñupiat and the Christianization of Arctic Alaska." In *Etudes/Inuit/Studies*. 18 (1-2), 81-108.
6. Rome had politically prepared the way for the spread of the Gospel. Vague expectations of coming change found utterance even from the lips of Roman courtier poets, and a feeling of unrest and anticipation pervaded society.
7. Burch, Ernest R. 1975. *Eskimo Kinsmen*. St. Paul: West Publishing Co., 25.
8. Wikipedia. "Amazon Rubber Cycle." http://en.wikipedia.org/wiki/Amazon_rubber_boom

# NOTES

9. Sparing-Chávez, Margarethe. 1999. *People of Peru*. Lima, Peru: SIL, 96. In Chácobo the word for father is *ïpa*, in Sharanahua it is *upa;* correspondingly for mother there is *ïhua* versus *uhua;* for fire, *chihi* versus *chii,* and for sun, *bari* versus *fari*. Also, in Chácobo, the word for a common cold is *natí*. *Natí* is also the word for killer. To catch a common cold meant your chances of living were very small.
10. Ibid., 96.
11. Burch, Ernest R. 1975. *Eskimo Kinsmen*. St. Paul: West Publishing Co., 25.

## 41. IÑUPIAT ESKIMOS

1. Chance, Norman A. 1990. "The Iñupiat and Arctic Alaska." Harcourt Brace. The quote appeared in *Ethnographic Portraits, People and the Land: Early Years*. 58-60. http://arcticcircle.uconn.edu/HistoryCulture/Inupiat/1800s.html
2. Burch, Ernest R. 1975. *Eskimo Kinsmen: Changing Family Relationships in Northwest Alaska*. St Paul: West Publishing Co., 22.
3. Arieti, Silvano. 1976. *Creativity, The Magic Synthesis*. New York: Basic Books, 71-73.
4. Ibid., 58-60.
5. Burch, Jr., Ernest, S., *Etudes/Inuit/Studies*, 1994, 18 (1-2), 81-108. http://www.alaskool.org/native_ed/research_reports/christianization/burch.htm
6. bid.
7. Ibid.
8. Ibid.
9. Ibid.
10. Ibid.

## 42. THE LIFE NEEDS NEW FORMS

1. Mayers, Marvin K. 1987. *Christianity Confronts Culture: A Strategy for Crosscultural Evangelism*. Grand Rapids, MI: Academie Books, 96.
2. Ibid., 96.
3. Meyer, Heinrich A. 1884. *Critical and Exegetical Handbook to the Gospel of Matthew*. New York: Funk and Wagnalls Co, 199-200.
4. Kraft, Charles. 2005. "Why Isn't Contextualization Implemented?" *Appropriate Christianity*. Pasadena, CA: William Carey Library, 257-258.
5. Kraft, Charles. 2005. *Christianity in Culture: A Study in Biblical Theologizing in Cross-Cultural Perspective*, 25th Edition. Maryknoll, NY: Orbis Books, 68.
6. Lingenfelter, Sherwood, 2005. "Power-Giving Leadership: Transformation for a Missional Church." *Appropriate Christianity*, edited by Charles H. Kraft. Pasadena, CA: William Carey Library, 285.
7. Lévi-Strauss, Claude. 1968. *The Savage Mind*. Chicago: The University of Chicago Press, 25

# NOTES

## 43. THE RULE OF EXOGAMY - PART II

1. Lévi-Strauss, Claude. 1969. *The Elementary Structures of Kinship*. Boston: Beacon Press, 479.
2. Fox, Robin. 1992 (1967). *Kinship and Marriage*. Cambridge: Cambridge University Press, 44.
3. Keil, C.F. and Delitzsch. Franz. 1951. *Commentary on the Old Testament, The Pentateuch*, Volume I, Grand Rapids, MI: Eerdmans, 116.
4. Lévi-Strauss, Claude. 1969. *The Elementary Structures of Kinship*. Boston: Beacon Press, 479.
5. Sug-in, Kweon. "The Extended Family in Contemporary Korea: Changing Patterns of Co-Residence." KS_ResourceBok.qxd. https://www.koreasociety.org/images/pdf/KoreanStudies/Monographs_GeneralReading/GettingtoKnowKorea/GTKK%207%20Sug-In%20Kweon%20Contemporary%20Extended%20Family.pdf
6. Nabhan, David. 2022. "Make No Mistake: The Nuclear Family is 'No Mistake.'" Newsmax. January 26, 2022. https://www.newsmax.com/davidnabhan/nuclear-family-mistake/2022/01/26/id/1054129/.
7. Mao Zedong. May, 1963. "Where do Correct Ideas Come From?" *Selected Works of Zedong*, Vol. IX.
8. Chinahighlights.com. 2024. "China's Development—How it Affects You, the Tourist." China Highlights. Updated January 17, 2024. https://www.chinahighlights.com/travelguide/developing-china.htm
9. The Jewish Agency for Israel. http://www.jewishagency.org/israel.
10. Barakat, Halim, 1993. *The Arab World, Society, Culture, and State*. Berkeley: University of California Press.
11. Patai, Raphael. 1976. *The Arab Mind*. New York: Charles Scribner's Sons, 282.
12. Ibid., 36.
13. Lévi-Strauss, Claude. 1969. *The Elementary Structures of Kinship*. Boston: Beacon Press, 479.
14. Marx, Karl. 1970 (1859). "It is not the consciousness of men that determines existence, but on the contrary, their social existence determines their consciousness." *A Contribution of the Critique of Political-Economy*. New York: International Publishers, 27.
15. Kraft, Charles. 2005. *Christianity in Culture: A Study in Biblical Theologizing in Cross-Cultural Perspective*. Maryknoll, NY: Orbis Books, 107.
16. Dooyeweerd, Herman. 1969. *A New Critique of Theoretical Thought*, Vol. III-IV. The Presbyterian and Reformed Publishing Company, 271.
17. παρεισῆλθον. Arndt, William and Gingrich, F. Wilbur. 1957. *A Greek-English Lexicon of the New Testament and Other Early Christian Literature*. Chicago: University of Chicago Press, 630.
18. Van Til, Henry R. 1979 (1959). *The Calvinistic Concept of Culture*. Grand Rapids, MI: Baker Book House, 32.

NOTES

## 44. FORMS HAVING NO PLACE IN THE DIVINE PLAN

1. Discover.hubpages.com. *What is Exogamy?* Updated Sept. 9, 2012. http://dialogue.hubpages.com/hub/What-is-Exogamy
2. Reuters, May 16, 2008. "Indian Village Proud After Double 'Honor Killing.'" https://freerepublic.com/focus/f-news/2017030/posts
3. Lingenfelter, Sherwood. 2005. "Power-Giving Leadership: Transformation for a Missional Church." In *Appropriate Christianity*, edited by Charles Kraft. Pasadena, CA: William Carey Library, 275-290.
4. Ibid., 271.

## 45. THE JÍVARO PEOPLE

1. Harner, Michael J. 1972. *The Jívaro: People of the Sacred Waterfalls*. Berkeley, CA: University of California Press.
2. Ibid.
3. Anitel, Stefan. 2008. Softpedia. "Jivaro: The Tribe of Shrunken Heads." Feb 29, 2008. https://news.softpedia.com/news/Jivaro-The-Tribe-of-the-Shrunken-Heads-79914.shtml
4. Lingenfelter, Sherwood. 2005. "Power-Giving Leadership: Transformation for a Missional Church." In *Appropriate Christianity*, edited by Charles H. Kraft. Pasadena, CA, 285.
5. Lévi-Strauss, Claude. 1969. *The Elementary Structures of Kinship*. Boston: Beacon Press, 479.
6. Harner, Michael J. 1972. *The Jívaro: People of the Sacred Waterfalls*. Berkeley, CA: University of California Press, 80.
7. Ibid., 94.
8. Ibid
9. Ibid., 79.
10. Ibid., 79.
11. Ibid., 97.
12. Ibid., 79.
13. Ibid., 85.
14. Dooyeweerd, Herman. 1969. *A New Critique of Theoretical Thought*, Vol. III. The Presbyterian and Reformed Publishing Company, 304.
15. Encyclopedia.com. Updated August 13, 2018. Jivaro. https://www.encyclopedia.com/history/latin-america-and-caribbean/mesoamerican-indigenous-peoples/jivaro.
16. Harner, Michael J. 1984 (1974). *The Jivaro: People of the Sacred Waterfalls*. Berkeley, CA: University of California Press.
17. Lévi-Strauss, Claude. 1969. *The Elementary Structures of Kinship*. Boston: Beacon Press, 479.
18. Dooyeweerd, Herman. 1969. *A New Critique of Theoretical Thought*, Vol. III. The Presbyterian and Reformed Publishing Company, 304.

19. Ibid., 80.
20. Harner, Michael J. 1972. *The Jívaro: People of the Sacred Waterfalls.* Berkeley, CA: University of California Press, 80.

## 46. SHARANAHUA

1. Siskind, Janet. 1980. *To Hunt in the Morning.* Oxford: Oxford University Press, 68.
2. Ibid., 116.
3. Ibid. 116.
4. Ibid., 68.
5. Hsu, Francis L. K.. 1972. "Kinship and Ways of Life." In *Psychological Anthropology*, edited by Francis L. K. Hsu. Cambridge, MA: Schenkman Publishing Co, 514.
6. Siskind, 76.
7. Ibid., 77.
8. Marx, Karl. 1970 (1859). "It is not the consciousness of men that determines existence, but on the contrary, their social existence determines their consciousness." *A Contribution to the Critique of Political Economy.* New York: International Publishers, 27.

## 47. MICCOSUKEE (MIKASUKI)

1. Kraft, Charles. 2005. *Christianity in Culture: A Study in Biblical Theologizing in Cross-cultural Perspective*, 25th Edition. Maryknoll, NY: Orbis Books, 107.
2. Belmont, Laura L. 1985. *Seminole Kinship System and Clan Interaction.* Mendoza, Argentina: Universidad Nacional de Cuyo, 29.
3. Jacobo, Julia. 2018. "Family of Newborn Taken After Birth Sues Hospital, Native American Tribe." April 13, 2018. https://abcnews.go.com/US/family-newborn-birth-sues-hospital-native-american-tribe/story?id=54446512
4. Ibid.

## 48. THE TROBRIAND ISLANDERS

1. Fathauer, George H. 1961. "Trobriand." In *Matrilineal Kinship*, edited by David M. Schneider and Kathleen Gough. Berkeley: University of California Press, 234.
2. Fathauer, George H. 1961. "Trobriand." In *Matrilineal Kinship*, edited by David M. Schneider and Kathleen Gough. Berkeley: University of California Press, 249.
3. Malinowski, Bronislaw. 1987 (1929). *The Sexual Life of Savages.* Boston: Beacon Press, 244.
4. Fathauer, 249.
5. Arens, W. 1986. *The Original Sin, Incest and Its Meaning.* New York: Oxford University Press, 15.
6. Malinowski, Bronislaw. 1987 (1931). *The Sexual Life of Savages.* Boston: Beacon Press, 439.
7. Fathauer, 247.

## NOTES

8. Fathauer, 250.
9. Darrah, Allan, 1972. "Is Beauty Skin Deep: The Ideology of Trobriand Fatherhood." Trobriand Islands Digital Ethnography Project. June, 1972. http://www.trobriandsindepth.com/Ideology%20of%20Fatherhood.html
10. Hoebel, E. Adamson. 1967. *The Law of Primitive Man.* Cambridge, MA: Harvard University Press, 191.
11. According to George Eldon Ladd, the Greek word "*Nomos* is fundamentally 'custom,' [eventually] hardening into what we call 'law.'" Ladd, George Eldon. 1974. *A Theology of the New Testament.* Grand Rapids, MI: Eerdmans Publishing Company, 504.

    When *nomos* occurs without the article, the writer informs the reader that he is speaking about law in the abstract, that is, whatever has the qualities of lawness. When "customary law" becomes "hardened" into the law, it becomes the law of such and such a nation.
12. Malinowski, 161.
13. Opposition to the idea of a Universal-Lexicon existing in the subconscious was expressed by Eugene Nida, who wrote: "There is a tendency to regard the 'true meaning' of a word as somehow related to some central core which is said to exist (in some Universal-Lexicon), either implicitly or explicitly, in each of the different meanings of a word or a linguistic unit. All the different meanings are supposed to be derivable from this central core of meaning." Nida, Eugene A. 1971. "Implications of Contemporary Linguistics for Biblical Scholar." In *Journal of Biblical Literature,* 91:73-89.
14. Malinowski, 159.
15. Pike, Kenneth, 1993. *Talk, Thought, and Thing: The Emic Road Toward Conscious Knowledge.* Dallas: SIL, 63.
16. *tama* = male ego's FaBr, FaMoBr.
17. Bruner, Jerome. 1990. *Acts of Meaning.* Cambridge, MA: Harvard University Press, 73.
18. Chomsky, Noam. 1980. *Rules and Representations.* New York: Colombia University Press, 48.
19. Fauther, 248.
20. Malinowski, Bronislaw. 1987 (1931). *The Sexual Life of Savages.* Boston: Beacon Press, 439.
21. Kraft, Charles, 2005. *Christianity in Culture: A Study in Biblical Theologizing in Cross-Cultural Perspective.* Maryknoll, NY: Orbis Books, 68.
22. Bruner, Jerome. 1990. *Acts of Meaning.* Cambridge, MA: Harvard University Press, 34.
23. Luskin, Casey. 2014. Evolution News & Science Today. "More Studies Show Children are Wired for Religious Belief: A Brief Literature Review." August 7, 2014. https://evolutionnews.org/2014/08/more_studies_sh/
24. Lingenfelter, Sherwood. 2005. "Power-Giving Leadership: Transformation for a Missional Church." In *Appropriate Christianity,* edited by Charles H. Kraft. Pasadena, CA: William Carey Publishing, 285.
25. Goodreads.com. https://www.goodreads.com/author/quotes/1466.Jean_-Paul_Sartre
26. Kraft, Charles H. 2005. "Meaning Equivalence Contextualization." In *Appropriate Christianity.* Pasadena, CA: William Carey Library, 163.

# NOTES

27. Malinowski, Bronislaw. 1987 (1931). *The Sexual Life of Savages.* Boston: Beacon Press, 4
28. Ibid.
29. Malinowski, 6
30. Ibid., 6.
31. Service, Elman. 1978. "The Trobriand Islander of Melanesia." In *Profiles in Ethnology*, Third Edition. New York: Harper & Row, 251.
32. Malinowski, 445.
33. Senft, Gunter. "Magic, Missionaries and Religion. Some observations from the Trobriand Islands." https://pure.mpg.de/rest/items/item_67156_2/component/file_468436/content.

## 49. KIOWA - APACHE

1. Eggan, Fred. 1955. "Methods and Results." In *Social Anthropology of North American Tribes*, edited by Fred Eggan. Chicago: The University of Chicago Press, 519
2. Ibid.
3. Keesing, Roger M. 1975. *Kinship Groups and Social Structures.* New York: Holt, Rinehart & Winston, 122.
4. WhiteWolfPack.com. White Wolf Pack. "The Horse's Role in Native American and Plains Indian Culture." http://www.whitewolfpack.com/2014/03/the-horses-role-in-native-american-and.html
5. Lévi-Strauss, Claude. 1969. *The Elementary Structures of Kinship.* Boston: Beacon Press, 479.
6. McAllister, 116
7. Ibid., 119
8. Ibid., 129.
9. Ibid., 130.
10. Dooyeweerd, Herman. 1969. "A New Critique of Theoretical Thought." Vol. III-IV. The Presbyterian and Reformed Publishing Company, 304.

## 50. DO SOUND WORDS EXIST

1. Kraft, Charles. 2005. *Christianity in Culture: A Study in Biblical Theologizing in Cross-Cultural Perspective*, 25th edition. Maryknoll, NY: Orbis Books, xxiii.
2. Kraft, Charles H. 2005. "Why Isn't Contextualization Implemented?" In *Appropriate Christianity.* Pasadena, CA: William Carey Library, 257-258.
3. Lenski, R.C.H. 1946 (1937). *The Interpretation of St. Paul's Epistle to the Colossians, to the Thessalonians, to Timothy, to Titus and to Philemon.* Wartburg Press: Columbus, Ohio, 770.
4. Kraft, 78.
5. Kraft, 107.
6. Yuan, Christopher. 2019. "He Made Them Male and Female: Sex, Gender, and the Image of God." desiringGod (blog). December 14, 2019. https://www.desiringgod.org/articles/he-made-them-male-and-female

# NOTES

7. Johnson, Ben. 2022. "Sports Star to be Jailed 10 months for 'Transphobic' Message that 'God Created Adam and Eve.' The Stream (blog). November 14, 2022. https://stream.org/sports-star-to-be-jailed-10-months-for-transphobic-message-that-god-created-adam-and-eve/
8. Zedong, Mao. "Mao Zedong Quotes." AZ Quotes (blog). https://www.azquotes.com/author/16154-Mao_Zedong
9. Rushdoony, Rousas John. 1975. "Hard Money and Society in the Bible." In *Gold is Money*, edited by Hans S. Senholz. London: Greenwood Press, 164.
10. Kraft, Charles H. 2005. "Why Isn't Contextualization Implemented?" In *Appropriate Christianity*. Pasadena, CA: William Carey Library, 76.
11. Plantinga, 16-17.
12. Kraft, Charles H. 2005. "Why Isn't Contextualization Implemented?" In *Appropriate Christianity*. Pasadena, CA: William Carey Library, 76.

## 51. NATURALIZING SINGING AND DANCING

1. Harner, Michael J. 1989. *The Jívaro*. Berkeley, CA: University of California Press, 70-72.
2. Simmons, Leo W. 1972 (1942). *Sun Chief - The Autobiography of a Hopi Indian*, edited by Leo. W. Simmons, 229.
3. Densmore, Frances. 1972. *Seminole Music*. New York: Da Capo Press. 176-177.
4. Lévi-Strauss, Claude. 1968. *The Savage Mind*. Chicago: The University of Chicago Press, 221.

## 52. WAR AGAINST THE LAW OF THE MIND

1. Radin, Paul. 1972. *The Trickster, A Study in American Mythology*. New York: Schocken Books.
   Books, 133.

## 53. EAT ME, AND YOU WILL DEFECATE

1. Radin, Paul. 1972. *The Trickster, A Study in American Mythology*. New York: Schocken Books, 25.

## 54. "HELP! I NEED TO BE CLEANSED!" AN ANALYSIS OF A WINNEBAGO STORY

1. Radin, Paul. 1972. "A Testimony of a Winnebago." *The Trickster: A Study in American Indian Mythology*. New York: Schocken Books, 149.
2. Jung, C.G. 1972. *On the Psychology of the Trickster Figure*. In *The Trickster*, 211.

# NOTES

## 55. THE CONTEXTUAL SHAPING OF MEANING

1. Leffel, Jim. "Postmodernism: The 'Spirit of the Age.'" Dwell Community Church (blog). https://www.dwellcc.org/essays/postmodernism-spirit-age
2. Levi-Strauss, Claude. 1966 (1962). *The Savage Mind*. University of Chicago Press: Chicago, 65.
3. Leach, Edmund. (1967) 1970. "Brain-Twister." *Claude Lévi-Strauss: The Anthropologist as Hero*. Hayes, E. Nelson & Tanya Hayes. Cambridge, Mass.: The M.I.T. Press, 129.

## 56. THE MYSTERY OF THE ONE-FLESH PRINCIPLE

1. Hsu, Francis L. K. 1972. "Kinship and Ways of Life." In *Psychological Anthropology*, edited by Francis L. K. Hsu. Cambridge, MA: Schenkman Publishing Co.
2. De Vos, George A. 1973. *Socialization for Achievement*. Berkeley, CA: University of California Press, 127-128.
3. Ibid.
4. Gail, Lee Bernstein. 1983. *Haruko's World: A Japanese Farm Woman and Her Community*. Stanford: Stanford University Press, xvii, 199.
5. Ibid.
6. Ibid.
7. Ibid.
8. Kraft, Charles. 2005. *Christianity in Culture: A Study in Biblical Theologizing in Cross-Cultural Perspective*, 25th Edition. Maryknoll, NY: Orbis Books, 107.
9. Dooyeweerd, Herman. 1969. *A New Critique of Theoretical Thought*, Vol 1. The Presbyterian and Reformed Publishing Company, 154.

## 57. CULTURAL DIVERSITY

1. Hsu, Francis. 1972. "Kinship and Ways of Life." In *Psychological Anthropology*, edited by Francis L. K. Hsu. Cambridge, MA: Schenkman Publishing Co., 518.
2. Kraft, Charles. 68.
3. Ibid.

## 58. DEMOLITION OF DIVINE MEANINGS IN PROGRESS

1. Levi-Strauss, Claude. 1966 (1962). *The Savage Mind*. University of Chicago Press: Chicago, 65.
2. Webster, 7.
3. Webster, Richard. 1995. *Why Freud Was Wrong, Sin, Science, and Psychoanalysis*. New York: Basic Books, 437.
4. Webster, 484.

5. Lévi-Strauss, Benoist, Jean-Marie. 1974. "Classicism Revisited: Human Nature and Structure." Lévi-Strauss and Chomsky. *The Limits of Human Nature*, edited by Jonathan Benthall. New York: E. P. Dutton & Co., 30.
6. Roach, Bill. 2017. "Carl H.F. Henry: A Theistic View of Language." May 25, 2017. https://williamroach.org/2017/05/25/carl-f-h-henry-a-theistic-view-of-language/ (blog).
7. Levi-Strauss, Claude. 1966 (1962). *The Savage Mind*. University of Chicago Press: Chicago, 65.
8. Jackendoff, Ray. 1994. *Patterns in the Mind, Language and Human Nature*. NY: Basic Books, 169.
9. Kraft, Charles. 2005. *Christianity in Culture: A Study in Biblical Theologizing in Cross-Cultural Perspective*, 25th Edition. Maryknoll, NY: Orbis Books, 27.
10. Clark, Gordon, 2004 (1973). *Christian Philosophy*. Unicoi, TN: The Trinity Foundation, 297.
11. Kraft, Charles. 2005. *Christianity in Culture: A Study in Biblical Theologizing in Cross-Cultural Perspective*. Maryknoll, NY: Orbis Books, 107.

## 59. THE PIRAHÃ OF BRAZIL

1. Sproul, R. C. 2000. *The Consequences of Ideas*. Wheaton: Crossway Books, 107.
2. Philip Lieberman. 1998. *Eve Spoke*. NY: W. W. Norton, xv.
3. Everett, Daniel. 2010. Freedom from Religion Foundation. "The Pirahã: People Who Define Happiness Without God." Volume 27, Number 3, April 2010. Free Thought Today. https://ffrf.org/publications/item/13492-the-pirahae-people-who-define-happiness-without-god (blog)
4. On Practice. 1937. "On the Relation Between Knowledge and Practice, Between Knowing and Doing." *Selected Works of Mao Zedong*, Vol. I, 299-30. July, 1937. https://www.marxists.org/reference/archive/mao/selected-works/volume-1/mswv1_16.htm
5. Kraft, Charles, 2005. *Christianity in Culture: A Study in Biblical Theologizing in Cross-Cultural Perspective*. Maryknoll, NY: Orbis Books, 231.
6. Radin, Paul. 1972. *The Trickster, A Study in American Mythology*. New York: Schocken Books, 28.
7. Clark, Gordon, 2004 (1973). *Christian Philosophy*. Unicoi, TN: The Trinity Foundation, 147.
8. Clark, 149.
9. Sproul, 38.
10. Kraft, Charles. 2005. *Christianity in Culture: A Study in Biblical Theologizing in Cross-Cultural Perspective*, 25th edition. Maryknoll, NY: Orbis Books, 27.
11. Carnell, Edward J. 1952. *An Introduction to Christian Apologetics*. Fourth Edition. Grand Rapids, MI: Eerdmans Publishing Co, 169.
12. Van Til, Cornelius. 1952. *An Introduction to Systematic Theology*, 152. Cited by Rousas J. Rushdoony in *By What Standard?* Philadelphia, PENN: The Presbyterian and Reformed Publishing Co., 146.
13. Clark, Gordon, 2004 (1973). *Christian Philosophy*. Unicoi, TN: The Trinity Foundation, 147.
14. Clark, 149.

15. Kraft, Charles, 2005. *Christianity in Culture: A Study in Biblical Theologizing in Cross-Cultural Perspective*. Maryknoll, NY: Orbis Books, 27
16. Carnell, Edward John. 1952. *An Introduction to Christian Apologetics, A Philosophical Defense of the Trinitarian-Theistic Faith*. Grand Rapids, MI: Eerdmans Publishing Co., 169.

## 60. THE NATURE OF ETIC DIVERGENCE

1. Plantinga Jr., Cornelius. 1995. *Not the Way It's Supposed to Be, a Breviary of Sin*. Grand Rapids, MI: Eerdmans Publishing Company, 24.
2. Kraft, Charles, 2005. *Christianity in Culture: A Study in Biblical Theologizing in Cross-Cultural Perspective*. Maryknoll, NY: Orbis Books, 304.
3. Lingenfelter, Sherwood. 2005. "Power-Giving Leadership: Transformation for a Missional Church." In *Appropriate Christianity*, edited by Charles H. Kraft. Pasadena, CA, 285.
4. Ibid., 64.
5. Farber, Bernard. 1968. *Comparative Kinship Systems*. New York: Wiley, 75
6. Kraft, Charles. 2005. *Christianity in Culture: A Study in Biblical Theologizing in Cross-Cultural Perspective*, 25th edition. Maryknoll, NY: Orbis Books, xxiii.

## 61. THE GLEANING OF MEANINGS

1. Sproul, R. C. 2000. *The Consequences of Ideas*. Wheaton: Crossway Books, 34.
2. Lyons, John. 1991 (1968). *Introduction to Theoretical Linguistics*. Cambridge: Cambridge University Press, 472.
3. Clark, Gordon. 1993 (1968). *An Introduction to Christian Philosophy*. Jefferson, Maryland: The Trinity Foundation, 30.
4. Wierzbicka, Anna. 1996. *Semantics, Primes and Universals*. Oxford, UK: Oxford University Press, 18.
5. Called "infrastructure" by cultural materialist Marvin Harris.
6. Bruner, Jerome. 1990. *Acts of Meaning*. Cambridge, MA: Harvard University Press, 34.
7. Kraft, 68.
8. Timsears69. Youtube.com. 2010. https://www.youtube.com/watch?v=UkX47t2QaRs

## 62. INNATE UNIVERSALS FROM THE FIELD OF PARTICULARS

1. Pike, Kenneth. 1993. *Talk, Thought, and Thing: The Emic Road Toward Conscious Knowledge*. Dallas: SIL, 63.
2. Nida, Eugene A. 1971. "Implications of Contemporary Linguistics for Biblical Scholar." In *Journal of Biblical Literature*, 91:73-89.

# NOTES

3. Pike, Kenneth. 1993. *Talk, Thought, and Thing: The Emic Road Toward Conscious Knowledge.* Dallas: SIL. 63. The quote reveals that Linguist Kenneth Pike was an innatist.
4. Sproul, R. C. 2000. *The Consequences of Ideas.* Wheaton: Crossway Books, 31.
5. Goodenough, Ward H. 1981. *Culture, Language, and Society.* Menlo Park, CA: The Benjamin/Cummings Publishing Company, 17.
6. Carruthers, Peter. 1995. *Human Knowledge and Human Nature.* Oxford, UK: Oxford University Press, 103.
7. Marx, Karl. 1970 (1859). *A Contribution of the Critique of Political-Economy.* New York: International Publishers, 21.
8. Carruthers, Peter. 1995. *Human Knowledge and Human Nature.* Oxford, UK: Oxford University Press, 1103.
9. Chan, Wing-Tsit. 1967. "The Story of Chinese Philosophy." In *The Chinese Mind*, edited by Charles A. Moore. Honolulu: East-West Center Press, 63.
10. Pike, Kenneth. 1993. *Talk, Thought, and Thing: The Emic Road Toward Conscious Knowledge.* Dallas: SIL, 76.
11. Beall, Todd S. 2016. Answers in Genesis. "Seven Principles from Genesis for Marriage and Family." April 30, 2016. https://answersingenesis.org/family/marriage/seven-principles-from-genesis/
12. Pike, Kenneth. 1993. *Talk, Thought, and Thing: The Emic Road Toward Conscious Knowledge.* Dallas: SIL, 38-39.
13. Pike, Kenneth. 1993. *Talk, Thought, and Thing: The Emic Road Toward Conscious Knowledge.* Dallas: SIL, 63.

## 63. SPECIES VERSUS KINDS

1. Robbins, John W. The Trinity Foundation. "The Trinity Manifesto: A Program for our Time." http://www.trinityfoundation.org/journal.php?id=1
2. Clark, Gordon. 1993 (1968). *An Introduction to Christian Philosophy.* Jefferson, Maryland: The Trinity Foundation, 149.
3. Pike, Kenneth. 1993. *Talk, Thought, and Thing: The Emic Road Toward Conscious Knowledge.* Dallas: SIL, x.
4. Kraft, Charles H. 1978. "Interpreting in Cultural Context." In *Journal of the Evangelical Theological Society*, 357-366.
5. Carruthers, Peter. 1995. *Human Knowledge and Human Nature.* Oxford, UK: Oxford University Press, 103.

## 64. DOES A DIVINE PLAN FOR LIVING EXIST

1. Fried, Morton H. 1976. "Chinese Culture, and Personality in Transition." In *Response to Change, Society, Culture, and Personality*, edited by George A DeVos. New York: D. Van Nostrand Co., 46.
2. Belmont, Laura L. 1985. *Seminole Kinship System and Clan Interaction.* Mendoza, Argentina: Universidad Nacional de Cuyo, 59.

# NOTES

3. Kraft, Charles. 2005. *Christianity in Culture: A Study in Biblical Theologizing in Cross-Cultural Perspective*, 25th edition. Maryknoll, NY: Orbis Books, 74.
4. Kraft, Charles H. 2005. "Why Isn't Contextualization Implemented?" In *Appropriate Christianity*. Pasadena, CA: William Carey Library, 76.
5. Plantinga Jr., Cornelius. 1995. *Not the Way It's Supposed to Be: A Breviary of Sin*. Grand Rapids: MI: Eerdmans Publishing Company, 16.
6. Plantinga, 16-17.
7. Plantinga, 16-17.
8. Campbell, Jonathan. 2005. "Appropriate Witness to Postmoderns: Re-Incarnating the Way of Jesus in 21st Century Western Culture." In *Appropriate Christianity*. Pasadena, CA: William Carey Library, 472.

## 66. THE MISSIOLOGICAL CROSSROAD

1. The family-of-five consists of either father, mother, sons, daughters, and incoming daughters-in-law, or, as in the case of the Chácobo, father, mother, sons, daughters, and incoming sons-in-law. The words of Jesus in Matthew 10:34-39, NASB) are: "Do not think that I came to bring peace on earth; I did not come to bring peace, but a sword. For I came to set a man against his father, and a daughter against her mother, and a daughter-in-law against her mother-in-law; and a man's enemies will be the members of his household. He who loves father or mother more than Me is not worthy of Me; and he who loves son or daughter more than Me is not worthy of Me. And he who does not take his cross and follow after Me is not worthy of Me. He who has found his life will lose it, and he who has lost his life for My sake will find it." Also, see Luke 12: 51-53.
2. McElhanon, Kenneth A. 2007. "Cognitive Linguistics, Biblical Truth and Ethical Conduct." In *Journal of Interdisciplinary Studies*, Vol. XIX No 1/2, 125.
3. Kraft, 277.
4. The paraphrase was given by Heinrich A. W. Meyer in 1884. *Critical and Exegetical Hand-Book to the Gospel of Matthew*. New York: Funk & Wagnalls, 199.

## 67. REQUIRES NEW FORMS

1. Mayers, Marvin K. 1996 [1974]. *Christianity Confronts Culture, A Strategy for Crosscultural Evangelism*. Grand Rapids, MI: Academic Books, 62.

## 68. CULTURAL RELATIVIST VERSUS CONCEPT-INNATIST

1. Mayers, Marvin K. 1987. *Christianity Confronts Culture: A Strategy for Crosscultural Evangelism*. Grand Rapids, MI: Academie Books, 62.
2. Kraft, Charles, 2005. *Christianity in Culture: A Study in Biblical Theologizing in Cross-Cultural Perspective*. Maryknoll, NY: Orbis Books, 78.

# NOTES

## 69. THE "YOKE OF SLAVERY" LONGS TO BE BROKEN

1. Dooyeweerd, Herman. 1969. *A New Critique of Theoretical Thought*, Vol. 1. The Presbyterian and Reformed Publishing Company, 276.
2. Dooyeweerd, 304.
3. Dooyeweerd, Herman. 1969. *A New Critique of Theoretical Thought*, Vol. III. The Presbyterian and Reformed Publishing Company, 304.
4. Fox, Robin. 1992 (1967). *Kinship and Marriage*. Cambridge: Cambridge University Press, 25.
5. Fox, Robin. 1992 (1967). *Kinship and Marriage*. Cambridge: Cambridge University Press, 12.
6. Grunlan, Stephen A. and Marvin K. Mayers. 1979. *Cultural Anthropology: A Christian Perspective*. Grand Rapids, MI; Academie Books, 206.
7. Kraft, 74.
8. Cloud, David. 4-20-16. Way of Life Bible College. "America's Founding Fathers and the Bible." https://www.wayoflife.org/reports/
9. Harris, Marvin. 1975 (1971). *Culture, People, Nature: An Introduction to General Anthropology*. New York: Thomas Y. Crowell, 59.
10. Hsu, Francis L. K. 1972. "Kinship and Ways of Life." In *Psychological Anthropology*, edited by Francis L. K. Hsu. Cambridge, MA: Schenkman Publishing Co, 514.
11. Ibid.

## 70. BREAKING THE YOKE OF SLAVERY

1. Meyer, Heinrich A. 1884. "A Paraphrase of What Jesus Declared." *Critical and Exegetical Handbook to the Gospel of Mathew*. New York: Funk and Wagnalls Co.
2. Bossen, Laurel & Hill Gates. 2017. *Bound Feet, Young Hands*. Stanford University Press, Stanford, CA.
3. Katie, Hunt. 2017. CNN.com "Work not Sex? The Real Reason Chinese Bound Their Feet." May 21, 2017. https://www.cnn.com/2017/05/21/health/china-foot-binding-new-theory/index.html
4. Fried, Morton H. 1976. "Chinese Culture, and Personality in Transition." In *Response to Change, Society, Culture, and Personality*, edited by George A DeVos. New York: D. Van Nostrand Co, 64.
5. Plantinga Jr., Cornelius. 1995. *Not the Way It's Supposed to Be: A Breviary of Sin*. Grand Rapids, MI: Eerdmans Publishing Company, 24.
6. Heinrich, August Wilhelm Meyer. 1884. *Critical and Exegetical Handbook to the Epistles to the Galatians*. New York: Funk and Wagnalls Co., 296.

# NOTES

## 71. THE BATTLE LINES ARE DRAWN

1. Sanday, William, & Arthur C. Headlam. 1896. *A Critical and Exegetical Commentary on the Epistle to The Romans.* Edinburgh: T & T Clark, 54.
2. Harris, Marvin. 1980. *Cultural Materialism: The Struggle for a Science of Culture.* New York: Vintage Books, 6.
3. Harris, 278.
4. Harris, Marvin, 1980. *Cultural Materialism: The Struggle for a Science of Culture.* New York: Vintage Books, 59.

## 72. YEAR 1998 IN GAINESVILLE, FLORIDA

1. "The proposition that existence precedes essence is a central claim of existentialism, which reverses the traditional philosophical view that essence (the nature) of a thing is more fundamental and immutable than its existence." —Wikipedia
2. TheGuardian.com Interview by Robert McCrum. "Daniel Everett: 'There is no such thing as universal grammar.'" https://www.theguardian.com/technology/2012/mar/25/daniel-everett-human-language-piraha
3. Bentley University Faculty, Daniel Everett. https://faculty.bentley.edu/profile/deverett

## 73. DISCOVERING "GOLD" AMONG THE PARTICULARS

1. Kraft, Charles. 2005. *Christianity in Culture: A Study in Biblical Theologizing in Cross-Cultural Perspective,* 25th Edition. Maryknoll, NY: Orbis Books, xxiii, 97.
2. A family of related tribes living in Peru, Brazil, and Bolivia whose language are derivatives of a prototype called "Pano."
3. Pike, Kenneth. 1993. *Talk, Thought, and Thing. The emic road toward conscious knowledge.* Dallas: SIL. 63. The quote reveals that Linguist Kenneth Pike was an innatist.
4. Maharishi Mahesh Yogi. 1990. *Maharishi Mahesh Yogi on the Bhagavad-Gita.* New York: Arkana. 175.
5. Ibid., 110.
6. Belmont, Laura L. 1985. *Seminole Kinship System and Clan Interaction.* Mendoza, Argentina. Universidad Nacional de Cuyo, 59.
7. Prost, Gilbert R. 1996. "The Structure of Mikasuki Selfhood." In MALC (Mid-America Linguistic Conference, 1994), edited by Francis Ingemann.Vol. II. Lawrence, KS: University of Kansas, 629-643.

# NOTES

## 74. ALLEGORY OF THE CAVE

1. InterestingLiterature.com. 2024. "A Summary and Analysis of Plato's Allegory of the Cave." Dr. Tearle, Oliver. (Loughborough University). https://interestingliterature.com/2023/03/plato-allegory-of-the-cave-summary-analysis/
2. Tearle, Oliver. Loughborough University. "A Summary and Analysis of Plato's Allegory of the Cave." Interesting Literature. https://interestingliterature.com/2023/03/plato-allegory-of-the-cave-summary-analysis/
3. Wikipedia. http://en.wikipedia.org/wiki/Worldview
4. Tearle, Oliver. Loughborough University. "A Summary and Analysis of Plato's Allegory of the Cave." Interesting Literature. https://interestingliterature.com/2023/03/plato-allegory-of-the-cave-summary-analysis/
5. Libre Texts Physics. 4.2: Newton's First Law of Motion: Enertia. https://phys.libretexts.org/Bookshelves/College_Physics/College_Physics_1e_(OpenStax)/04%3A_Dynamics-_Force_and_Newton's_Laws_of_Motion/4.02%3A_Newtons_First_Law_of_Motion_-_Inertia
6. Tearle, Oliver. Loughborough University. "A Summary and Analysis of Plato's Allegory of the Cave." Interesting Literature. https://interestingliterature.com/2023/03/plato-allegory-of-the-cave-summary-analysis/
7. Steinbach, Lori, M.A. Endnotes. Plato's Republic. "Why, in Plato's *Republic,* can't educators put knowledge in a soul that wasn't there before?" https://www.enotes.com/topics/platos-republic/questions/why-concluding-paragraph-does-plato-say-impossible-465860
8. Dr. Hamp, Douglas. 2022. "Intro: Old Gods, Ancient Aliens." *Corrupting the Image 3: Singularity, Superhumans, and the Second Coming of Jesus.* USA: Eskaton Media Group, 3

## 75. A REVOLUTION WITHOUT GUNS

1. Kraft, Charles. 2005. *Christianity in Culture: A Study in Biblical Theologizing in Cross-Cultural Perspective.* Maryknoll, NY: Orbis Books, 78.
2. I (Gil Prost) would add that Haiti is vying for that sad distinction.

www.ingramcontent.com/pod-product-compliance
Lightning Source LLC
Chambersburg PA
CBHW020451030426
42337CB00011B/78